"This is a fine study of class differentiation in rural Indonesia, the first by an Indonesian scholar for a long time. It is based on fieldwork in two villages, one centred on rice in Java and the other on palm oil in Sumatra. The book skilfully traces the dynamics of class and generational reproduction, including non-farming activities and earnings of different classes. It is of great interest and value to those studying rural change in other regions of the global South."

Henry Bernstein, *School of Oriental and African Studies, University of London, UK*

Capitalism and Agrarian Change

Small-scale agricultural producers in the peripheral world are often condescendingly assumed to be a single social class ('the peasantry') to be pitted against the state or corporation. This book challenges this rather idealistic view by demonstrating that under current capitalist social relations (competition, efficiency and productivity, and profit maximisation), these agricultural producers have been differentiated into different agrarian classes by exploitation. By comparing two different contexts of local agrarian change in Indonesia—rice cultivation in Java and oil palm in Sumatra—this book exposes the different class locations of the agrarian classes among petty agricultural producers and the class relations between them. These are often inextricably linked to gender, clanship and generational issues. The power of class dynamics crucially shapes how agricultural production in both rice and oil palm is organised. The share received by different agrarian classes from the production site then prominently shapes the different nature of class reproduction for each agrarian class. This analysis demonstrates that the different agrarian classes possess different capacities and responses in their relation to the state or corporations. Any real emancipation attempt in the Indonesian countryside (and beyond) must start from a proper understanding of these class dynamics. This book marks a significant contribution to the literature on agrarian change, the political economy of development, rural development and Marxist political economy.

Muchtar Habibi is a Lecturer in the Department of Public Policy and Management, Faculty of Social and Political Sciences at the Universitas Gadjah Mada, Indonesia.

Routledge Frontiers of Political Economy

Economics and Art Theory
Edited by Stratos Myrogiannis and Constantinos Repapis

Capitalism and Agrarian Change
Class, Production and Reproduction in Indonesia
Muchtar Habibi

Capitalist Agriculture and the Global Bee Crisis
Rebecca Ellis

China, Trust and Digital Supply Chains
Dynamics of a Zero Trust World
Warwick Powell

Macroeconomic Modelling, Economic Policy and Methodology
Economics at the Edge
Edited by Mikael Randrup Byrialsen, Hamid Raza and Finn Olesen

Economics, Anthropology and the Origin of Money as a Bargaining Counter
Patrick Spread

Bernard Schmitt's Quantum Macroeconomic Analysis
Alvaro Cencini

Blockchain and the Commons
Vangelis Papadimitropoulos

Globalization and the Decline of American Power
Cyrus Bina

For more information about this series, please visit: www.routledge.com/Routledge-Frontiers-of-Political-Economy/book-series/SE0345

Capitalism and Agrarian Change

Class, Production and Reproduction in Indonesia

Muchtar Habibi

Routledge
Taylor & Francis Group
LONDON AND NEW YORK

First published 2023
by Routledge
4 Park Square, Milton Park, Abingdon, Oxon OX14 4RN

and by Routledge
605 Third Avenue, New York, NY 10158

Routledge is an imprint of the Taylor & Francis Group, an informa business

British Library Cataloguing-in-Publication Data
A catalogue record for this book is available from the British Library

Library of Congress Cataloging-in-Publication Data
Names: Habibi, Muchtar, author.
Title: Capitalism and agrarian change: class, production and reproduction in Indonesia/Muchtar Habibi.
Description: Abingdon, Oxon; New York, NY: Routledge, 2022. |
Series: Routledge frontiers of political economy |
Includes bibliographical references and index.
Identifiers: LCCN 2022007382 | ISBN 9781032212173 (hardback) |
ISBN 9781032212180 (paperback) | ISBN 9781003267348 (ebook)
Subjects: LCSH: Agriculture–Economic aspects–Indonesia. |
Land reform–Indonesia. | Farms, Small–Indonesia. |
Social stratification–Indonesia. | Capitalism–Indonesia.
Classification: LCC HD2082 .H33 2022 |
DDC 338.109598–dc23/eng/20220519
LC record available at https://lccn.loc.gov/2022007382

ISBN: 978-1-032-21217-3 (hbk)
ISBN: 978-1-032-21218-0 (pbk)
ISBN: 978-1-003-26734-8 (ebk)

DOI: 10.4324/9781003267348

Typeset in Bembo
by Deanta Global Publishing Services, Chennai, India

For

Linda Sudiono
and classes of labour in agriculture and beyond

Contents

List of Figures x
List of Tables xi
List of Appendices xiii
Acknowledgements xiv
Abbreviations xvii

1 Introduction 1

2 Exposing Class Dynamics of Agrarian Change Under Capitalism 12

3 Agrarian Change in Indonesia and the State 41

4 Situating the Agrarian Change in Java and Sumatra 76

5 Class Dynamics of Agrarian Change in Java and Sumatra 89

6 Agricultural Production in Java and Sumatra 142

7 Class Reproduction in Java and Sumatra 187

8 Conclusion 230

Appendixes 247
Index 253

Figures

3.1 World CPO Price 1970–2018 (in $/metric ton) 62
4.1 The map of the village studied in Central Java and North Sumatera, Indonesia 79
7.1 Class and generational reproduction of the agrarian ruling class in the two villages 192
7.2 Class and generational reproduction of PCPs in the two villages 208
7.3 Class and generational reproduction of the classes of labour in the two villages 219

Tables

3.1 The rate of profit of wet paddy cultivation per hectare in Indonesia and Central Java 54
3.2 The change in total real revenue and total production cost of a hectare of wet paddy cultivation in Indonesia and Central Java (in thousands of rupiah) 55
3.3 The composition of wet paddy cultivation cost per hectare in Indonesia and Central Java (in percentages) 56
3.4 Indonesia's agricultural real wages in food crops (in rupiah per day) 57
3.5 Land productivity per hectare of wet paddy field per season in Indonesia and Central Java 58
3.6 Farm-gate price per kg of paddy in Indonesia (in rupiah) 58
3.7 The rate of profit per hectare of oil palm of farmer/smallholders 59
3.8 The change in total real revenue and total production cost of a hectare of oil palm production in Indonesia (in thousands of rupiah) 60
3.9 The composition of the oil palm production cost of oil palm farmers/smallholders per hectare in Indonesia (in percentages) 60
3.10 Agricultural real wages in estate crops (in rupiah per day) 61
3.11 Land productivity of oil palm per hectare in Indonesia and North Sumatera (in tonnes per month) 61
3.12 Agricultural landholders[a] in Indonesia, 1973–2003 (percentages) 64
3.13 Rice landholders in Indonesia, 1963–2013 (percentages) 66
5.1 Landholding in *Njomplang*, Central Java 1992 and 2017 (percentages) 93
5.2 Landholding in *Timpang*, North Sumatra 2018 (percentages) 94
5.3 Class location in *Njomplang*, Central Java 118
5.4 Class location in *Timpang*, North Sumatera 120
5.5 The wages for agricultural tasks in *Njomplang*, Central Java 130
6.1 Land tenure in *Njomplang*, Central Java 144
6.2 Land tenure in *Timpang*, North Sumatera 146

6.3 The trajectory of sharecropping in *Njomplang*, Central Java 148
6.4 The dynamics of the labour arrangement in *Njomplang*, Central Java 156
6.5 The dynamics of the labour arrangement in *Timpang*, North Sumatera 162
6.6 Credit provision in *Njomplang*, Central Java 164
6.7 Credit provision in *Timpang*, North Sumatera 167
6.8 Land productivity and the income from 'own-account' farming of agrarian classes in *Njomplang*, Central Java 175
6.9 Land productivity and the income from 'own-account' farming of agrarian classes in *Timpang*, North Sumatra 178
7.1 The net result of land transactions of each class in *Njomplang* Central Java, 2012–2017 188
7.2 The net result of land transactions of each class in *Timpang* North Sumatra, 2015–2017 190

Appendices

1	The Village Head and Family Ties in *Njomplang*, Central Java	247
2	The Village Head and Family Ties in *Timpang*, North Sumatera	248
3	Production Cost and Revenue in a Rice Cultivation Village	248
3.1	Production Cost and Revenue of Rice Cultivation of Capitalist Farmers per Season in *Njomplang*, Central Java	248
3.2	Production Cost and Revenue of Rice Cultivation of PCP per Season in *Njomplang*, Central Java	249
3.3	Production Cost and Revenue of Rice Cultivation of 'Semi-Proletariat Farmers' per Season in *Njomplang*, Central Java	249
3.4	Production Cost and Revenue of Rice Cultivation of 'Proletariat-Farmers' per Season in *Njomplang*, Central Java	250
4	Production Cost and Revenue in an Oil Palm Village	250
4.1	Production Cost and Revenue of Capitalist Farmers per Year in *Timpang*, North Sumatera	250
4.2	Production Cost and Revenue of PCP per Year in *Timpang*, North Sumatera	251
4.3	Production Cost and Revenue of 'Semi-Proletariat Farmers' per Year in *Timpang*, North Sumatera	251
5	Real Wage in *Njomplang* 2001 and 2017 (in Thousands Rupiah)	252

Acknowledgements

This book is the fruit of a long intellectual journey. I was born and grew up in the Javanese countryside, where my current worldview was largely forged. Raised in a 'white-collar worker' family but owning no land (paddy fields), I experienced a unique social position. Being 'white-collar workers', my family had quite a high social status in the village and was close to the circle of the village ruling class. However, owning no paddy fields separated my family from the rest of the village ruling class members, most of whom were landowners employing wage labour. In retrospect, this social distance provides me with a space to be critical of the landowners-cum-village ruling class. The fact that I mingled more with my distant relatives, who were mostly from 'blue-collar worker' backgrounds than with friends from ruling class upbringing, only added spice to my relationship with the village ruling class. For the freedom to choose with whom I played during my childhood and their abundant love, I am grateful to my parents. To my mother, Harmiyati, and my late father, Marino: your love is always in my heart. My deep love goes to my sister, Retno Dwi Rohaniyati, without whose financial support neither my undergraduate study at Universitas Gadjah Mada (UGM) nor my recent intellectual journey would simply not have been possible.

My current intellectual quest would not have been possible without meeting many friends, colleagues and comrades in Yogyakarta. My gratitude goes to Professor Erwan Agus Purwanto and Professor Agus Pramusinto in the Department of Management and Public Policy UGM for their encouragement to join academic life after I completed my undergraduate program at UGM and for their constant support for me to become a serious academician. Their commitment to academic freedom has provided me with a space to form my thoughts and perspectives, for which I can only be grateful. Comrades in the MAP Corner-Klub MKP UGM have been the home for my intellectual journey. Seeing many potential scholars-activists emerge from this community has always recharged my optimism of will despite my intellectual pessimism. It is perhaps at the hands of their generation that a more progressive and better future for this country and beyond can be collectively formed. Talking to dozens of speakers (from both academic and activist backgrounds) at the MAP Corner-Klub MKP UGM weekly discussion events on Tuesdays has forged and enriched my worldview. I am grateful to all of them; unfortunately, their names cannot all be mentioned. Thanks to comrades at the Social Movement Institute (SMI) for their friendship, and to Mas Eko Prasetyo, who inspired me with his 'explosive and stylish words' when I was an undergraduate student. Special thanks go to A.N. Luthfi for introducing me to critical agrarian studies, without which this book would not have been possible. Benny Juliawan has been a great comrade and intellectual partner. I am looking forward to collaborating with him again soon. Many thanks to Iwan, a life teacher, and Emil, an exceptional comrade to whom I talk with about almost everything. I am sorry for stealing much of his free time to listen to my nonsense. It is great to laugh at our foolishness with such ease.

My intellectual journey has also benefitted from meeting comrades elsewhere. Roy Murtadho, Rizky Affiat, Muhammad Azka and other comrades at Islam Bergerak have often made me rethink what I have taken for granted. Many thanks to comrades at the Indoprogress Institute for Social Research and Education (IISRE): Coen Pontoh, Ruth Rahayu, Inaya, Anto Sangadji and others with whom I have gained insights and lessons. For me, working for IISRE as a Research Coordinator is a great opportunity to engage with potential progressive young researchers and to apply Marxist concepts and frameworks empirically in Indonesia's context. I can only be grateful for this opportunity.

This book is based on my PhD thesis at the School of Oriental and African Studies (SOAS), University of London. This is the place where I have forged and formed my current thoughts and perspectives fully. This book would simply not have been possible without Jens Lerche. Working with him for about four years was a privilege. His approach makes him rather a comrade for me than a supervisor. It is only stating the obvious to say that my research project has greatly benefitted from his critical and constructive comments throughout my studies at SOAS. I can only be grateful for his relentless support. Many thanks also go to Ben White. He is the one who inspired me to study agrarian change from a critical perspective. When I first read his critique of Clifford Geertz, I realised how unrealistic Geertz's vision of a rural Javanese community is, which confirms my own experience of living in rural Java: class matters in the countryside. It puzzles me, though, that he rarely touches explicitly on class in his current writing. For my PhD thesis, I can only be grateful for his meticulous and insightful comments. While we do not always agree on everything, his unrivalled knowledge of agrarian change in Indonesia has prevented me from committing many unnecessary errors.

If there is a person who is responsible for the whole idea of this book, it is Henry Bernstein. It should be obvious for readers that the framework and argument developed in this book draw heavily on Henry's perspective on agrarian change. His 'little book but a tour de force' inspired me as a master's student at The International Institute of Social Studies (ISS) Den Haag. His catchy 'four political economy questions' challenge me to apply these questions in investigating concrete agrarian change in a specific social setting. This ambition, along with the attempt to clarify my thoughts about this subject, led to a PhD research project at SOAS which intends to cover all four political economy questions in a single analysis: class, production and reproduction. I am grateful that Henry was available to give comments on my PhD thesis. His critiques and suggestions have improved the thesis significantly. I am also grateful for his valuable input on the book's manuscript version.

Many people have helped my fieldwork in Java and Sumatra. In both locations, I am grateful for excellent assistance from Joko Susilo (Josu) in collecting secondary data in the village and district. The secondary data collection in Java and Sumatra would not have been possible without his continuing support. In Sumatra, many thanks to Sony, who helped me get into the villages I studied. My fieldwork would not have been possible without the warm welcome and kind support of the villagers in these two villages. In Java, I am grateful to Supadmi, Joko Suwito, Kasyanto and Rizal for treating me like a member of their own family. In Sumatra, Lilik, Gianto and R. Marpaung also made me feel at home. All of their support has greatly eased the tiring process of fieldwork. Living in the two villages for about eight months, which perhaps is a once in a lifetime experience, has taught me priceless life lessons.

I am also grateful to Andy Humphries, a Routledge editor who has supported and helped me through the editing process. Many thanks to the editor of *The Journal of Agrarian Change* and the editor of *The Journal of Peasant Studies* for their permission to reproduce significant amounts of material from their journals in this book (Chapter 5). My deep gratitude goes to Indonesia Endowment Fund for Education/LPDP for giving me the scholarship for my master and PhD studies. Without their financial support, this book would simply not have been possible.

An intellectual journey is only a part of a life journey. I am now blessed to enjoy a joyous intellectual and non-intellectual journey with my partner, Linda Sudiono. For her intellectual might, warm support and caring, I can only be grateful. Having a life partner who shares the same political view is a rare gift. While this book is presented for her, we agree to dedicate this book to Tarmi, Mulyono, Paijo, Agus, Suri, Lilik, Bintang, Lubis and other members of classes of labour in Java and Sumatra and beyond, the fruits of whose labour have not been enjoyed by themselves. It is to them that we dedicate this book.

Yogyakarta,
Department of Management and Public Policy,
Faculty of Social and Political Sciences,
Universitas Gadjah Mada
M.H

Abbreviations

BOS	*Bantuan Operasional Sekolah*/School Operational Assistance
BPD	*Badan Permusyawaratan Desa*/Village Body Representative
BPDPKS	*Badan Pengelola Dana Perkebunan Kelapa Sawit*/Endowment Fund Body for Palm Oil
BPS	*Badan Pusat Statistik*/National Statistic Agency
BRI	*Bank Rakyat Indonesia*/People's Bank of Indonesia
BSM	*Bantuan Siswa Miskin*/Cash Transfer to Student from Poor Households
BTI	*Barisan Tani Indonesia*/ Indonesian Farmer's Front
BTPN	*Bank Tabungan Pensiunan Nasional*/National Pension Savings Bank
CPO	Crude Palm Oil
CT	Capitalist Thesis
DI-TII	*Darul Islam-Tentara Islam Indonesia*/Darul Islam-Islamic Armed Forces of Indonesia
GAPKI	*Gabungan Pengusaha Kelapa Sawit Indonesia*/Indonesian Palm oil Business Association
GAPOKTAN	*Gabungan Kelompok Tani*/Association of Farmer Groups
GDP	Gross Domestic Product
HKTI	*Himpunan Kerukunan Tani Indonesia*/Indonesian Farmer Association
ILC	International Land Coalition
IMF	International Monetary Fund
KADIN	*Kamar Dagang dan Industri Indonesia*/Chamber of Commerce and Industry Indonesia
KBKI	*Konsentrasi Buruh Kerakyatan Indonesia*/Indonesian People's Worker Union
KORAMIL	*Komando Rayon Militer*/Military Sub-District Command
KPA	*Konsorsium Pembaharuan Agraria*/Consortium for Agrarian Reform
KPPA	*Koperasi Kredit Primer Anggota*/Member's Primary Credit Cooperative
KUD	*Koperasi Unit Desa*/Village Unit Cooperative

KUR	*Kredit Usaha Rakyat*/Credit for micro business
NES	Nucleus Plasma Scheme
PA	Primitive Accumulation
PCP	Petty Commodity Producer
PERTAMINA	*Perusahaan Pertambangan Minyak dan Gas Bumi Negara/* Indonesian State-Owned Oil and Natural Gas Company
PERTANU	*Persatuan Tani Nahdatul Ulama*/Nahdatul Ulama Farmer Union
PETANI	*Persatuan Tani Indonesia*/Indonesian Farmer Union
PKH	*Program Keluarga Harapan*/Conditional Cash Transfer
PKI	*Partai Komunis Indonesia*/Indonesian Communist Party
PNI	*Partai Nasional Indonesia*/Indonesian National Party
POKTAN	*Kelompok Tani*/Farmer group
PT KAI	Perusahaan Terbuka Kereta Api Indonesia/Indonesian State-Owned Railways Company
PTPN	*Perusahaan Terbuka Perkebunan Nusantara*/Indonesian State-Owned Agribusiness Company
PUSKESMAS	*Pusat Kesehatan Masyarakat*/Public Health Centre at Sub-District Level
RASKIN	*Beras Miskin*/Rice for the Poor
SARBUPRI	*Sarekat Buruh Perkebunan Republik Indonesia*/Estate Worker Union of Republic Indonesia
SFT	Semi-Feudalist Thesis
SPI	*Serikat Petani Indonesia*/Indonesian Peasant Union
TGHK	*Tata Guna Hutan Kesepakatan*/Consensus Forest Land Use Plan

1 Introduction

Agrarian Populism and the Partiality of Agrarian Change in Indonesia

A commonly held view of contemporary agrarian change in Indonesia is the inclination to perceive agrarian change mainly as the expansion of 'export crops' such as oil palm, cocoa and rubber in the outer islands.[1] One particular driver of such a dominant view has been the arrival of the so-called 'global land rush' in the early twenty-first century, which has accelerated global land enclosure, particularly in developing countries (White et al., 2012). Among other regions, Southeast Asia has been one of the main locations for such acquisitions, notably for oil palm production (Borras & Franco, 2011). As the biggest oil palm producer in the world, Indonesia is undoubtedly among the most important arenas in this quest for new frontiers. The other side of the coin is that agrarian conflicts have been a dominant feature in Indonesia since the downfall of Suharto's authoritarian regime at the end of the twentieth century, which opened up space for people's protests and grievances (Lucas & Warren, 2013). Most agrarian conflicts involve local people and farmers defending or claiming the land against the encroachment of the state or corporation (KPA, 2017). The oil palm sector is cited as the largest contributor to this conflict.

The widespread agrarian conflict between farmers and corporations or the state paves the way for the growing movement of 'land for the people' in Indonesia. *Consortium for Agrarian Reform* (Konsorsium Pembaruan Agraria/ KPA) is probably the most influential people's movement organisation for agrarian reform at the national level. It often unites a broad alliance of 'civil society' including farmer unionists, environmental activists, human right activists and the activists for 'indigenous people' under one banner to fight against land grabs orchestrated by corporations and the state (for instance, KNPA, 2019). At the grass-roots level, independent farmer unionists have been among the most prominent fighters against these land grabs since the growing number of independent farmer unions after political democratisation. The largest independent farmer union in the country, SPI, has consistently fought for 'land for the tillers', 'peasant rights' and 'food sovereignty'(SPI, 2021), echoing the global agrarian movements elsewhere in responding to the 'global land rush'.

DOI: 10.4324/9781003267348-1

The SPI is also a member of the *Via Campesina*, the largest 'peasant union' in the world, and the leader of the global agrarian movements. Together, they are fighting against the corporatisation of agriculture under the banner of 'the people of the land'. This agrarian populist struggle assumes that 'all farmers' are in great danger from the expansion of corporations (Bernstein, 2014).

The agrarian populism in the country has also retained its grip among intellectuals. One of the most exemplary contemporary manifestos, perhaps, is 'Petani dan Penguasa' (*Peasant and the Ruler*), a book written by a scholar-activist Noer Fauzi Rachman in the late 1990s. As the title indicates, *Peasant and the Ruler* (1999) emphasises the struggle of the assumed undifferentiated peasant against the ruler. The state and its partner, corporations, are described as the primary enemy of the peasants as they often legally or illegally dispossess peasant's land. By counterposing 'peasants' as a distinct class and the ruler (state and corporation), Rachman provides a foundation to the prominent role of 'peasant politics' and their struggle for land. This tradition is sustained by a more recent work edited by Lucas and Warren in their widely celebrated book *Land for the People* (2013). Again, in line with *Peasant and the Ruler*, *Land for the People* views corporations and the state as the main devils versus assumed undifferentiated 'people'. While this book may provide a detailed account of agrarian conflict, 'the book's populist commitments preclude a more substantial analysis of the agrarian conflict and the state in the context of the unique characteristics of Indonesia's capitalist development' (Pincus, 2015: 293).

The agrarian populism in Indonesia and its failure to take into account the country's unique capitalist development with its class dynamics has been partly sustained by the legacy of Suharto's authoritarian regime. The regime was responsible for the creation and promotion of the romanticised image of the 'harmonious village', where people in the village were described as an undifferentiated community and still performing reciprocal and mutual assistance (*gotong-royong*) for the common good (Pincus, 1996: 3). Clifford Geertz's classic work, *Agricultural Involution* (1963) and his concept of 'sharing poverty' stamps an intellectual might to such romanticised image of village life. In the broader landscape, Suharto banned any leftist traditions, including the study of Marxist political economy at the universities, which, effectively, prevented the development of critical social sciences (Hadiz & Dhakidae, 2005). While a Marxist political economy perspective is now allowed to be taught at the university, it still cannot be adopted by any social organisations. It is in this context that today, Marxist political economy and, particularly, class analysis remain predominantly absent (Farid, 2005), not only in the sphere of the social sciences but also among activists and social movements.

With some qualifications, agrarian populism has even arguably been sustained by the contemporary literature on agrarian change in Indonesia, which mainly pays attention to the land grabs and agrarian conflicts that have largely taken place in the outer islands. As far as land grabs are concerned, a growing number of studies have documented them along with the mechanisms involved in the process (Hall, 2011; McCarthy et al., 2012; Ito et al., 2014;

Astuti & McGregor, 2016; Rutten et al., 2017). Others have pointed out the impact of land grabs on indigenous people, on women and on the environment (Colbran, 2011; Julia & White, 2012; Goldstein, 2016). The impact of oil palm expansion on the livelihoods of the assumed undifferentiated smallholders has also been addressed (Rist et al., 2010; Feientrenie et al., 2010; Euler et al., 2016). Not least, the social movements against land grabbing have also drawn significant attention (Pye, 2010; GRAIN, 2014). Agrarian conflict, however, is not confined to the oil palm sector. There have also been major conflicts between farmers and the state or the corporations beyond oil palm, and social movements that demand agrarian reform (Rachman, 2011; Lucas & Warren, 2013). With the overwhelming concern regarding land grabs and agrarian conflict, the recurrent theme in this field tends to treat farmers or petty agricultural producers as an undifferentiated 'common people', in contest with either corporations or the state.

This partial bias towards agrarian change in the outer islands has left behind the study of agrarian change in Java, the most important island in the country, which up to the 1990s was instrumental in exposing the class dynamics of agricultural producers. During the height of political economy studies in rural Java in the last quarter of the twentieth century (for instance, Stoler, 1977a; 1977b; Hüsken, 1979; Hart, 1986; White & Wiradi, 1989; Hüsken & White, 1989; Pincus, 1996), research prominently highlighted the endemic land concentration along with proletarianisation on the one hand and the emergence of wealthier farmers in rural Java on the other. Those studies also threw some light on how class differentiation impacts on agricultural production. This included the focus on the dynamics of land tenure, labour arrangements, credit provision and technological development, which had been shaped by relations between agrarian classes. Last but not least, most studies at the time also investigated how different agrarian classes reproduced themselves through different mechanisms. Instead of treating undifferentiated 'people' as the main trait of agricultural producers, this literature exposed class dynamics in the countryside. The recent reversal of the focus of research into agrarian change from Java to the outer islands—as a result of the massive expansion of 'development projects' and social and environmental crisis in the outer islands and a shift in funding sources which favours studies outside Java (Peluso & Hart, 2005: 179)—marks a detachment from the focus of political economy in scrutinising the internal dynamics of agricultural producers to major attention on the agrarian conflict between presumably undifferentiated 'people' and the state and corporations.

Class Dynamics of Agrarian Change under Capitalism

An immediate major problem that can be identified from recent research into agrarian change in Indonesia is its failure to take into account the internal class dynamics of agricultural producers. Without this attention, one fails to acknowledge the existence of an employer-worker relationship among farmers/

smallholders in a capitalist system (Bernstein, 2010). This has neglected the exploitative relations between the propertied class within agriculture (capitalist farmers and 'landlord-capitalists') whose substantial possession of the means of production (particularly land) has enabled them to command the labour of others and the classes of labour (farmers-cum-workers) who, although they control or own marginal land, still have to sell their labour all the year in order to subsist. The omission of class relations among farmers/smallholders from the scene of agrarian change has disabled any meaningful understanding of different positions of farmers in the division of labour in agricultural production, access to credit and agricultural technologies. This eventually leads to a failure in comprehending the different agricultural outputs produced by each farmer and thus their different level of income from 'own-account' farming. Without a proper assessment of the production site, it is not possible to explain why some farmers manage to buy more land and agricultural technologies (e.g. tractors, combine harvester machines) or are able to send their children to university while other farmers lose their lands and struggle to send their children just to secondary school. This also holds true if one wishes to understand the different attitudes of farmers towards corporations and the state. The absence of class dynamics from the picture of agrarian change in Indonesia, as agrarian populism often suggests, has led to a misleading account of contemporary capitalist agrarian change in the country.

The partiality of researchers to studying agrarian change in the outer islands, which contributes to sustaining agrarian populism, has also failed to understand the contradictory nature of state intervention in agriculture. By looking only at the state policies towards export crops in the outer islands, where oil palm is the main commodity, agrarian populist supporters often emphasise the anti-smallholder/farmer nature of the Indonesian state (for instance, see SPI's statement in Kompas, 2016; and KPA, 2021). The fact that the state puts a levy on oil palm, its inability to protect the price from the global volatile market and its tendency to give premium care to the corporate-based palm oil producers (either private or state-owned) has easily fitted into the narrative of agrarian populism, pitting smallholders/farmers as a single class against the state or corporation. However, this picture of an anti-farmer state is contradicted by the continuing state support to rice farmers who are mostly located in Java. In rice cultivation, the state has long had a close relationship with the capitalist rice farmers as their clients, to control the countryside. Failing to identify the relations between the different agrarian classes and the way they relate to the state leads to the simplistic account of agrarian populism which only sees the relations between the state or corporation and the assumed homogeneous farmers.

This book intends to show the prominent role of class dynamics in shaping contemporary agrarian change in Indonesia. It first develops a proper framework for understanding the internal dynamics of agricultural producers in contemporary capitalist social relations and secondly, with this informed framework, investigates agrarian change not only in the outer islands of Indonesia but also in the neglected region of Java. We start from an understanding of agrarian change based on Marxist political economy, which posits that a proper account of agrarian change requires an examination of the class dynamics, production relations and the reproduction of agrarian classes in a specific setting. Of all these dimensions of agrarian change, the state's role in navigating such dynamics cannot be overlooked. The approach that has gained new momentum from current debates on the agrarian question, particularly Bernstein-Byres (Oya, 2013), is then used to chart agrarian change in Java and the outer islands. We will argue that the contemporary dynamics of capitalist agrarian change in Indonesia, both in oil palm in the outer islands and Javanese rice cultivation, owe much to the class dynamics which shape the nature of agricultural production and the pattern of class reproduction.

It will be shown that farmers/smallholders in Indonesia are not a single class. They are differentiated by an exploitative relation between farmer-employer (capitalist farmer or 'landlord-capitalist') and farmer-worker (classes of labour). Somewhere between these two distinct classes lie the Petty Commodity Producers (PCPs hereafter) who mostly employ their own family labour to till their land; thus neither command others' labour nor is their labour commanded by others. Our understanding of class as an exploitation relation differs itself from the mainstream gradational class stratifications. These different agrarian classes play different roles in agricultural production. Capitalist farmers decide what to grow and how to grow it, while farmers-cum-workers and workers must abide by the wishes of the employers who buy their labour. The forms of land tenure, labour arrangements credit provision and technological development in agricultural production are thus shaped by this class relation. While capitalist farmers generate income from 'own-account' farming that is considerably higher than their subsistence needs, the PCPs only earn income from 'own-account' farming sufficient for their subsistence, while the farmers-cum-workers' income from their 'own-account' farming is insufficient to meet their subsistence.

Given the different levels of income they receive from production, agrarian classes use their income for different purposes. With their high surpluses, capitalist farmers are able to purchase more substantial means of production for their farming, occupying village leader positions or financing their children's higher education. Differing from the activity of capitalist farmers to accumulate, the PCPs mostly use their income from farming for simple reproduction needs. They may buy or lease modest lands and send their children to secondary school. However, some of the PCPs may transform themselves into capitalist farmers when they seek to sell their labour all the year round, even though the income from their farming has already met their basic needs. Their willingness to sell their labour earns them substantial additional income, which enables them to buy a substantial amount of land within a certain period of time, making their transformation into capitalist farmers possible. The dream of becoming capitalist farmers is inconceivable for farmers-cum-workers (classes of labour), since their income from farming is much smaller than that of PCPs. Hence, although they sell their labour throughout the year, this income is only enough to sustain their subsistence level. In this situation, buying land is very difficult (especially in Java, more so than the outer islands) for the classes of labour, and when they want to send their children to secondary school, they must rely on state assistance.

By comparing agrarian change in two different contexts (oil palm and rice), we can comprehend the nature of state intervention on agrarian change. It will be argued that the Indonesian state is not simply an anti-farmers/smallholders institution, as is often argued by agrarian populists. It is true that the state has put a premium on corporate-based palm oil producers at the expense of farmers/smallholders. However, it is also true that the state has continued to provide input subsidies and price support mechanisms for rice farmers. The explanation for this contradictory state intervention must be sought in the broader class relations and capitalism in Indonesia. Historically, rice has been politically more crucial than oil palm, since it is the staple food for the majority of the Indonesian population, and it has been the most important currency involved in maintaining social stability. An affordable rice price for domestic workers is also crucial for the state to keep Indonesia's labour market 'competitive' for attracting foreign investors and boosting economic growth. It is no secret that the state is bound to support rice farmers. Nonetheless, this does not necessarily mean that all rice farmers receive the same benefit from the state. Capitalist rice farmers get most of the assistance, given that 'price-based' support means that larger cultivators receive larger input subsidies and higher sale revenues. Land redistribution programs that could deliver real benefit to the rice PCPs and classes of labour at the expense of rice capitalist farmers (and 'landlord-capitalists') are simply not an option for the Indonesian state. In return, rice capitalist farmers are meant to be the state clients in the countryside to maintain social stability. This indicates that the nature of the Indonesian state intervention in agriculture signals the complex class relations between the state, corporate agriculture and agrarian classes (capitalist farmers, PCPs and the classes of labour) in the context of peripheral capitalism, which is structured to attract foreign capital at all costs. In this understanding, the Indonesian state is rather a capitalist state in the peripheral world that needs to provide affordable staple food to maintain its low-wage working population while at the same time obliged to welcome corporate agriculture in non-staple foods and corporate non-agriculture to boost economic growth and capital accumulation. This implies that the Indonesian state is not simply anti-farmers/smallholders, but it is anti-workers both within and beyond agriculture.

In Chapter 2, this book starts by building a conceptual framework to grasp the internal dynamics of agricultural producers. This chapter argues that the emergence of capitalist social relations in agriculture has paved the way for the emergence of agrarian classes, which crucially shape production relations and class reproduction. Against agrarian populism, we argue that capitalist transition has transformed the 'peasantry' into farmers. Situated under the law of generalised commodity production (competition, efficiency, profit maximisation), farmers have been differentiated into different agrarian classes. In contrast with the Weberian class approach, which sees class as a matter of 'life chance', we argued that class is about exploitation. The class power of agrarian classes, then, plays a prominent role in shaping the nature of agricultural production. One particular aspect that sustains agrarian populism is the notion that in developing countries, capitalism has not developed properly as in the advanced world, and the 'peasantry' remains alive and kicking. The different nature of production relations in the peripheral world is often perceived as 'semi-feudalism'. We oppose this notion by arguing that the current nature of production relations in the developing world are capitalist, since the process of generalised commodity production has transformed the 'peasantry' into farmers and workers. Under capitalist agriculture, it is argued that the nature of land tenure, labour arrangements, agricultural productivity, wages and the income from 'own-account' farming are shaped by agrarian class relation. This emphasis on the social organisation of production challenges the neoclassical economics view of production dynamics, which is mainly understood from the technical aspect of production. The chapter will also argue that the production process has a different impact on the reproduction of different agrarian classes. While capitalist farmers manage to accumulate capital, the PCPs are mostly only able to maintain simple reproduction, and classes of labour struggle to survive at a subsistence level.

The book goes on to argue in Chapter 3 that the nature of the Indonesian state in mediating agrarian changes relates to broader class relations beyond agriculture which shape the nature of state intervention in agriculture over time. This has had a prominent impact on production relations and class reproduction throughout Indonesian history. With a strong and organised working class in the early independence up to Sukarno's era, the state was more inclined towards the working class by supporting a pro-labour policy in agriculture and initiating agrarian reform. This pattern was reversed when Suharto's authoritarian regime took power at the end of the 1960s, accompanied by the massacre of millions of leftist supporters and sympathisers. Since then, labour's platform of agrarian reform agendas has been neglected and replaced by the Green Revolution, which in various ways favours the capitalist farmers (especially rice producers) who serve as state clients in the rural areas. On the production side, mechanisation of rice cultivation was arrested, leading to a stagnation of productivity, and it has only been pushed through under Jokowi's administration since the mid-2010s. A similar intervention applies to oil palm production, where an intensification program to improve production techniques has only been implemented in the last few years, after decades of priority on extensification. However, there is a difference in how the state treats rice and oil palm production. As mentioned earlier, rice has enjoyed more support from the state than oil palm. Different from agrarian populism, which explains this bias as the manifestation of anti-farmers/smallholders orientation of the Indonesian state, we argue that this bias is closely related to the broader anti-workers approach of the Indonesian state to attract foreign investors, which has been the case since the ousting of leftist power in the mid-1960s. The limited state support in agriculture shapes the nature of class reproduction of the agrarian classes, where non-agricultural activities become increasingly important for all agrarian classes, although with different functions.

The empirical evidence on the dynamics of agrarian classes in Javanese rice cultivation and the outer islands' oil palm trees is presented in the second part of this book. In Chapter 4, we will first chart the historical trajectory of two sites of agrarian change, in a Javanese rice village and a Sumatran oil palm village. It serves as the background to explain the contemporary agrarian change in both villages which is elaborated in the subsequent chapters. It will show the nature of the 'old frontier' in the Javanese site, while the oil palm site in Sumatra is a 'new frontier'. This situates the different pattern of class dynamics in two contexts. In this chapter, we also briefly discuss our methodology, explaining the data collection techniques employed in the two villages studied.

In Chapter 5, to debunk the notion of a homogeneous 'peasantry' in recent years in the Indonesian countryside, we show the class dynamics of agrarian change in Java and Sumatra. Firstly, a grasp of the nature of class location of different agrarian classes is needed, and this emphasises the usefulness of a comparative study to position agrarian class location. It also highlights how land productivity for different crops is crucial to locate households in labour relations, which is key to understanding their class positions. The chapter subsequently attempts to patch the flaws of previous studies, which barely touch upon the internal segments of agrarian classes. The chapter then explains how capitalist farmers and classes of labour relate to each other, and the position of PCPs in this relation, in shaping wage levels and working conditions. The different setting between rice cultivation in Java and Sumatra's oil palm plantations provides a rich insight into how class relations reveal a different nature in a different social setting.

To understand the nature of agricultural production in rural Indonesia, something that has been overlooked by agrarian populist and neoclassical economics, in Chapter 6 we show how class relations shape the dynamics of land tenure, labour arrangements, technological development and credit provision in Javanese rice cultivation and Sumatran oil palm production. The comparison reveals the different nature of agricultural production dynamics in these crops. For instance, share-cropping is a prominent land arrangement in Javanese rice, while cultivation with wage labour is notable in Sumatra's oil palm production, with a different impact on production costs and income from 'own-account' farming. Thus, the chapter continues to assess land productivity and income from 'own-account' farming in both the rice and oil palm setting. Again, a comparative study proves to be useful to provide crucial insights. This chapter shows that while capitalist farmers in Sumatra's oil palm production generate higher income from 'own-account' farming than their compatriots in Javanese rice cultivation, the high volatility of oil palm prices and the stagnant land productivity in the last few decades have prevented them from depending solely on oil palm production.

In Chapter 7, to rectify agrarian populists who fail to grasp the differential nature of class reproduction of various farmers, we show how different agrarian classes utilise their income from production to serve different functions of reproduction. We expose how capitalist farmers and 'landlord-capitalists' are involved in accumulation activities, both in their 'own-account' farming and non-agricultural activities. We also highlight the competition between capitalist farmers and 'landlord-capitalists' which crucially shapes their strategy of accumulation. This has largely been overlooked in the literature. The comparison between Sumatra and Java reveals the specificity of class reproduction strategies and also applies to the reproduction of PCPs and the working classes, which respectively engage in simple reproduction and survival activity. The chapter will go on to illuminate how class reproduction intertwines closely with generation, gender and clanship in particular settings.

Note

1 This generally refers to the islands 'outside' Java (with Madura), such as Sumatra, Kalimantan and Sulawesi, and other smaller islands. Despite the statistical convention which dates back to the colonial period, the distinction between Java (with Madura) and the 'outer islands' also serves as a 'fairly accurate representation of the fault line between the core and periphery' (Dick, 2002: 3) given the overwhelming economic development in Java compared to the 'outer islands'. We use the term in both senses.

References

Astuti, R & McGregor, A 2016, 'Indigenous land claims or green grabs? Inclusions and exclusions within forest carbon politics in Indonesia', *The Journal of Peasant Studies*, vol. 44, no. 2, pp. 445–466.

Bernstein, H 2010, *Class dynamics of agrarian change*, Sterling, VA, Kumarian Press.

Bernstein, H 2014, 'Food sovereignty via the "peasant way": A sceptical view', *The Journal of Peasant Studies*, vol. 41, no. 6, pp. 1031–1063.

Borras, S.M & Franco, J 2011, *Political dynamics of land grabbing in Southeast Asia: Understanding Europe's role*, Amsterdam, TNI.

Colbran, N 2011, 'Indigenous peoples in Indonesia: At risk of disappearing as distinct peoples in the rush for biofuel?' *International Journal on Minority and Group Rights*, vol. 18, pp. 63–92.

Dick, H 2002, *The emergence of a national economy: An economic history of Indonesia, 1800–2000*, Honolulu, University of Hawaii Press.

Euler, M et al 2016, 'Oil palm expansion among smallholder farmers in Sumatra, Indonesia', *Journal of Agricultural Economics*, vol. 67, no. 3, pp. 658–676.

Farid, H 2005, 'The class question in Indonesian social science', in H Vedi & D Daniel (eds), *Social science and power in Indonesia*, Jakarta, Equinox Publishing, pp. 167–196.

Feientrenie, L et al 2010, 'Why do farmers prefer oil palm? Lesson learnt from Bungo District, Indonesia', *Small Scale Forestry*, vol. 9, pp. 379–396.

Geertz, C 1963, *Agricultural involution: The process of ecological change in Indonesia*, Los Angeles: University of California Press.

Goldstein, J.E 2016, 'Knowing the subterranean: Land grabbing, oil palm, and divergent expertise in Indonesia's peat soil', *Environment & Planning*, vol. 48, no. 4, pp. 754–770.

GRAIN 2014, '"Peasants" long fight to roll back palm oil land grab in Indonesia', *Against The Grain*, January, pp. 1–5.

Hadiz, V & Dhakidae, D 2005, *Social science and power in Indonesia*, Jakarta, Equinox Publishing.

Hall, D 2011, 'Land grabs, land control, and Southeast Asian crop booms', *The Journal of Peasant Studies*, vol. 38, no. 4, pp. 837–857.

Hart, G 1986, *Power, labor and livelihood: Processes of change in rural Java*, Berkeley, CA, University of California Press.

Hüsken, F 1979, 'Landlors, sharecroppers and agricultural labourers: Changing labour relations in rural Java', *Journal of Contemporary Asia*, vol. 9, pp. 140–151.

Hüsken, F & White, B 1989, '*Java social differentiation, food production and agrarian* control', in G Hart, A Turton & B White (eds), *Agrarian transformations: Local process and the state in Southeast Asia*, Berkeley, CA, University of California Press, pp. 234–265.

Ito, T et al 2014, 'Power to make land dispossession acceptable: A policy discourse analysis of the Merauke Integrated Food and Energy Estate (MIFEE), Papua, Indonesia', *The Journal of Peasant Studies*, vol. 41, no. 1, pp. 29–50.

Julia & White, B 2012, 'Gendered experiences of dispossession: Oil palm expansion in a Dayak Hibun community in West Kalimantan', *The Journal of Peasant Studies*, vol. 39, no. 3–4, pp. 995–1016.

Kompas, 2016, 'Kebijakan Pemerintah di Sektor Pertanian Belum Berpihak pada Petani', *Kompas* 25 September, viewed 29 September 2021, https://nasional.kompas.com/read/2016/09/25/06000051/kebijakan.pemerintah.di.sektor.pertanian.belum.berpihak.pada.petani?page=all.

KNPA 2019, *Bersatu Melawan Perampasan Tanah, Jalankan Reforma Agraria Untuk Keadilan dan Kesejahteraan Rakyat*, Pernyataan Sikap Peringatan Hari Tani Nasional (HTN) 2019 Komite Nasional Pembaruan Agraria, 24 September, viewed 29 September 2021, https://elsam.or.id/bersatu-melawan-perampasan-tanah-jalankan-reforma-agraria-untuk-keadilan-dan-kesejahteraan-rakyat/

KPA 2017, 'Cases of agrarian conflict rises in 2017: Consortium', *The Jakarta Post*, 28 December, viewed 29 September 2021.

KPA 2021, *Kala Petani Semakin Ditinggalkan*, Konsorsium Pembaruan Agraria, viewed 29 September 2021, http://kpa.or.id/media/baca/kegiatan/610/Kala_Petani_Semakin_Ditinggalkan/.

Lucas, A & Warren, C 2013, *Land for the people: The state and agrarian conflict in Indonesia*, Athens, OH, Ohio University Press.

McCarthy, J.F et al 2012, 'Trajectories of land acquisition and enclosure: Development schemes, virtual land grabs, and green acquisitions in Indonesia's outer islands', *The Journal of Peasant Studies*, vol. 39, no. 2, pp. 521–549.

Oya, C 2013, 'The land rush and classic agrarian questions of capital and labour: A systematic scoping review of the socioeconomic impact of land grabs in Africa', *Third World Quarterly*, vol. 34, no. 9, pp. 1532–1557.

Peluso, N.L & Hart, G 2005, 'Revisiting "rural" Java: Agrarian research in the wake of reformasi: A review essay', *Indonesia*, vol. 80, pp. 177–195.

Pincus, J 1996, *Class power and agrarian change: Land and labour in rural West Java*, London, MacMillan Press.

Pincus, J 2015, 'Book review', *Journal of Agrarian Change*, vol. 15, pp. 290–292.

Pye, O 2010, 'The biofuel connection – Transnational activism and the palm oil boom', *The Journal of Peasant Studies*, vol. 37, no. 4, pp. 851–874.

Rachman, N.F 1999, *Petani dan Penguasa: Dinamika Perjalanan Politik Agraria Indonesia*, Yogyakarta, Insist Press.

Rachman, N.F 2011, *The resurgence of land reform policy and agrarian movements in Indonesia* (Unpublished Doctoral Dissertation). Berkeley, CA, University of California, Berkeley.

Rist, L et al 2010, 'The livelihood impacts of oil palm: Smallholders in Indonesia', *Biodiversity and Conservation*, vol. 19, no. 4, pp. 1009–1024.

Rutten, R et al 2017, 'Smallholder bargaining power in large-scale land deals: A relational perspective', *The Journal of Peasant Studies*, vol. 44 no. 4, pp. 891–917.

SPI 2021, *Kedaulatan Pangan dan Perlindungan Hak Asasi Petani sebagai Fondasi Sistem Pangan yang Memenuhi Hak Atas Pangan dan Gizi*, Serikat Petani Indonesia, viewed 29 September 2021, https://spi.or.id/kedaulatan-pangan-dan-perlindungan-hak-asasi-petani-sebagai-fondasi-sistem-pangan-yang-memenuhi-hak-atas-pangan-dan-gizi/.

Stoler, A.L 1977a, 'Rice harvesting in Kali Loro: A study of class and labor relations in rural Java', *American Ethnologist*, vol. 4, no. 4, pp. 678–698.

Stoler, A.L 1977b, 'Class structure and female autonomy in rural Java', *Sign*, vol. 3, no. 1, pp. 74–89.

White, B & Wiradi, G 1989, 'Agrarian and nonagrarian bases of inequality in nine javanese villages', in G Hart, A Turton & B White (eds), *Agrarian transformations: Local process and the state in Southeast Asia*, Berkeley, CA, University of California Press.

White, B et al 2012, 'The new enclosures: Critical perspectives on corporate land deals', *The Journal of Peasant Studies*, vol. 39, no. 3–4, pp. 619–647.

2 Exposing Class Dynamics of Agrarian Change Under Capitalism

Introduction

There is a widespread notion that while the 'peasantry' in the advanced capitalist world has been transformed into farmers and workers, the 'peasantry' in the peripheral world[1] keeps its subsistence-oriented and egalitarian nature. To counter this populist narrative, this chapter argues that while the 'peasantry' in the advanced countries was transformed into farmers and workers during the capitalist transition, in the peripheral world, this transformation largely took place in the colonial era. In this understanding, the current expansion of capital in agriculture under neoliberalism should not be seen as the *creation* of capitalist social relations ('primitive accumulation') as many observers suggest. It is argued that today the peripheral world simply experiences the *expansion* and *deepening* of capitalist social relations in agriculture spearheaded by the neoliberal wave, given that 'primitive accumulation' was already taking place during the colonial period. The recent expansion of capital often delivers either further class differentiation of the farmers/smallholders or dispossession by displacement or both. Against the Weberian class approach, which understands class as 'life chance', this chapter argues that the Marxist understanding of class as exploitation is a more powerful tool to grasp the nature of agrarian classes. To maintain that the nature of today's agricultural production in the peripheral countries is already based on capitalist social relations, this chapter refutes the argument of 'semi-feudalist' thesis. We argue that under capitalist agriculture, the prominent aspects of production (land tenure, labour arrangement, credit provision and technologies) are shaped by class dynamics, and the different levels of agricultural outputs and incomes from 'own-account' farming of different agrarian classes shape the pattern of class reproduction.

Capitalist Agrarian Change and Class Dynamics

Capitalist Transition and Class Differentiation

There are several ways to delineate how the process of capitalist development shapes the nature of agricultural producers. One explanation comes from the tradition of 'commercial capitalism'. It argues that the key figures of the

DOI: 10.4324/9781003267348-2

development of capitalism are the classes of the landowners, of the merchants (Banaji, 2007) and of capital and financiers (Arrighi, 1994; Moore, 2003). This rather flexible usage of the notion of 'capital class' is presumably exploiting the no less ambiguous concept of labour in categories such as 'landless labour', 'tenant-farmers' and 'small peasants', terms which are used interchangeably (Bernstein, 2010: 32–33). Given this shallow treatment, the chief shortcoming of such an approach is that it fails to provide a useful account of the impact of capitalist development on class structure, since it mainly focuses on the cycle of financial capital and state formation.

Another approach is suggested by the so-called 'agrarian transition' approach. In this tradition, capitalist development in agriculture situates class relations in at least three mechanisms. At the beginning, the established Marxist understanding of primitive accumulation sees the separation of the agricultural producers from the means of production, particularly land (Marx, 1976). It marks the transformation of capitalist property relations, from the common and relatively inclusive to the private and exclusive access to land (Wood, 2002: 108). This separation deprives the producers (peasants) direct access (non-market) to the land and, therefore, their access to the means of production becomes mediated by the market. The result is, as Brenner puts it, that 'they had *no choice* but to respond to the rising market by competing with one another as effectively as possible by cost-cutting, and thus by specializing, accumulating their surpluses, and innovating' (Brenner, 1982: 91). Subsequently, the extensification and intensification of commodity relations (land and labour) transform the mode of surplus appropriation: from the 'extra-economic means' to the more purely 'economic means' (market) (Brenner, 1976). Surplus is no longer extracted from peasants through taxes and other traditional duties, but they become farmers (tenants) from whom surplus is extracted via economic means (fixed rents). Both tenant-farmers and landlords are now compelled by the market imperative to increase productivity and profit. As a result, 'market imperatives certainly accelerated the polarization of English rural society into larger landowners and a growing property-less multitude' (Wood, 2002: 103).

There is little doubt that the course of commodification in England and its impact on class formation (the typical capital-wage labour relation) is not necessarily universal. Indeed, commodification is the outcome of the capitalist transition which formed the fundamental social relation between capital and wage labour. Once established in England, commodification, with the help of Britain's imperialism, became unequivocally imposed around the world. However, in peripheral world, the vast number of agricultural producers (farmers) is neither primarily capitalist farmers nor simply wage-earning agricultural labour since they retain their small plot of land. This, for some, has been perceived as not being capitalist agriculture (Byres, 1996; Patnaik, 1986). Yet, as will be discussed further in the next section, capitalism in agriculture does not necessarily entail the *full-scale development* of typical capital-wage labour relations.

Capitalism may be seen 'as a system of generalized commodity production' (Bernstein, 2010: 124), in which the commodity relationship has become the dominant precondition in determining the production and the reproduction of agricultural producers. Although direct agricultural producers (farmers) may retain some plots of land (not-fully proletarianised), they have been obliged to generalise commodity relations as far as their reproduction depends on the production of the commodity to be sold in the market and their inputs are bought from the market while they are bound to be productive in order to compete with other farmers in the market. Commodification may not 'displace' the peasantry from the land as neo-populist supporters often propose (Desmarais, 2007; Ploeg, 2008). Yet, commodification has undoubtedly 'transformed' the peasantry into petty commodity producers (PCP) or farmers, which maintain characteristics very distinct from the 'old peasantry' (Bernstein, 2011). Commodification transforms the subsistence-oriented peasantry into commodity production-based farmers.

This generalised commodity production is precisely the nature of capitalist development that situates farmers in current peripheral world. Conceptually, as PCP, farmers face 'contradictory unity of class places' (Bernstein, 2010: 103). On the one hand, they are part of the capital in terms of possession of land, tools, seeds, fertilisers and other chemicals. On the other hand, they are also part of the labour since they provide their own labour (family labour) to perform the agricultural tasks. This contradictory class position implies the inherent contradiction of the reproduction of the farmers. Their income should be distributed to both reproduce the means of production (capital) by paying the replacement cost and rent, and reproduce the producer (family labour) through providing funds for the household's consumption, and thus provide generational reproduction. In generalised commodity production, the reproduction of PCP has always faced a threat from market dynamics. The higher cost of farming, fluctuating prices, technological changes, credit availability and indebtedness are some of the market sources which threaten the stability of PCP (Bernstein, 2010; Zhang, 2015). This is not to mention the state's intervention in setting the term of trade against agriculture, which may pose a direct threat of disintegration of PCP (Bernstein, 1988).

If farmers are able to meet the minimum requirements to reproduce both capital and labour at the same scale as they start the production, they reproduce themselves as PCPs who are able to perform 'simple reproduction' (Bernstein, 1988). At other times, PCPs might be able to accumulate productive assets on a larger scale than the minimum requirements to reproducing themselves. They then become capitalist farmers, involved in what Marx calls 'expanded reproduction'. Conversely, in difficult times, other sections of PCP may find themselves in a struggle (sometimes they succeed, sometimes fail) to meet the minimum requirement to reproduce both their capital and labour to the same scale, experiencing a 'simple reproduction squeeze' and joining the group of semi-proletarian farmers (Gibbon & Neocosmos, 1985) or 'marginal farmers' (Bernstein, 2010). They generally have to seek wage labour employment (both 'on-farm' and 'off-farm') and, at the same time, reduce their consumption levels in order to retain their small piece of the means of production (land). As with other farmers who fail completely to meet the basic requirements to reproduce their previous scale of both capital and labour, they are forced to join the landless wage labour, and thus marking the typical process of proletarianisation.

The theoretical proposition of class differentiation does not suggest that all PCPs have experienced, and would face, constant differentiation between capital and wage labour in all places at all times. It should be clear that, as Bernstein states, 'whether differentiation of PCP occurs, the extent to which it occurs, and the specific mechanisms through which it occurs, are always the effect of particular conditions of competition and class struggle requiring concrete investigation' (Bernstein, 1988: 264).

Capitalist Agrarian Change under Neoliberalism

The current expansion of capitalist accumulation under neoliberalism marks the new dynamics of market relations that govern all aspects of our life's aspect (labour, land, nature). There is the highly debated primitive accumulation (PA) process around the world precipitated by the neoliberal wave. In this debate, there is a strong tendency to see PA particularly in the current peripheral world as the *creation* of capitalist social relations. The issue, then, is to locate what capitalism is ('inside') and what it is not ('outside' of capitalism). A clear definition of capitalism is thus inevitably needed to capture the moment 'when people, ideas, land, and nature are moving from the 'outside' to the 'inside' of capitalism' (Hall, 2012: 1204). Yet, among others, David Harvey's popular conception of 'accumulation by dispossession' (2003), which equates to PA, lacks this clarity.

Other theorists (de Angelis, 2001; Byres, 2003; Webber, 2008; Patnaik & Moyo, 2011) provide a classical account of capitalism by understanding that capitalist social relations exist when the direct producers are separated from the means of production and they are proletarianised, while the capitalists control the means of production as private property. By this definition, PA means the first step of the creation of capitalist social relations: the separation of direct producers from the means of production. When direct producers are not yet fully separated from their land, and not fully employed as wage labourers elsewhere (by which means their surplus values are extracted), capitalism is considered incomplete or even non-existent. Yet, as Hall (2012) insists, the view that agricultural smallholders in the peripheral world (Southeast Asia in this case) live outside of capitalism because many of them are not fully proletarianised and are assumed to subsist in nature and avoid market relations is incorrect since it does not accurately represent the reality of the context of Southeast Asia. Theoretically, the more serious problem is the 'stereotypical' understanding of capitalism (Bernstein, 2016). This 'stereotypical' view provides a concrete analysis of contemporary capitalism based on capitalism 'proper' developed by Marx's work in the late nineteenth century without mediation ('concentration of many determinations'). Bernstein emphasises that the popularity of PA is due particularly to the implicit assumption that the contemporary peripheral world would follow the path of advanced capitalist countries, including that PA, as the 'original sin' of capitalism in Europe, must happen in the current peripheral world (which is presumably still pre-capitalist) if capitalist relations are deemed to exist. This argument, as Bernstein aptly highlights, is both teleological and less useful to understand the contemporary world under neoliberalism.

Avoiding the 'stereotypical approach', Bernstein (1977, 2010) develops his own account of capitalism. His understanding of capitalism is similar to that of Brenner (1976, 1982) and Wood (2002) in the sense that 'market dependence' marks the prominent nature of capitalism, which could exist without global full-scale proletarianisation. He depicts capitalism as 'generalized commodity production' where 'the reproduction of any class, social category or formation, [becomes] impossible *outside* capitalist commodity relations, even if reproduction is not constituted exclusively by them' (Bernstein, 2018: 18). This outcome was precipitated by primitive accumulation and proletarianisation in England and elsewhere to mark the beginning of the commodification of land and labour and then spread to everything else. In the peripheral world, however, Bernstein insists that primitive accumulation and, to a certain degree, proletarianisation (not necessarily fully-fledged) successfully established a 'generalization of commodity relations' by the end of colonial period in Asia and Africa. The 'commodification of subsistence' in the peripheral globe has meant that the reproduction of any social classes (notably farmers) is predominantly mediated by the market in the sense that they cannot reproduce themselves outside the circuit of commodity production (Bernstein, 2010). Because capitalist relations are considered to have been established since the 1940s–1950s, it would be contradictory to depict PA (the creation of capitalist relations) as having been developed since the neoliberal turn in the 1980s.

It is important to note then that the current phenomena of 'land grabbing', 'enclosure', privatisation and reproduction of capitalist relations through either violence or theft are not necessarily associated with primitive accumulation and the *creation* of capitalist social relations. What might be clear is that commodification has been intensified under the neoliberal wave, both in its spatial-scale and coverage-sphere and has thus *expanded and deepened* capitalist social relations. This has delivered some impacts on agricultural producers.

Apart from class differentiation that was discussed earlier, contemporary capital expansion under neoliberalism may also make agricultural producers/farmers experience what in the literature is referred to as 'dispossession by displacement' (Araghi, 2000, 2009). With the 'great global enclosure of our time' during the neoliberal era, non-corporate-agricultural producers or farmers (popularly called smallholders) are dispossessed and forced to move away from their land. The dispossessors are generally corporate-agricultural producers. In Indonesia's oil palm production, the literature suggests the 'twin processes' of both dispossession by displacement and class differentiation have occurred among the farmers (Fortin, 2011). However, in Indonesia's rice cultivation, class differentiation does not go hand-in-hand with dispossession by displacement because the majority of the rice producers are farmers, not corporates either state or privately-owned. It is likely that, when commodity production involves both corporate-agricultural producers and non-corporate-agricultural producers (farmers), the dynamics of commodification will lead to both dispossession by displacement and class differentiation, while this is not the case when it involves only 'corporate-agricultural producers' or 'non-corporate-agricultural producers'.

Approaching Class

While class differentiation of farmers/smallholders is the prominent trait of current capitalist expansion, there are several ways of understanding class. The Weberian approach sees class as a set of gradational categories across a social group. Commonly, it is based on differential access to 'life chances': the supply of goods, external living conditions and life experiences (Weber, in Gerth & Mills, 1958). Based on these indicators, a quantitative measurement is generally devoted to identifying class stratification. As a result, it describes the usual terms of class hierarchy in the capitalist society as being upper class, upper-middle class, middle class, lower-middle class, lower class, etc. In agrarian terms, one might be introduced to categories of poor farmers, middle farmers, rich farmers, etc.

The problems with such a categorisation are profound. In the first place, since the threshold of 'life chances' for each class is arbitrary, it tends to produce a large and indefinite number of classes without any substantial meaning (Gubbay, 1997: 77). What is the substantial difference between, for instance, 'middle class' and 'lower-middle class'? Moreover, this attempt is to give an impression that households are able to move relatively easily back and forth between the gradational class categories. Historically, however, households are bound by the more institutionalised social relations that limit their options to acquire class mobility. This type of class analysis fails to see the structural position of different classes in capitalism that have different lived experiences and opposing economic interests from each other (Oya, 2004).

Instead of 'life chances', the Marxist perspective proposes 'exploitation' as the key characteristic of class analysis (Marx, 1976). The established understanding of this concept perceives class as the social expression of exploitation that takes place through 'the appropriation of the labour of others: in a commodity-producing of what Marx calls "surplus value"' (Ste Croix, 1981: 43). The location of the exploiting and exploited classes is understood from their positions in the production relationship. The structural approach to class, however, brings this concept into an extreme position. Cohen (1978), for example, insists that 'a person's class is established by nothing but his objective place in the network of ownership relations'. As a result, looking at class structure alone, at any given moment, is seen as being sufficient to understand class and the rationale for generating class taxonomies, depicting a static account of class exploitation.

The main shortcoming of such an account is that it mistakenly treats class structure as a definitive characteristic of class, while discounting the fact 'that any relation to the means of production is simultaneously a social relation among human agents; that these agents are actors…coming to an awareness of such systemic relations these actors become class agents in the fullest sense' (McNally, 2015: 140). Perceiving class without human agents may only lead to 'empty dogmatism'.

In contrast to Cohen, E.P. Thompson (1966) proposed that class is a 'relation' and not a 'category' (Thompson, 1966: 9). Since class is basically a 'historical process', it can only be understood through time and can only be understood via a diachronic approach, instead of at a particular moment (synchronic). This 'relational approach' of class has ignited controversy since it seems to imply that when class has not happened at any given moment, 'objective exploitation' is not taking place. The standard critique to Thompson has been that to claim a class only exists in its relationship with another class may dangerously lead to voluntarism and idealism (Anderson, 1980; Hall, 1981).

However, as Wood (1982: 52) convincingly suggests, 'the difference between Thompson and his critics is largely a question of emphasis'. From this interpretation, class location through which production relations shape class formations has not been completely abandoned. Nonetheless, class location needs to be treated merely as a 'class situation' in which 'objective exploitation' based on productive relations is experienced and handled by people (Wood, 1982: 49). In this respect, 'class situation' itself is never a complete account of class. It should co-exist with the way people experience and react to their 'objective exploitation'. This process of class formation is the key to understanding class (McNally, 2015). It implies that the impoverished nature of seeing only the structural aspect of class needs to be accompanied by looking into the 'diverse life process of social class'. In analytical term, a combination of the synchronic and diachronic approaches to class is necessary. Camfield (2004: 427) has posited that 'class may be considered synchronically…however, class relations exist in time'. This suggests that class location could be a departure point to understanding class relations through time.

As far as agrarian class is concerned, the need to understand class both in its 'economic sociology' (location) and 'political sociology' (relation) aspect has also been suggested (Bernstein, 2010). When it comes to the 'political sociology of class', agricultural producers' experience of production relations, however, are not self-evidently and exclusively being perceived as a class. Their experiences are inextricably intertwined with other forms of social relations: race, gender, ethnicity, national identity, etc. (Bernstein, 2010). The combination of experiences and their impact on class relations is a matter of empirical investigation.

To identify agrarian class location, it is widely accepted that a single indicator of land ownership is highly inadequate (Oya, 2004; Zhang, 2015). Patnaik (1976), in the context of India's debate, suggests a combination of land possession and a labour ratio to identify class structure. A labour ratio captures the position of households in the labour market by looking at the ratio between the hours of hired in and sold in labour in agriculture. A similar account is proposed by Bardhan (1982). Zhang (2015) develops this approach further by combining property ownership and market relations to locate agrarian class location. While property ownership depicts the fundamental difference between those who dominate the means of production and the property-less labourers, market relations signal the consequences of such property relations.

Zhang (2015) identifies four different market relations (land, labour, product and means of production) through which exploitation and class reproduction take place. The labour relation defines the exploitation between those who buy and those who sell their labour power. Property-less workers are destined to sell their labour to the owners of the means of production, which enables the latter to appropriate the surplus value from the former. While on the contrary, land, product and means of production relations only provide a hint of how classes harness their share from production to reproduce themselves.

This approach is consistent in our understanding of class as a social expression of exploitation, as mentioned earlier. Our account of class location represents an attempt to see class as a 'distinct location in the production relations' (Wood, 2002). The emphasis is required to distance ourselves from the Weberian approach which emphasises the gradational nature of class. In this respect, the key point is rather identifying a distinct qualitative position of class-based on an individual's position in the production and their pattern of reproduction, rather than supplying a quantitative measurement of inequality. This suggests that a qualitative measurement of class is considered to be more useful than a quantitative one.

This qualitative approach is deployed to identify the nature of the household's involvement in each market relation. In the labour relation, attention is focused on seeing whether a household predominantly hires in or sells out their labour power. The pattern of whether a household is predominantly involved in purchasing or renting land or selling or leasing land is the main concern regarding the land relation and a household's participation. Regarding the product relation, it looks at the main trend, whether a household sells their products on the market or keeps them for their own consumption. Last but not least, the activity of a household in the means of production relation (buying or not) is a good way of identifying the different patterns of its reproduction.

While Zhang's approach is useful, it still focuses on agriculture in the narrow sense, discounting the analysis of agriculture beyond the farm. This critique is based on the understanding that, in modern capitalism, the agricultural sector may include 'agrarian capital beyond the countryside' and, at the same time, 'rural labour beyond the farm' (Bernstein, 2010: 110). Workers have increasingly engaged in the fluid social boundaries of jobs that are depicted in the literature as 'classes of labour' (Bernstein, 2010; Lerche, 2010; Mezzadri, 2017; Pattenden, 2018) 'who now depend—directly and indirectly—on the sale of their labour power for their own daily reproduction' (Panitch & Leys, 2000: ix).

However, the significance of the so-called 'off-farm' activities when discussing agrarian class location is still largely overlooked. Before continuing our discussion on the relationship between 'off-farm' activities and class, it is important to clarify the related terms that we will use throughout our study. 'Off-farm' activities often refer to activities outside 'own-account' farming, which is popularly described as 'on-farm'. The activities outside 'own-account' farming include both hiring/selling labour in farming and non-agricultural activities (hiring/selling labour and self-employment outside of agriculture). In this case, the term 'off-farm' activity tends to be confused with the activity outside of agriculture, although, in fact, it includes activities within agriculture but outside 'own-account' farming ('on-farm'). To avoid confusion, we maintain the categorisation of 'own-account' farming, hiring/selling labour in farming and non-agricultural activities. From our class perspective, this categorisation is also more useful for identifying the contribution of households' 'own-account' farming, hiring/selling labour in farming and non-agricultural activities for their overall class reproduction.

A burgeoning literature has captured the 'own-account' farming and non-agricultural activities issue in a discussion on part-time farming and pluriactivity (Gasson, 1986; Fuller, 1990; Evans & Berry, 1993). However, since their main concern is to understand the livelihood aspect of farming and non-farming activities in rural areas, they hardly bring their insight to bear on the theoretical discussion on class. Among the exceptions is, perhaps, Buttel (1982), who suggests, using the context of US agriculture, that the rise in part-time farming in the 1970s (the involvement of farmers outside 'own-account' farming) stalled class polarisation, to some extent, though only temporarily. Identifying agrarian class location-based not only on their position in property relations and production relations but also their engagement in selling out their labour to other's farms and non-agricultural activities, is crucial to grasping the complex nature of this location.

Following the conceptual approach of class as the social expression of exploitation, it is well-known that capital and labour represent the main exploiting and exploited classes. However, agrarian class location is much more complex and diverse given the variety of agricultural production relations in different settings. Firstly, the capitalist class includes many different scales, sectors and factions, so that we may speak of 'classes of capitalists' (Bernstein, 2010). This is equally true for labour. As mentioned before, the 'classes of labour' covers a wide range of those who predominantly depend on wages for their daily reproduction. Zhang (2015), for instance, has highlighted the component of class of labour in China when he discusses the 'semi-proletariat farmer', while Lerche (1999) alludes to the members of the classes of labour when he observes sharecroppers in India who are actually 'disguised wage labour'. Hence, the composition of the classes of labour depends on a particular context. Apart from capitalists and the classes of labour, however, structurally there are also PCPs who pose a 'contradictory unity of class place' (Bernstein, 2010) in agricultural production. Since their participation in the labour market is redundant, they do not easily fit into either the capitalist or working class.

The complexity of agrarian class location is even more pronounced when we take into account the 'own-account' farming and non-agricultural activities of the households in each agrarian class. For instance, capitalist farmers may comprise of different factions, signalled by their different activities in non-agricultural accumulation. This applies also to the case of PCPs and the classes of labour. While the literature has shed some light on the complexity of agrarian class location, so far there has been no systematic study to explore the complexity of the agrarian class itself.

Our study embarks on this task by looking into a combination of property relations and market relations (Zhang, 2015) and activities beyond 'own-account' farming (Buttel, 1982). Our systematic understanding of the complexity of agrarian class location is indispensable if we wish to adequately grasp the nature of class relations. As mentioned earlier, our identification of agrarian class location must be seen as a departure. This 'class situation' needs to be followed by an investigation into the complex processes through which people experience and handle their 'class situation'. Furthermore, there may be varied positions within similar class situations that complicate their response. The nature of class relations between capitalist farmers and the classes of labour in the countryside can be explained by looking at the complex 'class situation' in the specific setting and how this impacts on class relations over time. This historical treatment may enable us to see 'the making' and 'un-making' of class at different moments in time.

Class Dynamics and Production Relations

Agrarian Change and Generalised Commodity Production

It has already been noted that current capitalist agrarian change shapes class dynamics. Before we move forward to depict the impact of class dynamics on agricultural production relations, it is important to clarify further our understanding of capitalist agriculture as generalised commodity production. The debate over this stance began in the early 1970s with the argument between Andre Gunder Frank (1967) and Ernesto Laclau (1971) over the nature of the mode of production in Latin America, in which they disputed capitalism versus feudalism. This disagreement then attracted further participants in the context of the 'India Debate' (Thorner, 1982; Patnaik, 1990).

The 'India Debate' exposed two different views: the so-called 'Semi-Feudalist Thesis' (SFT) and the 'Capitalist Thesis' (CT). The main proposition of the SFT was that capitalist relations of production are not complete as far as they do not meet the full criteria of capitalism as it originated and developed in advanced capitalist countries. In agriculture, it is incomplete if there is no development of productive forces marked by the effectiveness of individual capitalist farmers to reduce production costs and improve productivity

(Patnaik, 1972; Byres, 1982). This view is sustained in their later work (Patnaik & Moyo, 2011; Byres, 2002, 2003, 2016). Bhaduri (1973), another leading adherent of the SFT, identified four aspects of these relations: (1) sharecropping, (2) the perpetual indebtedness of small tenants, (3) the concentration of two modes of exploitation: usury and landownership in the hands of the same economic class, and (4) a lack of accessibility to the market for the small tenant.

The main problem with the SFT is its confusion when distinguishing between the 'criteria' for capitalist relations and the 'indicators' of the process of capitalist development. It is historically true that the development of productive forces based on the capitalist relations of production. However, it is equally valid to say that the existence of capitalist relations of production in other contexts is not accompanied by the high-level development of productive forces. Patnaik and Byres' insistence that the existence of capitalist relations of production *should* manifest itself in the massive development of productive forces is, thus, misleading. As Rudra (1978a: 920) points out,

> the question, whether some relations of production can be characterised as capitalist or not, ought to be kept distinct from the question of whether development of the forces of production is taking place on the basis of such relations or not.

This does not suggest, however, that the distinct question means the production relations and the development of productive forces are necessarily separated in practice.

There are also serious problems identifying several archaic social relations hindering capitalist development in agriculture. Some argue that sharecropping is a flexible arrangement that could be either part of a feudal or a capitalist institution, depending on the nature of landowners: whether they are pure rentiers or eager to put their money into investment (Rudra, 1978b; Chakraborty, 1981). The same issue applies to perpetual indebtedness since usury does not always play a negative role in capitalist development (Rudra, 1978b). A strong rejection has also been made of the argument that a kind of 'labour bondage' is a characteristic of semi-feudal production relations. Firstly, Rudra (1978b) suggests that debt-bondage labour is not part of un-free labour in Marx's sense. Secondly, in his exchange with Patnaik, Brass (1995) proposes the misconception that un-free labour is always incompatible with capitalism. In fact, since the onset of capitalism, Brass argues, it has accommodated certain form of un-free labour to push forward the accumulation.

This study conceives agricultural production relations in the peripheral countries as a capitalist characteristic based on the existence of generalised commodity production in agriculture. By generalised commodity production, we mean that 'reproduction cannot take place outside commodity relations and the disciplines they impose' (Bernstein, 2010: 102). This formulation implies several mechanisms. In the first place, to build any commodity relation, there should be private ownership of the means of production. This requires the separation of independent producers from their means of production through land privatisation. In the second place, to reproduce themselves, those who lose their means of production possess only labour power to be sold in the labour market as a commodity. Since labour power appears as general wage labour, capitalists may buy it in the market to take control in the commodity production process. This also applies to the 'marginal farmers' who retain tiny plots of means of production (land) and yet depend on the wage labour to sustain their reproduction (Bernstein, 2010).

In this specific case, the employer and employee relation (the wage labour relation mediated by the market), capital appropriates the surplus labour (surplus value) through economic means. When there are several non-economic labour relations such as slavery and other forms of unfree labour involved, they should be situated within the broader capitalist production on the global scale (Brass, 1995, 2013). The principle is that, so long as the non-economic coercion of labour process *is introduced by capital* to generate surplus for accumulation elsewhere, it is consistent with the characteristics of generalised commodity production. This is also true for certain social relations, such as sharecropping, usury and incomplete access to the market which are incorrectly identified by the adherents of the semi-feudal thesis as pre-capitalist characteristics (Rudra, 1978a and b; Chakraborty, 1981).

The last characteristic, generalised commodity production implies the surpluses generated in the production process via economic means are allocated to expand the productive capacity of commodity production. This is, indeed, the process of extended reproduction (accumulation). However, whether or not the surplus is reallocated in the same farm, the same geographical areas or the same country is not a 'criterion' to define capitalist production. Instead, it is merely an 'indicator' of the process of capitalist development (Chattopadhyay, 1972; Rudra, 1978a and b). In the context of peripheral countries, the process of capitalist development (the development of productive forces) is shaped by its structural position in global capitalist imperialism (Alavi, 1981). This depends on the specific historical trajectory of a particular country.

Generalised Commodity Production and Production Relations in the Peripheral World

We will now look at the impact of class dynamics situated within generalised commodity production on agricultural production relations. There are many dimensions of production relations, though not all of them are relevant to the objectives of this study. This study focuses only on labour relations, the productivity of agriculture, wages and profit.

We shall begin with labour relations in agricultural production. Many empirical studies (Lerche, 1999; Ramachandran et al., 2010) have pointed out that the recalcitrant nature of sharecropping is explained as a better way of making profit out of agriculture. However, there has been little theoretical development of these studies. One of the more established theoretical accounts of sharecropping is proposed by neoclassical economists. They generally perceive sharecropping as an inefficient labour arrangement (Marshall, 1961). But, in later developments, some orthodox economists have argued that sharecropping is as efficient as other modern labour arrangements (Cheung, 1969; Newberry, 1975). In both cases, however, these economists have focused mainly on technical aspects and, thus, have failed to explain the pertinence of sharecropping in the context of unequal power relations (Pearce, 1983). For Pearce, the nature of sharecropping should be investigated through the social practices of relations between sharecroppers and landowners. Sharecropping represents the provision of the means of production (land, input) by one party in return for a share of the crop yield from another party. Landowners are the providers of the means of production, while those who do not have any means of production (landless labour) must provide services to landowners in return for the yield. In this respect, sharecropping is a mechanism by which the owners of the means of productions require access to others' labour. Opposing the mainstream view that sharecropping is merely a form of rent or labour remuneration, Pearce concludes that sharecropping is *a specific method of surplus appropriation* (1983: 53).

From this standpoint, Pearce develops his own framework to explain the nature of sharecropping under capitalism. For him, the nature of labour relations (sharecropping or wage labour) is shaped by two different related mechanisms. The first is what he calls 'class dominance', a situation where a class is dependent on another class's decision for its own reproduction, and the second is the nature of the 'labour process', the way in which labour and the means of productions are deployed in the productive activity (Pearce, 1983: 55–57). From the two variables investigated, he identifies four conditions where sharecropping is desirable. First, when 'class dominance' is high but the 'labour process' is under-mechanised. The second condition is where 'class dominance' is high but in the hands of tenants, and they are risk-averse. Thirdly, the conditions for sharecropping occur when 'class dominance' is lower but the 'labour process' is highly mechanised, and both landowners and tenants are risk-averse. Finally, suitable conditions for sharecropping are met when 'class dominance' is lower and, at the same time, the 'labour process' is under-mechanised. From the situations above, the biggest chance of sharecropping taking place is when 'class dominance' is lower and, at the same time, the 'labour process' is under-mechanised. This condition is, indeed, a familiar one in the peripheral world.

While this framework is extremely useful for understanding the pertinence of sharecropping, there are at least two caveats to Pearce's argument. First, it lacks an explanation of why the 'labour process' is under-mechanised and, thus, causes an increase in uncertainty and supervision cost. Pearce seems to treat the application of technology as a natural process parallel to the development of productive forces (capitalism). However, the adoption of any technologies is largely dependent on social relations, whether society approves of those technologies or not (Scott, 1985). The resistance to mechanisation in a particular context should receive more attention to understand the nature of the agricultural labour process.

There are also technical problems that need to be considered by landowners. As a cycle, each phase of agricultural production is equally important (from planting to harvesting). It implies that the adoption of any new technologies in certain phases of production which would replace labour must ensure the availability of a labour supply for the other stages of production. The classic example is provided by Byres (1995) in his assessment of sharecropping in the US. The second shortcoming relates to Pearce's narrow focus on internal 'own-account' farming accumulation. However, given that the importance of non-agricultural activities has grown significantly for farmers (Fuller, 1990; Evans & Llberry, 1993), the reason for the pertinence of contemporary sharecropping cannot be accorded exclusively to the economic calculation of both landowners and tenants. Rent-seeking activities, corruption and illegal charges for providing public services are some of the forms of popular non-agricultural accumulation pursued by capitalist farmers who become village officials (Hüsken, 1989). The pertinence of sharecropping should be sought in the political calculation as much as in the economic consideration.

In the literature, the 'patron-client' relationship between landowners and tenants, such as in sharecropping, continues to exist in contemporary capitalism for several reasons. Drawing on the Southeast Asia context, Scott (1972a) reveals that in a pre-capitalist setting (the pre-colonial period), the 'patron-client' relationship was much more traditional in nature: highly personalised, involving a more comprehensive level of exchange (including almost everything in life's affairs), enjoying a more affective relationship than merely acting as an instrumental tool and, thus, being more persistent (Scott, 1972a: 106). However, along with the pace of the commercialisation of the economy and the penetration of the nation state, Scott assesses that the 'patron-client' relationship was likely to become eroded, though not necessarily disappear.

For Scott, the legitimacy of the relationship is largely reduced when the commercialisation of the economy precipitates social differentiation and strengthens the landowner over the landless labour. With this rising bargaining power, the patrons no longer provide minimum social services for the tenants and, rather than seeing the relationship as more or less benefiting them, the tenants increasingly experience more the exploitative nature of the relationship (Scott, 1972b: 6). But, even when the patrons lose their legitimacy, they find another way to dominate farmers in the 'same template of the patron-client' relationship given, on the one hand, the resources they possess and, on the other hand, the disintegration of the tenant-farmers class. Instead of automatically wiping out the 'patron-client' relationship, the current expansion of commodification may simply transform it into a new form.

The next focus of production relations of this study is agricultural productivity. It was mentioned earlier that the orthodox economists believe that productivity is a result of the technical aspect of production (Hayami & Ruttan, 1985). However, 'technical divisions of labour and their effects for productivity require social organization' (Bernstein, 2010: 17–18). Agricultural productivity owes much to the form of the social organisation (the division of labour) of production, which is greatly shaped by property relations. Those who own the means of production, such as land and technology, pose the power to decide what to do to those who own none of the means of production (labour). These two parties may be in conflict over the production process due to their contradictory interests. For example, the landowners' inception of new farming technologies that could wipe out manual agricultural jobs is resisted by labour (Scott, 1985) and may significantly halt the advancement of agricultural productivity. Thus, agricultural productivity depends on the dynamics of both technical aspects and class relations in a specific context.

It is also crucial to see agricultural productivity as a result of a dialectical relationship between the technical aspects and the social organisation of production. In the capitalist economy, soil fertility might be enhanced through the application of chemical fertilisers in order to maximise the exploitation of nature for higher economic profit. In the long run, however, as the literature has indicated, too much chemical input decreases soil fertility, thus levelling down land productivity. This 'metabolic rift' takes place when the further social division of labour leads to the flowing of soil nutrients from rural to urban spaces and returns only in exceptional cases (Foster, 2000). It is clear that capitalist farming has a limit to increasing its productivity, given that the natural ingredients (soil nutrients) cannot be easily replaced by manufactured manipulation. When such a limit is met (soil degradation), it may force the reorganisation of the production process or not, depending on the balance of power of the agrarian classes and the pattern of accumulation at certain historical junctures.

This brings us to the next issue of wage and agricultural profitability. Orthodox economists tend to propose a simple equilibrium model in explaining wage levels (Hayami & Kikuchi, 1981; Hayami & Ruttan, 1985). There is much emphasis on the technical aspects (demography and technology) again, subject to severe limitations. Pincus (1996), who resurveys the two villages of Hayami and Kikuchi (1981) in Subang, provides a particular explanation. The main problem with Hayami and Kikuchi, according to Pincus, lies in their ignorance of social relations, especially the 'ownership structure' that determines the pattern of labour use, wage distribution (levels) and technological change. Pincus argues that 'ownership structure' is 'shown to be closely bound up with local variations in class structure and the capacity of contending classes to bring about or resist change' (1996: 189).

The explanation for wage levels is closely related to the level of profit. Pincus (1996) brings further forward his class perspective to examine the profit level of agricultural producers in the Javanese villages he studied. From this case study, Pincus shows that the profit levels (both in absolute value and in the share between capital and labour), instead of being determined merely by the supply and demand function, are shaped by class structure and class relations in a particular setting. This includes the need to take into account the state's intervention in the local dynamics.

Agricultural production relations also often reveal the unequal burdens and rewards received by women and men. The discussion of the 'feminisation of agriculture' suggests that the more women dominate in performing agricultural tasks, the more burdens they have to face, given their 'obligation' to do domestic jobs (Deere, 2005). However, discrimination against women intertwines with their class position since not all women are oppressed in the same way. There are several ways to conceive the entangled relations between gender and class. The most popular one is probably the intersectionality approach (Collins, 2015). It suggests that we cannot understand one form of oppression, such as gender-based oppression, without taking into account, at the same time, racialised and class domination. This is because race, gender, class and ethnicity are bound together and shaped by the intersectional system of society.

However, this view fails to see the coherent logic underlying many forms of oppression (McNally, 2017: 96). From this critique, 'social reproduction perspective' argues that, while class exploitation represents the oppression of capital in the production process as one sphere of capitalist social relations, other oppressions (sexual, racial) are located in the reproduction arena in the imperative of capital accumulation to bring ready/able labour onto 'capital's doorstep' (Bhattacharya, 2017). In agrarian terms, class exploitation and women's oppression take the form of unpaid domestic jobs such as taking care of labour reproduction (male) and, at the same time, they force women (particularly from the labouring class) to work as agricultural workers, often with lower wages than men. These are intertwined under the imperative logic of capital accumulation.

Agrarian Change and the Reproduction of Agrarian Classes

We discussed earlier the way in which capitalist agrarian change shapes class location and class relations and production relations. It is now time to see how this forms the pattern of reproduction of different agrarian classes. We shall look at the peculiar pattern of reproduction of capitalist farmers, PCP and the classes of labour. There are several approaches to discerning the reproduction of each agrarian class. The position of the study is hopefully well-demonstrated in the following discussion.

Capitalist Farmers and Accumulation

We may begin with capitalist farmers. The proponents of the neo-populist perspective maintain that, throughout history, all peasants have been subsistence-oriented (Chayanov, 1966). Hence, it is simply a deviation if certain peasants choose to pursue profit. Nonetheless, this view exhibits a chronic flaw, both theoretically and historically (Bernstein, 2010: 93). In generalised commodity production (capitalism), capitalist farmers who own the crucial means of production, like land and technology, tend to be capable of producing a larger surplus of product than other farmers. They may harness the surplus for consumption activities or for expanding their business to acquire more profit. In the latter activities, capitalist farmers engage in 'expanded reproduction' or 'accumulation'.

The accumulation in agriculture may express itself in two different forms. These are derived from the classic account of Lenin in analysing the capitalist trajectory in rural Prussia and the US. In Prussia, Lenin ([1908] 1962: 239) depicts how the 'feudal landlord economy slowly evolves into the bourgeois, Junker landlord economy, which condemns the peasants to decades of the most harrowing expropriation and bondage while, at the same time, a small minority of *Grossbauern* (big peasants) arises'. This 'Prussian path', as Lenin calls it, also implies that the differentiation of the peasantry was limited while the degradation of the peasant mass was pronounced. The nature of accumulation is 'from above' because 'the processes in question were controlled by the class of large feudal landlords' (Byres, 1986: 25). The state mediated the process through eliminating serfdom yet it provided room for the Junkers to acquire more peasant land in return for its removal.

A contrasting path is described by Lenin in the US. There, 'there is no landlord economy, or else it is broken up by revolution, which confiscates and splits up the feudal estates…the peasant predominates, becomes the sole agent of agriculture, and evolves into a capitalist farmer' (Lenin, [1908] 1962: 239). Accumulation was on the shoulders of the few peasants who were able to appropriate more agricultural surpluses at the expense of other peasants through a massive process of differentiation. In this 'American path', Lenin noted that these peasants would secure the greatest degree of prosperity possible, while other peasants were transformed into wage labourers. This process is perceived as accumulation from below since the initiative and control of the accumulation was in the hands of the peasants.

Albeit its origin is rooted in the problem of the transition to capitalism, the process of accumulation, both from above and from below, can be discerned as merely a descriptive term to distinguish a distinct feature of accumulation in agriculture, without necessarily being labelled as a kind of transition process as was argued in the previous sub-section. In a contemporary study, Mamdani (1987: 202) deploys the term accumulation from below in its descriptive sense to refer to accumulation brought about by 'a *relatively spontaneous* process whereby differentiation occurs through *internal* unequal relations, the result of *competition* generated by existing commodity relations'. In contrast, accumulation from above means that the accumulation is a 'result of an organised state connection, necessarily requiring a complement of extra-economic coercion' (Mamdani, 1987: 222). This conception is followed by Neocosmos (1993). However, Cousins (2013) simply indicates the scale of primary actors of accumulation as a foundation to distinguish between two kinds of accumulation. Hence, he sees accumulation from below as a process 'where small-scale farmers must compete with long-established, large-scale capitalist farmers (beneficiaries of a racially-based version of accumulation from above)' (Cousins, 2013: 136). On the contrary, accumulation from above take places when large-scale capitalist farmers, including agri-business, dominate the accumulation in agriculture. The state's intervention is crucial in promoting both types of accumulation. Zhang (2015) seems to provide a rather different emphasis. He sees accumulation from below as a process whereby indigenous capitalist farmers in a village accumulate both through increasing productivity (economic) and exploiting social ties (political networks) against 'outside capital, which is both bigger and more able to mobilise higher level political power' (Zhang, 2015: 353). In this respect, accumulation from above would refer to the accumulation led by bigger capital from the city.

The different emphasis in the contemporary studies on the characteristics of accumulation is, at least in part, due to the specificity of empirical investigations in the different social settings. Thus, we need to combine the rich data from contemporary empirical studies with the insight from the classic formulation of this issue. It should be clear that accumulation from below is part of a process in which the primary accumulators are capitalist farmers (actors) who are involved in market exchange and compelled by its logic (competition, productivity, profit). This leads to class differentiation, with or without direct assistance from the state and regardless of their spatial origin. In stark contrast to this, accumulation from above is being driven by agricultural corporate capitals or estate landlords with or without direct state intervention and regardless of the geographical setting.

The path of accumulation in a particular country, especially in peripheral countries, is situated by global market forces at a specific point of time in history which shapes the state's intervention to promote a certain type of accumulation. In the aftermath of World War II, to accommodate the widespread resistance of peasants, along with potential communist rebellions, global capital and post-colonial states initiated either land reform or the Green Revolution. These processes 'led to the emergence of capital-accumulating family farms producing overwhelmingly for the market and worked by owners with some hired labour' (Araghi, 2009: 128). In this respect, post-colonial states promoted accumulation from below in order to build a national economy. In the countries which underwent the Green Revolution, the emergence of capitalist farmers via class differentiation led to proletarianisation.

Neoliberal approaches since the 1980s have replaced the state-led to market-led agricultural development. It is often stated that the promotion of agro-export crops (cash crops) in the contemporary peripheral countries harms the domestic-oriented crops (food crops) (Watts, 2009). The state is compelled to facilitate the expansion of a 'corporate food regime' and the state is no longer able to provide adequate assistance to those who produce domestic-oriented crops (food crops) and, thus, is unlikely to expand accumulation from below. On the other side of the coin, the promotion of export crops may have a mixed impact on capitalist farmers who grow export crops, fluctuating between dispossession and expansion.

However, the expansion of export crops across the globe is often overstated since, in many parts of the world, export crops continue to play a limited role for domestic farmers (Bernstein & Campling, 2006). For the countries or the parts of a country which experience little export crop expansion, a different scenario applies. When the state's support to farmers is reduced because they do not enjoy the rise of global market prices, farmers would be unlikely to be able to promote accumulation from below. This suggests that whether the state in the peripheral countries under a neoliberal aegis is likely to promote accumulation from above or accumulation from below depends on the particular context in any given country.

When capitalist farmers see only bleak opportunities to accumulate further in their 'own-account' farming, they seek other avenues of accumulation outside agriculture. Capitalist farmers have increasingly engaged in 'diversification for accumulation' (Hart, 1994). The impact of such non-agricultural accumulation has been seen to halt agrarian class polarisation (Buttel, 1982). However, whether this strategy of accumulation chosen for the same reason and executed in the same way for all farmers or not require more empirical inquiries.

The Contingent Nature of PCPs' Simple Reproduction

It is often perceived that the main feature of the reproduction of PCPsis that it meets the requirements of 'simple reproduction'. Neo-populist supporters believe that the prime orientation of small producers is not to pursue profit but merely to meet subsistence by calculating the balance of 'labour-consumer ratio' within the household (Chayanov, 1966: 87).[2] They will only work harder if there are 'more mouths that need to be fed' (Ploeg, 2013: 33). When the market dynamics disadvantage petty producers, they will attempt to 'adapt' to the external disturbances without necessarily transforming their 'static/genuine' nature as subsistence producers. One important mechanism of adaptation is so-called 'self-exploitation' (Chayanov, 1966: 70).

This essentialist view on farmers is undoubtedly unrealistic since such an ahistorical approach fails to take into account the transformations of farmers throughout history (Bernstein, 2009: 65), which has been discussed earlier. Even when they succeed in maintaining their simple reproduction, their survival of differentiation[3] is merely a 'contingent resilience', without any references to its inherent supremacy (Zhang, 2015). This means that the survival of PCPs depends largely on a specific situation instead of it being attached to their inherent superiority in holding on to their land at all costs. While the term 'contingent resilience' may be useful in depicting the vulnerable nature of PCPs' reproduction, it may overstate the 'defensive' nature of PCPs while discounting the possibility of them transforming themselves into capitalist farmers.

The argument for the persistence of PCPs, but with a different reason, is provided by Kautsky ([1899] 1988). Like Lenin ([1899] 1956), Kautsky believes that class differentiation is an essential trait of capitalist agriculture. Nonetheless, unlike Lenin, he argues that class differentiation does not necessarily lead to the disappearance of PCPs. Capital tends to incorporate the PCPs into their circuit of accumulation, as long as they provide cheap food commodities that reduce the labour cost (wages) to capitalists elsewhere. Thus, in the interest of capital acquiring 'cheap' labour power, the existence of PCPs would be tolerated, and even encouraged, by capital. Rather than seeing this incorporation as merely a transitional phase, Kautsky believes that it could be sustained over time in capitalism.

This functionalist perspective, however, overlooks the salient role of resistance against proletarianisation that preserves PCPs. As Bernstein (1977, 2010) argues, the nature of the relationship between capital and PCPs involves competition and conflict. In order to gain control over the production process, farmers stage various struggles against either capitalist or state domination. The resistance of the PCPs manifests itself in several ways: a refusal to adopt new techniques of land cultivation; strikes in protest against the cultivation of new crops; temporary withdrawal from the commodity relation; or the search for alternative sources of cash income (Wolf, 1969; Scott, 1985). As the response to this resistance, capital tries to determine the conditions of production and exchange of PCPs through 'vertical concentration' (Bernstein, 1977: 70). In this respect, the survival of PCPs is not simply due to the interest of capital, but it is also a response of capital to their resistance.

Both the interest of capital to preserve PCPs and their struggle against capital are mediated by the dynamic power of the capitalist market (global) and the state. In the neoliberal era, the international food regime's interest is to keep the subsidy of agriculture in the metropolitan countries (the EU and the US) while, at the same time, promote the liberalisation, privatisation and deregulation of agriculture in the peripheral countries. The impacts of this development on PCPs are two-fold. First, there has been a significant decline in government subsidies and aid funding for agriculture and, in particular, direct assistance to PCPs that makes them barely able to compete with cheaper agricultural commodities (especially food crops) from the metropolitan countries since they are still heavily subsidised (Bernstein 2010: 84–85). This prompts further 'de-peasantization' when many PCPs lose the needed incentive to farm the land (Araghi, 2009). Second, the wave of liberalisation facilitates an 'enclosure food regime' to appropriate direct access to land and, therefore, displace PCPs (Araghi, 2009).

The penetration of the global market, however, has been challenged by widespread resistance. Neo-populist adherents seem to celebrate the global agrarian movement under the banner of 'the people of the land' when confronting the corporatisation of agriculture (Desmarais, 2007; McMichael, 2006; Ploeg, 2008). They assume that 'all farmers' are in great danger of penetration by corporate capital. This perspective tends to blur the differences and contradictory interests among the farmers themselves, as discussed in the first sub-section (Bernstein, 2010). Thus, the resistance of PCPs against corporate capital is only one among their other struggles against either capitalist farmers or classes of labour. These class dynamics need to be investigated further.

Given the minimum role of the state on the one hand and, on the other hand, the nature of class dynamics and the resistance to the interests of capital (the corporations) in this neoliberal period, PCPs in the peripheral countries have been increasingly unable to reproduce themselves without engaging in other jobs, sometimes through a complex combination of self-employment and wage employment, in both agriculture and non-agriculture (Bernstein, 2010: 111). In many cases, they also depend on remittances from their family members working in the city or abroad (Zhang, 2015). Under such circumstance, the households of PCPs tend to optimise their members involved in income generation.

Women generally do not play roles as merely housewives, taking care of domestic routines, but also active workers, providing extra income for their households (Deere, 2005). Due to their role in contributing to the household's revenue, women in PCP households may have more autonomy *vis-à-vis* their husbands (Stoler, 1977b). However, as suggested by the social reproduction perspective, they still must face the double burdens of taking care of unpaid domestic jobs to reproduce labour (her husband and sons) and attending to outside domestic waged jobs to serve the needs of capital.

It should be clear that, in contemporary neoliberal capitalism, the reproduction of the PCPs can hardly be designated to either their inherent tendency to persist or their destiny to disappear. One who wishes to understand the reproduction of PCPs needs to acknowledge that their reproduction is dynamically shaped, both by the interest of capital (mediated by the state) and their resistances in specific settings. The pattern of income generation of PCP households, from 'own-account' farming, selling labour out to other's farm and non-agricultural activities, including the women's role in that process, must also be examined in order to understand their reproduction.

The Classes of Labour Searching for Survival

Many farmers who own/control only a meagre quantity of land barely manage to meet their subsistence without selling their labour throughout the year. These 'marginal farmers' (Bernstein, 2010) must face a 'subsistence squeeze' that forces them to obtain extra incomes beyond 'own-account' farming to sustain their daily survival. A stereotypical view of the working class often classifies only those who have no possession of the means of production as the working class proper. Bernstein (2010) insists that 'marginal farmers' who still own a tiny plot of land and dispose of their labour elsewhere all year round are perceived as members of what we have discussed earlier, the classes of labour. 'Marginal farmers' join those who neither own nor control any land, depending on wages to reproduce themselves.

The reproduction of the classes of labour is mediated by the state's intervention within a broader class relationship between capital and labour. In the postwar period, the zeal of emancipation and 'developmentalism' increased social welfare for the classes of labour, either through subsidies or prices support mechanisms for 'marginal farmers', and through land reform for the landless. Pro-labour legislation to protect workers' wage and provide decent working conditions were also the norm in this period. This development, however, has been reversed since the neoliberal wave in the 1980s (Harvey, 2005). What has been left is only minimum state intervention to assist workers' reproduction. Social policies have been increased in many regions (Tillin & Duckett, 2017). However, those interventions have not touched upon the root of poverty, namely the unequal power relations transmitted from the past (land inequality), and in so doing, the social policies are only part of the 'management of poverty' by subsidising low wages and low productivity (Saad-Filho, 2015).

Given the limited assistance from the state during this neoliberal period, the classes of labour in the countryside are struggling to survive by employing several mechanisms. One common response is rural emigration, looking for better opportunities in urban areas (Araghi, 1995). However, due to limited well-paid employment available in the cities, the rural proletariat ends up being part of the 'global informal working class', living in the 'planet of slums' (Davis, 2006). Many others join 'circular migration' and become 'footloose labour' (Breman, 1996) whose livelihoods depend largely on flexible wage employment elsewhere. Another response to survival is resistance. The struggle of the rural landless workers, farmers and the indigenous movements in many parts of the world against neoliberal adjustment (land dispossession and the cuts in social welfare) is part of this resistance (Petras & Veltmeyer, 2013, Lerche, 2013). Another equally important response is the engagement of the classes of labour in 'rural income diversification' (Wise and Veltmeyer, 2016: 117). This includes the development of rural non-agricultural micro-businesses which rely on micro-credits. Women generally play a pivotal role in these businesses although they continue to be tied to the obligation of taking care of unpaid domestic jobs. In this case, not only do the female labourers contribute directly to production but they are also significantly responsible for reproduction by bringing their household labour onto 'capital's doorstep' (Bhattacharya, 2017). The dominant form of the response of the classes of labour depends on a particular context.

Conclusion

This chapter has dealt with the agrarian populism which keeps perceive the peasantry in the peripheral world as a subsistence-oriented and egalitarian community. We have argued that the peasantry in today peripheral countries has been transformed into farmers (commodity production-oriented) and workers since the end of colonial period. It has also been argued that the current phenomena of 'land grabbing' and 'enclosure' are not necessarily associated with primitive accumulation and the *creation* of capitalist social relations. It rather shows the intensification of commodification under the neoliberal wave, both in its spatial-scale and coverage-sphere, and has thus expanded and deepened capitalist social relations. Whether this expansion is accompanied by 'dispossession by displacement' or class differentiation of petty producers or both at the same time, depends on the specific setting. This was followed by a discussion on the way in which we empirically approach both agrarian class location and class relations. Class location is best understood from different perspectives from both property relations and four different market relations. Filling the gap of the existing literature, our approach to class location also takes into account the activities of the households beyond 'own-account' farming in order to capture the nuances of the agrarian class. As far as class relations are concerned, it has been argued that looking into the way people experience their class location is significant. This is especially crucial given that a complex agrarian class location may deliver different responses from people from the same class.

The class dynamics of agricultural producers, in turn, shape the nature of production relations. It has been argued that recent production relations are organised according to capitalist social relations instead of 'semi-feudal' social formations. Under capitalism, along with the technical aspects of production, class dynamics impact certain crucial labour relations (wage labour or sharecropping), agricultural productivity, wages and the level of profits. This dynamic largely depends on the particular setting. It is also indispensable to look at the dialectical relationship between the technical aspects of production and the social organisation of production. Agriculture has faced a metabolic rift due to the massive 'improvement of the technical aspects of production' through chemicalisation, the impact of which on agricultural production can be clearly seen. Male and female workers earn different levels of wages for the same tasks in the production relations. It is argued that gender and class are not an independent form of oppression as 'intersectionality' suggests. Class and gender oppression are intertwined in capitalist social relations, reflected in exploitation in the workplace (production) and oppression in the non-workplace (reproduction of labour) for the sake of capital accumulation.

The income from the production process, which is shared unequally, provides the background for different paths of reproduction for different agrarian classes. The extent to which capitalist farmers accumulate through either 'own-account' farming or non-agricultural avenues depends on specific circumstances. Their pattern of accumulation is also shaped by their relationship to the 'corporate-agricultural producers' and state intervention. Together, this trajectory in any given country along with a particular crop determines whether accumulation from below or accumulation from above will be the dominant form of accumulation. For PCPs whose capital is only equal to their labour, they are neither able to accumulate nor necessarily sell their labour for survival. However, their 'simple reproduction' remains 'contingent' on the specific circumstances related to their commodification, the activities of the 'corporate-agricultural producers' and state intervention. The classes of labour who either own a tiny parcel of land or no land at all are required to dispose of their labour for the sake of survival. Their reproduction depends mainly on the availability of employment, the working conditions, wage levels and the state support provided. Women and men play different roles in the household reproduction. For women from PCPs and the classes of labour households, they tend to experience double burdens, despite their relative autonomy from men. In all of these processes, under neoliberal capitalism, the state maintains its crucial role of facilitating commodification while, for several reasons that depend on specific contexts, it keeps providing some supports for PCPs and the classes of labour.

Notes

1 The term 'peripheral world' is used merely as a descriptive designation to signal the unequal power relations under current imperialism where 'core capitalist countries' have dominated the global political and economic institutions since the colonial period at the expense of the former colonised countries. The term is considered more useful than the generic term of 'global south', 'developing countries' or 'third world'.

2 Of those who are interested in the dynamics of peasant households, Deere and de Janvry (1981) take the dynamics of social forces outside the household more seriously. This makes their approach different from the mainstream neo-populist approach.

3 In replying to the critiques, Chayanov acknowledged that 'it is quite true that peasant farming is not homogenous; apart from peasant labour farms, it includes numerous semi-proletarian and semicapitalist farms' (1966: 47). He maintains that 'social differentiation' co-exists with 'demographic differentiation'. However, given his work at that time predominantly explained the latter, his theoretical stand cannot escape the critique that his focus on internal dynamics of the households made him ignore the wider social forces (the dynamics of commodity production in the national and global scale) that shape the dynamics of households, thus leading him to a rather static picture of peasant farming. Replying to this critique, Chayanov stated: 'in the next few years, on the basis of research into national economy problems, we will be able to explain to ourselves and to others what we will take up in our practical research work from the rich experience of Marxist methods' (Chayanov, 1966: 46). Daniel Thorner, a sympathetic reader of Chayanov's theory, eventually admitted, 'although it encompassed a very wide range of possibilities, Chayanov's theory of peasant farming remained essentially a static one' (1966: xxii).

References

Alavi, H 1981, 'Structure of colonial formations', *Economic and Political Weekly*, no. 10/12, pp. 475–486.

Anderson, P 1980, *Arguments within English Marxism*, London, Verso.

Araghi, F.A 1995, 'Global depeasantization, 1945–1990', *The Sociological Quarterly*, vol. 36, no. 2, pp. 337–368.

Araghi, F, 2000, 'The great global enclosure of our times: Peasants and the agrarian question at the end of the twentieth century', in *Hungry for profit: The agribusiness threat to farmers, food, and the environment*, New York, Monthly Review Press, pp. 145–160.

Araghi, F.A 2009, 'The invisible hand and the visible foot: Peasants, dispossession and globalization', in A.H Akram-Lodhi & C Kay (eds), *Peasants and globalization: Political economy, rural transformation and the agrarian question*, New York, Routledge, pp. 111–147.

Arrighi, G 1994, *The long twentieth century: Money, power and the origins of our time*, London, Verso.

Banaji, J 2007, *Agrarian change in late antiquity: Gold, labour and aristocratic dominance*, Oxford, Oxford University Press.

Bardhan, P 1982, 'Agrarian class formation in India', *The Journal of Peasant Studies*, vol. 10, no. 1, pp. 73–94.

Bhattacharya, T 2017, *Social reproduction theory: Remapping class, recentering oppression*, London, Pluto Press.

Bernstein, H 1977, 'Notes on capital and peasantry', *Review of African Political Economy*, vol. 10, pp. 60–73.

Bernstein, H 1988, 'Capitalism and petty-bourgeois production: Class relations and divisions of labour', *The Journal of Peasant Studies*, vol. 15, no. 2, pp. 258–271.

Bernstein, H 2009, 'V.I. Lenin and A.V. Chayanov: looking back, looking forward', *The Journal of Peasant Studies*, 36:1, 55–81

Bernstein, H 2010, *Class dynamics of agrarian change*, Sterling, VA, Kumarian Press.

Bernstein, H 2011, '"Farewells to the peasantry?" And its relevance to recent South African debates', *Transformation: Critical Perspectives on Southern Africa*, vol. 75, no. 1, pp. 44–52.

Bernstein, H 2016, 'Revisiting agrarian transition: Reflections on long histories and current realities', in B.B Mohanty (ed), *Critical perspectives on agrarian transition: India in the global debate*, London and New York, Routledge, pp. 67–91.

Bernstein, H. 2018. "Mainstreaming the Marginal? The Case of "Primitive Accumulation"." Paper for Workshop on the Marginal as Mainstream: Analytical Concepts for the Study of Contemporary Capitalism, Wolfson College, University of Oxford, July 2–3.

Bernstein, H & Campling, L 2006, 'Commodity studies and commodity fetishism I: Trading down', *Journal of Agrarian Change*, vol. 6, pp. 239–264.

Bhaduri, A 1973, 'A study in agricultural backwardness under semi-feudalism', *The Economic Journal*, no. 329, pp. 120–137.

Brass, T 1995, 'Reply to Utsa Patnaik: If the cap fits….', *International Review of Social History*, vol. 40, no. 1, pp. 93–117.

Brass, T 2013, *Labor regime change in the twenty-first century*, Chicago, IL and London, Haymarket.

Breman, J 1996, *Footloose labour: Working in India's informal economy*, Cambridge, Cambridge University Press.

Brenner, R 1976, 'Agrarian class structure and economic development in pre-industrial Europe', *Past & Present*, vol. 70, pp. 30–75.

Brenner, R 1982, 'The agrarian roots of European capitalism', *Past & Present*, no. 97, pp. 16–113.

Buttel, F.H 1982, 'The political economy of part-time farming', *GeoJournal*, vol. 6, pp. 293–300.

Byres, T.J 1982, 'India: Capitalist industrialization or structural stasis?' in M Bienefeld & M Godfrey (eds), *The struggle for development: National strategies in an international context*, Chichester, Wiley, pp. 135–164.

Byres, T.J 1986, 'The agrarian question, forms of capitalist agrarian transition and the state: An essay with reference to Asia', *Social Scientist*, vol. 14, no. 11/12, pp. 3–67.

Byres, T.J 1995, 'Political economy, agrarian question and comparative method', *Economic and Political Weekly*, vol. 30, no. 10, pp. 507–513.

Byres, T.J 1996, *Capitalism from above and capitalism from below: An essay in comparative political economy*, New York, Macmillan Press.

Byres, T.J 2002, 'Paths of capitalist agrarian transition in the past and in the contemporary world', in V.K Ramachandran & M Swaminathan (eds), *Agrarian studies: Essays on agrarian relations in less-developed countries*, London and New York, Zed Books, pp. 54–83.

Byres, T.J 2003, 'Structural change, the agrarian question and the possible impact of globalization', in J Ghosh & C.P Chandrasekhar (eds), *Work and well being in the age of finance*, New Delhi, Tulika Books, pp. 171–211.

Byres, T.J 2016, 'In pursuit of capitalist agrarian transition', *Journal of Agrarian Change*, vol. 16, no. 3, pp. 432–451.

Camfield, D 2004, 'Re-orienting class analysis: Working classes as historical formations', *Science & Society*, vol. 68, no. 4, pp. 421–446.

Chakraborty, A 1981, 'Tenancy and mode of production', *Economic and Political Weekly*, no. 13, pp. A5–A14.

Chattopadhyay, P 1972, 'Mode of production in Indian agriculture: An "anti-kritik"', *Economic and Political Weekly*, vol. 7, no. 53, pp. A185–A192.

Chayanov, A.V 1966, *The theory of peasant economy*, Homewood, Richard D. Irwin.

Cheung, S 1969, *The theory of share tenancy*, Chicago, IL, University of Chicago.

Cohen, G.A 1978, *Karl Marx's theory of history: A defense*. Princeton, NJ, Princeton University Press.

Collins, P.H 2015, 'Intersectionality's definitional dilemmas', *Annual Review of Sociology*, vol. 41, no. 1, pp. 1–20.

Cousins, B 2013, 'Smallholder irrigation schemes, agrarian reform and "accumulation from above and from below" in South Africa', *Journal of Agrarian Change*, vol. 13, no. 1, pp. 116–139.

Davis, M 2006, *Planet of slums*, London, Verso.

de Angelis, M 2001, 'Marx and primitive accumulation: The continues character of capital's "enclosures"', *The Commoner*, vol. 2, no. 1, pp. 1–22.

Deere, C.D 2005, 'The feminization of agriculture?: Economic restructuring in rural latin America', *Occasional Paper* 2005 No. 1. Geneva, United Nations Research Institute for Social Development.

Deere, C.D & de Janvry, A 1981, 'Demographic and social differentiation among northern Peruvian peasants', *Journal of Peasant Studies*, vol. 8, no. 3, pp. 335–366.

Desmarais, A.A 2007, *La Via Campesina: Globalization and the power of peasants*, London, Pluto Press.

Evans, N.J & Llbery, B.W 1993, 'The pluriactivity, part-time farming, and farm diversification debate', *Environment and Planning A: Economy and Space*, vol. 25, no. 7, pp. 945–959.

Foster, J.B 2000, *Marx's ecology: Materialism and nature*, New York, Monthly Review Press.

Fortin, C.J 2011, 'The biofuel boom and Indonesia's oil palm industry: The twin processes of peasant dispossession and adverse incorporation in West Kalimantan', paper presented at the *International Conference on Global Land Grabbing*, University of Sussex, UK 6–8 April.

Frank, A.G 1967, *Capitalism and underdevelopment in Latin America*, New York, Monthly Review Press.

Fuller, A.J 1990, 'From part-time farming to pluriactivity: A decade of change in rural Europe', *Journal of Rural Studies*, vol. 6, no. 4, pp. 361–373.

Gasson, R 1986, 'Part time farming: Strategy for survival?' *Sociologia Ruralis*, vol. 24, no. 34, pp. 364–376.

Gerth, H & C.W Mills 1958, *From Max Weber*, New York, Oxford University Press.

Gibbon, P & M Neocosmos 1985, 'Some problems in the political economy of "African socialism"', in H Bernstein & B.K Campbell (eds), *Contradictions of accumulation in Africa: Studies in economy and state*, Beverley Hills, CA, Sage, pp. 153–206.

Gubbay, J 1997, 'A marxist critique of weberian class analyses', *Sociology*, vol. 31, no. 1, pp. 73–89.

Hall, S 1981, 'In defence of theory', in R Samuel (ed), *People's history and socialist theory*, London, Routledge & Kegan Paul, pp. 378–385.

Hall, D 2012, 'Rethinking primitive accumulation: Theoretical tensions and rural southeast Asian complexities', *Antipode*, vol. 44, no. 4, pp. 1188–1208.

Hart, G 1994, 'The dynamics of diversification in an Asian rice region', in B Koppel, J.N Hawkins & W.E James (eds), *Development or deterioration?: Work in rural Asia*, London, L. Rienner Publishers, pp. 47–71.

Harvey, D 2003, *The new imperialism*, Oxford, Oxford University Press.

Harvey, D 2005, *A brief history of neoliberalism*, Oxford, Oxford University Press.

Hayami, Y & Kikuchi, M 1981, *Asian village economy at the crossroads*, Tokyo, University of Tokyo Press.

Hayami, Y & Ruttan, V.W 1985, *Agricultural development: An international perspective*, Baltimore, MD, Johns Hopkins University Press.

Hüsken, F 1989, 'Cycles of commercialization and accumulation in a central Javanese village', in G Hart, A Turton & B White (eds), *Agrarian transformations: Local process and the state in Southeast Asia*, Berkeley, CA, University of California Press. pp. 303–331.

Kautsky, K 1988 [1899], *The agrarian question in two volumes*, London, Zwan Publication.

Laclau, E 1971, 'Feudalism and capitalism in Latin America', *New Left Review*, vol. 67, pp. 19–38.

Lenin, V.I 1956 [1899], *The development of capitalism in Russia: The process of the formation of a home market for large-scale industry*, Moscow, Foreign Languages Pub. House.

Lenin, V.I 1962 [1908], *The agrarian programme of social-democracy in the first Russian revolution, 1905–1907*, in vol. 13 of *Collected Works*, Moscow, Foreign Languages Publishing House.

Lerche, J 1999, 'Politics of the poor: Agricultural labourers and political transformations in Uttar Pradesh', *The Journal of Peasant Studies*, vol. 26, no. 2–3, pp. 182–241.

Lerche, J 2010, 'From "rural labour" to "classes of labour": Class fragmentation, caste and class struggle at the bottom of the indian labour hierarchy', in B Harriss-White & J Heyer (eds), *The comparative political economy of development: Africa and South Asia*, London, Routledge, pp. 66–87.

Lerche, J 2013, 'The agrarian question in neoliberal India: Agrarian transition bypassed?' *Journal of Agrarian Change*, vol. 13, no. 3, pp. 382–404.

Mamdani, M 1987, 'Extreme but not exceptional: Towards an analysis of the agrarian question in Uganda', *Journal of Peasant Studies*, vol. 14, no. 2, pp. 199–225.

Marshall, A 1961 [1890], *Principles of economics*, London, Macmillan.

Marx, K 1976, *Capital: A critique of political economy*, Harmondsworth, Penguin Books.

Mezzadri, A 2017, *The sweatshop regime: Labouring bodies, exploitation, and garments made in India*, Cambridge, Cambridge University Press.

McMichael, P 2006, 'Reframing development: Global peasant movements and the new agrarian question', *Canadian Journal of Development Studies/Revue canadienne d'études du développement*, vol. 27, no. 4, pp. 471–483.

McNally, D 2015, 'The dialectics of unity and difference in the constitution of wage-labour: On internal relations and working-class formation', *Capital & Class*, vol. 39, no. 1, pp. 131–146.

McNally, D 2017, 'Intersections and dialectics: Critical reconstructions in social reproduction theory', in T Bhattacharya (ed), *Social reproduction theory: Remapping class, recentering oppression*, London, Pluto Press, pp. 94–111.

Moore, J.W 2003, 'Nature and the transition from feudalism to capitalism', *Review*, vol. 26, no. 2, pp. 97–172.

Neocosmos, M 1993, *The agrarian question in Southern Africa and 'accumulation from below': Economics and politics inthe struggle for democracy*, Uppsala, Nordiska Afrikainstitutet.

Newbery, D 1975, 'Tenurial obstacles to innovation', *Journal of Development Studies*, vol. 2, no. 4, pp. 263–277.

Oya, C 2004, 'The empirical investigation of rural class formation: Methodological issues in a study of large and middle-scale farmers in Senegal', *Historical Materialism*, vol. 12, no. 4, pp. 289–326.

Panitch, L & Leys, C 2000, *Working classes, global realities*, London, Merlin Press.

Patnaik, U 1972, 'On the mode of production in Indian agriculture: A reply', *Economic and Political Weekly*, vol. 7, no. 40, pp. A145–A152.

Patnaik, U 1976, 'Class differentiation within the peasantry: An approach to analysis of Indian agriculture', *Economic and Political Weekly*, vol. 11, no. 39, pp. A82–101.

Patnaik, U 1986, 'The agrarian question and development of capitalism in India', *Economic and Political Weekly*, vol. 21, no. 18, pp. 781–793.

Patnaik, U 1990, *Agrarian relations and accumulation: The 'mode of production' debate in India*, Bombay and Oxford, Published for Sameeksha Trust by Oxford University Press.

Patnaik, U & Moyo, S 2011, *The Agrarian question in the Neoliberal era: Primitive accumulation and the peasantry*, Oxford, Pambazuka Press.

Pattenden, J 2018, 'The politics of classes of labour: Fragmentation, reproduction zones and collective action in Karnataka, India', *The Journal of Peasant Studies*, vol. 45, no. 5–6, pp. 1039–1059.

Pearce, R 1983, 'Sharecropping: Towards a Marxist view', *The Journal of Peasant Studies*, vol. 10, no. 2–3, pp. 42–70.

Petras, J & Veltmeyer, H 2013, *Social movements in Latin America*, Basingtoke, Palgrave Macmillan.

Pincus, J 1996, *Class power and agrarian change: Land and labour in rural West Java*, London, MacMillan Press.

Ploeg, J.D 2008, *The new peasantries: Struggles for autonomy and sustainability in an era of empire and globalization*, London, Earthscan Food and Agriculture Series.

Ploeg, J.D 2013, *Peasants and the art of farming: A chayanovian manifesto*, Winnipeg, Fernwood Publishing.

Ramachandran, V.K. Rawal, Vikas & Swaminathan, Madhura (eds) (2010), *Socio-economic Surveys of Three Villages in Andhra Prades, A Study of Agrarian Relations*, New Delhi: Tulika Books.

Rudra, A 1978a, 'Class relations in Indian agriculture: I', *Economic and Political Weekly*, vol. 13, no. 22, pp. 916–923.

Rudra, A 1978b, 'Class relations in Indian agriculture: II'. *Economic and Political Weekly*, vol. 13, no. 23, pp. 963–968.

Saad-Filho, A 2015, 'Social policy for neoliberalism: The Bolsa família programme in Brazil', *Development and Change*, vol. 46, no. 6, pp. 1227–1252.

Scott, J.C 1972a, 'Patron-client politics and political change in Southeast Asia', *American Political Science Review*, vol. 66, no. 1, pp. 91–113.

Scott, J.C 1972b, 'The erosion of patron-client bonds and social change in rural Southeast Asia', *The Journal of Asian Studies*, vol. 32, no. 1, pp. 5–37.

Scott, J.C 1985, *Weapons of the weak: Everyday forms of peasant resistance*, New Haven, CT, Yale University Press.

Ste Croix, G.E.M 1981, *The class struggle in the ancient greek world: From the archaic age to the arab conquests*, Ithaca, NY, Cornell University Press.

Stoler, A.L 1977b, 'Class structure and female autonomy in rural Java', *Sign*, vol. 3, no. 1, pp. 74–89.

Thompson, E.P 1966, *The making of the English working class*, New York, Vintage Books.

Thorner, A 1982, 'Semi-feudalism or capitalism? Contemporary debate on classes and mode of production in India', *Economic and Political Weekly*, vol. 17, no. 49, pp. 1961–1968.

Tillin, L & Duckett, J 2017, 'The politics of social policy: Welfare expansion in Brazil, China, India and South Africa in comparative perspective', *Commonwealth & Comparative Politics*, vol. 55, no. 3, pp. 253–277.

Watts, M.J 2009, 'The southern question: Agrarian questions of labour and capital', in A.H Akram-Lodhi & C Kay (eds), *Peasants and globalization: Political economy, rural transformation and the agrarian question*, New York, Routledge, pp. 262–287

Webber, M 2008, 'Primitive accumulation in modern China', *Dialectical Anthropology*, vol. 32, pp. 299–320. doi:10.1007/s10624-008-9039-8

Wise, R.D & Veltmeyer, H 2016, *Agrarian change, migration and development*, Rugby, Practical Action Publishing.

Wolf, E.R 1969, *Peasant wars of the twentieth century*, New York, Harper and Row.

Wood, E.M 1982, 'The politics of theory and the concept of class: E.P. Thompson and his critics', *Studies in Political Economy*, vol. 9, no. 1, pp. 45–75.

Wood, E.M 2002, *The origin of capitalism: A longer view*, London and New York, Verso.

Zhang, Q.F 2015, 'Class differentiation in rural China: Dynamics of accumulation, commodification and state intervention', *Journal of Agrarian Change*, vol. 15, no. 3, pp. 338–365.

3 Agrarian Change in Indonesia and the State

Introduction

It is common among the agrarian populist movements to perceive the Indonesian state as anti-farmers/smallholders. This chapter casts doubt on this simplistic view by elaborating class relations in the country both within and beyond agriculture, which have shaped the nature of state intervention in agriculture over time. To comprehend current capitalist agrarian change and class relations under neoliberalism, the first section of this chapter discusses the process of 'primitive accumulation' and the emergence of capitalist agriculture in Indonesia that took place during the colonial period. This understanding is crucial to assessing the extent to which 'primitive accumulation' characterises contemporary agrarian change in Indonesia. The following section will explain the national class dynamics and how the country's annihilation of leftist power in the past has led to the current disorganisation of classes of labour throughout the country. This annihilation has paved the way for the anti-worker bias of the state, both in agriculture and beyond. In contrast to agrarian populism, we argue that the bias of the state towards rice farmers at the expense of oil palm farmers relates to the broader nature of the Indonesian capitalist state, to provide affordable staple food (rice) in order to maintain cheap domestic labour to boost capital accumulation. The chapter also describes the limited support of the state to increase agricultural profit for both rice and oil palm farmers. The last section discusses the impact of limited state support in agriculture on the general pattern of agrarian class reproduction at a national level.

Primitive Accumulation and the Emergence of Capitalist Agriculture in Indonesia

The emergence of capitalist agriculture in Indonesia, as in any other peripheral countries, dates back to the colonial period. There has been debate about the nature of the 'mode of production' under Dutch rule. Geertz (1963: 89), for instance, insists that the labour supply for industrial plantations in Java was not proletariat simply because they 'had one foot in the rice terrace and the other in the mill', indicating the role of a 'pre-capitalist' labour arrangement in the

DOI: 10.4324/9781003267348-3

capitalist industry. More explicitly, under the influence of the 'Asiatic mode of production', Tichelman (1980) contends that Java's sugar industry under the cultivation system represented the application of a certain pre-capitalist form of labour. He highlights 'the prolonged use, even until the twentieth century, of pre-capitalist methods of appropriating agrarian surplus, whether in kind or in labour' (1980: 122–123). A similar view is developed by Gordon (1982), who argues that the expansion of the sugar plantations was only possible because of the cheap land and labour provided 'by the colonial state through its extra-economic functions' (1982: 174) and thus represents a 'colonial mode of production'.[1] This applies also to the plantations in East Cost Sumatera, where the indentured labour regime served the Dutch companies' accumulation, although it was more a plantation in the 'classic model'. The paradigm of 'peasant-plantation' in Java is inextricably linked to the intellectual epoch of anti-colonial nationalism and dependency theory in the mid-twentieth century, which was highly influential though not unchallenged (Knight, 2000: 220–221). No doubt Meillassoux's notion of the 'articulation of mode of production' (1972) was the popular approach.

However, as has been argued in the theoretical chapter, this approach fails to distinguish between the 'criteria' of capitalism and the 'indicator' of capitalist development. Knight has aptly noted in his critique of Gordon (1982) that

> if the use of state power to force access to resources rules out the 'purity' of capitalist enterprise, colonial or otherwise, then there would be few such enterprises which at one time or another in their history would pass this test.
>
> (1988: 247)

One might think that even the contemporary neoliberal state would not pass such a test. Knight observes further that what happened in late colonial Java was 'a stage of capitalist development, not a peculiarly "colonial" form of quasi-capitalism'. It is indeed the case that the colonial period in Indonesia marks the initial stage of the capitalist development of what Marx calls primitive accumulation. This was the moment of the creation of capitalist social relations which are generally persecuted with 'blood and fire'.

The advance of capitalist agriculture during this time undoubtedly owes much to the Dutch colonial state. In Java, the first wave of primitive accumulation took place in the early nineteenth century when the Dutch colonial state that had replaced the VOC as the ruling class in the colony introduced the cultivation system (1830–1870). Under this system, Javanese villagers and a few other places in the outer islands were obliged to grow export crops on a portion of their cultivated land. Although land appropriation for export crops did not entirely displace farmers from their land, it does not necessarily mean that commodification of subsistence, though in its early phase, was not taking place. Cash began to circulate increasingly in rural Java after the inception of the cultivation system (Alexander & Alexander, 1979: 32). After several decades of the cultivation system, there was little doubt that there 'was a rapid monetarisation of the village economy' (Fasseur, 1986: 144). Labour commodification also took place in this period, where there was 'ample evidence that proletarianization…had been going on in rural Java since the mid-nineteenth century' (Knight, 1989: 53).

In 1870, after endless pressure from the Dutch capitalists at home, the colonial state eventually abolished the cultivation system to give the way to the private capitalists exploiting the colony. Since the 1870s, private companies were given a prominent role in exploiting Java and its outer islands. In the highland areas of coffee, tea and rubber, and the plantations on the outer islands, the private capitalists were given the rights to lease land for 75 years from the native inhabitants. The companies were also able to lease the land on customary rights of tenure (Kahn, 1980: 173). In the lowland sugarcane areas in Java, the companies were supposed to rent the paddy fields on a short-term rotational basis. Liberalisation implied the abolishment of forced labour, where the private companies were impelled to recruit and manage their own workforce from voluntary 'free labour'. However, in practice, forced labour in some areas remained the norm for sugar production until the 1890s and even up to the 1910s for coffee. A growing body of literature in Java has suggested that the first step of 'full commoditization' of labour power and land had taken place by the end of World War I after proletarisation began in the mid-nineteenth century (Elson, 1984, 1986; Knight, 1989; Hüsken, 1988; Boomgaard, 1990; Fasseur, 1992). In rural Java, liberalisation also meant the beginning of massive land privatisation (Elson, 1984: 219; Hüsken, 1988: 129; Gordon, 1999: 6). This paved the way for land appropriation with displacement and the increasingly growing proletariat both in rural and urban areas, making it the centre of social unrest during 'an age of motion' (Shiraishi, 1990). In 1926–1927, the first national revolt against the Dutch rule was organised under the communist leadership of PKI (McVey, 2006). Although it was crushed fiercely by the Dutch, the PKI survived and later became one of the largest political forces in the 1960s. For the outer islands (Sumatera), liberalisation marks the outset of 'primitive accumulation' with the expansion of corporate plantations in the frontier land. After indentured labour was abolished in 1911 and the practice had largely disappeared in the 1930s (Stoler, 1995), commodity relations expanded considerably.

Proletarianisation both in Java and Sumatera continued rapidly until the end of World War II, which was followed by the political independence of the country. By the early 1940s, around half a million labourers were looking for wages in the plantations in Java and other outer islands (mainly Sumatera), while hundreds of thousands of industrial workers filled the Javanese urban areas (Sidel, 2015: 19). By the mid-twentieth century, primitive accumulation for at least Java and Sumatera had been largely completed, as a certain degree of proletarianisation in the last century had successfully established generalised commodity production. Agricultural producers in Java and Sumatera since then have *predominantly* been dominated by 'market dependence' for their reproduction. After this moment, we may speak of 'the end of peasantry' where the 'peasantry' has been transformed 'into that of farmer and worker' (Elson, 1997: 238). One might think that this timeline is too early for the emergence of generalised commodity production in Java and Sumatera. However, the regions' path indeed reveals the unusual process of primitive accumulation by Southeast Asian standards. Sidel notes that

> compared to the Philippines and much of the rest of Southeast Asia at the turn of the twentieth century, the Dutch East Indies was distinguished by the relatively early emergence of a class of wage labourers concentrated in large-scale agricultural production and processing and key modes of modern transport.
>
> (Sidel, 2015: 19)

This suggests that primitive accumulation and the emergence of generalised commodity production of agriculture, at least in Java and Sumatera, precedes the neoliberal wave that started in the 1980s. Under current neoliberalism, we witness the *expansion* of capitalist agriculture instead of the *creation* of capitalist agriculture spearheaded by primitive accumulation (Chapter 2). Nonetheless, by suggesting that primitive accumulation in Java and Sumatera had *predominantly* already taken place by the mid-twentieth century, we do not suggest that prior to the neoliberal era every corner of the area had been ruled by commodity production. Some areas remained disconnected from national or global commodity production and a subsistence economy was the norm in these areas before the expansion of commodity production had reached them. As will be discussed in the next chapter, our village studied in North Sumatera is a 'new frontier', which only experienced its primitive accumulation in the 1980s when the palm oil companies expanded their commodity production. Since then, land and labour commoditisation have been generalised to serve the capitalist model of agriculture.

Class Dynamics and the State

Class relations and the nature of the Indonesian state have been transformed overtime. In the early days of independence, the flourish of revolutionary ideas provided fertile ground for the development of political organisations, including farmer's unions and labour unions in agriculture. Among the best known were the BTI (Indonesian Farmer's Front) and SARBUPRI (Estate Workers' Union of the Republic of Indonesia). Both the BTI and SARBUPRI were closely related to the PKI (the Indonesian Communist Party), which was the largest left-wing political party in the country (Pelzer, 1982: 45). By way of membership, the PKI became the fourth biggest party in the country after the 1955 election, making it 'the largest non-ruling communist party in the world' (Mortimer, 2006: 19).

With a strong and well-organised working class amidst the aspirations of a newly-established state set to reorganise the legacy of colonial order, two central progressive agrarian policies were instituted at this time. First, the state, in 1958, agreed to the nationalisation of foreign-owned plantations that was initiated by the labour unions, including SARBUPRI (Pelzer, 1982). However, this progressive attempt was abruptly ended when the army took control of plantation management. This arrangement was later to become the nest of rent-seeking and corruption activities (Mackie, 1967). At the sixth party congress in 1959, the PKI launched its agrarian program, which proposed the following: the confiscation of landlords' lands (both foreign and Indonesian owned) without compensation; free land redistribution to the landless and the 'poor farmers'—'land must be distributed to each member of the peasant family individually, the landownership system must be a peasant landownership system, or in other words, private ownership by the peasants of the land' (quoted in van der Kroef, 1963: 58); long-term and cheap credit to farmers, and the abolition of the 'feudal slavery system' (*pologoro* and *ijon*).

The state responded by introducing agrarian reform under the basic sharetenancy law (BSTL) in 1959 and the Basic Agrarian Law (BAL) in 1960. The laws were the product of long formulation following the establishment of an agrarian commission, set up in 1948 by Sukarno. Under the BSTL, the share of the yield between the landowner and the sharecropper was supposed to be decided at the district level. At that time, the general share was 50-50 (Van der Kroef, 1963: 58), where sharecroppers bore the production cost. The BSTL stated that the landowner must also bear the production cost, and, thus, the yields divided between landowner and sharecropper were the total outputs minus production costs, except the self-labour of the cultivator. As for the BAL, its prominent characteristic was the mandate to regulate the maxima and minima of arable land ownerships: a minimum of two hectares of land for each farmer, while in terms of the maximum, it ranged from five hectares in the most densely populated areas to 15 hectares in the least populated. The maximum also applied to the land at one's disposal through land mortgage and land lease (Utrecht, 1969: 75). From the beginning, the PKI condemned the law but not because it promoted private land ownership, as one author has suggested (White, 2016: 4).[2] As is clearly stated above, the PKI had already promoted private land ownership themselves in their 1959 Congress. Their opposition to the law was simply that it failed to meet the 'radical reform' whereby all the landlords' landholdings were confiscated and the land was handed over to the tillers. The existence of the BSTL only meant the continuation of sharecropping and the failure of the farmers' unions to convert their demands into law. Thus, in practice, the PKI kept calling on the sharecroppers in the field to demand a 60 percent share. The party eventually accepted the reform since they perceived that it would provide a sound basis to provoke the farmers into action and raise their political consciousness (Mortimer, 2006).

The implementation of the laws progressed at a snail's pace. At the same time, in late 1963, the 'harvest in Java had been heavily depleted by the worst drought and rat plague in living memory' (Mortimer, 2006: 300). In 1964, dissatisfied with the progress of agrarian reform and the deterioration of the rural economy, the PKI and BTI organised an offensive in the rural areas of Central Java, East Java and Bali to forcefully seize the lands that were seen to be the object of land reform. This move was labelled by their opponents as 'one-sided actions' (*Aksi Sepihak*). Landless labourers, with the support of the BTI, occupied the land without waiting for the decision of the local Land Reform Committee. In the case of the sharecroppers, they did not give up the harvest from the fields to the landowners because they had filed an application for these fields to the Committee and thought that they now belonged to them, despite there being no decision by the Committee (Utrecht, 1969: 81–82).

Their formidable opponents were the low-rank landed gentry (*priyayi*) at the village level, who affiliated themselves with the PNI (Sukarno's party), and the local elite of traditional Muslim figures under the banner of the *Nahdatul Ulama* party (Wertheim, 1966: 117). The local landed class, who received backing from both the parties and their farmers union's affiliations (PETANI and PERTANU), fought against the *Aksi Sepihak* of the PKI. In fact, the landowners themselves had also committed to the *Aksi Sepihak* when they took the initiative to cast out, at will, their labourers or sharecroppers who were members of the BTI before the Committee had come to register the land. With the severe economic conditions and the massive mobilisation by the PKI along class lines, the patron-client relationship was greatly weakened (Utrecht, 1972). Moreover, the state, through Sukarno, also gave its support to the movement. The state had no choice but to support the labourers' struggle as they had been the backbone of support for President Sukarno. The result was overt class struggle in the countryside (Wertheim, 1969).

The revolutionary action of the landless labourers and the BTI faced a counter-revolutionary backlash a year later. After the failure of the coup on 30 September 1965, the pendulum swung to the conservative parties. To destroy leftist power, General Suharto deceived the public with false news about the torture of generals to incur public anger against the PKI. In the Cold War atmosphere, the Allied forces provided assistance in the form of weapons, logistics and lists of communist members to the army (Melvin, 2018; Robinson, 2018). The combination of misleading public over the PKI and the continuing class struggle in the countryside served as a pretext for the mass murder of at least half a million members of the PKI and their sympathisers across the country from 1965 to 1966 (Cribb, 2004; Roosa, 2006). The brutal killings swept through Java and the outer islands. The army assisted the militias who had quarrelled with the PKI over the land reform process and let them execute anybody alleged to be related to the PKI, including BTI members. In North Sumatera, the mass murder wiped out the BTI and other PKI supporters. The members and officials of SARBUPRI were also slaughtered, with the help of the plantation companies (White, 2016: 7).

The annihilation of communist power in Indonesia after 1965 turned around the short-lived class struggle of the previous years. The vanguard party of the labouring class completely vanished. The organisers of the classes of labour in the countryside were no longer available. Without such an organised labour party, the 'nationalist-socialist' state under Sukarno, which had navigated agrarian reform and the nationalisation of plantations, had gone (Habibi & Juliawan, 2018).

Under Suharto's New Order, the revolutionary atmosphere was depleted following the mass murders, and the urgent need was to address the deteriorating economy. Socialist-nationalist ideology was jettisoned and a state-capitalism approach of 'developmentalism' was adopted (Chalmers & Hadiz, 1997). The resistance against the old imperial powers, exemplified in the nationalisation of industries, for example, was replaced by benevolent cooperation, with the new global powers (primarily the US and Japan) as 'the senior partners'. Class-based social conflict in the countryside, which had 'harmed' the economy, was supplanted by state patronage over rice capitalist farmers. The state during the early Suharto period overwhelmingly focused on economic growth and stability to legitimise its establishment.

In agricultural term, this meant there was a pressing need to increase production and to stabilise rural areas. Given this imperative, the main economic policy in the early Suharto period was to ensure food availability at relatively stable prices (Hüsken & White, 1989: 249). Affordable staple food (rice) is also crucial to maintaining cheap domestic labour. The availability of cheap workers is just too strategic for the New Order's focus on attracting foreign capital and boosting economic growth (Hadiz, 1997). In doing so, the state had to provide the food through domestic production because the international rice market was extremely risky (Hart, 1986: 45). Consequently, the Suharto regime attempted to increase domestic agriculture productivity. The Green Revolution was the most appropriate answer since international aid, flowing mainly from the US and the World Bank, was greatly available, and the oil boom in the 1970s provided the resources needed. Suharto completely neglected the agrarian reform agenda of the Sukarno era, although he never revoked the Basic Agrarian Law No. 5/1960.

In order to implement the Green Revolution complete political control over rural areas was required. In the context of the 'unreformed agrarian structure' (Hüsken & White, 1989), it was important to tame any potential unrest in the countryside. With this caution, first, the state depoliticised the rural areas by introducing the 'floating mass' by 'banning all political party branches below the level of the district' (Hüsken & White, 1989: 256). Secondly, the state provided material benefits to the rural elites, mainly to 'a rural landlord/kulak class through the provision of rural credit and infrastructure' (Robison, 1982: 58). This included continuing to provide them with salary land (*tanah bengkok*) which had been officially granted since the colonial period (Kammen, 2003) and was meant to have been abolished during the short-lived overt class struggle in the mid-1960s. In return, the rural elites had to maintain political control over the rural areas on behalf of the state (Hart, 1986: 44).

The role of the state under the New Order, as a patron to the local rice capitalist farmers-cum-village officials, effectively re-established the patron-client relationship at the village level (Hüsken & White, 1989). Since then, the rice capitalist farmers/'landlord-capitalists'-cum-village officials have regained the role they held during the colonial period, acting as patrons to their clients in the village. This negates the anti-farmers/smallholders sentiment of the Indonesian state perceived by agrarian populist movements. At the national level, the HKTI, as the state-sponsored farmers union, was dominated by capitalist farmers and provided the legitimacy for the New Order for being pro-farmer. The dominance of the HKTI effectively prevented a more independent and radical farmers' union to develop. At the same time, the Green Revolution greatly improved agricultural productivity and effectively prevented any severe economic deterioration of the rural economy. This strengthened the patrons' capacity while also preventing their clients from taking drastic measures against them. Furthermore, the strict authoritarian rule stopped any potential radical organisation from developing in the countryside. All of this has contributed to the absence of an overt class struggle in the rural areas, despite the continuation of rapid class differentiation, since the 1970s (Stoler, 1977; Hüsken, 1988: White & Wiradi, 1989; Pincus, 1996).

In the outer islands, like Sumatera, the state initiated the expansion of plantations in the late 1970s. In 1977, the government established the first NES program to improve the rural economy and diversify the state's revenues. To serve this expansion, in 1980, the state announced the Consensus Forest Land Use Plan (*Tata Guna Hutan Kesepakatan* or TGHK) which classified 143.8 million hectares (approximately 75 percent of the nation's land area) as 'forest land' (McCarthy, 2000: 94). This classification meant that the Ministry of Forestry's jurisdiction extended over areas inhabited or used by some 60 million people (McCarthy, 2000: 99). With this absolute control, the state was able to distribute logging concessions for agricultural plantations to the private companies. Timber and oil palm plantations were among the most common concessions. For Suharto, concessions created large revenue 'to benefit loyal military officers, appease potential opponents and bolster the military budget' (Dauvergne, 1997: 7). This enclosure largely took place without consultation with the local inhabitants (Peluso, 1995). This marked the beginning of 'dispossession by displacement' in post-Independence Indonesia.

Liberalisation took place in the mid-1980s when the state experienced an increasing deficit in the balance of payments. The acute dependence on oil revenues and the poor performance of non-oil exports during the 1970s ended tragically in an economic crisis when oil prices plunged in 1982 (Soesastro, 1989: 854). Following instructions from the World Bank and the IMF, the government initiated limited liberalisation in the form of tariff and non-tariff reductions and capital market reforms to increase non-oil and gas exports. The adjustments were directed mostly at manufacturing and much less at agriculture (Rada et al., 2011: 868). The most important agriculture liberalisation at this period was the granting of permission for foreign investors to build their chemical fertiliser plants in the country. However, even when the international donor agencies failed to urge further agricultural liberalisation in the mid-1980s, the state's expenditure on agriculture was notably reduced because the oil boom, as the biggest source of state revenues, had gone (Simatupang & Timmer, 2008: 67). This marked the end of the 'developmental state' of the New Order, to be replaced by a more 'neoliberal state' with an authoritarian political regime.

For rice cultivation in Java, liberalisation in the 1980s meant the decline of the state's support for rice production. One might have expected that this would reduce the local patrons' capability of serving their clients (sharecroppers) and, thus, add impetus to their conflict. However, more than a decade of accumulation under the Green Revolution had enabled 'large farmers' to invest in lucrative non-agricultural business: local trades, transportation services, money-lending and political accumulation (Pincus, 1996). The relative independence of the 'large farmers' from the state was also assisted by the remittances sent from their children who occupied prosperous salaried jobs elsewhere. This might negate Hart's contention (1986) which tends to overemphasises the dependency of the 'large farmers' on the state.

For agriculture in the outer islands, liberalisation expanded the plantation activities that had started some years earlier. There is a paradox here. On the one hand, integration with the global market via liberalisation was required since the Indonesian state had increasingly relied on agricultural exports as their main revenue source. At the same time, the state kept protecting the export sectors from foreign players to maintain the interest of Suharto's cronies (McCarthy, 2010). Since the forestry and plantations had been among the sectors most highly protected from liberalisation, in 1986 the state began to support the expansion of the estates with easy credit access at concessional rates (Larson, 1996). In oil palm, the state's support also signalled its response to the growing prices and demand for oil palm since the mid-1970s (Sanders et al., 2014). As a result, the plantations increased immensely, from only 133 thousand hectares in 1970 to one million hectares in 1990, a few years after the first neoliberal adjustment was taken (DJP, 2016: 3). The expansion of plantations mainly benefitted the corporations owned by the cronies of Suharto at the expense of rural inhabitants, and this 'dispossession by displacement' frequently incited resistances from the local people (Peluso, 1995).

At the same time, liberalisation also increased the prominent role of smallholders. Their share of the total acreage of oil palm grew immensely from a mere 3,125 hectares in 1979 to 200,000 in 1990, and around one million hectares in 2000 (DJP, 2016: 17). The NES scheme was largely responsible for the growth of oil palm production in the hands of smallholders. Under the NES, the state granted 'concession land' to state-owned and private companies where 80 percent of this land had to be given to the smallholder as 'plasma'. The state provided the credits for smallholders to plant, their initial living expenses and housing. The companies, as 'nucleus estates', were responsible for delivering extension services, and collecting and processing the crops (McCarthy, 2010). Only in 1995–1998, when the state's budget became more limited, was the scheme replaced by the KPPA (Prime Cooperative for Credit Members), following pressure from the World Bank. In this period, the increased exposure of the smallholders to the global market precipitated class differentiation, although only in its early phase (McCarthy, 2010).

The second phase of liberalisation, since 1998, has not greatly transformed class relations and the state. The only change has been the political democratisation after the end of the authoritarian New Order regime. The state's main concern remains largely to maintain social stability and boost economic growth. The general bias of the state towards capital at the expense of non-capital (labour and the environment) continues. The need to provide affordable staple food (rice) to cheap domestic workers remains the norm to facilitate accumulation both in agriculture (e.g. corporate-based agriculture outside staple foods) and beyond (e.g. manufacture). The neoliberal state in the post-Suharto era is only required to operate within a politically democratic regime. There has been little change in the power structure in the country, since the old elites nurtured under Suharto have managed to hold their power through the new liberal parliamentary politics (Robison & Hadiz, 2004).

At the same time, class-based political organisations that existed before Suharto have not been re-established. During the three decades of its rule, the New Order developed an astonishingly effective anti-communist propaganda machine through manipulating the education system, mass media, popular culture and the religious credo (Farid, 2005). Suharto not only annihilated communist members and sympathisers physically but also erased the memory and ideas of communism or socialism, which, together with nationalism and Islamism, were the backbone of the country's political ideology in the colonial and pre-Suharto period (McVey, 2006). The strong sentiment of anti-communism after the Suharto period has provided a great obstacle to building class-based political vehicles, particularly in the countryside where the remnant of the old gentry and traditional Islamist figures are located. What has been developed is the 'populist' farmers unions, such as the SPI, a member of the *Via Campesina*. Their main concern, however, is to establish 'food sovereignty' rather than deal with the exploitation present in agricultural production itself.

The state patronage of the rural ruling class (especially the rice capitalist farmers) was strengthened when its financial capacity recovered in the early 2000s following the bailout from IMF in return for further liberalisation. Since 2005, the state fertiliser subsidy has returned to its level prior to the crisis (see the next section). The continuing state assistance to rice farmers disproves the simplistic notion of the agrarian populists that the Indonesian state is anti-farmers/smallholders. In 2007, the government introduced the Association of Farmers Groups (GAPOKTAN)[3] to 'nurture the farmers groups' to improve their welfare (Ministry of Agriculture, 2007). Each GAPOKTAN should fill out an application to receive certain grants (for seeds, tractors, water pumps, etc.) from the government. Obtaining such a grant greatly depends on the skill of the GAPOKTAN's leader to 'lobby' the local government officers and political figures. The leaders and the administrators of such GAPOKTANs are overwhelmingly large landowners and/or village officials.

The patron-client relationship with the state was arguably fostered after the inception of the Village Fund policy ('Dana Desa') in 2015. Each village, on average, receives 700 million to 1.2 billion rupiah per year. While the program is not designated to the development of agriculture, it provides lucrative sources for the accumulation of the village officials-cum-large landowners, both legally and illegally. Between 2015 and 2018, more than 900 village officials have been arrested on corruption charges. Legally, the village officials who dominate the decision-making process concerning the fund's allocation often designate money that benefits them, such as the luxurious renovation of the village offices at the expense of labouring poor workers in the village.

In the outer islands, the post-Suharto period marked the acceleration of 'dispossession by displacement' and class differentiation. The IMF-led economic liberalisation required the country to generate revenues from overwhelmingly export-base activities (Feintrenie et al., 2010). The rise in exports of natural resources (ultimately, coal) and agricultural products, such as oil palm, rubber and cocoa, have precipitated the enclosure of vast areas of lands. For oil palm alone, the extent of plantations rose from 4.1 million in 2000 to 8 million hectares in 2010, and 12 million hectares in 2017 (DJP, 2018: 3). Many rural inhabitants have been displaced because of this expansion. However, the share of land held by oil palm farmers has increased three-fold, from around one million hectares in 2000 to 3.3 million in 2010, and then again it increased to more than four and a half million in 2017. This is equal to around 40 percent of total oil palm acreage. Overall, around 2.6 million households of oil palm farmers contribute around a third of the total oil palm production in 2017 (DJP, 2018: 16). The growth in the number of oil palm smallholders during this period has no longer depended on the state's assistance. The state even reversed the regulations regarding the obligation of the companies to provide 80 percent of total concessions for smallholders in previous years to 20 percent since the 2000s (McCarthy, 2010). The growing number of oil palm smallholders has increased the wealth of a few large smallholders, while others have lagged behind, marking the acceleration of class differentiation (McCarthy, 2010; Fortin, 2011; Li, 2014).

However, different from the rice capitalist farmers who have been effectively incorporated into state patronage since the New Order, oil palm capitalist farmers have not been included, for several reasons. As mentioned in the introduction, the rice crop is politically more important than oil palm. Moreover, as will be shown in the next section, the power of the 'corporate-scale plantation' in the oil palm sector prevents the state from providing adequate assistance to oil palm farmers (smallholders), including the capitalist farmers. This implies that the oil palm capitalist farmers are economically more vulnerable to global volatility than the rice capitalist farmers and politically weaker than the rice capitalist farmers since they may face land dispossession through the expansion of the 'corporate-scale producers'.

The State and Agricultural Production

Class dynamics also show up when looking at its impact on agricultural production. They have a particular impact on labour arrangements (sharecropping and wage labour) and agricultural profits (which closely relate to land productivity, production costs and commodity prices) over time.

The State and Labour Arrangements

In Java, the incidence of sharecropping in paddy cultivation has been the norm, stretching back to the pre-colonial period. In this paper, limited space prevents us from providing details (see Breman, 2015). During this era, sharecropping in Java was built on the *cacah* system, a stratified household system of land ownership and cultivation. In the early nineteenth century, under the Dutch Cultivation System, sharecropping was reorganised, leading to the disintegration of the *cacah* system (Breman, 2015). With the disintegration of the *cacah* system and the beginning of proletarianisation, the patrons of sharecropping were no longer traditional landowners (*sikep*), but landowner farmer-cum-village officials who began to be commoditised in their subsistence but yet not necessarily commoditised as agricultural producers (Breman, 1982). This owes much to the failed attempt at rice commercialisation by the colonial state in the 1820s (Hugenholtz, 1986: 156).

By the early twentieth century, land concentration and proletarianisation in Java had reached a considerable level (Knight, 1989; Boomgaard, 1990), while monetisation and integration into the global market had penetrated deeper into the interior of Java (Burger cited in Hüsken, 1988). Rice commercialisation grew, though insignificantly. In the end, it was only a short-lived attempt at agricultural and rice commercialisation in Java because the conditions became unfavourable during 1930–1950 when monetised trade disappeared because of economic depression, war and revolution (Hüsken, 1979: 142). In the mid-1950s, the big farmers only gradually strengthened their position over the landless and petty farmers, while sharecropping remained the prominent mechanism of surplus appropriation.

Meanwhile, in North Sumatera, free wage labour had become the norm in the 1930s. This not only applied to the plantations owned by corporations, but also to 'small growers' who hired wage labour. The domination of wage labour over sharecropping in Sumatera relates to several considerations. First, Sumatera, during the colonial period, was a vast wasteland with very few inhabitants. The norm was an abundance of land with a shortage of labour. It was only with the help of the repressive labour regime that the colonial accumulation maintained their labour supply (Breman, 1989: 38; Stoler, 1995). Second, the nature of the crop has played a distinctive role. Rubber or oil palm crops have been the dominant crops on this island. For oil palm, its cultivation is not labour-intensive and, thus, the need to secure a labour supply through sharecropping is negligible. When there is a sharecropping arrangement in the oil palm field, as will be seen in North Sumatera (Chapter 6), it is generally because of the desire of the absentee landowners to lower maintenance costs.

While the labour relation of production in oil palm on Sumatera was transformed into free wage labour, this was not the case for the Javanese paddy cultivation in the 1950s. In Java, large farmer-patrons had failed to substantially commercialise their rice cultivation processes and had to face the abolition of landlordism (the sharecropping arrangement) under the mobilisation of the left-wing organisations of the BTI and PKI. However, as explained in the previous section, the PKI, in the end, accepted a compromise by allowing sharecropping to continue in return for an increased share for sharecroppers (van der Kroef, 1963).

This proved to be a missed opportunity to abolish sharecropping once and for all from the country when the annihilation of the communists in the mid-1960s changed everything. Following this, the Green Revolution successfully delivered full-scale rice commercialisation. As the attempt to modernise agriculture production through the inception of new technologies successfully boosted production, there was no longer any need for the state to transform sharecropping. Moreover, the state's clients in the rural areas (the large farmers) were in favour of sharecropping, as it was more desirable for both political and economic reasons (Hüsken, 1979).

When the state's economic support for the Green Revolution gradually declined after the neoliberal adjustment in the mid-1980s, sharecropping was left untouched. Again, the state had no interest whatsoever in curtailing it as long as the rice production faced no acute crisis and patron-farmers continued to see the benefits of sharecropping. Nonetheless, there has been a new development since the mid-2010s, where the state has initiated the inception of machines to assist in the planting and harvesting of rice to regain the high annual production rate of the early 1980s. The growing sense of crisis has been precipitated by the fact that the current rate of population growth, combined with stagnation in rice production in the last three decades, has resulted in a quite significant rise in rice imports over these years. Similar to the early New Order state, rice dependency on the global market has been seen as risky business for the current government in a country where rice is the most prominent currency for social stability.

Moreover, Jokowi, leader of the current administration who has been associated with the symbol of 'new hope' (*Time*, 2014), needed to make a breakthrough for his populist image. Since 2014, Jokowi's administration has delivered thousands of combine harvesters to rice farmers throughout the country. In 2017 alone, the administration distributed 2,641 harvesters through GAPOKTAN. The use of both planting machines and combine harvesters has decreased labour costs by around 30 percent (see Chapter 6), which could facilitate capitalist farmer's accumulation. With the use of these machines, the demand for labour has also been drastically reduced, and there is no longer a need for sharecropping to secure labour.

Sharecropping, which has been considered the clinical instrument for accumulation over the last century, for the first time, is increasingly being seen by capitalist farmers as an obstacle to accumulation. However, the option of capitalist farmers to replace sharecropping is not a straightforward choice, considering both the resistance from the agricultural labourers and the technical problems with the existing machines. The state itself has only limited resources to channel rapid mechanisation. Thus, while some areas have mechanised their rice cultivation, others have not (Ambarwati et al., 2016). It is, indeed, the struggle between the labourers and the capitalist farmers and the technical barriers of mechanisation in the specific setting that determine the results of such efforts. This requires further investigation in the local context.

The State and Agricultural Profit[4]

The Indonesian state has also played a prominent role in shaping the agricultural profit that is closely related to production costs, land productivity and commodity prices. In the last three decades, there has been a declining trend in the profit rate per hectare of wet paddy cultivation, both in Indonesia and Central Java. The data is drawn from the agricultural census, conducted regularly by the BPS. The data collection method follows international standards is believed to yield reliable data. To our knowledge, a discussion on the agricultural profit rates and their underlying causes in Indonesia has largely been neglected.

As shown in Table 3.1, the revenue per cost ratio in Indonesia has plummeted by almost a half, from 3.4 in 1983 to 1.8 in 2017. This means that in 2017, every rupiah that was put into production only generated 1.8 rupiah in return. This is only about half of the ratio in 1983. A similar trend can be found in Central Java. The rate of profit is even lower when we include the land rent in the production cost. The BPS has only started including the land rent in the production cost since the 2003 census. This has prevented us from

Table 3.1 The rate of profit of wet paddy cultivation per hectare in Indonesia and Central Java

	1983	*1993*	*2003*	*2013*	*2017*
Indonesia	3.4	2.9	2.4	1.9	1.8
Central Java	3.2	2.6	2.0	1.9	1.7
Adjusted by adding land rent cost					
Indonesia			2.3	1.4	1.4
Central Java			1.9	1.3	1.2

Source: calculated by the author from the BPS

Note: The time frame for the tables in this whole section follows the agricultural census periodisation, except for the last year indicated, which represents the time when our research was carried out. The method and the number of samples covered in the survey are similar to the agricultural census.

Table 3.2 The change in total real revenue and total production cost of a hectare of wet paddy cultivation in Indonesia and Central Java (in thousands of rupiah)

		1983	*1993*	*2003*	*2013*	*2017*
Indonesia	Total revenue	8008	8067	10495	14699	13022
	Total cost	2333	2787	4315	7606	7094
				(4612)	(10844)	(9536)
Central Java	Total revenue	8506	8974	10776	14638	12675
	Total cost	2687	3516	5303	7784	7445
				(5748)	(11617)	(10764)

Source: calculated by the author from the BPS

Note: The consumer price index (CPI) index to estimate real total revenue and total cost is based on World Bank data, with 2010 as the base year. The figure inside the bracket is the adjusted figure created by adding land rent costs.

comparing it with previous years. However, by including land rent cost, it is clear that there has been a significant decline in the profit rate between 2003 and 2017. Since the BPS census only covers the average of rice farmers from different sizes of land cultivation, it is not a straightforward way of looking into the different rate of profit for each agrarian class. This will be investigated in the village level study.

The plummet in the rate of profit relates to the trend where the increased production cost has exceeded the rise in total revenue. Table 3.2 clearly demonstrates how, in the last three decades, in the real terms, the rise in production cost has become five times that of the increase of total revenue. While the total revenue has only increased by 60 percent, the total cost has spiked to 300 percent in the last three decades. This trend applies to both Indonesia and Central Java, although the latter has experienced a slightly lower climb in production cost.

This trend begs an explanation. On the one hand, the sky-rocketing production cost needs to be seen in the changing nature of the composition of the production cost. It is clear that the share of labour cost to total production cost has dropped by 15 percent in the last three decades, from around 60 percent in 1983 to about 45 percent in 2017 (Table 3.3). The decline is even higher in Central Java, amounting to 40 percent. The drastic fall in labour cost in 2003 was related to the rise in input cost due to the zero input subsidies provided at the time (see below).

The fall in the share of labour cost to total cost is happening despite the fact that the real wages of agricultural workers in the food crops sector (such as paddy) has increased around three-fold in the same period (Table 3.4). This suggests that there has been a decline in the number of workers per unit of land cultivated. The burgeoning literature has highlighted the reduced number of workers needed for crucial rice cultivation tasks, such as planting and harvesting. As will be shown, our study in Central Java adds to this understanding (Chapter 6).

Table 3.3 The composition of wet paddy cultivation cost per hectare in Indonesia and Central Java (in percentages)

	1983		*1993*		*2003*		*2013*		*2017*	
	Indonesia	*Central Java*	*Indonesia*	*Central Java*	*Indonesia*	*Central Java*	*Indonesia*	*Central Java*	*Indonesia*	*Central Java*
Labour cost	60.7	63.1	51.2	53.6	30.9	36.1	68.8*	70.6*	46.3	39.0
Input cost	22.3	23.2	28.6	30.2	43.4	43.6	22.0	21.8	23.4	23.3
Adjusted by adding land rent cost										
Labour cost	-	-	-	-	28.9	33.3	48.2*	47.3*	31.2	27.0
Input cost	-	-	-	-	40.6	40.2	15.5	14.6	17.4	16.1
Rent cost	-	-	-	-	6.4	7.7	29.9	32.9	25.6	30.8

Source: calculated by the author from the BPS

*The BPS mixes together labour and services cost, including transport cost for harvesting. This makes the labour cost in 2013 significantly higher than the figure in 2003 and 2017. For the sake of consistency, it is useful to see the figure in 2017.

Table 3.4 Indonesia's agricultural real wages in food crops (in rupiah per day)

Agricultural tasks	*1983*	*1993*	*2003*	*2013*	*2018*
Hoeing	10,799	13,065	20,024	37,039	37,382
Planting	8,663	10,094	16,749	31,699	32,040
Weeding	8,820	10,836	17,111	30,490	30,104

Source: calculated by the author from the BPS
Note: The CPI index to estimate real wages is based on World Bank data, with 2010 as the base year. The three agricultural tasks chosen are the only ones with data available since the 1980s. The BPS has only just begun collecting wage data on other agricultural tasks (applying fertilisers, ploughing, harvesting, etc.) since 2009.

Meanwhile, input cost has stagnated at around 22 percent in the last three decades (Table 3.3). A similar trend can be found in Central Java. The only substantial increase in input cost took place between 1993 and 2003, when there was 150 percent increase of inputs cost in this period. This dramatic rise owes much to the IMF-led liberalisation policies in 1998–2003 which forced Indonesia to provide zero subsidies for fertilisers and pesticides from 2000 to 2003. Since the mid-2000s, when the government returned to paying subsidies, the contribution of input cost to total cost has declined to a level similar to that of the 1980s.

Along with the decline in labour cost and the stagnation of input cost, the decline of profit in the last three decades is explained by another factor. Table 3.3 indicates a significant rise in land rent cost between 2003 and 2017 (about 25 percent) while labour cost stalls and input cost significantly drops. The rise of land rent cost may be related to several conditions. One common trigger is a massive agricultural land conversion to non-agricultural business, mostly housing and industry. Between 2000 and 2015, the rate of paddy fields being converted into non-agricultural activities reached 96,512 hectares per year (Mulyani et al., 2016). If the average yearly conversion continues and no new rice fields are created, by 2045, Indonesia will have lost about three million hectares of paddy field. This worrying figure is more than four times higher than the conservative estimate made by the BPS. Land conversion in Java has driven a surge in land value and, thus, land price (Rondhi et al., 2018). With the spike of land price in the rural areas, land rent cost is also rising.

The spike in total cost that has mainly been caused by the increase in land rent cost has occurred at a time when total revenue has barely increased. This halt owes much to the stagnation in land productivity over the last three decades and the minimal rise in the farm-gate rice price. Land productivity of wet paddy field in Indonesia has stalled, increasing from 4.5 tonnes per hectare in 1983 to only 4.6 in 2017 (Table 3.5). Although land productivity has always been higher in Central Java than in Indonesia, Central Java has also experienced arrested development of wet paddy productivity. While this land productivity for rice cultivation is parallel to the global average (4.6 tonnes/ha),

Table 3.5 Land productivity per hectare of wet paddy field per season in Indonesia and Central Java

	1983	*1993*	*2003*	*2013**	*2017*
Indonesia	4.5	4.7	5.5	5.2	4.6
Central Java	4.8	5.3	6.1	5.6	5.0

Source: calculated by the author from the BPS
*The figure is an average combination between wet and dry paddy which is slightly lower than the figure for wet paddy alone.

it is only around two-thirds of major rice producing countries such as South Korea, China and to a certain degree Japan (FAOSTAT, 2017). The stagnation of production volume per hectare prevents any substantial rise in total revenue. The literature suggests that the state's failure to maintain and expand the irrigation system as the basic infrastructure of rice cultivation and the inability to introduce new production techniques have been responsible for the stagnant land productivity of the last few decades (Simatupang & Timmer, 2008). This is not to mention land soil degradation, which requires higher inputs (fertilisers) yet only generates similar levels of output.

At the same time, the farm-gate rice price has only increased slightly in the last three decades. If the total revenue is equal to land productivity times rice price—while land productivity has halted—the increase in total revenue is mostly explained by the rise of the paddy price (Table 3.6). This indicates that the 60 percent increase in total revenue between 1983 and 2017 in Indonesia (and about 50 percent in Central Java) has been caused by the change in paddy price. The increase in the farm-gate paddy price has lagged far behind the total cost which, in the same period, rose two-fold for Indonesia and almost two-fold for Central Java (Table 3.2).

Expecting the farm-gate paddy price to increase substantially in the near future seems inconceivable. The Indonesian state has always provided price support to rice farmers. Up until the late 1990s, state assistance kept domestic price rice largely in parallel with the global price. Only since the mid-2000s, has the state extensively applied restrictions on rice imports through both import banning (only occasional imports are allowed) and tariffs that put domestic rice prices at around 25 percent higher than global price (Dawe, 2008: 117). Any further increase in the domestic rice price would have a disastrous effect on rice

Table 3.6 Farm-gate price per kg of paddy in Indonesia (in rupiah)

	1983	*1993*	*2003*	*2013*	*2017*
Indonesia	1449	2831	-	-	3995
Central Java	1364	2775	-	-	3617

Source: calculated by the author from the BPS

consumers who comprise the majority population of non-rice producers, such as labourers. This puts a limit on state support. It is claimed that the lobbying activity of the state-sponsored farmers association, the HKTI, is responsible for the state price support (McCulloch, 2008). However, overemphasising the role of the HKTI ignores the state's consideration of the declining rate of profit since the 1990s (Table 3.1). With the rising production cost and stalled land productivity, which the state, for whatever reasons has failed to cope with, the easiest way it can help its client is through price support. This 'necessary but limited support' characterises recent state intervention to aid rice producers, especially capitalist farmers.

Our discussion reveals the 'defensive' nature of current rice capitalist cultivation in Indonesia. The declining rate of profit is partly due to ambiguous state intervention. At the production site, it keeps providing input subsidies similar to the Green Revolution era. However, the state permission to allow massive land conversion has driven the surge of land price and, thus, land rent cost, though this may benefit those who sell their land. On the other hand, given its limited resources have been spent on supplying input subsidies, the state has failed to promote innovation in rice cultivation and to maintain and expand its basic infrastructure, namely the irrigation system. This has been mostly responsible for the halted land productivity in the last three decades. A 'metabolic rift' in the form of land degradation in Indonesia's paddy fields has also contributed to the stalled land productivity. The only counterbalance to further profit decline has been the rise of the domestic rice price that is now higher than the global standard, which is maintained by the state patronage over capitalist farmers.

Oil palm farmers have also experienced profit decline, though it has been less dramatic than for the rice farmers. The revenue per cost ratio in oil palm has dropped by about a quarter, from 3.9 in 1993 to 3 in 2013 (Table 3.7). The current oil palm profit rate is still higher than in rice cultivation. Given the data at the provincial level is unavailable, we cannot compare the profit rate between North Sumatera and the national average. As with the rice data, the BPS has excluded land rent cost from total cost of oil palm in data earlier than the 2000s. This means calculating a comparison of profit rate between before

Table 3.7 The rate of profit per hectare of oil palm of farmer/smallholders

	1993	*2013*
Indonesia	3.9	3.0
Adjusted by adding land rent cost		
Indonesia	-	1.8

Source: calculated by the author from the BPS
Note: data for 1983 and 2003 is not available. Data at the province level is not available either. Hence, we have no figure for North Sumatera.

Table 3.8 The change in total real revenue and total production cost of a hectare of oil palm production in Indonesia (in thousands of rupiah)

	1993	*2013*
Total revenue	9261	11203
Total cost	2358	4488 (6390)

Source: calculated by the author from the BPS
Note: The CPI index used to estimate real total revenue and total cost is based on World Bank data, with 2010 as the base year. The figure inside the brackets is the adjusted figure calculated by adding land rent cost.

and after the 2000s is not a straightforward option. Excluding the land rent cost in 2013 is required to make such a comparison. In class terms, again, since the BPS only provides the average figure of profit rate across oil palm farmers, it does not reveal the profit rate for different agrarian classes at the national level. This will be investigated in the village study.

Compared to rice cultivation, the modest decline in the oil palm profit rate owes much to the modest divergence of the changing total revenue and total cost in the last two decades (Table 3.8). The total revenue of oil palm production has increased by 20 percent, while total cost has risen by 50 percent. The two-times divergence is lower than the five-times discrepancy in rice cultivation.

The rise of total cost seems to be due to the upsurge in the labour cost. The data limitation prevents us from reaching a firm conclusion. If we look at the trend between 1993 and 2013, by excluding land rent cost, it is clear that there is a huge increase in labour cost to total cost and a substantial drop in the contribution of input cost to total cost (Table 3.9). In 2013, land rent cost contributed a third of the total cost. However, since we have no evidence of

Table 3.9 The composition of the oil palm production cost of oil palm farmers/ smallholders per hectare in Indonesia (in percentages)

	1993	*2013*
Labour cost	21.6	45.1
Input cost	41.9	31.2
Adjusted by adding land rent cost		
Labour cost	-	35.3
Input cost	-	21.9
Land rent cost	-	30.9

Source: calculated by the author from the BPS

Table 3.10 Agricultural real wages in estate crops (in rupiah per day)

	2009	*2013*	*2018*
Hoeing	33,960	37,495	35,321
Planting	32,847	34,586	32,488
Weeding	32,699	33,273	32,179

Source: calculated by the author from the BPS
Note: The consumer price index (CPI) index to estimate real total revenue and total cost is based on World Bank data, with 2010 as the base year. The BPS only began to collect the wage data on estate crops in 2009.

the share of land rent cost in 1993, it is not possible to see its trend over time. What we know is that both labour cost and land rent cost are now the main components of the total cost of oil palm production.

The surge of the labour cost in the less labour-intensive oil palm crop seems to be explained by the rise of real wages. Since the BPS only started their survey on estate crop wages in 2009 (Table 3.10), it is not straightforward to see the trend of oil palm's real wages in the last few decades. Nonetheless, as shown earlier in the food crop's wages, the three-fold rise in real wages may indicate the general trend in the agricultural real wage. If we compare the real wage in food crops (Table 3.4) with estate crops (Table 3.10) in 2013 and 2018, it is clear that they share a similar level. It seems not implausible to expect that the spike of the real wage in food crops in the last three decades also the case in estate crops.

While the total cost per hectare of oil palm has risen in the last two decades, the total revenue has only climbed a little. As opposed to rice cultivation, land productivity in oil palm has doubled in the last two decades (Table 3.11). However, the land productivity of oil palm farmers is around 20 percent lower

Table 3.11 Land productivity of oil palm per hectare in Indonesia and North Sumatera (in tonnes per month)

	1993		*2003*		*2013*		*2018*	
	North Sumatera	*Indonesia*	*North Sumatera*	*Indonesia*	*North Sumatera*	*Indonesia*	*North Sumatera*	*Indonesia*
Farmers/ 'small-holders'	-	1.6	3.1	2.7	3.6	3.2	3.4	3.1
'Corporate-scale producers'	-	2.3	3.8	3.2	4.3	3.8	4.5	3.9

Source: calculated by the author from the BPS
Note: land productivity for 'corporate-scale producers' is the average land productivity of both private and state-owned companies.

than 'corporate-scale producers'. Furthermore, the current level of land productivity is much lower than the international standard. Malaysia, the closest neighbour and also the second-biggest oil palm producer in the world, has around three times higher land productivity (10 tons per hectare/month) than Indonesia, who are the biggest oil palm producer (*Kompas*, 20/6/2017). Moreover, Indonesia's land productivity has developed little in the last decade. The expansionist strategy of Indonesia in the raising of oil palm production rather than its intensification may explain this stagnation (Varkkey et al., 2018). Meanwhile, the government points to the rampant use of bad seeds, the ageing oil palm plants and poor production maintenance of the oil palm mechanical infrastructure as the main sources of the stalled productivity.

However, the state has done very little to address the problems. Out of the targeted 2.4 million hectares of replanting of oil palm trees, only 33.000 hectares had been replanted by the end of 2018. The government complained about the low contribution of the oil palm sector in terms of taxes. Between 2011 and 2015, the annual average contribution of taxes from oil palm amounted to only 2.2 percent of total tax revenues (DJP, 2016). Thus, in 2015, the government established the BPDP (Endowment Fund Body for Oil Palm) to earn extra revenue from oil palm through a non-tax instrument. The state puts a levy of $50 per ton of exported oil palm, regardless of the global price of CPO. The yearly earning from this levy is approximately half of the revenue from taxes. A main criticism, however, is that most of the fund collected from the levy (about 90 percent) has been allocated to subsidise the bio-fuel industry, in which the beneficiaries are giant corporations (former Suharto cronies) instead of the smallholders. For instance, from the total levy earning of around Rp10 trillion in 2017, only Rp 400 billion was allocated to the replanting program (*Detikfinance*, 18/2/2018).

The pressure caused by the falling rate of profit in oil palm production has been counteracted by the rise of the CPO price. In the last two decades (1993–2013), the price of CPO has more than doubled, from 377 to 870 $/mt (Figure 3.1 below). This price spike has been much higher than with rice. This partly

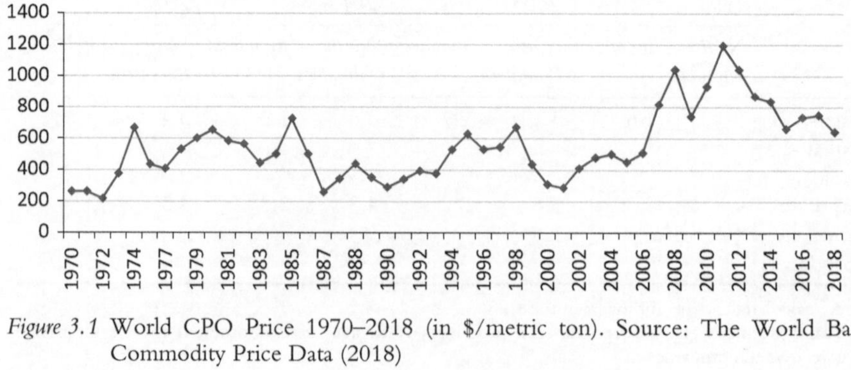

Figure 3.1 World CPO Price 1970–2018 (in $/metric ton). Source: The World Bank Commodity Price Data (2018)

explains why the falling rate of profit in oil palm is less dramatic than in rice cultivation. Though the general trend of the CPO price has been to rise in the last few decades, it has also widely fluctuated. At the end of 2018, the CPO price fell, for the first time, back to the level of 2007 (below 600 $/mt). This drastic fall, after a decade of high prices, delivered a detrimental impact to oil palm exporter countries like Indonesia. The Indonesia Oil Palm Business Association (GAPKI) desperately urged the state to abolish the export levy. They threatened that the price of fresh fruit bunches of oil palm (FFB) at the farm-gate (the farmer) would be much lower if such levies were not lifted and that this would notably harm oil palm farmers. In early December, the state removed the export levy as the CPO price was below 570 $/mt (*Kompas*, 5/12/2018).

This shows the power of the 'corporate-scale producers' over the oil palm farmers (smallholders). The need to accommodate the 'corporate-scale producers' in oil palm production prevents the establishment of state patronage over oil palm capitalist farmers as is the case with rice capitalist farmers. Not only is the state unable to avoid the pressure from the 'corporate-scale producers', who control some 60 percent of total oil palm fields in the country, but also several key state officials, especially those with a military background, are part of the oil palm conglomerates themselves (CNN Indonesia, 2019).

What we see in the current oil palm production in Indonesia is the continuing expansion of the sector under a declining rate of profit and a fluctuating global CPO price. Oil palm farmers face a greater challenge than 'corporate-scale producers'. At the production site, the land productivity of oil palm farmers is lower than that of the 'corporate-scale producers'. Instead of helping the farmers to improve their land productivity, the state reallocates the state fund from the export levy to 'corporate-scale producers' in the bio-diesel industry. The state, for the reasons mentioned above, has also facilitated the expansion of 'corporate-scale producers', often at the expense of farmers/smallholders. The oil palm farmers/smallholders have also been exposed to global price volatility, given limited state protection. This, however, does not characterise the anti-farmers/smallholders of the Indonesian state. As discussed earlier, the continuing state support to rice farmers has contradicted this agrarian populist view. The state bias to provide more support to rice farmers than oil palm farmers signals the pro-capital state (anti-workers) consideration to boost capital accumulation both within (e.g. corporate-based agriculture) and beyond agriculture (e.g. manufacture) by providing affordable staple food (rice) to maintain cheap domestic labour, as discussed in the previous section.

At the same time of the limited state support to oil palm farmers/smallholders, the production cost has increased, exceeding the rise of revenue, due mainly to a spike in the labour cost and land rent. The rise of the CPO price in the last few decades has helped control the decline in the profit rate. However, since the end of 2018, the fall in the CPO price has hit the sector, putting the oil palm farmers in a more vulnerable position than the 'corporate-scale producers'. If the CPO price continues to decline in the foreseeable future, oil palm farmers, especially PCPs and classes of labour, will be hit hardest by the volatility of the global capitalist market.

Agrarian Class Reproduction and the State

Agrarian Classes in Indonesia

With the declining trend in the agricultural profit rate for both rice and oil palm, it is now time to look at the impact of this on agrarian class reproduction. The discussion of agrarian classes in Indonesia may not be straightforward given the limited literature which deals explicitly with class categorisation. This is particularly the case when we talk about agrarian classes at the national level. The general approach has been to base social differentiation on the agricultural landholding that has been regularly reported by the agricultural census since 1963. Table 3.12 shows an attempt to record social differentiation provided by Bachriadi and Wiradi (2013). From the census, they report the substantial increase in numbers of the 'near-to-(absolute) landless' over the last three decades. Apart from this rapid change in the smallest landholding category, other categories have tended to experience a less dramatic development. The proportion of 'small peasants' (farming less than a half hectare) shows only a slight increase. This stagnant trend can also be found for the numbers of 'middle peasants' (farming 1–1.99 hectares), which have slightly declined in the past three decades. For 'large landholders', which Bachriadi and Wiradi (2013: 64) categorise as those holding between two and five hectares, the numbers have barely risen.

The problem with such an interpretation lies in their treatment of taking for granted the category of 'agricultural landholders' offered by the census. To focus only on the broad category of 'agriculture' may be more misleading than illuminating. Land productivity in one crop is different from another. As

Table 3.12 Agricultural landholders[a] in Indonesia, 1973–2003 (percentages)

Landholding (hectares)	*1973*	*1983*	*1993*	*2003*
< 0.10	3.4	7.3	8.1	10.9
0.10–.20	12.5	10.4	12.3	12.4
0.20–0.49	29.8	26.8	28.2	27.9
**Sub < 0.50*	*45.7*	*44.5*	*48.6*	*51.2*
0.5–0.99	24.7	23.4	22.2	19.7
1.00–1.99	18.1	18.6	16.8	16.1
2.00–5.00	9.4	11.2	11.0	11.4
> 5.00	2.1	2.3	1.4	1.6
Total	100	100	100	100

Source: Bachriadi and Wiradi (2013: 64)
*The sub-row has been added by the author
[a]Landholding refers to the BPS category of 'operated farm size'.

will be shown from our village study in Chapter 5 and 6, different levels of land productivity between rice and oil palm implies different degrees of profit and, thus, different forms of participation in the labour market. Those who cultivate between one and two hectares of rice field would be considered a capitalist farmer, meaning they are able to hire other's labour throughout the year. However, the cultivators of the same scale of land for oil palm production would be insufficient to sustain basic subsistence, forcing the landholders to sell their labour all year round. They would be considered as members of the classes of labour. Putting together landholders of various crops in a single category based on their landholding is fallacious.

If we look at it closer, the census delivers an account of rice landholding over time. The trajectory of landholding in this particular crop offers a very different conclusion from the broad category of 'agricultural landholders'. As shown in Table 3.13, rice landholding has shown a dramatic change in landholding pattern over the last five decades. This extreme trajectory of rice landholding could not have been seen if one only looked at the general pattern of agricultural landholding. A similar procedure, unfortunately, cannot be applied to oil palm since the census has barely recorded landholding in the oil palm sector.

However, the census should be treated with caution. It offers data of landholding categories (BPS refers to operated farm size), but these are mixed between land control and landownership. It includes 'land owned' plus 'land originating from another party' (via land lease, sharecropping, or pawning), minus 'land which is held by another party' (via land lease, sharecropping, or pawning).[5] This definition is in line with the definition provided by, for example, the Cambridge English Dictionary of a landholder, even if more colloquially a 'landholder' tends to be mean someone who owns land. The census does mention the proportion of agriculture landholders by status. The census from 1963 onwards shows that the landholders who are owner-operators make up between two-thirds and three-quarters of the total landholders, while the number of 'owner-operators-cum-sharecroppers' varies between a third and a quarter. The smallest portion is the 'landless tenants'. Their share has been relatively stable at around 5 percent (Bachriadi & Wiradi, 2013: 61). This indicates that the majority of rice landholders are also landowners themselves.

The data might be used to roughly indicate the class composition of Indonesian rice farmers.[6] Based on an empirical application of the class categories, as will be established in Chapter 5, we can categorise landholders based on our understanding of class, instead of taking for granted the categorisation made by the census. We categorise those owning more than a hectare of paddy field as capitalist farmers while those owning between half a hectare and a hectare are PCPs, and as members of the classes of labour if they own less than a half hectare of paddy field. While our class categorisation is based on a local study, it may be used to roughly gauge the national trend, although it is far from being perfect.

From this class categorisation, Table 3.13 suggests that the proportion of rice capitalist farmers has shrunk dramatically from about 30 percent in 1983

Table 3.13 Rice landholders in Indonesia, 1963–2013 (percentages)

Landholding (hectares)	*1963*	*1973*	*1983*	*1993*	*2003*	*2013*
< 0.50	41.4	42.3	47.7	50.0	74.6	87.4
0.5–0.99	28.8	26.5	25.7	22.9	16.1	8.0
> 1.00	29.8	31.2	30.6	27.1	9.3	4.6
Sub 1.00–1.99	*19.8*	*19.0*	*18.8*	*15.9*	*7.1*	*3.4*
> 2.00	*10.8*	*12.2*	*11.8*	*11.2*	*2.2*	*1.2*
Total	100	100	100	100	100	100

Source: calculated by author from the agricultural census, multi-years

to less than 5 percent in 2013. At the same time, the number of members of the classes of labour has almost doubled (from almost 50 to almost 90 percent), while the proportion of PCPs has declined from 25 to 8 percent. In absolute terms, the number of rice capitalist farmer households in the country was estimated at 1.2 million households in the last census. This tiny number of households employs the labour of about 22.8 million households of members of the classes of labour and about 2.1 million households of PCPs. The period between 1983 and 2013 was a time when land productivity of paddy fields was relatively stagnant, making our estimation throughout the period plausible. Land productivity between 1963 and 1973 was only half of that from 1983 onwards. Based on this, to be a rice capitalist farmer in the 1960s and 1970s would require twice as much land as a contemporary rice capitalist farmer. The same conditions apply to PCPs and members of the classes of labour in this period.

A similar analysis for the trajectory of class composition in oil palm cannot be made because the census has never provided figures for landholding in the oil palm sector. Under such constraints, we are unable to estimate the size of each agrarian class in oil palm.

Class Reproduction

Capitalist Farmers

The shrinking proportion of rice capitalist farmers has been accompanied by rapid land concentration of landholding. The Gini index of landholding reveals an alarming increase in inequality over the last four decades. While, in 1983, the Gini index stood at 0.50, it soared to 0.64 a decade later. The inequality reached its peak in 2003 when 1 percent of the population controlled 72 percent of total land (Gini index 0.72). It only slightly declined in 2013 to 0.68. While the Gini index for rice landholding is not available, it is quite clear that land concentration, including in rice cultivation, had taken place rapidly. This suggests that the sharp fall in the rice capitalist farmers' segment goes hand-in-hand with the bigger landholding they hold. Other rice capitalist farmers who ceased to be capitalist farmers may have other explanations for choosing to exit agriculture. The decline of the profit rate of rice cultivation, which the state has done little to rectify (see previous section), is maybe one explanation.

In the early 1980s, when the Green Revolution was at its peak, non-agricultural revenues for rice capitalist farmers accounted for about half of their total income (White & Wiradi, 1989). Since then, local trade, transportation services, political accumulation via being village officials and sending children to university have become common non-agricultural activities of capitalist farmers (Pincus, 1996). The avenues of non-agricultural accumulation have continued and developed into new forms in the twenty-first century.

In the post-Suharto period, political accumulation through village offices (receiving salary, land, being involved in corruption, illegal charges) for instance, has remained one of the most prominent instruments of non-agricultural accumulation, for both rice and oil palm capitalist farmers. Given this crucial privilege, the state's decision under Jokowi's administration to abolish salary land and replace it with a monthly salary in 2014 was opposed by thousands of well-organised village official-cum-capitalist farmers across the country. A year later, salary land was restored, and the monthly salary was added to the income for the convenience of the state's clients in the rural areas. As will be shown in the village study (Chapter 7), this state intervention provides lucrative non-agricultural incomes for capitalist farmers.

Agrarian accumulation in Indonesia may not appear unusual to other peripheral countries. In the 'domestic-oriented crop' of rice, capitalist farmers have accumulated more significantly since the inception of the Green Revolution in the late 1960s. The germ of what Lenin called 'accumulation from below' can be seen in this development. However, the germ has not developed into fully-fledged capitalist accumulation from below due to the falling income from 'own-account' farming that has been discussed in the previous section. In this case, capitalist farmers find themselves more comfortable investing in non-agricultural activities than the riskier 'own-account' farming avenues. Their non-agricultural activities and the reason for engaging in them, however, may vary in different contexts. This will be investigated in the village study.

In the 'export-oriented crop' of oil palm, the 'accumulation from above', led by corporations and the state, has been accompanied by 'accumulation from below' enjoyed by the oil palm capitalist farmers. While we have no clear knowledge of the national figure since the data is unavailable, the literature (McCarthy, 2010; Fortin, 2011) indicates that the oil palm capitalist farmers have been involved in accumulation and have expanded greatly in the 2000s. Similar to rice farmers, oil palm capitalist farmers combine their 'own-account' farming accumulation with non-agricultural activities. Whether the reasons for and types of non-agricultural activities are similar to their fellow farmers in rice cultivation or not will be investigated in the village study (Chapter 7).

PCP

As far as PCPs are concerned, their dwindling numbers may be seen as a result of their narrow options: on the one hand, the rate of profit has fallen, and on the other hand, engaging in a business outside rice cultivation is problematic given their limited capital. As mentioned earlier, PCPs in rice cultivation have largely relied on state support for their reproduction. Under the Green Revolution, the assistance from the state helped them to 'consolidate' their position (White & Wiradi, 1989). However, since the 1980s, the proportion of PCPs has shrunk. It is easier to explain the decline from the 1980s to the mid-2000s, given that during this period, state assistances declined. But the continued fall in the number of rice PCPs since the mid-2000s, when support from the state returned to previous levels, or even higher, can only be explained by the fall of the profit rate that has persisted over the last two decades, as discussed above.

The dissolution of the rice PCPs may also be related to the wide-scale agricultural land conversion to non-agricultural business that took place, as mentioned earlier. Paddy field conversion had an impact on all the agrarian classes, not only on PCPs. However, given their smaller scale of land cultivation, it is reasonable to expect that PCPs possess a lower capacity to refuse either the threats or the allurements to exit agriculture than capitalist farmers. Nonetheless, the literature has barely dealt with the current response of the rice PCPs in their attempts to reproduce themselves. Whether they depend more on 'own-account' farming or non-agricultural activities for their reproduction requires further investigation. This will be covered via the village study.

If rice has been domestically protected from the volatile of the global market, this has not been the case for oil palm. For oil palm PCPs, the NES program, combined with the transmigration program, granted each participant family two hectares of land. This marked the transformation of the landless proletariat from Java into the PCPs of oil palm in Sumatera. Some of them failed to retain their land until the boom in the 2000s and, thus, were forced to join the classes of labour in selling their labour, both to individual capitalist farmers and plantation corporations (McCarthy, 2010, Fortin, 2011). The decline of state support since 1998 has contributed to this process. Others, nevertheless, have been able to not only retain their initial land but have also added to their land ownership, since the boom, at the expense of other landowners. What constitutes the ability to achieve this, either from 'own-account' farming or non-agricultural activities, needs further study at the local level.

State intervention on PCPs in Indonesia might signal what Harris-White has called 'the incoherent state project for PCPs' (Harris-White, 2012: 136). On the one hand, the state provides agricultural input in the form of subsidies granted to both rice and oil palm PCPs as part of the broader state assistance to farmers. For oil palm farmers, the pressure to accommodate 'smallholder' agriculture, which includes capitalist farmers as opposed to 'corporate-based producers', serves the state's goal in assisting oil palm PCPs. On the other hand, the state has done little about the large-scale land conversion in Java, from paddy field to non-agricultural activities, or the dispossession of the oil palm 'non-corporate based producers' due to the expansion of the 'corporate-based producers'.

Classes of Labour

The fall in the rice PCPs share implies a marked increase in the size of the rice classes of labour. Nonetheless, the resilience of the existing members of the classes of labour in staying in rice cultivation requires an explanation. The reproduction strategies and state intervention are crucial in this regard. For the classes of labour, increasing wages and improving working conditions are the most prominent demands. In Javanese rice cultivation, in the early years of independence and under the 'nationalist-socialist state' of Sukarno, the agrarian classes of labour owned their vanguard political organisations in the form of the BTI and PKI. As shown in the first section, the political struggle against capitalist farmers and the redistributive land reform played a prominent role in their 'political strategies of reproduction' at the time. However, following the destruction of leftist power in the mid-1960s and the inception of the Green Revolution, the reproduction strategies of the classes of labour have since been transformed. A bourgeoning literature has defined their 'non-political strategies' as being: migration (both permanent and circular), non-agricultural activities (petty trades, petty home handicrafts, casual jobs outside of agriculture) and remittances, etc. However, few mention 'subtle resistance' by the classes of labour against the capitalist farmers (Pincus, 1996).

After the political democratisation in 1998 that coincided with the second neoliberal cycle, little has changed. The classes of labour still have no effective organisation to advance their interests. Their main responses have been 'non-political strategies of reproduction'. Since 1998, the state has provided food assistance relief for the poor (RASKIN/Rice for the Poor) both in rural and urban areas to cope with the devastating effects of the Asian financial crisis. Since the mid-2000s, the state has also provided a subsidy for education up to high school (see Chapter 7). The state also launched the Village Fund ('Dana Desa') program in 2015 to create additional employment in the countryside, particularly during the off-season. These 'poverty management' programs have become crucial non-agricultural relief for the classes of labour and they are increasingly dependent on such relief from the state simply because the political struggle to demand a structural change at the production site (land reform) is neglected. The same situation is being faced by the classes of labour in oil palm production.

Conclusion

This chapter has shown that class dynamics at the national level have shaped state intervention in agriculture, over time. The strong and well-organised labouring class, until the mid-1960s successfully forced the state to introduce several pro-classes of labour measures, from nationalising foreign plantations and protecting agricultural workers to introducing agrarian reform. Only since the annihilation of the leftist powers in the country, has state's bias to capital become more apparent, due to the classes of labour having become severely disorganised. Under the New Order, the state completely ignored the agrarian reform agenda by pursuing the Green Revolution and introducing state patronage over capitalist farmers as their clients in the countryside. This situation remains the norm today. The support to rice farmers, especially capitalist farmers, negates the image of anti-farmers/smallholders of the Indonesian state embraced by agrarian populism. However, unlike the rice capitalist farmers, the oil palm capitalist farmers are not well-incorporated into this patronage because of both the pressure from 'corporate-scale producers' in the oil palm sector and the lesser importance of the oil palm crop in the state's political consideration. This state bias has little to do with

> the concentration of power in the hands of military and civilian bureaucracies dominated by the Javanese, who tend to associate agriculture with wet-rice cultivation, and have little knowledge of, or sympathy for, cash crops producers belonging to non-Javanese ethnic groups in the more remote parts of the archipelago

as one author suggests (Booth, 1988: 237). The state bias rather indicates the anti-worker sentiment of the Indonesian state both within and beyond agriculture since the ousting of leftist power in the mid-1960s. This anti-workers measure requires affordable staple foods (rice) for maintaining cheap labour to facilitate accumulation within agriculture (e.g. corporate-based agriculture outside staple food) and beyond.

The state patronage over capitalist farmers, especially the rice capitalists, explains the continuing support of the state for agriculture, particularly rice cultivation. State assistance is largely confined to agricultural inputs and the rice price. Despite this support, rice cultivation has experienced a fall in profit rate in the last few decades. The state has barely managed to improve land productivity or, at the same time, control the rise in land rent cost. Ironically, oil palm farmers have experienced a lower decline of profit, although they have received minimal state assistance (mostly agricultural inputs). The booming price of oil palm in the last decades has helped to ease the rise in production cost. However, when the boom is over, they will be hit hardest.

The different state interventions in the rice and oil palm sectors have shaped the different nature of agrarian class reproduction. Rice capitalist farmers now increasingly depend on non-agricultural avenues because they face a more drastic rate of profit fall. Thus, they anticipate combining their rice cultivation with their more profitable non-agricultural businesses. Many of them have exited from agriculture completely. Oil palm capitalist farmers have also taken up non-agricultural activities for reasons we need to delineate further through the village study (Chapter 7). For both oil palm and rice capitalist farmer, apart from the subsidy for agricultural inputs, the only major help from the state at the production site has been the contra-land reform policy that has helped maintain the capitalist farmers hold on their privileges in the countryside. The state support to PCPs and the classes of labour is redundant at best (Harris-White, 2012). Although it keeps providing agricultural input subsidies, the state has done little to prevent land conversion and land dispossession by displacement. Nor has it provided price support, particularly for the oil palm sector. Against such a background, non-agricultural activities have become crucial for PCPs and the classes of labour, although the extent of its importance in the overall reproduction strategies remains to be seen from the village study.

Notes

1 In his later article (1999), Gordon abandoned his previous position and perceived that sugar plantations were capitalist in nature, though with the qualification of 'colonial capitalism' (Gordon, 1999: 5).

2 Indeed, in its 1945 Program and repeated by Muso's 'New Road' strategy in 1948, the PKI preferred to promote a communal land tenure system. However, under Aidit leadership (started in 1954), in order to 'draw peasants into the united national front', PKI began to prioritise land reform ('land to the peasants') with private land ownership as its basis. See Van der Kroef (1963, 55–56).

3 GAPOKTAN consists of several POKTAN (farmers groups). The membership of each POKTAN varies between 10–30 farmers. Each village is supposed to have several POKTANs but only one GAPOKTAN. In 2020, there were 646,293 POKTANs and 64,241 GAPOKTANs in Indonesia (Ministry of Agriculture, 2020: 7–9). Some villages do not have a GAPOKTAN.

4 The official data (BPS) uses the term 'profit' to describe the net income from total value produced minus total production cost in 'own-account' farming of the average farmers (no class distinction is made). In the following chapters, we rather use the descriptive term of income from 'own-account' farming' than 'profit'. The term 'profit' seems to be misplaced for non-capitalist farmers who do not involve in the expanded reproduction.

5 If one only looks at this data, the obvious problem is shortly recognised. For instance, 'landowner' of two hectares who sharecrops out her/his land to ten sharecroppers will be registered as zero 'landholder'.

6 We also need to emphasise that the landholding *or* landownership alone is imperfect when indicating class location. As will be discussed in Chapter 5, apart from *only* landholding or landownership, class location can also be indicated through a complex combination of landholding and landownership.

References

Alexander, J & Alexander, P 1979, 'Labour demands and the "involution" of javanese agriculture', *Social Analysis*, vol. 3, pp. 22–44.

Ambarwati, A et al 2016, 'Land tenure and agrarian structure in regions of small-scale food production', in J.F McCarthy & K Robinson (eds), *Land and development in Indonesia: Searching for the people's sovereignty*, Singapore, ISEAS-Yusof Ishak Institute, 265–296.

Bachriadi, D & Wiradi, G 2013, 'Land concentration and land reform in Indonesia interpreting agricultural census data, 1963–2003', in A Lucas & C Warren (eds), *Land for the people: The state and agrarian conflict in Indonesia*, Athens, OH, Ohio University Press, 42–92.

Boomgaard, P 1990, 'Why work for wages? Free labour in Java, 1600–1900', *Economic and Social History in the Netherlands*, vol. 2, pp. 37–57.

Booth, A 1988, *Agricultural development in Indonesia*, Sydney, Allen & Unwin.

Breman, J 1982, 'The village on Java and the early-colonial state', *The Journal of Peasant Studies*, vol. 9, no. 4, pp. 189–240.

Breman, J 1989, *Taming the coolie beast: Plantation society and the colonial order in Southeast Asia*, Delhi and New York, Oxford University Press.

Breman, J 2015, *Mobilizing labour for the global coffee market: Profits from an unfree work regime in colonial Java*, Amsterdam, Amsterdam University Press.

Chalmers, I & Hadiz, V (Eds.) 1997, *The politics of economic development in Indonesia: Contending perspectives*, London and New York, Routledge.

CNN Indonesia 2019, 'Jejak Para Purnawirawan di Pusaran Bisnis Tambang dan Sawit', 20 Februari 2019, viewed 7 March 2019, https://www.cnnindonesia.com/nasional/20190220063330-32-370896/jejak-para-purnawirawan-di-pusaran-bisnis-tambang-dan-sawit.

Cribb, R 2004, 'The Indonesian Massacres', In S Totten, W Parsons & I Charny (eds), *Century of genocide: Eyewitness accounts and critical views*, 2nd Edition, London, Routledge, 233–262.

Dauvergne, P 1997, *Weak states and the environment in Indonesia and the solomonislands*, Department of International Relations Working Paper No. 10, Canberra, Australian National University.

Dawe, D 2008, 'Can Indonesia trust the world rice market?' *Bulletin of Indonesian Economic Studies*, vol. 44, no. 1, pp. 115–132.

Detikfinance, 18 February 2018, 'Alokasi-dana-sawit-dinilai-tak-tepat-sasaran', Available at https://finance.detik.com/industri/d-3872884/alokasi-dana-sawit-dinilai-tak-tepat-sasaran

DJP 2016, *Statistik Perkebunan Sawit 2015-2017*, Jakarta, Direktorat Jenderal Perkebunan Kementerian Pertanian.

DJP 2018, *Statistik Perkebunan Indonesia 2017–2019*, Jakarta, Direktorat Jenderal Perkebunan Kementerian Pertanian.

Elson, R.E 1986, '*Sugar* factory workers and the emergence of 'free labour' in nineteenth-century Java', *Modern Asian Studies*, vol. 20, no. 1, pp. 139–174.

Elson, R.E 1984, *Javanese peasants and the colonial sugar industry: Impact and change in an East Java residency, 1830–1940*, Singapore, Oxford University Press.

Elson, R 1997, *The End of the peasantry in Southeast Asia: A social and economic history of peasant livelihood, 1800–1910s*, New York, ST. Martin's Press.

FAOSTAT 2017, Available at https://www.fao.org/faostat/en/#country

Farid, H 2005, 'Indonesia's original sin: Mass killings and capitalist expansion, 1965–66', *Inter-Asia Cultural Studies*, vol. 6, no. 1, pp. 3–16.

Fasseur, C 1986, 'The cultivation siaterm and its impact on the dutch Colonial Economy and the Indigeous Society in Nineteenth Century Java', in C.A Bayly & D.H.A Kolff (eds), *Two colonial empires: Comparative studies in overseas history*, Dordrecht, Springer, pp. 137–154.

Fasseur, C 1992, *The politics of colonial exploitation* (translated and edited by Elson, R. E., Kraal, Ary). Ithaca, NY, Cornell University, Southeast Asia Program.

Feintrenie, L et al. 2010, 'Are local people conservationists? Analysis of transition dynamics from agroforests to monoculture plantations in Indonesia', *Ecology and Society*, vol. 15, no. 4, pp. 37–51.

Fortin, C.J 2011, 'The biofuel boom and Indonesia's oil palm industry: The twin processes of peasant dispossession and adverse incorporation in West Kalimantan', paper presented at the *International Conference on Global Land Grabbing*, University of Sussex, UK 6–8 April.

Geertz, C 1963, *Agricultural involution: The processes of ecological change in Indonesia*, Berkeley, CA, University of California Press.

Gordon, A 1982, 'Indonesia, plantations and the 'post-colonial' mode of production', *Journal of Contemporary Asia*, vol. 12, no. 2, pp. 168–187.

Gordon, A 1999, 'The Agrarian Question in colonial Java: Coercion and colonial capitalist sugar plantations, 1870–1941', *Journal Of Peasant Studies*, vol. 27, no. 1, pp. 1–34.

Habibi, M & Juliawan, B.H 2018, 'Creating surplus labour: Neo-liberal transformations and the development of relative surplus population in Indonesia', *Journal of Contemporary Asia*, vol. 48, no. 4, pp. 649–670.

Hadiz, V 1997, *Workers and the state in Indonesia*, London, Routledge.

Hart, G 1986, *Power, labor and livelihood: Processes of change in rural Java*, Berkeley, CA, University of California Press.

Harriss-White, B 2012, 'Capitalism and the common man: Peasants and petty production in Africa and South Asia', *Agrarian South: Journal of Political Economy*, vol. 1, no. 2, pp. 109–160.

Hugenholtz, W.R 1986, 'Famine and food supply in Java 1830–1914', in C.A Bayly & D.H.A Kolff (eds), *Two colonial empires: Comparative studies in overseas history*, Dordrecht, Springer, 155–188.

Hüsken, F 1979, 'Landlors, sharecroppers and agricultural labourers: Changing labour relations in rural java', *Journal of Contemporary Asia*, vol. 9, pp. 140–151.

Hüsken, F 1988, *Masyarakat Desa Dalam Perubahan Zaman : sejarah diferensiasi sosial di jawa 1830–1980*, Jakarta, Grasindo.

Hüsken, F & White, B 1989, '*Java social differentiation, food production and agrarian* control', in G Hart, A Turton & B White (eds), *Agrarian transformations: Local process and the state in Southeast Asia*, Berkeley, CA, University of California Press, 234–265.

Kahn, J.S 1980, *Minangkabau social formation: Indonesian peasants and the world- economy*, Cambridge-London-New York-New Rochelle-Melbourne-Sydney, Cambridge University Press.

Kammen, D 2003, '*Pilkades*: Democracy, village elections and protest in Indonesia', in J.T Siegel & A.R Kahin (eds), *Southeast Asia over three generations: Essays presented to benedict R. O'G Anderson*, Ithaca, NY: Cornell University Press, pp. 303–330.

Knight, G.R 2000, 'The sugar industry of colonial java and its global trajectory', *South East Asia Research*, vol. 8, no. 3, pp. 213–238.

Kompas 2017, 'Produktivitas Sawit Indonesia masih Kalah dari Malaysia', 20 Juni 2017, viewed 7 March 2019, https://money.kompas.com/read/2017/06/20/131900726/produktivitas.sawit.indonesia.masih.kalah.dari.malaysia?page=all.

Kompas 2018, 'Harga Minyak Sawit Anjlok, Pemerintah Nolkan Pungutan Ekspor', 26 November, viewed 7 March 2019, https://ekonomi.kompas.com/read/2018/11/26/182113526/harga-minyak-sawit-anjlok-pemerintah-nolkan-pungutan-ekspor.

Knight, G.R 1988, 'Peasant labour and capitalist production in late colonial Indonesia: The 'campaign' at a North Java sugar factory, 1840–70', *Journal of Southeast Asian Studies*, vol. 19, no. 2, pp. 245–265.

Knight, G.R 1989, 'Sugar, peasants and proletarians: Colonial Southeastern Asia, 1830–1940', *Critique of Anthropology*, vol. 9, no. 2, pp. 541–572.

Larson, D.F 1996, '*Indonesia's* palm oil subsector', *Policy, Research working paper*, WPS 1654, Washington, DC, World Bank Group.

Mackie, J.A.C 1967, 'The government estate', in T.K Tan (ed), *Sukarno's guided Indonesia*, Melbourne, Jacaranda Press, 58–72.

Melvin, J 2018, *The army and the Indonesian genocide: Mechanics of mass murder*, New York, Routledge.

McCarthy, J.F 2000, 'The changing regime: Forest property and *reformasi* in Indonesia', *Development and Change*, vol. 31, no. 129, pp. 91–128.

McCarthy, J.F 2010, 'Processes of inclusion and adverse incorporation: Oil palm and agrarian change in Sumatra, Indonesia', *The Journal of Peasant Studies*, vol. 37, no. 4, pp. 821–850.

McCulloch, N 2008, 'Rice prices and poverty in Indonesia', *Bulletin of Indonesian Economic Studies*, vol. 44, no. 1, pp. 45–64.

McVey, R.T 2006 [1965], *The rise of Indonesian communism*, Jakarta, Equinox Publishing.

Meillassoux, C 1972, 'From reproduction to production', *Economy & Society*, vol. 1, no. 1, pp. 93–105.

Ministry of Agriculture, 2007, *Ministry of Agriculture Regulation No. 273/2007: Pedoman Penumbuhan dan Pengembangan Kelompoktani dan Gabungan Kelompoktani I*. Jakarta: Ministry of Agriculture.

Ministry of Agriculture, 2020, *Data Statistik Penyuluhan Pertanian 2020*. Jakarta: Ministry of Agriculture.

Mortimer, R 2006 [1974], *Indonesian communism under Sukarno: Ideology and politics 1959–1965*, Jakarta, Equinox Publishing.

Mulyani, A et al 2016, 'Analysis of conversion of rice paddy fields: High-resolution spatial analysis shows fast conversion', *Jurnal Tanah dan Iklim* (J. Land and Climate), vol. 40, pp. 121–133 (in Indonesian).

Li, T.M 2014, *Land's end: Capitalist relations on an indigenous frontier*, Durham and London, Duke University Press.

Peluso, N.L 1995, 'Whose woods are these? Counter-mapping forest territories in Kalimantan, Indonesia', *Antipode*, vol. 27, no. 4, pp. 383–406.

Pelzer, K.J 1982, *Planters against peasants: The agrarian struggle in East Sumatra 1947–1958*, Springer Netherlands.

Pincus, J 1996, *Class power and agrarian change: Land and labour in rural West Java*, London, MacMillan Press.

Rada, N.E, Buccola, S.T & Fuglie, K.O 2011, 'Government policy and agricultural productivity in Indonesia', *American Journal of Agricultural Economics*, vol. 93, pp. 867–884.

Robison, R 1982, 'The transformation of the state in Indonesia', *Bulletin of Concerned Asian Scholars*, vol. 14, no. 1, pp. 48–61.

Robison, R & Hadiz, V.R 2004, *Reorganizing power in Indonesia: The politics of oligarchy in an age of markets*, London, Routledge Curzon.

Robinson, G.B 2018, *The killing season: A history of the Indonesian Massacres, 1965–66*, Princeton, NJ and Oxford, Princeton University Press.

Roosa, J 2006, *Pretext for mass murder: The September 30th movement and Suharto's coup d'état in Indonesia*, Madison, University of Wisconsin Press.

Rondhi, M et al 2018, 'Agricultural land conversion, land economic value, and sustainable agriculture: A case study in East Java, Indonesia', *Land*, vol. 7, no. 4, pp. 148.

Sanders, D.J, Balagtas J.V & Gruere, G 2014, 'Revisiting the palm oil boom in South-East Asia: Fuel versus food demand drivers', *Applied Economics*, vol. 46, no. 2, pp. 127–138.

Shiraishi, T 1990, *An age in motion: Popular radicalism in java, 1912–1926*, Front Cover, Cornell University Press.

Sidel, J.T 2015, 'Primitive accumulation and 'progress' in Southeast Asia: The diverse legacies of a common(s) tragedy', *TRaNS: Trans-Regional and -National Studies of Southeast Asia*, vol. 3, no. 1, pp. 5–23.

Simatupang, P & Timmer. C.P 2008, 'Indonesian rice production: Policies and realities', *Bulletin of Indonesian Economic Studies*, vol. 44, no. 1, pp. 65–80.

Soesastro, M.H 1989, 'The political economy of deregulation in Indonesia', *Asian Survey*, vol. 29, no. 9, pp. 853–869.

Stoler, A.L 1977, 'Rice harvesting in Kali Loro: A study of class and labor relations in rural Java', *American Ethnologist*, vol. 4, no. 4, pp. 678–698.

Stoler, A.L 1995, *Capitalism and confrontation in Sumatra's Plantation Belt, 1870–1979*, Ann Arbor, MI, University of Michigan Press.

Tichelman, F 1980, *The social evolution of Indonesia: The Asiatic mode of production and its legacy /by Fritjef St. Tichelman*; translated from the Dutch by Jean Sanders, Boston, Martinus Nijheff.

Time, 'A New Hope', 27 October 2014.

Utrecht, E 1969, 'Land reform in Indonesia', *Bulletin of Indonesian Economic Studies*, vol. 5, no. 3, pp. 71–88.

Utrecht, E 1972, 'Class struggle and politics in Java', *Journal of Contemporary Asia*, vol. 2, no. 3, pp. 274–282.

Van Der Kroef, J 1963, 'Peasant and land reform in Indonesian communism', *Journal of Southeast Asian History*, vol. 4, no. 1, pp. 31–67.

Varkkey, H et al 2018, 'Palm oil intensification and expansion in Indonesia and Malaysia: Environmental and socio-political factors influencing policy', *Forest Policy and Economics*, vol. 92, pp. 148–159.

Wertheim, W 1966, 'Indonesia before and after the Untung Coup', *Pacific Affairs*, vol. 39, no. 1/2, pp. 115–127.

Wertheim, W 1969, 'From aliran towards class struggle in the countryside of Java', *Pacific Viewpoint*, vol. 10, no. 2, pp. 1–17.

White, B 2016, 'Remembering the Indonesian Peasants' Front and Plantation Workers' Union (1945–1966)', *The Journal of Peasant Studies*, vol. 43, no. 1, pp. 1–16.

White, B & Wiradi, G 1989, 'Agrarian and nonagrarian bases of inequality in nine Javanese villages', in G Hart, A Turton & B White (eds), *Agrarian transformations: Local process and the state in Southeast Asia*, Berkeley, CA, University of California Press, 266–302.

4 Situating the Agrarian Change in Java and Sumatra

Introduction

This chapter presents the socio-economic characteristics of the two villages studied in Java and Sumatra and the historical background of the main crop production in both villages. It will show that the village in Central Java is an 'old frontier' while the village in North Sumatra is a 'new frontier'. We argue that this shapes different class dynamics in the two villages studied. This chapter will begin by looking into the socio-economic nature of the villages in Java and Sumatra. The next section will depict the process of 'primitive accumulation' and the inception of the main crops in the two villages. The oil palm village receives much greater attention since its 'primitive accumulation' has taken place within the period covered in this book (since the 1960s). In the rice village, 'primitive accumulation' had already taken place many centuries earlier, putting it beyond the scope of our study (see Chapter 3 for general pattern in Java). The transition from the former main crop to the current main crop is discussed in the next section. Again, the oil palm village needs more explanation, since its recent oil palm crop has just replaced the previous main crop of rice. This is not the case in the rice village, where rice has been the main crop for centuries. This chapter also briefly discusses the data collection process in the villages studied.

Socio-Economic Features of *Njomplang* and *Timpang*

Our comparative study was carried out in two villages in Central Java and North Sumatra. Central Java is one of the largest rice baskets in the country, and its economic and political importance is indisputable. Among the districts (*kabupaten*) of the province, Purworejo is one of the main suppliers of rice. As many other rice basket producers in the country, the district also experienced the Green Revolution in the 1970s. In this district, '*Njomplang*' (pseudo name) is one of the largest rice producers and possesses the most irrigated rice field cultivation in the areas as a result of a Green Revolution program in the 1970s. Studying this village would provide a good chance to see the agrarian change of the last couple of decades.

DOI: 10.4324/9781003267348-4

In contemporary rural Java, *Njomplang* may be classified as an 'agrarian village', where more than half of the household heads' occupations remain related to agriculture, and the majority of village lands are dedicated to agricultural production. Almost all the total area of *Njomplang* is comprised of paddy fields (112 hectares) while the rest (15 hectares) is dedicated to housing and public facilities. More than half of the employment (almost 60 percent) in *Njomplang* is involved in the rice-related economy. While a significant number of villagers own no land, many of them hold land controlled through sharecropping arrangements.

This access to land control keeps many villagers in agricultural employment. Only about 15 percent of the villagers work for private companies, while less than 10 percent have set up their own petty businesses. It is difficult to find petty traders or petty service providers in the village. The number of villagers who are part of the civil service (teachers, nurses, policemen and military officers) is only about 5 percent. As will be clear in Chapter 6, many civil servants are landowners themselves, being the patrons for the sharecroppers. They should be regarded as being involved in agriculture as well.

In *Njomplang*, more than three-quarters of its paddy fields are served by a proper irrigation system. Paddy is harvested twice a year. Tractors have replaced manual hoeing over the last three decades. At the same time, the use of chemical fertilisers and herbicides has grown rapidly. Land productivity per hectare is higher than the average for Central Java and Indonesia (see Chapter 7). All of these characteristics signify an agrarian village with a well-developed production technique, of which *Njomplang* is an example.

Paddy and agriculture in the district (Purworejo) remain important for the local economy. The share of agriculture in Purworejo's GDP is much higher (25 percent) than the average national figure (15 percent). The contribution of agriculture to employment is also higher than the national average, although not a great deal higher (35 percent compared to 30 percent) (BPS Purworejo, 2018). Purworejo follows the national pattern of agrarian change where the share of agriculture in GDP has declined in parallel with the fall of agriculture's contribution to employment, although to a lesser degree.

Meanwhile, North Sumatra is the oldest and one of the largest producers of oil palm in Indonesia. In this region, small growers (farmers) cultivate the largest share of total palm oil areas, exceeding fields operated by either state-owned or private companies (BPS, 2018). Langkat district is well known as one of the largest palm oil producers of the province. Langkat, like other largest palm oil producers in the region (Labuhanbatu Utara and Asahan), depicts the prominent nature of small growers in palm oil production within the island. A village, '*Timpang*' (pseudo name), has among the largest number of 'smallholders' in the district. They hold small pieces of land (several to dozens of hectares), albeit the size is considerably larger than that of rice agriculture in Java, and the production is inextricably linked to global market dynamics. To study this village is strategic to understanding the agrarian change of small palm oil farmers and their interaction with the global market and capitalist expansion.

In Sumatra, we may find several types of village as far as agriculture, particularly oil palm, is concerned. There are villages where 'corporate-based producers' (either private or state-owned) play a larger role than 'non-corporate producers'/'smallholders'. We may call it 'corporate-based oil palm village'. Other villages witness the prominent role of 'non-corporate producers'/'smallholders' although it does not necessarily mean that the total oil palm they cultivate is larger than those managed by 'corporate-scale producers'. National figures state that the total oil palm fields owned by 'smallholders' is about 40 percent (BPS, 2018). In this regard, we consider the villages in which oil palm 'smallholders' cultivate around such figures as 'smallholders palm oil village'. Since our concern is looking at the internal dynamics of oil palm 'smallholders', *Timpang* represents this type of village in Sumatra. *Timpang* also depicts the village type where oil palm production has been the norm for a longer period of time than the relatively new villages of 'smallholders' oil palm (see the details in Chapter 4). This 'older small-holders oil palm village' provides us a better chance to understand a longer process of capitalist trajectory in oil palm production.

In *Timpang*, unlike *Njomplang*, where most of the land is used to grow the main agriculture crop (paddy), only about a quarter of the total land area is used for oil palms (2,720 hectares) as the main crop. While paddy is the second most important crop, it now takes up only a tenth of the total land area of smallholders oil palm production. A large part of the land in *Timpang* is still either forest or wetlands. The northern border of the village is a bay that flows from the Indian Ocean/Malaka Strait (see Figure 4.1). From the total oil palm areas, 40 percent belongs to 'non-corporate based producers'/'smallholders', while 60 percent is owned by the 'corporate-based producers'. Since this split matches national figures (see Chapter 5), *Timpang* is considered a 'smallholders oil palm village'. As far as the population density is concerned, *Timpang* has a much lower density (38/km^2) than the rice village in Java (725/km^2). There is little doubt that *Timpang* is a 'new frontier', a place where the number of inhabitants is low in relation to the total land area it covers, although this does not necessarily mean that the land distribution is not skewed.

As a 'small-holders oil palm village', *Timpang* is quite different from *Njomplang*. Here, agriculture only accounts for about 40 percent of total employment (including fishery) while the rest of it is non-agricultural jobs. In *Timpang*, the most popular non-agricultural employment (about 35 percent) is 'self-employed' petty business, involved in trades and services. Such employment is much easier to be found here than in *Njomplang*. A further 8 percent are employed in private companies. About the same number are those with no permanent jobs. Similar to *Njomplang*, civil servants number the least of those employed in *Timpang*.

In Langkat itself, the share of those employed in agriculture is about 35 percent (BPS Langkat, 2017). This is only 5 percent higher than the national figure. However, the contribution of agriculture to Langkat's GDP is still significant (about 40 percent), much higher than the national average (15

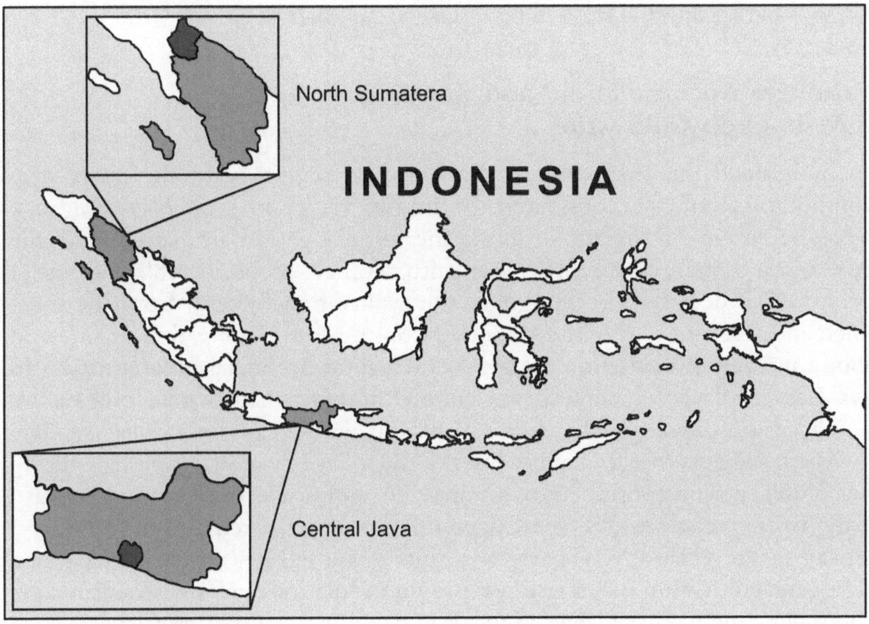

Figure 4.1 The map of the village studied in Central Java and North Sumatera, Indonesia. (Source: author)

percent). Paddy cultivation used to be the most popular crop until the early 2000s when oil palm replaced it. Oil palm is now the most popular crop in Langkat, with about 50 thousand hectares of land dedicated to it and about two-thirds of a million tons harvested per year (BPS Langkat, 2017). Although rubber takes up a similar amount of land, it produces only less than a fifteenth of the oil palm.

Apart from the role of agriculture in the villages, a prominent characteristic shared by *Njomplang* and *Timpang* is their social diversity, although *Njomplang* may be considered socially 'narrower' (culturally homogeneous) than *Timpang*. In *Njomplang*, as in many Javanese villages, most villagers (more than 90 percent) are of Javanese descent and are Muslims. With such a configuration, ethnicity and religion may not be a crucial social concern in *Njomplang*. For *Timpang*, the Batak, although in the majority, must live together with Javanese, Acehnese and Malay. Since many Batak are Muslims, the configuration between Muslims and Christians/Catholics is almost identical. The composition in *Timpang* is considered exceptional in Langkat, where the majority population is Muslim. While ethnicity and religion are undoubtedly pivotal concerns of the villagers, there has been no overt social conflict based on such dimensions. The stereotyping of different ethnicities and religions is common, but it has never resulted in open conflict. Stereotyping is crucial, mainly in the case of a family wishing to marry into another family from a different ethnic or religious background. This will be discussed in Chapter 5.

'Primitive Accumulation' and the Origin of Main Crop Cultivation

To understand the two villages, the historical trajectory of the main crop commodity should be considered. As in any village in Java, *Njomplang* first encountered capitalist relations during the colonial period, primarily under the Cultivation System in the early nineteenth century. A considerable amount of literature has depicted the impact of the Cultivation System, from the mid-nineteenth century to the mid-twentieth, on the commodification of land and labour and the monetisation in Java (see Chapter 3). Social differentiation in Java was greatly accelerated at this time although it had begun long before the Cultivation System. This seems to have been the case for *Njomplang*. The fieldwork suggests that the family lines of the village head of *Njomplang* during the colonial period continued to dominate the political economy until the turn of the twenty-first century (see Chapter 5). From what remains of the (lorry) railway in the village, *Njomplang* was among the villages which experienced sugar cane cultivation when rice was grown in rotation cycles with sugar cane. The sugar cane in the village might only have been entirely replaced by rice in the 1930s, during the decline of the colonial sugar industry in Java after the Great Depression.

Rice has been the sole main agricultural crop since then. With this background, when we look at the agrarian change in *Njomplang* over the last six decades (since the 1960s, the same period we are applying for *Timpang*), capitalist rice production has been the main commodity crop. In the 1960s, in *Njomplang*, as in other Javanese villages, individual land ownership was widespread and the land market was well advanced. We will discuss the changes in the labour system, land arrangement, credit provision and technology in Chapter 6. What is required here is to emphasise that *Njomplang* as 'an old frontier' village had been experiencing 'primitive accumulation' long before the period of agrarian change we are discussing is concerned.

Meanwhile, as a new frontier village, our fieldwork informs us that the 'primitive accumulation' in *Timpang* only took place in the 1980s, when corporations expanded into the plantations in the village. However, the advent of oil palm production in this village is older than in other areas in the country, where it only began in the 2000s. The earlier contact with oil palm production qualifies *Timpang* as an 'older small-holders oil palm village'.

The earliest social formations in *Timpang* date back to the 1960s when the first settlers come to the village. The settlers were mostly Acehnese, working as forest loggers. There were also some Acehnese who moved to *Timpang* to avoid the Islamic rebellion in Aceh in 1958 (DI-TII). Considering the distance from Aceh to *Timpang* is only a few kilometres, there is little surprise that Acehnese were the first settlers there. The Malay, who was the descendants of

Sultan Langkat, the King of Langkat, only went to *Timpang* after the Acehnese. In the first decade of its existence, the population in *Timpang* numbered only in the dozens. The common agriculture practices were the shifting cultivation of second crops (cassava, corn) and paddy. Farmers often left their cultivated lands due to attacks on their farms by wild animals (tigers, pigs and elephants) or the failure of the yield to provide basic subsistence. However, for whatever reason, they continued to open up new fields. A family could open up to 20 hectares, depending on their capability (family labour or money to hire in wage labour). The abandoned lands were opened again for the next settlers who wished to stay and cultivate the land. Individual-permanent land ownership was not recognised. The land market was virtually invisible.

This gradually changed in the 1970s, when the second wave of settlers arrived. Most of them were Batak, from both Toba and Karo, and Javanese. With the growing incoming migration into the village, swidden agriculture was gradually replaced by sedentary cultivation, and paddy cultivation became the common agricultural practice, along with growing second crops, cloves and indigo. When cloves and indigo failed, farmers started to grow rubber. For paddy cultivation, they built their own simple irrigation systems (small dams and narrow ditches) and managed to harvest their paddy once a year. The first rice huller was introduced by a capitalist farmer who owned 10 hectares of land. The economic value of land rose. Individual land ownership was acknowledged and the land market developed.[1] *Timpang*'s population grew into the hundreds.

Land value soared after the expansion of companies' plantation in *Timpang*. In 1979, the oil palm company offered the NES scheme to the villagers in *Timpang*. Only a few of them accepted, while many turned the offer down. They were not sure about the prospect of oil palm or about the scheme. Another reason for refusal was that the villagers could not afford to wait for four years for the oil palm crop to mature without other sources of income. In the mid-1980s, one of the companies (PT. SBI) began to purchase land from the villagers. While no direct violence was involved during the land acquisition, the company did spread the rumour that the villagers' land rights would be withdrawn by the government if they did not cultivate it. Some farmers noted that their parents sold the land for Rp. 100 thousand per hectare to PT. SBI. They were not aware of the potential value of land in *Timpang* at the time. At the same time, other farmers sold their lands to other villagers, either for survival or to pay gambling debts. For those who sold their lands, either to companies or other villagers, they left limited parcels of land, or even no land at all, to their children. Most of their children migrated out of the village to become manual labourers elsewhere while others became the classes of labour in the village. However, some farmers retained their land and did not sell it becoming the capitalist farmers currently in *Timpang*.

A quite different mechanism was employed when the oil palm companies used violence to take over the lands. In 1987, PT. PH, known by the villagers as the company owned by Mrs. Tien (Suharto's wife), threatened the villagers in

Timpang if they did not give up their lands to the company. The company mobilised the military in the acquisition and told the villagers that 'this land belonged to the Mother (Ibunda), Mrs. President Suharto, as one villager recalled. The company only paid compensation of Rp. 30 thousand per hectare, and each household were entitled to only two hectares of compensation (Rp. 60 thousand). About 180 households who were evicted from their land held a protest. They were beaten up by the military and arrested, and then to the KORAMIL (the Sub-district Military Office) for interrogation. Some farmers lost 10 to 20 hectares of their land. Others lost up to five hectares. Those who lost all of their land had to migrate elsewhere if they did not want to be employed by the company which had robbed them of their property. This could be described as proletarianisation in the form of 'dispossession by displacement'. This was also the case when around the same time another company, PT. RPL, intimidated *Timpang* villagers who owned land in the neighbouring villages into giving it up. While they were granted higher compensation (Rp. 100 thousand per hectare), they were forced into the sale. The threat of forced eviction was issued to those who did not accept the compensatory offer.

In both cases, some farmers managed to retain their land. They were fortunate because their land was not on the company maps. Some of the current capitalist farmers in *Timpang* emerged because of this. Even when their lands were on the company plans, a few farmers managed to negotiate their compensation. One of them was Sofian (see Chapter 5). Owning about 20 hectares of land, which was the largest plot on PT. PH's map, Sofian negotiated with the head of the land acquisition project. He was granted Rp. five million compensation for his land, the highest compensation for any landowners in *Timpang*. With his big compensation, Sofian purchased new land, not far from the national Medan-Banda Aceh highway.

After the land acquisition, the companies started to produce oil palm in the late 1980s. Land values soared. The third wave of settlers came to *Timpang* in search of better opportunities. The first type of settlers were employees of private companies who had very high monthly salary which they used to buy large areas of land in the village. Bungaran and Budi, two capitalist farmers in contemporary *Timpang* (see Chapter 5), were classic examples. Conversely, many workers from the surrounding regions moved to *Timpang* in this period with unskilled labour power. Land was becoming scarcer and more expensive. They had little money, and some of them had to live in a hut in the middle of their *sawah*. Only after years of saving were they able to rent or buy a small home and yard in the village. Many of them worked as daily labourers for rice growers or as rubber tappers because the oil palm companies had not yet started to harvest the fruit. Paddy cultivation was also thriving in the late 1980s due to the introduction of modern rice seeds (IR 64) in *Timpang* (1987). While the inception was much later than in *Njomplang*, the introduction of IR 64 in *Timpang* doubled the harvesting to twice a year. Tractors were first introduced to *Timpang* in the mid-1990s. Since then, *Timpang* has become one of the main rice producers in the sub-district. Despite these developments, for the classes of labour in *Timpang*, life was 'barely subsistent', they recalled. Many of them, mostly the youth, migrated out to Medan, Riau, Aceh and Malaysia to find better-waged employment.

The Transition to the Oil Palm Economy

In the early 1990s, the companies harvested their oil palm for the first time. The villagers who worked for the companies spread the word to other villagers about 'the success of oil palm'. Before growing their own oil palm, however, the villagers were told by the companies that no one would buy it from the farmers. The threat was ignored by Sofian and other capitalist farmers, who were the first oil palm growers in *Timpang*. They learned about growing oil palm from the villagers who worked for the companies. Their concern about the difficulty of selling oil palm proved to be meaningless when, in the mid-1990s, the first local trader/agent of oil palm (*Toke*, literally meaning 'capital owner') established his business. His initiative was followed by other farmers (capitalist and PCP) to start buying oil palm from fellow farmers and sell it to local processing plants.

The number of farmers growing oil palm increased. For those landowners who had not grown any perennial crops, they chose to grow oil palm instead of rubber, because the waiting period for harvesting oil palm was much shorter (four years compared to eight years). Even the rubber farmers replaced it with oil palm. While the price of rubber was higher than oil palm (about 30:1), cultivating the oil palm was much more practical than cultivating rubber. Oil palm only needed to be harvested once every two weeks and could be sold immediately, while rubber had to be harvested every day and it would need a week before the harvest was large enough to be sold to local agents. The shift to oil palm was dominated by capitalist farmers and some PCPs. For the classes of labour, replacing rubber or *sawah* with oil palm was not an easy option. The initial capital to buy oil palm seeds and other inputs was not in their hands, while the waiting period for the first harvesting of at least four years, with little or no other revenue, was not feasible.

In 1996, there was a significant administrative change in *Timpang*. Because of its growing population, *Timpang* was formally separated from the previous village administration (Halban). Administratively, the history of current *Timpang*, until 1996, was the history of a Halban village. As the new administration was installed, opportunities to occupy village political and administrative positions opened. As we will see in Chapter 7, a capitalist farmer, Sofian, managed to hold the position of village head for two periods (2008–2017).

The main road in the village that connects Medan to Banda Aceh has always been important for the local economy. As early as the 1970s, the village was notorious for their 'Village Thieves' since so many thefts took place there. The thieves would climb onto the moving trucks and steal their loads. People called them 'jumping squirrels'/*Bajing Loncat*, since they had to jump onto the trucks to steal the loads. With the growing paddy economy, the impact of the road became more crucial. Since the 1980s, local villagers, in cooperation with procurers from the city, set up as street vendors along the main road to disguise their prostitution businesses. Along with prostitution, the selling of alcohol and drugs soared. While the 'squirrel jumpers' and prostitution have declined over the last few years, the drug business has been on the rise.

The significant agrarian change only took place in the 2000s. The oil palm price had reached an unprecedented level, leading to a boom period. The farmers in *Timpang*, from the capitalist farmer to the classes of labour, replaced their rubber and paddy with oil palm. There were some conditions that made such a shift possible, especially for the classes of labour. When oil palm was developed in the previous decade (during the 1990s), the jobs for harvesters, both with the companies and individual farmers thrived such that they provided an alternative income for the classes of labour while they were waiting for their oil palm to be ready for harvest. For seeds, they bought the lower quality at a lower price. To minimise production cost, they barely applied fertilisers to their land.

It should be noted that many farmers in *Timpang* would keep their paddy field as for as long as they could. However, in the 2000s, the expansion of oil palm in the village reduced the water available for rice cultivation. Without a proper irrigation system and the oil palm crop absorbing most of the water available, the *sawah* in *Timpang* faced a bleak future. Many of the rice farmers were forced to grow oil palm because paddy cultivation was virtually impossible owing to the water issue. By the mid-2000s, the 'golden era of rice' in *Timpang* was over. Only a few trucks since have come to *Timpang* to pick up the dry stalk paddy, compared to the dozens of trucks in the previous decade.

The final blow took place in the 2010s. With the expansion of oil palm, the water crisis was exacerbated. Oil palm that had been grown only in the hilly areas of *Timpang* had since been planted in the lowland areas, which had previously been used only for paddy. Many farmers, including the classes of labour, remember the rice era was 'barely subsistence', but they also remember the clean river. In contrast, since the inception of oil palm, the rivers are dry most of the time and not as clean as they used to be. The villagers also now have to dig much deeper for their wells just to find good fresh soil water. But, even for the classes of labour, since the oil palm era, their economic welfare has become 'not bad' (a euphemism for good enough). They can find daily wage jobs, both in the companies and with individual farmers, with the same or even higher wages than daily labourers in the big city of Medan. Permanent migration out of the village has declined even though not all the classes of labour are well off. Many of them practise temporary migration to find sufficient capital to buy their own land in *Timpang*, wishing to live and retire in their home village. One would not be surprised at the ambiguity in contemporary *Timpang*. While many of the villagers condemn the environmental degradation of the village, as many of them celebrate their general economic improvement, despite the companies and capitalist farmers who initiated the shift to oil palm taking the largest share of the wealth.

We now have established the historical background of the main crop cultivation and the socio-economic features of the two villages studied. It has been explained that *Njomplang* represents the 'old frontier', while *Timpang* exhibits the characteristics of the 'new frontier'. This has allowed us to better explain the class dynamics of 'primitive accumulation' and transition to main crop cultivation in the oil palm village rather than in the rice village. We have also depicted the nature of the 'agrarian village' represented in the two villages. How the crop development and the recent socio-economic changes have featured in their development provides the impetus for the contemporary class dynamics will be the subject of the subsequent chapters.

Data Collection

Data collection for *Njomplang* was conducted from September to December 2017, while for *Timpang* it took place from March to May 2018. I lived in each village throughout the times indicated. A research assistant in each village helped me to make early contact with the villagers and establish the technical requirements for the fieldwork. They also helped me to collect the secondary data in the district offices. They were not living in the villages during the fieldwork. I did the main data collection comprising the interviews, survey and participatory observations.

The interviews were carried out both before and after the survey. At the beginning of the research, the interviews were designated to provide an understanding of the rough pattern of class structure in the two villages. At this phase, the interview focused on the pattern of land ownership, labour relations, output relations and means of production relations. We randomly interviewed landowners/landholders from different sizes to get a crude hint of class location. Combining this interview with the wider observation in both villages, we eventually found three categories of land ownership/control which reflected different modes of activity in the four social relations (land, labour, output and means of production). In *Njomplang*, the stratification includes those who owned and/or controlled more than a hectare of *sawah*, households who owned and/or controlled between a half and one hectare of land and those who owned and/or controlled less than half a hectare of *sawah*. Because of the distinct land productivity between paddy and oil palm, the stratification in *Timpang* is quite different from that of *Njomplang*. In *Timpang*, we found a rather different class location between those who owned and/or controlled more than four hectares of oil palm fields, landowners/landholders between two and four hectares and those who owned and/or controlled less than two hectares of land.

To acquire more systematic information and exemplify the pattern of class dynamics, we conducted a household survey. The survey was mainly designed to collect data on basic household profiles, their activity in the four social relations (land, labour, output and means of production), income from 'own-account' farming, the participants' access to credit and their activity outside farming. One of the main aspects of our survey was to estimate the different levels of income from 'own-account' farming of different agrarian classes. In estimating the income from 'own-account' farming, we approached the calculation by focusing on what farmers *actually* spend on production cost and what *actually* they receive from the sale of their output. This provides a more realistic picture than that of conventional economics which includes 'shadow cost' such as land rent cost that farmers might neither actually pay nor consider as a cost.

Given the relatively small size of our survey (see below), it is not our intention to calculate the precise income from 'own-account' farming for each agrarian class. Nonetheless, our estimate provides a reasonable illustration of the different income from 'own-account' farming for the different agrarian classes. This is indispensable for the main objective of our study, the capturing of class dynamics of agrarian change in the two villages.

The respondents of the household survey were chosen through a purposive process. They were picked from three different land strata established from the interviews and the wider observations in the villages. This sampling method was chosen to capture the different nature of the various social groups (classes) in the village. The problem with using a purely random sampling procedure, in this case, is that it may exclude important features of households for the sake of formality. Thus, pure random sampling was not only deemed inadequate, but it could lead to a misleading analysis of the processes and mechanisms of agrarian change (Pincus, 1996: 25).

The respondents for each land stratum were chosen purposively to capture the possible variation within each stratum. In *Njomplang*, there were seven respondents who owned more than a hectare of paddy field. In class terms (to be established in Chapter 5), they were capitalist farmers. This includes four households who owned between a hectare and two hectares of *sawah* and three households who owned more than two hectares. The former are defined as 'modest' capitalist farmers while the latter will be defined as 'big' capitalist farmers. The number of respondents for this land stratum was deemed adequate to cover variation within this category: it was not possible to find respondents of a nature different from these two groups within this category.

Apart from capitalist farmers, there are 'landlord-capitalists' in *Njomplang*. They were excluded from the survey since they did not make production process related decisions. This makes them irrelevant to one of the main aspects of survey, namely the estimate of income from 'own-account' farming. Information about them on other aspects was gathered through interviews.

There were 11 households in the survey who owned/or controlled between a half and one hectare paddy field. In class terms, in the following chapter, they will be categorised as PCP. Four of them owned the land while seven of them only controlled the land (i.e. leased in the land they tilled). In class terms, the former is here called 'substantial PCPs' and the latter 'formal PCPs'. There are fewer respondents from the 'substantial PCPs' category than from the 'formal PCPs' category, simply because it was difficult to find additional respondents from this group.

As for the respondents who owned/or controlled less than half a hectare of *sawah*, there were 26 households. They are part of the 'class of labour' in class terms. We eventually identified two variants in this group of respondents. The first group owned a tiny plot of land (0.1 ha–0.34 ha) and controlled (sharecropped) a tiny plot of land (less than 0.34 ha) or owned no land but controlled (sharecropped) a little land (0.35 ha–0.84 ha). They mostly sold their output. This later we identify as 'semi-proletariat farmers'. The second group is those who owned no land and controlled (sharecropped) a tiny plot of land (0.1 ha–0.34 ha). They mostly did not sell their output but used it for own consumption. We label this group 'proletariat-farmers'. For each of these groups, we had 13 respondents. The numbers of respondents were deemed to be sufficient to capture the variation within each group.

In *Timpang*, there were nine respondents who owned/controlled more than four hectares of oil palm. In class terms, they were part of the capitalist farmers category. Six of the households owned/controlled between four and eight hectares of oil palm, and three households owned/controlled more than eight hectares. Comparable to *Njomplang*, the former we label, later, as 'modest' capitalist farmers and the latter 'big' capitalist farmers. We decided that the number of respondents from this class was adequate, since we could not identify other variations than the two groups mentioned. As for the respondents from those who owned/or controlled between two and four hectares of oil palm, the number of households surveyed was 13. All of them were landowners, and none of them were *only* landholders; we could not find such households in this land category. This, in class terms, means all the PCP respondents in *Timpang* were 'substantial PCPs' (owned the land they tilled). Meanwhile, the number of respondents from those who owned/or controlled less than two hectares of oil palm was 23. In class terms, similar to *Njomplang*, they were a member of 'classes of labour'. We were, in the beginning, expecting some variations within this group of respondents, as we found in *Njomplang*. However, we did not find any substantial variation. Because they owned land, though only miniscule plots, we later describe them as part of the 'semi-proletariat farmers' category, just as their compatriots in Java. We found only a negligible number of 'proletariat-farmers', and thus they were excluded from our survey. Nonetheless, we gathered different aspects of information about them through interviews.

It should be noted that our survey was not designed to proportionally represent the population of each social group identified, as is often the case when using a positivist approach. The main goals of the survey were to collect more information to highlight the different characteristics of each social group when capturing the processes and mechanisms of class dynamics in the village. This is also partly the reason why we did not conduct a baseline census of all households. Another reason was that a single researcher simply does not have the resources to complete such a major undertaking. This, however, does not necessarily mean that we knew nothing about the size of each social group in the village. Exercising caution, land registration in the village offices of both settlements provided us with a rough estimate of the size of each social group selected. After adjusting the data from the land registration along with our survey and interview results, we were able to make reasonable estimations of the size of each class in the village (see Chapter 5).

After the survey, the interviews took place immediately with the same respondents to grasp a number of thematic issues (the negotiation of wages and working conditions, the changes in land arrangements, the labour system, credit provisions, technological development over time, the trajectory of their activities beyond 'own-account' farming, such as trade and services, and the education of the children). Interviews were also conducted with key informants who were not participants in the survey to collect information on certain topics (the historical trajectory of the village, the political contests for the election of the village head, etc.). The interview was also employed to capture the life histories of the respondents from each different agrarian class to illustrate the nature of the agrarian class structure and its reproduction. In *Njomplang*, we overall interviewed 76 participants, while in *Timpang*, there were 82.

Apart from the primary data, we also collected secondary data. This included land ownership/control and the land transactions registered in the village office. Other relevant information was also gathered, such as a village profile and, in the case of *Njomplang*, documents related to the 'village meeting' that recorded the wages for different agricultural tasks. I asked for the data from the village officials. Since I had lived in the villages for quite some time, it was not difficult getting this secondary data. We crosschecked the secondary data with our data from the surveys, interviews and observations. To estimate the real wage in *Njomplang*, we also collected data related to the price of rice from the local office of the Indonesia Logistics Bureau (BULOG). This data was collected by a research assistant. The procedure of estimating the real wage can be found in Appendix 5. The estimation of the real wage could not be made for *Timpang* since the wage data for the previous decades was not available.

Note

1 It is beyond the scope of our study to investigate in detail the process and mechanism of the transformation from communal land property towards individual land ownership. See Li (2014) for a proper investigation of this process in a different context of agrarian change in Indonesia.

References

BPS 2018, *Statistik Kelapa Sawit Indonesia 2017*, Jakarta, BPS.

BPS Langkat 2017, *Produk Domestik Regional Bruto Kabupaten Langkat Menurut Lapangan Usaha 2012-2016*, Langkat, BPS.

BPS Purworejo 2018, *Purworejo Dalam Angka*, Purworejo, BPS.

Li, T.M 2014, *Land's end: Capitalist relations on an Indigenous frontier*, Durham, NC, Duke University Press.

Pincus, J 1996, *Class power and agrarian change: Land and labour in rural West Java*, London, MacMillan Press.

5 Class Dynamics of Agrarian Change in Java and Sumatra

Introduction

To demystify the notion of homogeneous farmers/smallholders in Indonesia, this chapter shows the power of class dynamics of agrarian change in Java (*Njomplang* village) and Sumatra (*Timpang* village). For the class location in the two villages, we show that farmers/smallholders are differentiated into different agrarian classes. However, they are not differentiated simply across different level of incomes ('life chance'), as a Weberian class approach often perceives. Our Marxist understanding of class shows how Javanese rice farmers and oil palm smallholders in Sumatra are differentiated by exploitation into capitalist farmers (and 'landlord-capitalists' in Java), PCPs and classes of labour. Unlike previous studies of agrarian class which tend to treat a class without any several different groups inside it, this chapter shows the internal complexity of class categories. This includes a discussion of family ties within the agrarian class. In the second part of the chapter, we show the class relations between the agrarian ruling class (capitalist farmers and 'landlord-capitalists') and classes of labour including PCPs in shaping the rate of wages and working conditions. We also depict the historical trajectory of class relations in the villages to identify their changing nature overtime. This chapter offers the most systematic analysis of internal differences within class location and their impact on class relations, one of which has hardly been done before.

Class Location in the Two Villages

Land Ownership and Land Control in Njomplang and Timpang

Before identifying class location, it is important to first note the crucial difference between land ownership and access to land cultivation owned by others. The latter is normally called 'land control only' or, in short, 'land control'. It is often mentioned that land control under a fixed-rent tenancy offers an incentive for tenants to increase land productivity[1] and, thus, profits, as much as land ownership. In fact, historically, some capitalist farmers during the agrarian transition in England were tenants (Wood, 2002). This, to some, extent offers a reason to overlook the difference between land ownership and land control.

DOI: 10.4324/9781003267348-5

However, the gap between land ownership and land control held under different arrangements such as sharecropping (in the form of normal sharecropping, not reverse sharecropping[2]) is more substantial. In *Njomplang*, under normal sharecropping, land control is much less valuable than land ownership. The nature of sharecropping has changed over time but, in recent times, it has involved much higher rent (in-kind) than fixed-rent leasing. Here, the share is 50-50 between landowners and sharecroppers, with the latter bearing the production cost. This means that land control under sharecropping in *Njomplang* should be considered to be only half as valuable as land ownership. For the same unit of land, the revenues received by sharecroppers are much lower than tenants with fixed-rent. As will be shown in the next section, this is crucial when we try to identify class location in the village.

Timpang in North Sumatra is a contrasting case. Here, the sharecropping arrangement is negligible, and the difference between land ownership and land control is less pronounced. In fact, most land is under land ownership, although it is not necessarily equally distributed.

Class Location in Two Villages and Its Composition

Chapter 2 argued that land ownership/control alone is inadequate in identifying class location. Along with land ownership/control, we locate farmer's households in relation to four different production relationships: land, labour, product and means of production. As we will see, land ownership/control shapes the activity of households in all these relationships. Using these classifications, we now establish the class categories on the ground in the two study villages, based on empirical fieldwork insights. As mentioned in the methodology (Chapter 2), we will first identify the different classes through qualitative insights and then use a survey to provide more information.

In *Njomplang*, we find that farmers who own at least one hectare[3] of paddy field (*sawah*) never sell their labour, while they hire labour all year round. The same land-labour relationship applies to tenants in a fixed-rent land-leasing arrangement (with more than 1.8 hectares in our study). Other farmers who own at least a hectare of *sawah* also never hire out their labour. However, they do not hire in labour but sharecrop out their lands. The paddy crop of these groups is well above their annual consumption needs (see Chapter 7). They sell almost all they produce. The revenue can be harnessed to buy substantial means of production, such as land or a tractor. The workers perceive two groups of farmers as '*juragan*' (employers). We conceptualise them as capitalist rice farmers and 'landlord-capitalists'. The former hire in labour throughout the year and never hire out their own, sell all their rice output and buy substantial means of production. The latter share the last three features of the former and yet do not hire in labour but extract rent from sharecroppers. Some of this '*juragan*' have only negligible non-agricultural activities while others undertake skilled artisan jobs (e.g. stone-masons) or are professional careerist and village political-bureaucratic leaders.

Other rice farmers in the village owning a considerable plot of *sawah* (between one-half and a hectare) or owning no land but sharecropping a large plot of land (0.85 ha–1.79 ha) are not compelled to engage in labour markets and depend mainly on family labour in rice cultivation. Sometimes they may dispose of their labour all year-round at will, i.e. not through economic compulsion, to meet beyond subsistence aspirations, while, at other times, they may hire in labour. They sell most of their rice output, which secures their subsistence. The earnings from rice cultivation, however, only enable them to buy basic agricultural technology, such as water pumps or threshing machines. Villagers from different social backgrounds often see them as a group of *cukupan* (moderate) farmers. Given their position in the four production relationships, we categorise them as PCPs. Some PCPs engage in non-agricultural work as masons, in petty self-employment or other casual jobs. A number of them occupy village officials positions, although only lower-ranked ones.

Another group of rice farmers in *Njomplang* sell their labour all year round out of market compulsion, while never hiring in the labour of others. Some of them own only a tiny plot of land (0.10 ha–0.34 ha) or control a tiny plot of land (less than 0.34 ha) or own no land but sharecrop in a small *sawah* (0.35 ha–0.84 ha). Others sharecrop on negligible measures of land (0.10 ha–0.34 ha), while having no land ownership at all. The rest of them neither own nor control any *sawah*. They sell only a little or none of their rice output as their earnings from rice cultivation barely meets their subsistence. They are compelled to sell their labour throughout the year to survive. Even with the wage-earning, they can only manage to buy basic agricultural technology. They generally consider themselves as *wong mburuh* (workers). Their shared characteristic of selling labour all year-round out of market compulsion, even though they share different positions in the land and output relations, points towards them being what is known as the classes of labour. Their non-agricultural activities are similar to the PCPs. Unlike the PCPs, however, the classes of labour have not been able to occupy positions as village officers.

Class locations in *Timpang*, North Sumatra is quite similar. The main difference is the nature of land ownership/control. As discussed in Chapter 1, land productivity—which is crucial for surplus generation—is varied, depending on the specific setting. We found that farmers in *Timpang* need to own or control (with fixed-rent, not sharecropping) at least four hectares of oil palm to hire in other labour all year round and not sell their labour to others. They can also buy more substantial means of production, such as land and trucks. These capabilities qualify them as capitalist farmers. Local labourers working for them often call this group of farmers as *bos* or *toke* (employer). Similar to their peers in Java, oil palm capitalist farmers in *Timpang* are involved in non-agricultural avenues.

Other oil palm farmers in the village occupy similar a position as that of the PCPs in Java. Here, farmers who own or control 2–3.99 hectares of oil palm enables them to be independent from the labour market. Occasionally, they may sell their labour or hire other's labour. They sell all their oil palm output, since it is not used in their daily food consumption. The sale meets their subsistence. As in Javanese rice cultivation, PCPs in oil palm sell their labour all year round *at will* to achieve beyond subsistence aspirations rather than out of market compulsion. Their earnings enable them to purchase basic agricultural technology, like fibre fruit picker poles and motorcycles for harvest transport. However, unlike their fellow workers in *Njomplang*, some PCPs in *Timpang* manage to buy plots of land given the land price in Sumatra is cheaper than in Java. They also undertake non-agricultural activities in petty self-employment (trade), rice trading, and acting as low ranked village officials.

We also find villagers selling their labour all year round out of market compulsion. In the oil palm context, some of them only own or control a small parcel of land (less than two hectares). Others neither own nor control any oil palm fields. Similar to PCPs, they also sell all their oil palm outputs. However, their miniscule outputs are insufficient to meet their basic needs. This compels them to sell their labour throughout the year. They mostly see themselves as *buruh* (worker), similar to those in the Javanese village. Again, the characteristic of selling labour all year round out of market compulsion qualifies them as members of the classes of labour. None of them holds any position of village official. An important difference between *Timpang* and *Njomplang* is the presence of oil palm companies. Many members of the classes of labour in the village work for the companies, as well as sell their labour to individual employers, or work in petty self-employment.

Our qualitative study indicates that in the two villages, the size of each agrarian class is comparable. The number of capitalist farmers is the smallest group. The group of PCPs is larger than that of the capitalist farmers but smaller than that of the classes of labour. To figure out the precise size of each is a more challenging task. As mentioned in the methodology (Chapter 2), estimating the proportion of each agrarian class is not a main concern of this study. Our primary goal is to understand the processes and mechanisms of agrarian changes through which class dynamics are affected.

However, we are able to provide some estimates of the composition of the agrarian classes in the villages by using the official landholding data. Land registration may not be regularly updated. However, after we adjust the data from land registration with our survey and interview data, land registration could provide some reasonable estimations of class composition in the villages, although it is far from perfect. This approach has been used by other researchers in Indonesia (Ambarwati et al., 2016).

The official land registration mixes together landholdings in the village owned by village-residents and non-residents. Taken together, as shown in Table 5.1 (left column), there has been no substantial change in class composition in the last two and a half decades: neither a significant shift in the proportion of each class nor the total land either of them hold. The composition is similar to the national picture, recorded by the agricultural census (Chapter 3).

However, in the village, where about half of the land is registered as non-residential property, it is important to see the pattern of landholding for

Table 5.1 Landholding in *Njomplang*, Central Java 1992 and 2017 (percentages)

Landholding (hectares)	*Village resident and non-resident*				*Village resident only*			
	1992		*2017*		*1992*		*2017*	
	Proportion of household	*Total land-holding*	*Proportion of household*	*Total land-holding*	*Proportion of household*	*Total land-holding*	*Proportion of household*	*Total land-holding*
< 0.5	89.4	57.0	89.7	41.1	89.5	59.1	85.3	52.1
0.5–0.9	6.4	16.8	6.6	27.2	5.5	14.4	11.2	27.1
≥ 1.0	4.3	26.2	3.8	29.7	5.0	26.5	3.5	20.8
Sub								
1–1.9	*3.8*	*23.2*	*3.3*	*25.8*	*4.7*	*24.9*	*2.3*	*13.7*
≥ 2.0	*0.5*	*3.0*	*0.5*	*3.9*	*0.3*	*1.6*	*1.2*	*7.1*
Total	100	100	100	100	100	100	100	100

Source: calculated by author from village land registration

residents only, since they decide the agricultural practices in the village, from wages and working conditions for all agricultural tasks through to the village meeting (see the next section). Looking at their class composition is crucial to understanding the local dynamics of agricultural practices. As shown in Table 5.1 in the column on the right, both the proportion of PCPs and their total landholding as increased two-fold. This rise owes much to the declining proportion of capitalist farmers, from about a quarter to a fifth, while for the classes of labour, they have declined from almost 60 to 50 percent.

In 2017, the tiny group of capitalist farmers and 'landlord-capitalists' (less than 5 percent) dominated a fifth of the total land in the village. In contrast, the members of the classes of labour (about 85 percent of households) only shared half of the total land. Meanwhile, the PCPs' share of total land was around a quarter, while their proportion to total households was about 10 percent, a two-fold increase from the previous two decades. The growth of both the PCPs' proportion and their total landholding could indicate that there was little further class polarisation. However, PCPs may not necessarily own their land and, thus, a nuanced account of the PCPs is required. The fieldwork suggests that, in the last two decades, many landholders have gained additional land control through sharecropping. As will be shown in the next chapter, this is largely due to the changing nature of the labour markets and class relations in the village.

Similar to *Njomplang*, village resident and non-resident landholding is combined in *Timpang*. However, the landholding in *Timpang* registered as non-residents' property only accounts for a third of the total land. This may explain how there is no significant divergence between the two versions of land registration (Table 5.2 in both left and right columns). On either side, capitalist farmers in the village comprise the smallest proportion of households, but still, their landholding (around 15 percent) is about three times that in *Njomplang*. What stands out from *Timpang* is that the number of PCPs (about a fifth of

Table 5.2 Landholding in *Timpang*, North Sumatra 2018 (percentages)

Landholding (hectares)	*Village resident and non-resident*		*Village resident only*	
	Proportion of households	*Total landholding*	*Proportion of households*	*Total landholding*
< 2.0	64.6	16.6	65.5	18.1
2.0–3.9	18.5	19.9	19.6	23.3
≥ 4.0	16.9	63.5	14.9	58.6
Sub				
4.0–7.9	*13.1*	*53.3*	*11.8*	*29.5*
≥ 8.0	*3.8*	*10.2*	*3.1*	*29.1*
Total	100	100	100	100

Source: calculated by author from village land registration

total households) is similar to that of the oil palm capitalist farmers. This makes the proportion of PCPs in *Timpang* much larger than their compatriots in *Njomplang*. The larger number of PCPs implies a smaller proportion of the classes of labour in the oil palm village (around two-thirds). Given the larger number of PCPs and capitalist farmers and the smaller proportion of classes of labour in *Timpang* than *Njomplang*, we may suggest that the agrarian class composition is more skewed in the latter than the former.

In *Timpang*, however, capitalist farmers, who constitute about 15 percent of all households, dominate more than half of the total landholding (Table 5.2), which is much more dominant than in *Njomplang*. As for PCPs, comprising a fifth of total landholders, they only share around a quarter of total landholding. For the classes of labour, their proportion of total landholders is about two-thirds, and yet they share less than one-fifth of total landholding. However, the historical trajectory of the composition of landholding in the village cannot be depicted given the data from the last two decades of *Timpang* is unavailable. Nonetheless, from our fieldwork (Chapter 4), there are some indications that the parents of the current landless households used to own land. That some 'semi-proletariat farmers' retain plots of land today indicates that they used to own more. This may suggest that the proportion of the 'semi-proletariat farmers' and PCPs might have been larger in the past than in the present.

The Nature of the Agrarian Ruling Class[4]

It is common to treat farmers owning enough land to enable them to hire other's labour or extract rent as a distinct class. However, the assumption that they are a unified unit may not hold true. We now show that there are several groups within the agrarian ruling class that differ from each other as far as their role in the production process and their pattern of class reproduction are concerned. This has been overlooked by the current literature, and this has prevented us from looking at the nature of cooperation and competition among factions within the agrarian ruling class, and the implication for class relations. To our knowledge, our study is the first to attempt to systematically investigate the distinct groups within the agrarian ruling class, and what impact this categorisation has on class relations.

In the Javanese village, the first part of the agrarian ruling class is landowners who mainly extract their surpluses through hire wage labour. There are several types among this group. Firstly, we find a group of landowners who play a direct role in supervising production activities on a daily basis and decide everything about the production processes (the type and volume of seeds, choice of fertiliser, labour, methods of planting, timing of each phase of production, etc.). Some of them are involved in the production processes themselves, though only in applying fertiliser and weeding. They are only doing it to spend their free time (i.e. fulfilling a hobby) rather than to earn additional income. By and large, they have little non-agricultural business. When they are involved in rice trading, this should be viewed as an extension activity of their 'own-account' farming. Rice trading, which takes place only during and after the harvesting period, provides them with adequate space to focus on their agricultural production. Their structural position makes them the group most willing to improvise and adopt new technology to increase land productivity. They also tend to manage their own land by employing wage labour rather than sharecrop it out to their neighbours, given their capability to mobilise wage workers for their land. Their shared characteristic of 'risk taker' may recall our understanding of the notion of the 'entrepreneur' embraced and promoted by mainstream economists. We consider them to be 'typical capitalist farmers'. Let's take Cokro for example:

> Cokro, a 62-year-old man owns about five hectares of *sawah*. He employs wage labour to take care of almost all of his land. Less than a half hectare is sharecropped out to his nephews out of 'family pressure'. Cokro and his wife love to supervise the daily activities in their rice cultivation. His business instinct sees the promising benefits of new production techniques, such as planting and combine harvester machinery. But, because of 'warnings from the labourers' and technical problems, he has not bought those machines. He had advised his daughter to stay away from village politics (because some people in the village encourage her to run for village head position), since being a leader is a 'complicated thing' and it is easier to focus only on business. Cokro himself is one of the key representatives of capitalist farmers in the village because of his active and vocal role during the 'village meetings' to determine the agricultural wages and working conditions.

Another group of rice capitalist farmers are both farmers *and* political leaders, or they maintain a bureaucratic position that significantly shapes their decisions on the production process. They sharecrop out some of their lands for political reasons and are less directly involved in the daily supervision of the production process. While technically, their political-bureaucratic positions still provide them with sufficient spare time to supervise daily production activities, they choose to sharecrop out some of their land to cultivate potential political supporters. The village head is elected via direct local elections. Anyone who wishes to occupy this position needs to create supporters by sharecropping out their land. Their dual occupations and the impact they have on the organisation of the production process defines them as another distinct group of capitalist farmers; we shall call them 'politico-bureaucrat capitalist farmers'.

Their structural position involves the contradiction between having economic considerations as a capitalist farmer and political considerations as a politico-bureaucrat. From a purely economic perspective, the adoption of a combine harvester machine is much more profitable than the current practice of manual labour. However, the adoption of new production techniques that will eliminate the jobs of manual harvesters is unfeasible for anyone considering holding a political position in the village. Holding a political position in the village is still a lucrative avenue for wealth creation (see Chapter 7). This persuades farmers who are politico-bureaucrats to be risk-averse in matters of agricultural production. At the production site, they will let 'typical capitalist farmers' take the lead. We may see this in the case of Karto:

> Karto is a 60-year-old man. After occupying the position of village head and receiving four hectares of salary land, Karto only sharecrops a tiny part of this land to his followers while left most of the land to be cultivated by wage labour. Every year, six people are allowed to sharecrop a half hectare of the land (900 m each) and in the past six years, 36 different people have received land cultivation rights from Karto. Due to political considerations, he also has had to face economic loss. Since 2016, the migrant planters' have not come because they have been offered more promising jobs in their villages of origin. However, Karto's younger brother has managed to attract migrant planters to come because he grants exclusive harvesting rights to these planters. Karto, as a village head, simply cannot do this, since giving the exclusive rights of harvesting to migrant labourers is highly unpopular and would trigger large protests from local village workers. As a result, Karto must be prepared to queue for available workers to plant his land. This sometimes causes planting delay, which might result in a damaged harvest yield. Unlike Cokro and Mantili, Karto, as the village head, is required to act as a mediator between employer and worker at the 'village meetings'. This position often puts him in the centre of a dilemma.

The last group of rice capitalist farmers in the village share different characteristics. There are teachers and medical workers (nurse, doctor) who are also farmers. Inheriting paddy fields from their parents makes them farmers, while their education (thanks to the wealth of their parents) enables them to be professionals in the village. They view being a farmer as a side-job. Although they are occupied by their professional jobs, they try to supervise agricultural production in their spare time. Most of their parcels of land are cultivated by wage labourers, not sharecroppers. A small portion of their lands are sharecropped out to their poor relatives, out of pity. Their limited spare time prevents them from involving themselves too much in agricultural production. This qualifies them as 'professional-capitalist farmers'. Given their limited involvement in the production process, they are more risk-averse than 'typical capitalist farmers'. Due to their higher education, they are considered by other local capitalists to be the village intellectuals or, to be more precise, the intellectuals of the ruling class in the village. Rosyid is one example:

> Rosyid is a 55-year-old teacher at the public secondary school and a farmer. His wife, Mutinah, works as a civil servant at the PUSKESMAS. Besides being a teacher, Rosyid is also known as a community leader. He was the initiator and co-founder of the Projo Seliro cooperative, whose membership is dominated by capitalist farmers and PCPs. As a teacher holding a

> bachelor's degree, he is often asked to prepare the test for the selection of village officials below the level of village head. This shows his key role as an intellectual for the village administration and the local ruling class members, who are mostly only high school graduates. As a teacher who is still active and busy as a community leader, he only has a limited amount of time to supervise the daily rice cultivation of his hectare of *sawah*, inherited from his mother-in-law. He occasionally monitors his wage labourers in his spare time after working hours. While he is the intellectual of the ruling class and a religious figure, he says nothing at the 'village meetings'.

Apart from capitalist farmers, within the member of agrarian ruling class in the village, there are landowners who mostly extract their surpluses via rent (mostly in-kind). Instead of hiring wage labour, they mainly sharecrop out most of their land due to their inability to supervise and control their large parcel of land on a daily basis. Given their indirect involvement in the production process, they are mostly risk-averse in their approach to adopting new technology and farming methods for optimising their land productivity. They prefer to support their children as village officials (especially village secretary or village headman) or send them to college to later be skilled employees in the city. We may characterise them as 'landlord-capitalists'. They are landlords given that their primary means of extraction is via rent (in-kind) from their sharecroppers but they are not pre-capitalist landlords. They are landlords in a capitalist setting in that generalised commodity production shapes their agricultural production activity. In today's *Njomplang*, when sharecropping is less profitable than cultivating one's land by wage worker (Chapter 6), they are compelled to continue being 'landlords' only because of their failure to mobilise wage workers for their land.

Within this 'landlord-capitalists' group, we can also distinguish between two different camps based on their inability to mobilise wage labour for their land. The first is the 'absentee landlord-capitalists'; they do not reside in the village although they used to live there, or their family members are still living in the village. Their absence from the village prevents them from hiring wage labour. They are not 'contracting out' (paying a fixed rate cost per hectare to a contractor who takes care of the whole cultivation process) their land because it is too risky without a trustworthy contractor.[5] Sharecropping out the land secures loyal workers and guarantees an acceptable yield from the land, even though it is seen less profitable than cultivation via wage labour (Chapter 6). Their absence also means they are in no position to initiate a change in the agricultural practices in the village (including wages and working conditions) unless they have influential family members in the village that can do so on their behalf. It can be seen from the absent Turi, who is represented by Sari:

> Turi is a doctor and lives in Yogyakarta (about 60 km from *Njomplang*). She is the first daughter of Prapto, whose father was the village head in *Njomplang* during the colonial period. Doctor Turi was very active in

> land-buying in the 1980s and 1990s when land prices were cheap. She owns about ten hectares (some of which are beyond the village border) which all are sharecropped out to villagers through the intermediary Sari, her sister-in-law who lives in *Njomplang*. The 56-year old Sari is usually called Mrs. Prawiro. Prawiro is the third child of Prapto. Prawiro used to cultivate his land with wage labour (about 2.7 ha). After Prawiro passed away in 2016, limited knowledge and experiences led to Sari contracting out most of her land (2 ha), since it was more profitable than sharecropping. Sari currently also has to negotiate the terms and conditions of sharecropping with 25 sharecroppers on behalf of her absentee sister-in-law. This is the largest number of clients owned by a single patron. While her own parcel of land is not as large as the villagers think, they see Prawiro and Sari as the 'biggest landlord' who plays a prominent role at the 'village meetings'.

The second sub-group amongst 'landlord-capitalists' are those residing in the village. We may call them 'present landlord-capitalists'. Their inability to mobilise adequate wage labour from the village owes much to the changing nature of the local labour market, whereas their failure to mobilise labour from outside the village relates to their limited social networks (Chapter 6). At the same time, they find it difficult to hire a local reliable 'farming contractor' to cultivate their land at the fixed rate cost. In some cases, being a widow with limited knowledge and experience of farming may be the main reason for their inability to mobilise wage labourers, requiring them to sharecrop out their land. Mantili is one such landowner:

> She is the 67-year-old widow of Joyo. When Joyo was alive, most of their land (around 2.5 hectares) was cultivated using wage labour. Mantili initially sought out farming contractors to manage the land following Joyo's death. She lives with her daughter, who works as a nurse, and her son-in-law, who is a private company employee. Her other children live comfortably outside of the village. Dealing with such a large piece of land in her ageing years has become troublesome. The practice of contracting out, which was only introduced into the village in the 2000s, is known to be more profitable than sharecropping. However, she can only find a contractor to manage some of her land. Because of this, she sharecrops out most of her land among fifteen sharecroppers. Along with Cokro and Prawiro (Sari), Mantili is well-known as the main representative of employers ('*juragan*') at the 'village meetings'.

It may be noted that the distinct groups within the agrarian ruling class should not be seen as a static and permanent positions. Households may transform from one into another group category quite flexibly from time to time. As illustrated above, some current 'landlord-capitalists' in the village were previously capitalist farmers. Only due to the changing nature of labour market and their inability to mobilise wage workers for their land, were they forced to be 'landlord-capitalists'. A similar fluidity also applies within the group of capitalist farmers. 'Typical capitalist farmers' might transform themselves to be 'politico-bureaucrat capitalist farmers' if they find a way to occupy village official positions whereas 'professional-capitalist farmers' could also do the same when they resign or retire from their employment and fill in the ranks of village officials. Apart from the dynamics of commodity production in the village, the transformation into different groups of the agrarian ruling class is also closely related to the nature of generational reproduction (see Chapter 7).

We also find distinct groups of capitalist farmers in the oil palm village of Sumatra. Here, we have identified a group of oil palm capitalist farmers who directly supervise daily production, while being involved in the production process themselves, carrying out such tasks as applying fertiliser and weeding, although only on an occasional basis. They are similar to the 'typical capitalist farmers' in *Njomplang*. This involvement in the production process makes them more likely to take a risk in increasing their production output. One example is Bungaran:

> He is a 65-year-old man, born into a Batak capitalist farmer family in Binjai. In 1986, he went to Langkat to work as a supervisor in a private company. His earnings enabled him to buy land. In the early 2000s, he resigned from his job and started to grow six hectares of oil palm. He used to be involved in the production process himself as far as applying fertiliser. However, since he has had to take care of his brothers' and sisters' land since the mid-2000s, he gave up that role to wage labourers, working under his close supervision. Bungaran is meticulous in growing oil palm. He only uses premium fertiliser, where its price is more than four times higher than regular fertiliser. In terms of productivity, he does not allow the application of herbicides but hires labourers to cut the grass and weeds regularly. He also prefers to harvest his oil palm every ten days, instead of the common practice of 14 days, to minimise lost fruit. With this premium care, his land productivity is above the average in the village (1.2 ton/hectare/harvest). Occupied with oil palm production, he is not interested in local politics.

A different group of oil palm capitalist farmers in the village do not reside in the village but extract a surplus from the direct hiring of wage labour through 'farming managers'. The 'farming manager' may be either a family member or just a local villager. In the case of the latter, they supervise production by visiting their fields twice a month during the harvesting time or once every few months at other times of the year. If their farm managers are family members who live in the village, they have no need to visit the fields so frequently, since they can entrust the oil palm production to their family. We may label this group as 'absentee-capitalist farmers'. They share characteristics with 'present-capitalist farmers' in that they extract surplus through wage labour. However, because they live outside the village, they do not have any direct political influence in the village the way their compatriot 'present-capitalist farmers' do, except if they have family members living in the village who can represent their material interests. This may be seen in the case of Bungaran's family:

> Bungaran is the oldest among six siblings. All of his siblings are salaried employees. His younger brother, a policeman, bought 15 hectares of land and grew oil palm in 2004. Another of Bungaran's younger brothers, who is a staff member at PTPN II in Medan, planted five hectares of oil palm in the mid-2000s. Since 2015, Bungaran has had to take care of 20 hectares of oil palm owned by his other younger brother, who is working at PERTAMINA. Bungaran is also taking care of four hectares of oil palm land belonging to his second child (a policeman). In total, Bungaran is a 'farming manager' for more than 40 hectares of oil palm belonging to his absentee family members. Bungaran is responsible not only for organising wage labourers for daily maintenance, such as weeding, fertilising and harvesting, but also for the sale of the fresh fruit bunches to the oil palm factories. The family has purchased him a mini-truck to deliver the oil palm bunches. Thanks to the consolidation of the family land, Bungaran is able to be a holder of SPs (a cover letter) from the processing plant factories that offer him a better price for his oil palm than if he sells to the local agents.[6] Bungaran's role is similar to that of Sari in Java in that he represents absentee landowners in the village.

Another group of oil palm capitalist farmers with distinct characteristics are those who are both farmers and who hold politico-bureaucratic positions. They may be regarded as 'politico-bureaucrat capitalist farmers', as in Java. However, as opposed to the Java context, they do not sharecrop out their lands. Sharecropping is economically unfeasible for oil palm production as its non-intensive cultivation does not require a constant labour supply. Since sharecropping is negligible in the village, its political function to attract political supporters is also unimportant. Thus, the 'politico-bureaucrat capitalist farmer' needs to spend their cash money on winning political support (see Chapter 7). This means they do not face the contradiction of economic versus political consideration, as do their compatriots in *Njomplang* do. In terms of technological development, they have no problem with the inception of new technology that may replace manual labour. However, due to the opportunities offered by companies operating in the village, they are more inclined to be involved in non-agricultural activities (land brokerage, acting as political intermediaries between the company and the villagers, and informal security providers/'goons'). Given this overwhelming level of non-agricultural activities, they largely remain risk-averse as far as innovation in agricultural production is concerned. Luhut is an example:

> Luhut, a 56-year-old man, only obtained his high school diploma in his forties. He owns seven hectares of oil palm field, one hectare of shrimp

> farm and 0.72 hectares of paddy field. He is also notorious as a *preman* (goon) in the village. Harnessing a Batak family-clanship network, he successfully secured the position of village head from 2000 to 2007. During his administration, there was a rumour that he was involved in the illegal selling of village marshlands to plantation companies. He has also been a local public relations (PR) officer for Pertamina Gas, PT KAI and the Kelantang Hotel in the village. He was once arrested by the police for drug trafficking but was released shortly afterwards. He hires in wage labourers to manage his oil palm field, under his son's supervision, while he is busy with other business. With his greater focus on non-agricultural activities and less concern with the oil palm, his land productivity is much lower than Bungaran's (only 0.9 ton/hectare/harvest). While he lost in the two previous local elections (2007 and 2013), he intends to run for village head again in the next election. This ambition seems to be futile given his notorious track record. However, as a 'politico-bureaucrat capitalist farmer', where farming is not really of great interest while the political avenue is the field in which he is more interested and capable, whatever the illusion might be, Luhut sees it as an opportunity.

Finally, there is also a group of oil palm capitalist farmers who, at the same time, work as teachers, nurses or doctors. Their characteristics are akin to the 'professional-capitalist farmers' in Java. In the oil palm village, however, due to the non-intensive nature of oil palm cultivation, their ability to supervise daily production is higher than that of their compatriots in Java. Another difference between Java and Sumatra is the path to being a 'professional-capitalist farmer'. In Java, professionals continue to be rice capitalist farmers mainly due to their large land ownership inherited from their parents. In Sumatra, many professionals become oil palm capitalist farmers by harnessing their lucrative earnings from professional positions to finance oil palm production (buying oil palm fields and hiring other's labour), even though their land-holding may not be that large (less than four hectares). This shows that non-agricultural jobs (professional employments) play a crucial role—more so than their initial land ownership—in converting households into capitalist farmers in the oil palm sector. Ucok is one example:

> Ucok is a 50-year-old teacher at the public elementary school. Ucok was lucky enough to inherit 2.5 hectares of land from his parents, the same amount as his only brother. Their seven sisters did not receive any land inheritance because of the patrilineal Batak land custom. Ucok depends entirely on the production of wage labourers. To supervise the harvesting, Ucok moves the harvesting day to Sunday, when he is not at work. His job as a teacher prevents him from fully concentrating on agricultural production. Hence, instead of buying more oil palm fields, he has purchased a house in a strategic location to open a trading business. As a teacher, he is a well-respected figure in the village. However, he is not the

most influential member of the intellectuals of the ruling class, as Rosyid in *Njomplang* is. This role is played by older teachers than Ucok and who also hold a bachelor's degree. However, they neither own oil palm fields nor are interested in farming. They are more typically professional than the capitalist farmers.

In our oil palm village, there is a negligible number of landowners extracting their surplus via rent (in-kind or fixed). To be 'landlord-capitalists', they have to extract rent from sharecroppers or tenants cultivating significantly large oil palm fields (four hectares is required as the minimum land ownership to be a capitalist farmer). In *Timpang*, only in rare cases do farmers sharecrop or rent out oil palm fields of more than four hectares. If it is more than four hectares, it is more profitable for landowners to hire a local 'farming manager' to organise the production process through wage labourers. The only exception to the 'landlord-capitalists' we find is an absentee landowner who sharecrops out his five hectares of land to a distant relative living in the village.

Similar to the rice village, the distinct groups within the agrarian ruling class in the oil palm village is not permanent positions either. Farmers from one distinct group may move into another group. However, given that the number of 'landlord-capitalist' in the oil palm context is negligible, such transformation is largely confined to the different groups of capitalist farmers.

The Agrarian Ruling Class and Family Ties

In rural settings, family ties are important. Even when capitalist social relations have penetrated, the extended family, as the main structure of family organisation in the countryside, remains a crucial determinant of social relations. The importance of family ties, however, is inextricably linked with class position. For the ruling class, family ties play a prominent role in identifying potential allies or competitors for the struggle over material resources in the village. By looking at family ties, we may see the internal dynamics of the ruling class in the village which shape the nature of their cooperation and competition.

In *Njomplang*, as may be in other Javanese villages, family ties are mainly established by close-knit extended families under the banner of Javanese ethnicity. Extended families are well-developed in the densely populated villages in Java, where development of the structure dates back to the colonial period. In this setting, one might expect to see the family ties of the whole ruling class in a village.

In *Njomplang*, Prawiro and Sari occupy the village secretary position through their son, Agung. Prawiro is a close relative to Cipto, since Cipto's father (Condronegoro) is the nephew-in-law of Prawiro's father (Prapto). Cipto's son, Supri, is the owner of the only rice huller in the village. Furthermore, Supri, an important 'typical capitalist farmer' is the son-in-law of Guntur, a 'landlord-capitalist' whose father is the older brother of Joyo's father. We can see the close blood relationship between Prawiro, Cipto, Guntur and Joyo.

Cipto himself was the village headman from 1998 to 2012. His nomination was fully supported by those other three influential families. Cipto even agreed to marry his son, Supri, to Guntur's daughter after Cipto officially occupied the village headman position. We may call them the Prawiro family block. They dominated the post of village headman from colonial times until 2012 (see Appendix 1).

The current village headman, Karto, a 'politico-bureaucrat capitalist farmer' in the village, comes from beyond the dynasty of Prawiro's block. His father was a religious figure who had no close connections to the family's establishment. Many of Karto's relatives are from a working class background. Their power lies more in numbers than in the possession of material resources. Karto is politically isolated to some degree, since he has only a younger sister, Wati, who occupies one of the village official positions. Wati's husband is an influential *penebas* (local paddy buyer, paying in advance and bearing the harvesting cost) in the village. Karto's son is abroad, working onboard a ship, whose remittances are crucial for Karto. It is only through a particular strategy that Karto managed to win the local election in 2012 (see Chapter 7).

Another important family block is that of the Hadikusumo. Hadikusomo, a big 'typical capitalist farmer' and former policeman, is the owner of the only fertiliser shop in the village. His father was a village official. Hadikusumo ran in the first village headman election under the New Order regime in 1990, only to lose to Probo, the son-in-law of Condronegoro. Hadikusomo's son-in-law, Wawan, is the head of the BPD (Village Body Representative). If this family block wishes to run for local election, Wawan is the only eligible candidate, since Hadikusumo is already too old (74), while his children live comfortably as employees elsewhere (mostly policemen). Another crucial connection for Hadikusomo is his younger brother-in-law, Dwi, who is the owner of a construction material shop.

Cokro, a 'typical capitalist farmer' has his own family block. Because Cokro's family background was set in the classes of labour, his current close relatives are mostly from the classes of labour, but their numbers in the village are considerably lower than Karto's relatives. Cokro has no close relatives in a village official position. As a member of the nouveau riche in the village, Cokro is politically isolated, while economically strong through the help of his son-in-law. This limited family network (both in numbers and political positions) is probably the reason why Cokro and his family are not interested in running for the local election.

The economic resources and political power in *Njomplang*, a village with 314 households, are dominated by ten families. As the ruling class, the different nature of the individual capitalist farmers is downplayed by their general class interest to keep wages low and minimise working conditions to maximise profit. Their cooperation can be seen in the village meetings, where they deny the demands of the classes of labour. This will be discussed in the next section.

Family ties are only crucial as far as they provide economic benefit. The capitalist households who actually have a close blood relationship with households from the classes of labour would not acknowledge this, since it would only bring them more burdens than opportunities. Soon after Karto occupied the post of village headman, many of his relatives from the classes of labour were disappointed with him. He only gave limited cultivation rights for his salary land, while keeping the majority of it for himself, cultivating it by using wage labourers. In the words of one of his relatives, Karto 'has forgotten his relatives after becoming rich'. From Karto's point of view, having close relatives from the classes of labour has been more of a burden than an opportunity, in terms of wishing to compete with the other capitalists in the village. For him, and others (Cokro, Mantili), class interest overrides family ties.

This tendency might also be seen in the Sumatra oil palm village, although with several qualifications. *Timpang*, as explained in Chapter 4, is a very diverse community, where Javanese, Batak, Malay and Acehnese, who are either Muslim or Christian (both Catholic and Protestant), have been living together for some five decades. Family ties are often closely linked with ethnicity (particularly, clanship) and religion, besides class. Certain families would only marry certain other families, based on either their stereotypical ethnicity or religion. For the ruling class in the village, then, the son/daughter of a Christian Batak capitalist farmer, for instance, cannot just marry the daughter/son of a Muslim capitalist farmer, from whichever ethnicity.

The marriage among capitalist families is mostly limited by religion and, to some extent, by ethnicity. This has effectively prevented the amalgamation of extended capitalist families and, thus, the concentration of families within the ruling class of the village. As a result, instead of developing family ties along class lines, capitalist farmers in *Timpang* may maintain their family ties along ethnicity-clanship lines, across different classes (PCPs and the classes of labour). This means our focus on agrarian ruling class family networks in *Timpang* would not represent the *overall* ruling class in the village, as it does in *Njomplang*.

The first important family-clanship block in the village is headed by Luhut. His brother-in-law is an important typical capitalist farmer who is also the head of GAPOKTAN in the village, which controls 15 POKTAN. One of Luhut's daughters is the owner of a minimarket near the village office, a strategic location on the national highway from Medan to Banda Aceh. The rest of his network lies in the clanship line of Batak PCPs and classes of labour, especially from Batak Tapanuli's line, which numbers among the largest in the village. This is the network that he harnessed in the 2000 local election which brought him to power.

Luhut was defeated by Sofian both in 2007 and 2013. When Sofian passed away in 2017 due to a lung infection, he was 49 years old. His parents, who were among the first settlers in the village, had left him 20 hectares of land. As a 'politico-bureaucrat capitalist farmer', Sofian was also an oil palm trader agent, one of the biggest in the village. He was also the biggest broker for agricultural inputs. Sofian was from the Batak Karo clanship, whose numbers in the village are fewer than Tapanuli's clan. Sofian's family networks were also limited. This family block seems to have found it difficult to find an eligible candidate to run for village head since the death of Sofian.

A strong contender against both Luhut and Sofian was Budi, a 54-year-old man. He came to *Timpang* in the late 1980s and worked as a supervisor at a privately-owned oil palm company which had enabled him to buy 20 hectares of oil palm and three hectares of paddy field. Of Javanese descent, Budi's family-clanship networks are much more limited in a village where the number of Javanese is small. His wife, however, is a Batak. Budi's father-in-law, Agam, is one of the most important local oil palm traders in the village, with dozens of loyal farmers who sell their oil palm to him. However, his network is much smaller than Luhut's. Moreover, Budi's economic resources are limited given the priority he has given to the education of his family. In the late 2000s, Budi had to sell five hectares of his land to finance his first daughter at medical college in Medan. He sold another five hectares in 2017 to finance his two other children. His priority of his family's education also means Budi no longer applies fertilisers to his oil palm fields. These limited economic resources may explain why Budi is no longer interested in being village head.

For all of these families, their family-clanship networks that are harnessed for political competition can easily be overridden by their general class interests when they face workers in agricultural production. There was widespread disappointment among the workers, including those who are in the same clan as Sofian, because he was a mean employer. One of the workers recalls, 'if we had to wait for water from him (Sofian), we would have died of thirst'.

As in *Njomplang*, only a very few families dominate the political-economic power in *Timpang*. What is important in *Timpang* is the inextricable link between family ties and clanship. Nonetheless, when it comes to agricultural production and dealing with labour, the capitalists still favour maximum profit at the expense of the workers who are in the same clan as them. This is similar to *Njomplang*, where extended family ties are only relevant to the capitalist farmers as far as they bring more economic opportunities than burdens.

Petty Commodity Producers and Their Characteristics

The dynamics of the PCPs are generally absent from the literature. On the one hand, Neo-populist supporters pay most attention to the internal household dynamics (demographic composition) of PCPs (Chayanov, 1966: 69; van der Ploeg, 2013: 33). As discussed in the theoretical chapter, this narrow focus is limited to explain the PCPs' transformation into capitalist farmers. On the other hand, some Marxists focus more on the result of the class differentiation of the two opposing classes (capital and labour). This prevents an understanding of the internal dynamics of PCPs. To analyse these, we will take the same approach as we did for the capitalist farmers, and focus on the different groups within the PCPs, in both *Njomplang* and *Timpang*, based on their production activities and their patterns of class reproduction.

In *Njomplang*, there is a group of PCPs who individually own a considerable amount of paddy field (between 0.5 and 0.9 hectare of *sawah*) that enables them to reproduce themselves as PCPs without selling their labour or hiring other's labour all year round. The earning from their land ownership mostly provides them with 'simple reproduction'. They do not have to sharecrop in land from 'landlord-capitalists'. Given their considerable land ownership, their ability to be independent of the labour market to sustain their subsistence, and the absence of dependence on patrons, we may speak of this group as 'substantial PCPs'. Some of them remain in this situation and have no interest in exchanging their 'autonomy from the labour market' for more economic gains. In that sense they tend to be satisfied with their subsistence life. This might resonate the 'classical PCPs' as literature has indicated. One example is Sutarno:

> After completing secondary school in the 1980s, 54-year-old Sutarno worked as a factory worker in Jakarta, Bogor and Semarang. He went back to *Njomplang* in the early 2000s to cultivate the 0.5 hectares of *sawah* he inherited from his parents. In the last few years, only out of pity, Sutarno sharecrops 0.24 hectares of *sawah* with his relative's widow because she cannot take care of the land by herself. With his wife, Yati, they use their own labour for all paddy cultivation phases. At the same time, they do not sell their labour for agricultural tasks; they prefer to tend goats. They also grow green beans during the off-season (August–October), both for their own consumption and for sale. All of their three children have completed high school and work elsewhere, as a factory worker, a mechanic and in casual labour. Sending their children (or one of them) to college was considered too difficult for them. They are grateful for their '*cukupan*' (moderate) life and are not interested in exchanging their 'autonomy from the labour market' for more economic gain by more intensively selling their labour.

However, others are willing to sell their labour or work harder by renting-in more lands to meet aspirations beyond subsistence, such as sending children to college. We may call this group as 'aspiring PCPs' given their relentless effort to meet their aspirations beyond subsistence. Along the way, they may sometimes hire in labour *at will*, in the sense that their economic sources allow them to hire in labour rather than simply being compelled to do so, as the members of classes of labour are (see below). This can be seen from Sutikno:

> Sutikno, a 56-year-old man inheriting 0.53 hectares of *sawah* from his parents. He and his wife take care of their *sawah* by their own labour. In the early 2000s, with the initial capital from his savings, they started to rent-in *sawah* (at its peak, it reached 1.5 hectares) that was cultivated mainly by family labour (sometimes they also hire in some wage labourers). Their land leasing activity is done to send their children for college education.

> They want to prevent their children from working in laborious jobs as they did. With such hard-working activity, they managed to pay Rp. 50 million for their son to enter the Military Academy and send their daughter to a college, majoring in nursery care.

A different group of PCPs are those who own no land but who control a large *sawah* (0.8 to 1.8 hectare) through sharecropping. As already mentioned, this land control is only half as valuable as land ownership. Nonetheless, this land control has enabled them to satisfy their subsistence and made them independent from the labour market. In this sense, they share similar characteristics with the 'substantial PCPs'. Unlike the 'substantial PCPs', however, their land control status via sharecropping makes their reproduction more vulnerable. Their land control could be withdrawn by landowners at will, though generally, sharecropping may last almost forever, and sharecroppers are able to leave their land control to their heirs. Given their relationship with their patrons, we regard them as 'formal PCPs'. Their numbers are greater than that of the 'substantial PCPs' in the village. Despite living at subsistence level, many 'formal PCPs' are prepared to sell their labour throughout the year. They deliberately exchange their 'autonomy from the labour market' for more economic gains, illuminating their character as 'aspiring PCPs'. This owes much to the accumulation dynamics in the village that generate new hopes, and pressures them to catch up with what capitalist farmers in the village are doing, primarily regarding matters of consumption: housing improvement or the possession of electronics and automobiles (motorcycles) are considered to be 'progress'. Their activities in selling their labour mean that they share common interests with the classes of labour. However, their relationship with their patrons might prevent them from openly expressing this. This may be seen in Adnan:

> Adnan, a 43-year-old man, and his wife have no land and, thus, sharecrop in 1.1 hectares of *sawah* from three different 'present landowners'. They cultivate the land with their own labour. However, during the off-season, they hire in workers to grow watermelons. If there is not a total harvest failure due to bad weather, they can make a net profit of between Rp. 7 million to Rp. 25 million in one watermelon harvesting season (depending on the damage to the watermelon). At one time, after selling their labour all year round as agricultural workers and growing watermelon, they thought to send their first son to college. But with the unpredictable nature of growing watermelons, their dream was abandoned. His son, a high school graduate, is currently working as a casual worker, while Adnan and Tanti keep working as labourers throughout the year. Having already exchanged their 'autonomy from the labour market' for selling labour all year round, they spend their disposable income on house improvement (installing tile floors), buying a new motorcycle and a leisure hobby, that of rearing expensive ornamental birds (several hundreds of thousands of rupiah per bird).

Similar groups of PCPs are also found in *Timpang*. The most important difference is that in our oil palm village, sharecropping and fixed rent are rare. This means that the group of PCPs who only control their land is negligible. This group of 'formal PCPs' is exceeded by the group of PCPs who own their considerable land (2–3.9 hectares). Sometimes, these 'substantial PCPs' of oil palm combine their land ownership with leasing-in several pieces of paddy field. Akin to the PCPs in the rice village, the PCPs in the oil palm village are able to meet their subsistence (Chapter 6) and enjoy 'autonomy from the labour market'. Similar to their fellow in Java, PCPs in *Timpang* also may sometimes hire in labour *at will*. Nonetheless, given the un-intensive nature of oil palm, PCPs hiring in labour is a less pronounced tendency than in the paddy village.

However, both 'substantial' and 'formal' PCPs in *Timpang* are resolute in selling their labour throughout the year, for both agricultural and non-agricultural jobs. Working as agricultural labourers, either at the company plantations or in individual capitalist farmer's oil palm fields is the main option for agricultural jobs. They also work as masons, labourers in the village project, on railway projects, and in local processing plants or factories, either as clerks or security officers. Unlike in Java, where some 'substantial PCPs' maintain their 'autonomy' by avoiding harder work (becoming 'classical PCPs'), most 'substantial PCPs' in Sumatra deliberately pursue extra income instead of keeping their 'autonomy from the labour market'. They share the features of 'aspiring PCPs' in *Njomplang*. In contrast to Java, however, the case of 'classical PCPs' in Sumatra is negligible. This owes much to the different nature of capitalist expansion in the two villages. As a 'new frontier', *Timpang* offers relatively cheaper land than the 'old frontier' of *Njomplang*. For PCPs, buying more lands in the oil palm village is more conceivable than in the paddy village. Moreover, the un-intensive nature of oil palm cultivation also provides more space for PCPs to sell their labour all year round either at the individual or company plantations. Hence, the expectation of the PCPs in Sumatra to pursue aspirations beyond subsistence (to become capitalist farmers or at least sending the children to college) is more pronounced than in Java.

The desire of 'substantial PCPs' in *Timpang* to sell their labour signals their response to the accumulation dynamics in the village, which are even more dramatic than in *Njomplang*, given the accumulation was only started about three decades ago. The aspirations to and pressures for following the success of the capitalist farmers are paramount. Some of the PCPs have succeeded in purchasing more land that has transformed them into capitalist farmers. This may be seen in the case of Subandi:

> 70-year-old Subandi worked as a 'farming manager' in 1991 for an absentee-capitalist. Besides taking care of 15 hectares of oil palm as a 'farming manager' and receiving a monthly salary, Subandi worked as a labourer in the fields to obtain daily wages. To earn extra income, he and his wife borrowed the barren land of their neighbours to grow second crops and vegetables on. From the savings, they managed to buy their first land in

> 1991. They bought 1.5 hectares of land for Rp. 700 thousand, in two instalments. They grew paddy for a year to collect the adequate initial capital to grow oil palm. A year later, they purchased another 1.5 hectares and started to grow oil palm in 1995. Through owning three hectares of oil palm in the mid-1990s, Subandi is one among those who have enjoyed the oil palm boom since the 2000s. Subandi and his wife have managed to send their second daughter to college and now she is a teacher in Aceh. They used to take care of their oil palm using their own labour, except for harvesting, when they hired in workers. Since 2016, their oil palm fields have become four hectares plus 0.4 hectares of paddy field. The additional land ownership has led them to hiring in labour for all the agricultural tasks in both oil palm and paddy, except for applying fertilisers, given the trust issue over the workers. With this quantitative change that has led to a qualitative transformation, Subandi has been transformed from a PCP into capitalist farmer since 2016.

Other PCPs in the village, however, face land fragmentation that transforms them into the classes of labour. We may see this in Rustam's case:

> Rustam, a 62-year-old man, has owned 1.5 hectares of oil palm since 1997. He also sharecrops in five hectares of oil palm owned by his distant relative who is an 'absentee landlord-capitalist' living in Medan. From this, he earns a third of the yield. He has three children. He takes care of their oil palm fields with his oldest son, Ari. The two other children work elsewhere in the village to earn a higher income. When Ari married in the early 2010s, Rustam granted his 1.5 hectares to him. His two other children protested this decision, but Rustam did not change his mind. Since then, Rustam has depended solely on his sharecropping field for his family reproduction (four members who are still living in his house). While previously he may been considered to be a PCP, he is now practically transformed into a member of the classes of labour, one who must keep working at labour jobs to meet his subsistence.

This illuminates how PCPs have no inherent superiority in maintaining their 'subsistence reproduction', as neo-populists often argue. On the contrary, they are subjected to class differentiation due to generalised 'commodification of subsistence' (Bernstein, 2010). Both in *Njomplang* and *Timpang*, market dependence clearly provides both constraints and opportunities by which the reproduction of the PCPs is shaped. Many of them meet their 'simple reproduction' comfortably, some of them successfully engage in expanded reproduction as capitalist farmers, while others must face the 'subsistence squeeze' as members of the classes of labour.

As far as their class politics is concerned, PCPs in Java and Sumatra reflect their contradictory nature. In our oil palm village, both 'substantial' and 'formal PCPs' are 'aspiring PCPs' who have no hesitation in selling their labour throughout the year to achieve their aspirations beyond subsistence. This makes them share the interest with workers in aspiring to higher wages and better working conditions. Many of them openly express their complaints about insufficient wages and inadequate working conditions, both with regard to the individual capitalist farmer's fields and the company's plantations. The eagerness of large numbers of 'substantial PCPs' to be exploited by selling their labour to become capitalist farmers themselves, illuminates a contradictory situation. It seems that for them, 'only by selling more of our labour power, can we become closer to being capitalist farmers'.

This characteristic is quite different from our rice village. Here, 'substantial PCPs' are fewer in number than 'formal PCPs'. Furthermore, only a few 'substantial PCPs' in the village are 'aspiring PCPs' who are willing to exchange their 'autonomy' for higher economic gains. This prevents some of them from sharing interests with workers. At the same time, while 'formal PCPs' in the village are basically 'aspiring PCPs' who sell their labour all year round and definitely identify their interests with labour, yet, given their land control is arranged under sharecropping, they are in a patron-client relationship with the 'landlord-capitalists'. Contradicting or overtly criticising their patron is not an option if they wish to keep their land control. Consequently, as will be shown in the next section, they tend to be passive at 'village meetings'.

The Traits of the Members of the Classes of Labour

The members of the classes of labour are the ruled class in rural Java and Sumatra. With little or no means of production, they are compelled to dispose of their labour all year round. While the concept of the 'classes of labour' greatly helps us to see the common characteristics of fragmented labourers who mostly depend on wages for their reproduction, it may discount their internal dynamics. Harris-White and Gooptu (2000) have highlighted the 'struggles over class' that signal the competition among the workers for their reproduction. This suggests that understanding the internal dynamics of classes of labour is crucial when looking at their internal tensions and cooperation, and how these impact on their relationship with capital.

In *Njomplang*, the first group of farmers selling their labour throughout the year out of market compulsion is those owning an insignificant plot of land (0.10 ha–0.34 ha), or controlling one (less than 0.34 ha), or owning no land and controlling merely a small *sawah* (0.35 ha–0.84 ha). They normally manage to sell most of their output to market. Nonetheless, their output alone is not sufficient to support their subsistence. This group of farmers may be called 'semi-proletariat farmers' given their land possession/control enables them to produce agricultural surplus output, while they must dispose of their labour all year round to satisfy their basic needs. At the same time, they do not hire in labour *at will*. They may only hire in labour from their neighbouring classes of labour households for planting and harvesting[7] when the number of their family labour is inadequate at the moment of the land cultivation phase of their tiny land (due to sickness or other reasons). This occasional 'horizontal labour hiring' (see more in Chapter 6) does not move them out of the classes of labour. Nevertheless, since their land control is crucial, either to complement their tiny land ownership or constitute their very nature, they have 'something to lose'. Furthermore, given their land control is largely tied to a patron-client relationship with a 'landlord-capitalist', being vocal in the negotiation process between capital and labour (at the 'village meetings') is not an easy option. Mulyono is one such farmer:

> Mulyono, a 53-year-old man, had been working as a plantation worker in Sumatra and factory worker in Jakarta before returning to *Njomplang* in 1992. He started farming by cultivating his 0.08 hectares *sawah* inheritance from his parents. His parents also left him land rights cultivations (sharecropping). Mulyono sharecrops in 0.08 hectares from Prawiro (Sari) and the same amount from Joyo (Mantili), both members of the most powerful families in the village. Since the 2000s, he has also sharecropped in 0.16 hectares from another capitalist farmer. Mulyono and his wife Karti cultivate their *sawah* using their own labour. Mulyono also disposes off his labour throughout the year as an agricultural labourer, while Karti engages in self-employment by producing *tempe* (a form of fermented soybean). For a 'semi-proletariat farmer' like Mulyono, higher wages and better working conditions are logical demands. Nevertheless, since their land control is crucial in complementing their negligible land ownership, and this land control is entirely dependent on a patron-client relationship with a 'landlord-capitalist', being vocal at the 'village meetings' is not a straightforward option.

Another group of farmers who are compelled to sell their labour all year round are those controlling a negligible amount of land (0.10 ha–0.34 ha) while owning no land at all. Like semi-proletariat farmers, they do not hire in labour *at will*. They may sell a portion of their output but, in many cases, they sell none at all because they only produce enough for their own consumption. Their almost zero output sales separates them from the 'semi-proletariat farmers'. They may be seen as 'proletariat-farmers', since they share the feature of the proletariat in not owning land; yet, their involvement in agricultural commodity production, although miniscule, to some extent, qualifies them as farmers. With their tiny sharecropping, the 'proletariat-farmers' are those within the classes of labour in *Njomplang* who have 'nothing to lose'. With no hesitation, they would give up their land control if they no longer found the benefits from it. Let's take Tarmi for example:

> Tarmi is a 42-year-old woman. After finishing high school in 1991, she worked as a factory worker in Bandung and then Bekasi, the biggest industrial complex in the country. In 2008, Tarmi and her husband, Juki, came back to *Njomplang* and sharecropped in *sawah* from one 'absentee

> landlord-capitalist' based in Yogyakarta and one politico-bureaucrat capitalist farmer living in the village: 0.16 hectares from each of them. They are hardly able to sell the output from such little cultivation, being only able to produce enough for their own consumption. They harness their own labour to cultivate their *sawah* and both of them sell their labour as agricultural labourers all year-round. For 'proletariat-farmers' like Tarmi and her husband, with so little land control and no land ownership, they have nothing to lose to advance their class interests. 'If they wish to take my land (control) back, let it be', Tarmi once challenged. Tarmi is very vocal at the 'village meetings' (see the next section) and this makes her one of the most important spokespersons of the classes of labour in *Njomplang*. While Tarmi never joined a labour union when she was working at the factory, living more than a decade in the industrial milieu may have shaped her courage to express her opinions.

The third group of farmers in *Njomplang* compelled to sell their labour throughout the year are those who neither own nor control any land. Since their survival depends entirely on disposing of their labour without any agricultural output generation, they may be perceived as a 'fully fledged proletariat' (here after FFP). Their zero land control and land ownership are sometimes because they deliberately declined any offer from capitalist farmers to sharecrop their land given they were offered a tiny plot of *sawah* (less than 0.33 ha), from which the earnings are lower than in non-agricultural activities, such as raising livestock or opening up a petty self-employed business. Some of them, however, received no offer to sharecrop in *sawah*, although they wanted one. In such cases, they are willing to work as agricultural workers, since agriculture is the main occupation available in *Njomplang*. They expected, after working for certain capitalist farmers, they would be offered sharecropping. As a member of the FFP working in agriculture, they are deeply concerned about their wages and working conditions and they are more a group of 'nothing to lose' than even the 'proletariat-farmers'. However, since the numbers of the FFP working in agriculture are lower than the 'proletariat-farmers' and 'semi-proletariat farmers' (most villagers involved in rice cultivation hold sharecropping rights, while many of the FFP are working outside of agriculture), their role in the negotiations between the classes of labour and the capitalist farmers in the village is limited. An example of a member of the FFP can be seen in Paijo:

> Paijo, a 52-year-old man, was born of landless parents. After marrying Pinah in the early 1990s, they have sharecropped in a 0.32 hectares *sawah* located in the northern part of *Njomplang*, owned by a capitalist farmer from the neighbouring village. In 2014, they returned the land because the cost of maintaining it was higher than the profit due to the need to use a water pump and the fact that much more fertiliser needs to be applied in the *sawah* in northern *Njomplang*. However, their aspirations to sharecrop in *sawah* in the southern section of *Njomplang* were never realised.

> Paijo eventually accepted a job as a tractor driver. Paijo and Pinah sell their labour as agricultural workers throughout the year for their survival. During the off-season, Paijo joins the village project as a coolie, while Pinah must accept unemployment. As a member of the FFP, Paijo's main concern is about wages. However, their role at the village meeting is less significant than that of the 'proletariat-farmers'.

We have also identified different groups of those disposing of their labour all year round out of market compulsion in *Timpang*. In the oil palm context, some of them only own tiny parcels of land and control little land (less than two hectares). They may be seen as 'semi-proletariat farmers', as their fellow workers in Java. Unlike in *Njomplang*, where some 'semi-proletariat farmers' only control land, in *Timpang*, most of them own their own tiny plots. Their land ownership provides some hope of obtaining more land and makes them a group that has 'something to lose'. They complement their income by selling their labour elsewhere and share interests with other classes of labour. Moreover, since 'semi-proletariat farmers' in *Timpang* have no patron-client relationship with the landowners (sharecropping), they are in a stronger position to advance their labour interests. Nonetheless, given that they have 'something to lose', the extent to which they are vocal in promoting their interests depends on the way in which they complement their main income from their own cultivation. Those complementing their earnings entirely by working only for individual capitalist farmers tend to be more antagonistic towards this class. This may be seen in Nardi:

> After completing his secondary school education, Nardi, a 40-year-old man, went to Riau as a casual worker, and came back to *Timpang* and got married in 2003. His parents left him 0.65 hectares of oil palm field. Nardi combines his own cultivation with selling his labour as a harvester for individual capitalist farmers. After 15 years, he now receives 14 *ancak* (permanent rights to harvest certain oil palm fields owned by a certain landowner), the highest number in the village. With these *ancak*, Nardi has no need to work for the corporate plantations. He is enjoying his work at the individual capitalist farmers given that 'no one orders us around and we can arrange our own work time'. The landowners only care that their oil palms are harvested at the right time and in the right volume (no stealing) and no close supervision is needed to the trusted harvesters. Without the patron-client relationship, Nardi is also freer to express his interests. He and his fellow workers frequently openly demand a rise in their wages.

Others who complement their revenues by working for oil palm companies in the village tend to be less vocal against individual capitalist farmers. Agus is one of them:

> Agus, a 33-year-old man, owns 0.5 hectares of oil palm. After working as an oil palm plantation worker in Riau and as a construction coolie in Aceh

> in the early 2000s, he went back to *Timpang* in 2007. Since then, he has worked as a harvester for individual capitalist farmers in the village. Until 2010, he successfully received five *ancak*. This harvesting job, combined with the yield from his tiny land ownership, was inadequate in meeting his household's needs. In the same year, Agus started working for PT. RPL as a company worker harvesting oil palm. He is aware that working at the company means having too many rules to abide by. He would be happy to work only for individual capitalist farmers, work which offers more autonomy, if he had at least eight *ancak*. However, with so many workers available while the oil palm fields of individual capitalists in the village are limited, looking for more *ancak* is not an easy task. Occupied with the company job, Agus tends to accept the wages and working conditions at the individual oil palm fields owned by the capitalist farmers.

In *Timpang*, another group who must sell their labour all year round are those owning no land and controlling only a tiny plot of land. They are part of the 'proletariat-farmers', like their Javanese comrades. However, the number of 'proletariat-farmers' in *Timpang* is negligible, given the incidence of land-leasing and sharecropping is rare. Bintang is one of them:

> He is a 40-year-old man who rents 0.4 hectares of oil palm. The landowner is a villager who needs money to improve his house. The contract runs for eight years, from 2015 to 2023, and the rent is only Rp. 10 million, a half of the normal rent. This gives Bintang extra income (on average, about Rp. 1 million per month) that is crucial in complementing his income from being a harvester for an individual capitalist farmer. Starting his career in the mid-2000s, Bintang has come to receive seven *ancak*. These *ancak*, combined with the revenues from renting-in oil palm, is considered sufficient to meet the basic needs of his wife and their three children. Under these circumstances, Bintang is not interested in working for oil palm companies and proudly declares that he 'does not like to be ordered around'.

The majority of members of the classes of labour in *Timpang* are those neither owning nor controlling any land. Their full dependency on selling their labour for survival qualifies them as members of the FFP, similar to their fellow workers in Java. Some of them work in agriculture (both oil palm and paddy), while others sell their labour in non-agricultural work or open self-employed petty businesses. The most-favoured agricultural employment is to work for individual capitalist farmers and to occupy a considerable number of *ancak* (around seven or eight) that is equal to company wages, but with more autonomy. Nonetheless, given that the number of harvesters looking for *ancak* exceeds the number of *ancak* available, many workers must find jobs elsewhere. Being a 'farming manager' is another desirable option. It provides workers with a steady income, since they are paid monthly, plus they receive a 'premi' (premium) per kg of oil palm in each harvesting session. It also gives them a sense of 'control' (over their own work process) because they have to organise daily production activities, such as hiring and supervising workers. Lubis is an example:

> Lubis is 40 years old. His parents were landless. Lubis did not complete his secondary school and worked as a casual worker immediately upon leaving school. In the early 2000s, he became a bus driver on the Aceh-Langkat route. Since 2013, he has occupied a 'farming manager' position, replacing the previous 'farming manager' who had been involved in oil palm theft. As a 'farming manager', he has to take care of 25 hectares of oil palm for an 'absentee-capitalist farmer' in Medan. He is in charge of hiring workers for weeding, applying fertilisers and pesticides and harvesting. Lubis plays a role as a security guard as well, during the night, to prevent theft. For doing this job, he receives a regular monthly salary (Rp. 2 million) and a premi of Rp. 10 for each kilogram of oil palm harvested. He is extremely grateful to be working as a 'farming manager'. He swears he will never work for a plantation company given that they only 'extract our labour and do not give us any autonomy!'

However, the 'farming manager' positions are limited in the village. Many of the FFP must work for plantation companies. Togar, a 32-year-old man, is one of them:

> Togar's parents were landless. After completing his secondary school, he went to Riau, to work as a harvester for a plantation company. In the early 2010s, he came back to the village. Once, he said that 'the company is actually cruel, they only extract our sweat!' Nonetheless, given that the chances of working for an individual capitalist farmer and of occupying the position of a 'farming manager' are bleak, he has had little option but to sell his labour again to a plantation company. He works for PT. KRA, a modest oil palm plantation company. Togar's status is that of 'company worker', receiving neither regular monthly salary nor any pension rights. He only receives 'premi' for each kilogram of oil palm he harvests. Having a wife and three children, Togar must struggle everyday to meet the basic needs of his household. He would like someday to work for a bigger company (such as PT. RPL in the case of Agus above) who will offer him a regular salary and pension rights.

For both the 'proletariat-farmer' and FFP in *Timpang*, having a job in oil palm production, even though it may be the less desirable option (working for the company), is still considered better than having no job at all or working at paddy cultivation, which is the least desirable option in agriculture. Hence, the opposition to the oil palm companies is more about wages and working conditions than about the presence of the companies themselves. Most workers express their comfort at the advent of oil palm in *Timpang*, which has been introduced by the companies, given the stagnation in paddy cultivation that only offered low wages. This distinguishes these groups from the 'semi-proletariat farmers', who may be against the presence of the companies as their land may be jeopardised. The presence of both the state and the privately-owned companies has also complicated the political orientation of the workers. Those working for the company tend to underplay the worker's concerns at the individual oil palm fields while the latter generally overlook the worker's issues at the plantation companies. This shows that the class location of the classes of labour is more complex than is commonly assumed.

The complexity of class location in the two villages is summarised in Tables 5.3 and 5.4. In both villages, we can see three main agrarian class locations: capitalist farmer, PCP and classes of labour. The complex nature of each class location has also been shown. For capitalist farmers in *Njomplang*, we identify three different sub-groups, namely the 'typical capitalist farmer', 'politico-bureaucrat capitalist farmer' and 'professional-capitalist farmer'. Apart from capitalist farmers, there is also a group of 'landlord-capitalists'. We also find similar groups of capitalist farmers in *Timpang*. Different types of capitalist farmers have different perspectives on the production process. Their differences are also reproduced through family ties which, importantly, shape the nature of cooperation and competition among them. We have also seen different groups within the PCPs in the two villages. A 'substantial PCP' is characterised by owning land and having no relationship with patrons. This separates them from the 'formal PCP', who only controls land and is generally tied to a patron. The different positions within similar class locations can also be found within the classes of labour in both villages. The 'semi-proletariat farmer', 'proletariat-farmer' and FFP share a similar general class location but they occupy different positions in land, labour, work and output relations. As will be shown in the next section, an understanding of the varied positions within similar class locations is crucial to understanding the nature of class relations in both villages.

Class Relations in the Two Villages

It should be noted that our treatment of class location above is only a point of departure to depict the nature of agrarian classes in the two villages. As we have mentioned in the theoretical discussion (Chapter 1), class location in the two villages must be seen merely as class situation (Wood, 1982), where people share similar situations in the production relationship. Nonetheless, they may experience and handle their class situations differently. We are now looking at how the agrarian classes in the two villages have responded to their class situations over time.

Class Struggle in the Villages before 1965 and Its Legacies

As shown in Chapter 3, overt class struggle in the Indonesian countryside took place in the 1960s when the BTI and PKI were the vanguard organisations

Table 5.3 Class location in *Njomplang*, Central Java

Property Possession	*Land relation*	*Labour relation*	*Product relation*	*Means of Production (MoP) relation*	*Non-agricultural occupation*	*Class*
Neither owns nor controls any land	-	No hire in of labour Hires out labour throughout the year	No sale	Buying limited basic MoP (rice threshing tool)	Construction worker, casual labourer, petty self-employment	**FFP (classes of labour)**
Owns no land and controls (sharecrops) a tiny plot of land (0.1 ha–0.34 ha)	Sharecrops in and does not sharecrop out May lease-in, does not lease out	No hire in of labour ***at will*** Hires out labour year-round	Sells little output (a half of total produced) or does not sell	Buying limited basic MoP (rice threshing tool)	Construction worker, casual labourer, petty self-employment	**Proletariat-farmer (classes of labour)**
Owns a tiny plot of land (0.1 ha–0.34 ha) and controls (sharecrops) a tiny plot of land (less than 0.34 ha) or owns no land but controls (sharecrops) a little land (0.35 ha–0.84 ha)	Sharecrops in and does not sharecrop out land May lease-in and lease out land	Does not hire in labour ***at will*** Hires out labour throughout the year	Sells most of the output	Buys some basic MoP (rice threshing tool and water pump)	Construction worker, casual labour, petty self-employment, mason	**Semi-proletariat farmer (classes of labour)**

Owns a considerable piece of land (0.50 ha–0.99 ha) or owns no land but controls (sharecrops) a large plot of land (0.85 ha–1.80 ha)	May sharecrop in and does not sharecrop out land May lease-in and lease out land	May hire in seasonal labour ***at will*** May hire out seasonal or year-round labour ***at will***	Sells most of the output	Buys some basic MoP (rice threshing tool and water pump)	Mason, petty self-employment, casual labourer, village official (low-rank)	**Petty commodity producer (PCP)**
Owns a large amount of land (over 1 ha) or controls (fixed-rent) a vast amount of land (over 1.80 ha)	May lease-in or lease out land May sharecrop out a tiny portion of the total land and no sharecrop in land	Hires in year-round labour Does not hire out labour	Sells all of the output	Buys substantial MoP (land, tractor)	Professional (teacher, nurse, doctor); political leader (villagehead); bureaucrat (village higher official, civil servant); craftsman; substantial trade	**Capitalist farmer (the ruling class)**
Owns a large amount of land (over 1 ha)	Does not sharecrop in and sharecrops out land (most of the total land) May lease out but no lease in land	No hiring in labour Does not hire out labour	Sells all of the output	Buys substantial MoP (land, tractor)	Professional (teacher, nurse, doctor); political leader (village head); bureaucrat (village higher official, civil servant);	**Landlord-capitalist (the ruling class)**

Source: author classification from the fieldwork

Table 5.4 Class location in *Timpang*, North Sumatera

Property Possession	*Land relation*	*Labour relation*	*Product relation*	*MoP relation*	*Non-agricultural occupation*	*Class*
Neither owns nor controls any land	-	Does not hire in labour Hires out labour all year round	No sales	Buys basic MoP (fibre fruit picker pole, motorcycle for harvesting)	Casual labour, petty self-employment	**FFP (classes of labour)**
Owns no land and controls a small plot of land (less than 2 ha)	May lease/sharecrop in land and does not lease out or pawn out land	Does not hire in labour ***at will*** Hires out labour all year round	Sells all output	Buys basic MoP (fibre fruit picker pole, motorcycle for harvesting)	Casual labour, petty self-employment	**Proletariat Farmer (classes of labour)**
Owns or controls a small plot of land (less than 2 ha)	May lease/sharecrop in land or pawn out land	Does not hire in labour ***at will*** Hires out labour all year round	Sells all output	Buys basic MoP (fibre fruit picker pole, motorcycle for harvesting, small amount of land)	Casual labour, petty self-employment, craftsman	**Semi-Proletariat Farmer (classes of labour)**
Owns or controls a considerable piece of land (2 ha–3.99 ha)	May lease/sharecrop in land or pawn out land	May hire in seasonal labour ***at will*** May hire out labour seasonally or throughout the year ***at will***	Sells all output	Buys basic MoP (fibre fruit picker pole, motorcycle for harvesting, considerable amount of land)	Craftsman, petty self-employment, rice trader, village official (low-rank)	**PCP**

Owns or controls (via fixed-rent) a large piece of land (over 4 ha)	May lease/pawn in or lease/pawn out land	Hires in year-round labour Does not hire out labour	Sells all output	Buys substantial MoP (a large amount of land, mini-truck)	Professional (teacher, nurse, doctor); political leader (village head); bureaucrat (village higher official, civil servant); craftsman; substantial trader (oil palm and non-oil palm)	**Capitalist Farmer**

Source: author classification from the fieldwork

for the classes of labour. In *Njomplang*, the PKI was the biggest political party and 'almost all of the villagers were PKI supporters'. Only a few of them were members of the PNI, one of the main rivals of the PKI at the national level. Among these few, Joyo was the chairman of *Pemuda Marhaen* (the Youth organisation of PNI) in the village, while Guntur and Hadikusumo were members. Since the numbers and followers of the PNI and *Pemuda Marhaen* were so few, they had no regular meetings or activities. In contrast, the PKI and its affiliated organisations (Pemuda Rakyat, BTI, LEKRA) held regular meetings and cultural activities in *Njomplang*. 'The organisation was very strong', some informants revealed. Their meetings were part of the campaign to promote the PKI's program, including land redistribution. Speakers at the meetings often condemned the 'rich farmers' and the village officials for not being pro-poor. The village head at the time was Condronegoro, a member of the PNI and the grandson-in-law of Darsuki, the village headman before independence (see Appendix 1). To attract villagers, the PKI performed traditional theatrical performances of 'Human Wayang' and 'Ludruk'. The events were always filled with PKI supporters (also coming from other villages), although some of the attendees had often only followed the crowd (*ikut-ikutan*). Many villagers were attracted to the PKI events because PKI members were articulate in promoting their views. A worker who was a former member of *Pemuda Marhaen* (PNI) in *Njomplang* ambiguously complimented them: 'I admit that PKI members were smart, but they were too radical'.

When radical action as part of the so-called '*aksi sepihak*' (one-sided action) was taking place in other parts of Java in 1964–1965 (Chapter 3), *Njomplang* and Purworejo did not participate. Still, the capitalist farmers experienced serious threats from BTI members in the village. Hardjo, an 81-year-old man, one of the village officials at the time and the older brother of Hadikusumo (a typical capitalist farmer) recalls that if they refused to redistribute their land, 'in their meeting and campaigns, they (the PKI) threatened to kill us'. Class antagonism between capital and labour was rife, although there were no violent class-based conflicts in the village. It is clear that in this period, the classes of labour in the same 'class situation' shared similar responses in terms of their material position by overtly opposing the capitalist farmers and 'landlord-capitalists'. Here, we see 'class in the making' in *Njomplang*.

However, the failed coup in September 1965 provided a pretext for the mass murder of PKI members and supporters throughout the country (Chapter 3). During this 'Killing Season' (Robinson, 2018), however, there were no mass killings in *Njomplang*. The absence of 'one-sided action' may explain why this was the case in this village and the surrounding villages. However, more than half of villagers in the village were arrested by the military sub-district command (KORAMIL). Among the arrested, between 6 and 12 were sent to jail. Meanwhile, the rest went home, followed by the mandatory visit to KORAMIL every month ('compulsory report'/'*Wajib Lapor*'). Their identity cards were stamped with E.T (*Eks Tapol*/ex-political prisoner) to mark their involvement in or support for the PKI.

The fate of the former PKI figures in the village is unclear. According to some informants, one of them went back to *Njomplang* after had been released from prison due to his illness. He died and was buried in the village. None of the heirs of the PKI figures are living in *Njomplang* anymore. They seem to have left the village not long after 1965. As only the winners have continued to live in *Njomplang*, the New Order's narratives have been well-developed there. What is left about the PKI are only their allegedly vicious characteristics of 'atheist, cruel, traitorous and radical'. There is no memory of how the classes of labour under the PKI became strong against the capitalist farmers and 'landlord-capitalists'. This has signalled 'the un-making of the working class' in the village, and elsewhere in the country.

On the other hand, the power of the capitalist farmers and 'landlord-capitalists' in *Njomplang* has been strengthened since the founding of the New Order. After the massacre, at the national level, Suharto reformed all the farmers' unions into one state-sponsored body (HKTI) to ease the Green Revolution (Chapter 3). At the village level, POKTAN and GAPOKTAN were mere objects to receive training and counselling from government agents about modern techniques of rice production. The state assistance in the form of modern inputs, credits and farming toolkits were distributed through the Village Unit Cooperative (KUD), dominated by capitalist farmer-cum-village officials. Across the country, corruption and mismanagement were rampant in the operations of the KUD (see, for instance, Lucas, 2009). This was no exception in *Njomplang*. When, in the 1980s, the KUD in the village faced an acute repayment failure from its debtors, they were predominantly capitalist farmers and 'landlord-capitalists'. 'Most of the rich farmers did not pay their debt at the KUD', some villagers recalled.

Since the downfall of Suharto's regime, the KUD has lost its mandate to distribute state assistance to farmers. Recently, state support in the form of agricultural inputs (seeds) and production tools (tractors, water pumps) are channelled directly through the POKTAN and GAPOKTAN. In *Njomplang*, all the POKTANs are headed by capitalist farmers. Many PCPs and members of the classes of labour (semi-proletariat farmers and proletariat-farmers) are well-incorporated into the network of state patronage exercised by the GAPOKTAN through the leadership of capitalist farmers to receive state assistance. For example, in August 2018, the POKTAN received two tractors after making a political contract with a local legislative member from GOLKAR (political party).[8] They agreed to vote for him at the national election in 2019. One of the POKTAN's members, who is also a 'semi-proletariat farmer', justified this pragmatic move because 'it is better to vote for a legislative member who clearly benefits us than other candidates, who can only promise and we do not know much about them'.

Class relations in *Timpang*, North Sumatra, are quite different, given the specific history of the village. As discussed in Chapter 4, the first settlers only went to *Timpang* in the 1960s, where the inhabitants numbered only dozens. As a result, this village had neither strong well-organised classes of labour under the BTI and PKI nor the mass killings. However, in 'Bukit Perak' (Silver Hill), about six kilometres from *Timpang*, there was a private timber company (PT. PK, that now is PT. RPL, which produces oil palm) where the majority of the workers were members of SARBUPRI (the PKI organisation for plantation workers). At the company, SARBUPRI represented the workers to make sure the company was delivering all the workers' rights, and they negotiated with the management. SARBUPRI also campaigned for land redistribution.

One of the former workers at the company, who now lives in *Timpang*, praised SARBUPRI's performance in promoting workers' interests, although he did not join any labour unions at that time. At the time, workers were granted regular allowances for the household (monthly rice, weekly milk, puddings, sugar, cooking oil and cloth once in every three months), allowances for their children, good health care facilities and pension rights, since all of them were permanent employees (SKO). Another former plantation worker in Tanjungpura (about 60 kilometers from *Timpang*), who is now living in *Timpang*, also remembered how he received a monthly allowance for all of his ten children. He recalled that the 'workers, at the time, lived in luxury'. Although he was a member of KBKI (the PNI labour union), he also praised SARBUPRI for their role in 'defending labour interests'.

Everything changed after the 'killing season' in 1965. In 'Bukit Perak', Qodir, a former worker, recalled:

> Thousands of people were slaughtered and thrown into a cave at Bukit Perak (today, people call it PKI Hill). People from around Langkat and Aceh were brought there. Every Sunday and Wednesday evening, the hill was packed with people. At least five trucks jammed with PKI members were sent there. Before slaughtering them, the *Algojo* (executor) drank alcohol. Some of the victims asked permission to have an Islamic prayer (*Sholat*) performed before being killed. Some were granted permission, while others were not and were killed because the *Algojo* was already drunk.

Many of the *Algojo* were foremen at the companies. This pattern was also the case in Tanjung Pura and other places in North Sumatra, where thousands of corpses were thrown into the river Ular after having been executed. This has been documented in Joshua Oppenheimer's films: *The Act of Killing* and *The Look of Silence*. One former labourer at a company plantation near the Ular, who moved to *Timpang* in the 1970s, saw many of his colleagues being slaughtered at the riverside. He wailed as he described when the 'luxury of my life as a worker' was brought to an end by the mass killing.

While in *Njomplang* the mass killings practically erased the history of class struggle in the village, in Timpang, there was no such history to tell. Most villagers in *Timpang* have no memories of labour organisations and the struggle against the plantation companies in their neighbouring villages. Only a few people who worked at the company in the 1960s, including the informants above, have such experiences. However, since they were too old to work at the plantation companies in *Timpang*, their experiences have not been passed to the next generation of workers. It explains how the current workers at the companies in *Timpang* have few ideas on how to advance their grievances (see next section).

In contrast, the corporate capitalists have been facilitated by the state to occupy land in *Timpang* since the early 1980s (Chapter 4). Repressive measures against workers at the plantations also took place during Suharto's authoritarian regime. 'The luxury of the workers' in the form of regular allowances, even for their children, and the job security of permanent work were withdrawn. The companies have dominated class relations with their workers since then.

Regarding class relations within the group of 'non-corporate producers', the state assistance for rice farmers in *Timpang* was both too late and too little. As already discussed, modern input, such as seeds (IR 64), were only introduced in *Timpang* in the late 1980s, when general state support to rice cultivation had declined significantly. Meanwhile, the KUD in the now *Timpang* was operating in the now neighbouring village of Halban (see Chapter 4), which meant rice capitalist farmers in *Timpang* had only few avenues for rent-seeking.

Only after Suharto's power was broken and POKTAN and GAPOKTAN became the direct channels for state grants were capitalist farmers in *Timpang* able to engage in lucrative rent-seeking. At the time of the fieldwork, there were 15 POKTAN in the village. None of them, however, held frequent meetings. Some of them held only an annual meeting. All the POKTAN were headed by a capitalist farmer. The rampant rent-seeking activity was the misuse of tractor grants. Many chairmen charged farmers a fee for using the tractor owned by the POKTAN. As opposed to *Njomplang*, where the fees go to POKTAN's account, in *Timpang*, these go to the chairman's pocket.[9] The rent-seeking of POKTAN in *Timpang* has spread to the distribution of seeds. Some of POKTAN's chairmen have abused the subsidised sale of seeds by selling the seeds as rice and reaping some millions of rupiah. With all of these aberrations, it is no surprise that there is widespread apathy towards POKTAN in *Timpang* and, thus, no regular meetings are held. One 'proletariat-farmer' who is not a member of any POKTAN even states that 'joining POKTAN only makes other people (the chairmen) richer'.

Many farmers other than the group of capitalist farmers have condemned the rampant corruption in the POKTAN and GAPOKTAN in *Timpang*. However, most of the grievances have only been expressed as gossip to avoid overt violent conflict with the POKTAN chairmen. The oil palm boom since the 2000s has also diverted the attention of the villagers away from such malpractices. Recently, villagers involved in paddy cultivation have become a minority compared to those who engage in oil palm. At the same time, the POKTAN and GAPOKTAN remain biased toward paddy cultivation, although they have recently opened up for other crop farming. The POKTAN in *Timpang* is basically a farmers group for rice farmers, not oil palm farmers.

Similar to *Njomplang*, the POKTAN and GAPOKTAN in *Timpang* exercise state patronage over the capitalist farmers in paddy cultivation. Nevertheless, given that the number of rice farmers in *Timpang* is much smaller than oil palm farmers, the PCPs and members of the classes of labour are mostly not incorporated into this state patronage network under the capitalist farmers' leadership. This means that the state patronage over the oil palm farmers in *Timpang* is weaker than over the rice farmers in *Njomplang*.

Contemporary Class Relations in Njomplang and Timpang

The Exceptional 'Village Meeting' in Njomplang and Class Relations

A peculiar aspect of the class relations in *Njomplang* is the presence of a 'village meeting' (*rembug desa*), at which agricultural wages and working conditions are negotiated. The practice is an exception rather than a rule in Indonesia. It can be found in neighbouring villages and, in the past, such meetings could also be found in other parts of the district (Wiradi, (2009[1961]), although it is unclear whether such a practice continues today. In other regions of Java, however, the village meeting discussing agricultural issues is hardly found. To our knowledge, the contemporary literature on agrarian change in Java never mentions such a practice. The *rembug desa* might have its root as an assembly of landholding villagers (*kuli kenceng/kuli gogol*) in the colonial period. In some or many villages, this institution may have survived post-independence despite its formal absence in the structure of village government (Ben White, 2021, personal communication). In the neighbouring sub-districts of *Njomplang*, such *rembug desa* originated in the colonial era and survived post-independence (Wiradi, (2009[1961]: 145–190). In *Njomplang,* while our fieldwork indicates that the *rembug desa* was formed in 1979, it is likely a revival of a long-standing institution stretching back into the colonial period, as in other sub-districts, and it was only re-introduced after the inception of a new rice seed, IR-64, in 1979.

Previously, the farmers had planted PB-5 and Pelita, which had a long paddy stalk and required an *ani-ani* (a hand-held knife) to harvest it. With the long varieties, the seeding process was done by *sambatan* (i.e. labour exchange). Labour exchange was still practiced by some farmers for land preparation (hoeing and ploughing). The introduction of IR-64 led to the replacement of *sambatan* practices, being replaced by wage labour (particularly contracted by task) (Chapter 6). Labour exchange in land preparation was also replaced by contract by task (tractors were only introduced in 1982). When all the agricultural tasks had been assigned to wage labour, there was a need to reorganise the way wages and working conditions were stipulated. The 'village meeting' (*rembug desa*) was designed to cater to this new dynamic.

All adult villagers are invited to the village meeting. The sub-district head was also invited to witness the meeting. The village head played the role of intermediary between the workers and the capitalist farmers. The decision-making mechanism was based on consensus (*musyawarah*), not voting. This was a part of the New Order's ideology: to preserve stability and order by discounting any possibility of social unrest and conflict in rural areas, a policy similar to corporatist industrial relations being used to tame urban unrest (Hadiz, 1997). In this rather manipulative setup, the meeting results during the Suharto period seemed predictable. Since the downfall of Suharto, the common villagers (classes of labour) have been freer to express their views, although the decision-making mechanism of the *musyawarah* has made it problematic for them, since their voices have not been seriously heard.

This is the context in which we are now reviewing the village meeting in 2016. It was held on Wednesday, 2nd of March. The village hall was packed with hundreds of villagers; many more stood outside. The meeting had been proposed by the tractor drivers[10] (members of the classes of labour and PCPs) who demanded the adjustment of tractor service fees. Fuel prices had soared by up to 36 percent[11] in 2014 and the tractor drivers were insisting on a bigger share of the total earnings from the tractor owners. They generally received 35 percent of the earnings from tractor services, after deductions for fuel costs, while the tractor owners (capitalist farmers) received 65 percent.[12] However, the tractor owners had told their drivers 'if you want higher returns, just ask for higher fees for tractor services'. The capitalist farmers' strategy, to pit labourers against each other, seemed to have worked. The village meeting was held in response to the driver's grievances.

Karto, the village head-cum-capitalist farmer, opened the meeting. From the outset, he emphasised that 'I cannot decide in this meeting, I am only a witness'. The villagers well understood this act. A 'politico-bureaucrat capitalist farmer' like Karto was trying to play safe in front of the villagers. He could not lose his popularity by taking sides too strongly for the capitalist interest in the village, since he was planning to hold on to his position in the next local election. Cokro, the 'typical capitalist farmer' first raised his hand to propose an increase from Rp. 120 thousand per *iring* (1/6 hectare) to Rp. 150 thousand. His proposal was supported by one tractor owner and Salim, a 'formal PCP', who was a driver for another tractor owner.

The classes of labour in the hall were soon shouting 'that is too expensive!' Ramdhan, another 'formal PCP' but not a tractor driver, even walked in front of the stage, challenging Cokro to write down his baseless calculations. Ramdhan proposed an increase to Rp. 140 thousands per *iring*, of which Rp. 10 thousand belonged exclusively to the driver (before any deductions for fuel costs). Cokro turned down the challenge and kept insisting on his proposal. He said: 'my tractors were not going to the field if the fee was not Rp. 150 thousand per *iring*'. The hall was loud with the grumbling of the attendees. Salim, who wanted to support Cokro, was prevented from doing so by his boss, the tractor owner. His boss seemed to withdraw support for Cokro's proposal leading to wide disappointment in the hall. Karto, as the moderator, was passive, saying: 'So, what is it to be?' Many attendees eventually opposed Cokro's proposal and welcomed the suggestion of an increase to Rp. 140 thousand. Later, it turned out that Cokro kept his own tariff for his two tractors, ignoring the decision at the meeting. While most of the villagers, mainly from the classes of labour, condemned his arrogant move, Cokro did not care as only a few villagers used the services of his tractors. The village officials did nothing about Cokro's behaviour. However, to respond to Cokro's sabotage, Karto bought two tractors that same year to anticipate the lack of tractors during the planting season. He was well aware that his inability to take a firm stance during the meeting had to be compensated by a heroic gesture to save his popularity.

The raise in the tractor tariff was not easily forgotten by the classes of labour, who bore the increased production cost. Tarmi, a 'proletariat-farmer' and a female planting worker, raised her hand to urge that 'if the tractor tariff was to be increased, so must the planting fees!' She demanded an increase from Rp. 100 thousand per *iring* to Rp. 120 thousand, plus free lunch. The proposal was well-supported by other planting workers (all of them were female). Not only did the provision of lunch by landowners save the time of planting workers by way of them not having to cook in the morning, but it also indicated the respect the landowners held towards them (*Nguwongke liyan*/to humanise other people). The provision of lunch that had been abolished at the 2014 meeting was tried to be brought again in 2016, since it was still common practice in the neighbouring villages. Cokro, however, did not accept this proposal. He argued that such a wage plus lunch was too high. He agreed to Rp. 120 thousand fees but without lunch. Mantili, a 'landlord-capitalist' fully supported Cokro's proposal. In fact, Mantili was the one who had taken the initiative to dismantle free lunches for planting workers two years earlier.[13] Sinah, another planting labourer, replied: 'that offer was not enough'. She compared it to the tariff in the neighbouring villages that has reached Rp. 150 thousand plus free lunch! Karto, again, played safe: 'So, how is this?' The fact that many of his relatives were members of the classes of labour did not make him take the side of the worker. The floor barely responded to Karto's question. Only a few planting workers expressed their view, along with some non-planting workers. The meeting eventually agreed to accept Cokro's proposal, despite the dissatisfaction of the planting workers. One of them could not hide her rage: 'The rich only care about what pleases them. Even though labourers like us proposed our views, we were not taken seriously. Only the proposal from the employer (*juragan*) matters'. With the rise in tractor fees being accepted but the demand of planting workers being rejected, Tarmi concluded, 'it was too obvious (*nyolok moto*) that the rich only want to be richer'.

Tarmi's insistence on an increase in the planting tariff led to the demand for levelling up other agricultural tasks' fees. Noto, a proletariat-farmer who is also a seeding worker, walked to the front stage with confidence and threatened that 'if the wage for seeding does not rise, the increase of tractor fees must be cancelled!' His rather bold move was precipitated by the fact that none of his colleagues (seeding workers) dared to speak of their interests. Noto proposed an increase from Rp. 50 thousand per *iring* to Rp. 70 thousand without the provision of lunch, or Rp. 60 thousand plus lunch. Again, this demand was only to follow the common practice in the neighbouring villages. However, only a few attendees in the hall supported this proposal. Even Noto's seeding worker colleagues were silent when asked about their opinion, not to mention other classes of labour who were not seeding workers. By contrast, Cokro, who represented the capitalists' interests, turned down that demand because 'it was too high'. In the end, the 'musyawarah' decided that the tariff for seeding was Rp. 60 thousand per *iring* without lunch. Noto was disappointed, not only with the result, but with the fact that his own colleague workers did not openly support him when 'little people (*wong cilik*) like us are being pressed over and over again'.

The debate continued on the daily wage for weeding. Weeding is the only main agricultural task that is organised with daily wage labour instead of contract by task (see the next chapter). The working hour is divided into two sessions: a morning session from 6.30 a.m. to 9.30 a.m. and an afternoon session from 12.30 p.m. to 3.30 p.m. Each session is called 'one go', and a worker who completes two sessions in a day has done 'two go' or simply 'daily labour'. The weeding workers are all female and they are mostly the same people who carry out the planting tasks. They insisted that the tariff should be raised from Rp. 12 thousand to Rp. 17.5 thousand for males, and Rp. 11 thousand to Rp. 16.5 thousand for female workers for 'one go'. It should be noted that they expressed their demand for daily wages for males, while female wages were then adjusted accordingly (lower than male wages by about 8 percent). In fact, these weeding workers did not urge equal pay between male and female workers in the first place. Therefore, the daily wage labour refers to male workers. The demand from workers was basically to catch up with the practice in the neighbouring villages. One labourer mentioned that the wage in those villages was already Rp. 20–25 thousand for 'one go'. Nevertheless, Mantili, Joyo's wife (the 'landlord capitalist') was not concerned about it and only agreed to pay Rp. 15 thousand. She even threatened labourers in the hall: 'if you do not want it, you do not need to sell your labour (*mburuh*)'. Prawiro supported Mantili's proposal. Both of them were indeed well-known by the labourers as the fussiest person as far as wages are concerned. As in the debate about planting fees, however, many weeding workers were only silent when asked about their response after capitalist farmers like Mantili made their offer. Karto, the moderator, could easily interpret the silence as an agreement to the capitalists' proposal. The wage for weeding was set at Rp. 15 thousand for males and Rp. 14 thousand for female workers for 'one go'.

Other agricultural tasks such as applying fertilisers and herbicides were also increased to catch up with the aforementioned tasks, as shown in Table 5.5 However, the increase in the wages for each agricultural task was lower than the 36 percent rise in the price of oil.

The results of the village meeting in 2016 show how the capitalist farmers successfully rejected the classes of labour's proposals while advancing theirs. We see the very active and direct action of the typical capitalist farmers (Cokro) and the landlord-capitalists (Mantili) in representing their class interests, while the 'politico-bureaucrat capitalist' (Karto) was less straightforward

Table 5.5 The wages for agricultural tasks in *Njomplang*, Central Java

Agricultural tasks per iring *(except weeding)*	*Wages*	
	2014	*2016*
Tractor services	120	140
Planting	100	120
Sowing	50	60
Serving planters (*tempah*)	20	25
Applying fertilisers by 'putting them in the holes'	35	40
Applying fertilisers by 'scattering' them	-	20
Applying herbicide	15	20
Spreading straw	40	50
Daily male labour (weeding)	24	30
Daily female labour (weeding)	22	28

Source: *Njomplang*'s Village Meeting in 2014 and 2016

in doing so because of his official position, and the 'professional-capitalist' chose to say nothing. At this point, the silence of the majority of the classes of labour at the meeting, although no intimidation or violence threats were involved, needs an explanation. There was a widespread feeling among the classes of labour that 'our voices as merely little people would not be heard'. The apathy towards the consensus ('*musyawarah*') instead of voting may indeed explain some elements of it. However, this does not explain why those who did dare to speak at the meeting were only 'proletariat-farmers' and 'fully-fledge proletariats' while the members of the 'semi-proletariat farmers' and PCPs were largely silent.

There was indeed a voice from the PCPs in the debate about the tractor fees. However, they were exceptions to the rule. The patrons of Salim and Ramdhan were not living in the village ('absentee landlord-capitalists'). This absence provided the space for Salim and Ramdhan to express their aspirations during the meeting. However, most of the other PCPs in *Njomplang* were 'formal PCPs' (like Adnan), who were tied to 'present landlord-capitalists' who resided in the village. Meanwhile, the 'substantial PCPs' (such as Sutarno) only wished to 'wait and see', and thus they kept silent. Even the 'semi-proletariat farmers' could not show their open support for the interests of the classes of labour, since they were tied to their patrons via sharecropping. Moreover, unlike either the 'proletariat-farmers' or the FFP, the 'semi-proletariat farmers' had 'something to lose' given their larger land control.

In contrast, the 'proletariat-farmers', like Tarmi, were actively vocal at the meeting because they had nothing to lose, given their tiny land control (less than 0.35 ha), even though their patrons were present in the village. The fact that only a few of them were brave enough to advance their interests in the meeting as related to the general de-politicisation policy exercised under the

New Order, and its legacy that entangled political struggle in many sectors, such as the industrial context (Hadiz, 2002).

The 'village meeting' in 2016 also disputed the decision of the previous meeting (2014) about the bonus in harvesting. In *Njomplang*, there was the so-called '*Ngurup*' (exchange), where the harvesters exchanged their share from harvesting (*bawon*) in the form of dry paddy stalks with drinks, usually a traditional drink (*dawet*), offered by local petty traders. This practice dates back to the Sukarno period. The practice, however, had changed in the early 2000s, when traders from outside the village (some of them even from other towns) offered their commodities, only this time the trade was not confined only to drink but also to food (snacks and lunch) and daily household needs such as sugar, onions, garlic and other foodstuffs. The harvesters welcomed such an abundant offer, especially given that after harvesting they are 'exhausted, thirsty and hungry', as one harvester recalls. In the early 2000s, they improvised by not exchanging their share from harvesting (*bawon*), but they took dry paddy stalks that had not been calculated as their share. In other words, they exchanged capitalist farmers' dry paddy stalks with the goods as they pleased. Some of them even ordered motorcycle tyres from the traders. One of the harvesters recalls how fortunate she was at the time, because for a small piece of harvested land (two *iring*, which equals to 0.32 ha), she and one of her harvesting partners could exchange 30 to 40 kg of dry paddy stalks with the traders. From this, we may calculate that for every hectare of harvested land, there were about 180 to 260 kg of landowner's dry paddy stalks that were taken away by the harvesters. Capitalist farmers even had to pay for the harvesters' *bawon*.

With such significant harm to the yield, capitalist farmers started to ban the practice of 'Ngurup'. At the village meeting in 2014, they succeeded in formally prohibiting the exchange. Nonetheless, the labourers did not easily give up their interest. In return for the abolition of 'Ngurup', they demanded that the landowners must provide lunch and drinks for the harvesters. This was agreed upon in the 2014 meeting. However, it turned out that none of capitalist farmers abided by the regulation. Facing this rule's violation, the classes of labour confidently protested in the 2016 'village meeting'. Tarmi asked, 'Why did no-one provide us with lunch and drinks for harvesting?' Mantili, the 'fussiest person' in the village, replied coldly, 'Who said that?' Not wanting to be undermined, Tarmi quickly answered, 'From the previous agreement in our previous meeting'. However, Mantili coldly replied again, 'Fine, we will send drinks'. During the meeting, again, the majority of classes of labour were silent, although capitalist farmers such as Mantili had clearly violated the previous agreement and one-sidedly changed the stipulation by erasing the provision of lunch in her promise. In fact, Mantili's promise and that of the other capitalist farmers in *Njomplang* were unfulfilled after the meeting. Responding this, one harvester condemned: 'That is outrageous!' Another harvester could not stand anymore: 'They (employers/capitalist farmers) are too stingy and too parsimonious!'

The open negotiation at the *rembug desa* highlights the important moment when the daily class relations in the village come to the surface and represents a crucial conjuncture when class contradictions are experienced, raising the class consciousness of agrarian classes. In *Njomplang*, daily class relations often take form more subtly. Classes of labour mostly gossip about capitalist farmers and 'landlord-capitalists' behind their backs to channel their grievances, including their loss at the 'village meeting'. They condemned the 'stingy employers (*Juragan*)' like Mantili and Cokro. Among the exceptions was Darsam (see Chapter 7), a modest 'typical capitalist farmer' who was known as a generous employer. Another way of protesting was through holding a boycott. The workers put the 'stingy employers' on a waiting list and only sold their labour to them when they had completed the planting for their 'top priority list' of 'generous employers'. This protest may have disturbed the production cycle of rice cultivation and endangered production. A boycott was also used as a way of giving back the right to cultivate a piece of land to the landowners because the share was too small (see Chapter 6). The threat to boycott production also took place against the plans of the capitalist farmers to introduce combine harvester machines and planting machines.

From the point of view of the classes of labour, their resistance was less organised collectively than through individual initiatives. This, however, does not mean that the classes of labour did not cooperate or coordinate at all. Debating at the village meeting, boycotting planting and sharecropping while threatening the application of machinery, required to some extent cooperation and coordination among the members of the classes of labour. This is known in the literature as 'everyday resistance' (Scott, 1989) or 'subtle resistance and negotiations' (Pincus, 1996). This is in contrast to the more collectively overt and well-organised class struggle that took place in the village in the 1960s. While its cumulative effect on class relations may not be overlooked, we may not need to glorify such disorganised struggles.

Class Relations and the Variation between Timpang's Central and Peripheral Hamlets

The first important feature that is absent in *Timpang* is the village meeting. This means there has been no open debate between the capitalist farmers and classes of labour in *Timpang* over agricultural wages and working conditions. Another pivotal difference is the varied nature of the class structure and labour market within the village. There are hamlets located around the main national highway from Medan to Banda Aceh. The terrain is much less hilly, with a few extreme ravines that are planted with oil palm. With the development of the village (see Chapter 4), these central hamlets have a much higher population than their counterpart hamlets in the periphery (about four times higher). Many villagers living in these hamlets are attracted to the easier access to public services and the market. They do not care so much that land is already scarce and expensive, and that landlessness is widespread in these central hamlets. Non-farming activities, such as trades and services, are more developed here.

In contrast, the peripheral hamlets are located about 3–7 km from the central hamlets, far from the highway. In this remote area, the terrain is more hilly with many extreme ravines. Population numbers are very low, and people have limited access to public services (one hamlet even has no electricity). However, the villagers remain here because most have their own oil palm fields. Land is some 30 percent cheaper and landlessness is less widespread than in the central hamlets. Non-farming activities, such as trades and services, are negligible here. It should be noted that the central hamlets, however, are much larger, both in terms of population and total land area, than the peripheral hamlets.

In the central hamlets the wage for harvesting oil palm is about Rp. 150/kg on average. The villagers call the payment for harvesting the 'premi' system. This means, for every kilogram of oil palm that is harvested, the harvester receives Rp. 150. If, on average, a worker can harvest a ton of oil palm a day, he receives Rp. 150 thousand/day. In practice, only a few workers have many *ancak* harvests almost every day (see previous section). Many of them harvest less than four days a week because they hold fewer than eight *ancak*. In the peripheral hamlets, the wage for harvesting is much higher, around Rp. 200/kg on average, even though there are a few capitalist farmers who still pay their harvesters through the daily wage labour system, not by 'premi'. In both types of hamlets, lunch for the harvesters much depends on the generosity of the capitalist farmers. The oil palm workers employed by individual capitalist farmers in *Timpang* have no restrictions on working in any hamlets. One might expect that workers from the central hamlets would have flooded into the peripheral hamlets in search of better wages. However, such an opportunity is small given the limited harvested area in the peripheral hamlets and the availability of their own labourers. Another crucial caveat to working in the peripheral hamlets is harvesting in the extreme ravines which involves a much higher risk of work-related accidents. One harvester noted how he gave up his *ancak* in the peripheral hamlets due to a work-related accident he suffered. As a result, there are only a few workers from the central hamlets working there.

With this hampered mobility and the lack of available land in the central hamlets, labourers in this area are forced to accept lower wages than their compatriots in the peripheral hamlets. This does not necessarily mean that protests there are virtually non-existent. Harvesters for Sofian's oil palm field, led by Nardi, a 'semi-proletariat farmer', once urged Sofian (a former village head) to increase their 'premi' from Rp. 125/kg to Rp. 150/kg. The workers were just trying to catch up with the standard wage of Rp. 150/kg in the hamlets. However, Sofian refused this demand. The next day, Nardi and his fellow harvesters were surprised when their places had been replaced by new harvesters, recruited by Sofian. Nardi and his friends condemned both Sofian and the workers who had replaced them. For the new workers, it was the only opportunity they would have to acquire more *ancak*, and, thus, a more steady income.

Sofian is notorious for his lack of generosity. On another occasion, his workers who cut off the midribs of the oil palm demanded a wage increase from Rp. 1500/midrib to Rp. 2000/midrib. Sofian again turned down the demand and made his workers leave their jobs, only to be replaced by their own fellow workers in the same hamlet. Kelik, a 'semi-proletariat farmer' who was the leader of the protest workers, recalled that 'we were deeply hurt because our own friends took over our positions'. With the recurrent failure in increasing their wages, workers in the 'central hamlets' have been cynical about their power. They generally view that the 'labourers here (the central hamlets) cannot solidly unite'.

However, this situation may also depend on the capitalist farmers. There was a case where an absentee-capitalist farmer in the central hamlets had to accommodate the harvesters' demands. Tobi, a young capitalist who lives in Medan, inherited 25 hectares of oil palm in *Timpang*. His father was among the key figures in North Sumatra's Chamber of Commerce and Industry Indonesia (KADIN). To take care of his land, Tobi hired in a local 'farming manager'-cum-foreman (Lubis). There were eight harvesters with a premi of Rp. 100/kg working for him. However, his harvesters, one of whom was Kelik, insisted on raising the premi to Rp. 150/kg. Tobi replied, in his Batak style: 'I am unable to agree to such a raise'. However, Tobi was unable to replace his workers, unlike Sofian. He was not part of the village and his network of workers in *Timpang* was limited. He eventually compromised by increasing the premi to Rp. 125/kg, half of what the workers had demanded. He also agreed to pay Rp. 200/kg at some extreme locations where it was more dangerous and exhausting for the harvesters to work. It seems that an absentee-capitalist farmer such as Tobi, without any family connection in the village, is more vulnerable than a present capitalist farmer—like Sofian. However, absentee-capitalist farmers who employ members of their own family as farming managers, such as Bungaran, are able to negotiate with their workers. Once, Bungaran's weeding workers, mostly female, urged him to increase their daily wage to more than Rp. 45 thousand. Bungaran told them persuasively: 'Come on please, the wage is there every day for you, this is not only once every three days'. The workers only accepted this and returned to work after hearing his reply.

With the exception of absentee-capitalist farmers without family connections in *Timpang*, capitalist farmers in the central hamlets are in a good bargaining position compared to the classes of labour. Here, workers openly envy their compatriot classes of labour in the peripheral hamlets who are more united in demanding wage rises. This power, however, is only made possible because many harvesters in the peripheral hamlets are PCPs who own considerable amounts of land. They also work for companies as daily wage labourers, which grants them more flexibility when arranging their time and reduces their need to sell their labour to individual capitalist farmers. However, their power is checked by the harvesters from the central hamlets. On one occasion, harvesters in the peripheral hamlets demanded an increase of premi from Rp. 200/kg to Rp. 250/kg. The capitalist farmers responded to this by inviting in workers from the central' hamlets who were happy enough to be paid Rp. 200/kg, which is already higher than the wages in their hamlets.

When the premi system is not applied and capitalist farmers pay the harvesters through the daily wage system, the dynamics of class relations are quite different. Damsik, a 'typical capitalist farmer' in the peripheral hamlets, owns ten hectares of oil palm. He is reluctant to pay Rp. 200/kg premi, which he considers too expensive, and offers a daily wage payment (Rp. 100 thousand/day) that he thinks would reduce labour costs. The workers accept it because they know they can play with it. For the workers, harvesting that can be completed in one day, for instance, is delayed for up to at least three days. The workers spend their time smoking, hanging around and chatting with each other, and taking a long break in the middle of the field. One of the workers, from a PCP background, proudly declares that: 'We are working as we please, outsmarting Damsik'. Their innocent justification for their action is based on their view regarding the 'stinginess' of Damsik. He never provides drinks, not to mention lunch. He is also notorious for being cunning by asking workers to perform tasks they are not supposed to.

For both central and peripheral hamlets, the PCPs in *Timpang* are more inclined to the interest of labour than capital. The PCPs in *Timpang* are mostly substantial PCPs, owning their own land; thus, they have no patron-client relationships with capitalist farmers. Moreover, since they are eager to sell their labour all year round *at will* to meet their beyond subsistence aspirations, they identify themselves as part of the classes of labour.

While harvesting is the most important agricultural task in oil palm production and it is fully dominated by male workers, female workers play a crucial role in weeding (cutting away the grass and weeds) and, sometimes, applying herbicides. Their daily wage, however, is lower by about 20 percent compared to the men. For weeding, working for capitalist farmers, female workers receive Rp. 45 thousand/day, while men receive Rp. 55 thousand/day. One of the female workers from a semi-proletariat background complained: 'We simply have no idea why our wage is lower than the men's while, in fact, our work is more diligent and tidier'. For the same job, the companies offer Rp. 62 thousand/day, the same for both male and female workers, with the status of daily casual labour. In this case, the female workers are more eager to work for the companies than individual capitalist farmers. However, the opportunities are limited.

The struggle between the capitalist farmers and the classes of labour plus the PCPs also includes disputes over working conditions. The first issue they have concerns autonomy and flexibility when completing agricultural tasks. Most harvesters in *Timpang* do not like to be ordered around by the capitalist farmers. They are prepared to leave capitalist farmers who supervise them too closely. For the workers, this supervision not only threatens their autonomy but also signals a level of distrust to them. Another crucial issue relates to the provision of services to workers. Workers appreciate the 'generous capitalist farmers' who provide them with drinks, snacks and even lunch. Bungaran is seen as one of these generous bosses. He provides drinks and snacks and, since 2014, has provided lunch. By contrast, Sofian is a 'stingy' boss who provides none of this. The workers tend to complain about the 'stingy boss' both in the fields and at home. Here, as in *Njomplang*, complaining about capitalist farmers is the means whereby the workers protest their losses in their wage negotiations.

Along with complaining, the workers are also involved in pilfering. However, not all pilfering is a form of protest. There is the pilfering of oil palm, where the thieves steal any oil palm available without considering the owners (against both companies and individual farmers, regardless of their class). Mostly it is youths who are stealing to buy fun (alcohol, drugs, and cigarettes). Pilfering that may be considered to be a form of protest is mostly conducted by women from the classes of labour. They mostly take *brondolan* (the scattered oil palm kernels which fall from the fruit bunches), not the bunches of oil palm as the youths do, from the companies and individual capitalist farmers. This practice is quite widespread in *Timpang*. If women workers come to work carrying a sack, they are mostly looking for *brondolan*.

While this is illegal, they continue doing it for their survival. One of the semi-proletariat farmers, 53-year-old Suri, continues to look for *brondolan* because she needs the money for her daughters at school. She can collect 10 kg of it per day, which she can sell for Rp. 130 thousand. This is similar to a day's wages for a harvester. Many other women looking for *brondolan* are members of the FFP and target the companies. Once, one was caught collecting *brondolan* and was fined Rp. 5 million. The villagers accept it if the victim of pilfering is the company. However, when the thieves target an individual's oil palm field, the villagers declare 'no peaceful resolution' for the thieves, although the culprits are from poor households and the victims are rich landowners.

Looking for *brondolan* on the companies' plantations is a response of the local classes of labour (female) who have not been absorbed into company workforces. For those who work for the companies, they have a different response. Workers at the companies are generally passive. No progressive labour unions operate here. Only the New Order's state-sponsored labour union the SPSI has been established in big companies. Nevertheless, there was a large workers' protest against PT. RPL in 2017. The dispute was precipitated by the promise of the company in 2016 that they would provide a bonus of double the monthly salary for each worker if the oil palm production reached two thousand tonnes in that year. However, the company failed to grant the bonus, without giving any reason. Hundreds of company workers conducted a protest. The company responded by ignoring them. The SPSI stepped in, offering to assist the workers. This yellow labour union and rent-seeking organisation asked for fees of Rp. 300 thousand per worker if they succeeded in delivering the bonus to the workers. However, after the SPSI had met the management of the company, they revoked their promise to help the workers. Many workers were suspicious of the SPSI, claiming that they 'had been bought' by the management.

The workers, in fact, did almost nothing to channel their dissatisfaction toward the company. A recurrent complaint the workers have is about the higher risk of harvesting oil palm. Recently, the company increased the target per harvester to about 450 kg/day, from only 300 kg/day in 2010. The drastic rise of the target means the worker must work more quickly. With such pressure, work accidents have increased. Some workers have been horribly injured after oil palm bunches fell onto them, while others have died due to terrible head wounds. The workers have responded by quitting their jobs because they realise that the risk of having an accident is increasing.

Another problem is that the pension rights, which have been one of the main attractions in joining a company, have not been properly delivered. Workers in their sixties have difficulty processing their pensions. 'The company makes it difficult for us to get our pension', one worker stated. The company offers the excuse that these workers are still able to work. However, the workers know that such an excuse is the only way the company can avoid paying out of the pension fund. As the workers get older, they are expected to quit of their own accord, leaving the company free from having to pay any pension. Again, the workers' response is neither to protest nor go on strike. Many of them choose to quit from the company and look for jobs or *ancak* at individual plantations, ones that are already packed with so many harvesters. This, by extension, has strengthened the bargaining power of the capitalist farmers in the village.

As in *Njomplang*, class-based disputes over agricultural wages and working conditions in *Timpang* largely take the form of negotiations, boycotts, 'slowing down the work', complaints and pilfering. They had no chance to encounter and witness the strong labour-farmer fronts like the BTI in the 1960s. In the current *Timpang*, few workers know how to organise collectively and to solve their grievances with the capitalist farmers. They cannot rely on the farmers group (POKTAN), which is dominated by capitalist farmers, and which spends most of its time accumulating state assistance. For the workers at the companies, they only know about the 'yellow labour union', the SPSI, while they know nothing about the power of the SARBUPRI in the 1960s. Although they may one day be involved in a large protest, without experience and knowledge to organise themselves collectively, their spontaneous struggle may only end up with them complaining or quitting their jobs.

Conclusion

This chapter has illustrated the class dynamics of agrarian change in two different villages in Java and Sumatra by looking at both the economic aspects of class (class location) and the sociological dimensions of class (class relations). We have identified three different agrarian class locations in the two villages: capitalist farmers (with 'landlord-capitalists' in the case of *Njomplang*), PCPs and classes of labour. The size of the capitalist farmer class is the smallest, while the classes of labour constitute the largest grouping. The proportion of PCPs who face a contradictory unity of class place is larger than the capitalist farmer class but smaller than the classes of labour. Class composition in *Njomplang* is more skewed than in *Timpang*. In the last two and half decades in *Njomplang*, there has been an increase in the size of the PCP and its total landholding that may signal an arrested class polarisation in the village. The unavailability of data for the previous decades prevents us from looking at the trajectory in *Timpang*. We have also looked closely into the nature of each agrarian class location to sufficiently grasp their internal differences. Understanding this complexity is crucial if one wishes to understand their different patterns of involvement in production, and the impact on class relations. In the past, this has been overlooked by the literature of agrarian change, both in Indonesia and elsewhere.

Class location is merely a 'class situation' (Wood, 1982) through which people share similar positions in the production relationship. Sharing similar class situations, however, may not automatically unite a response, especially given the varied positions within similar class situations. We have shown that in *Njomplang*, there are several groups within the agrarian ruling class. For capitalist farmers, there are 'typical capitalist farmers', 'politico-bureaucrat capitalist farmers' and 'professional-capitalist farmers'. Apart from capitalist farmers, there are also 'landlord-capitalists' (both present and absentee). Similar types are found in *Timpang*, although here, the 'landlord-capitalists' are negligible, given the limited practice of sharecropping and land-leasing in the village. The 'varied positions within similar class situations' prominently shape different attitudes by classes when promoting their class interests. It has been shown that certain capitalist farmers ('politico-bureaucrat capitalist farmer') are less obvious when advancing their class interests, given the consideration they give to keeping their village official positions, while 'typical capitalist farmers' and 'landlord-capitalists' (in *Njomplang*'s case) are more antagonistic towards the classes of labour. The 'varied positions within similar class situations' of the agrarian ruling class is also crucially reproduced through family ties, which shape their competitive nature, particularly in occupying village positions of official power.

A similar situation is faced by PCPs. Most PCPs in *Njomplang* ('formal PCPs') are more inclined to entertain the interests of the 'landlord-capitalist' because they depend on the latter for their land control via sharecropping. In *Timpang*, most PCPs share their interests with labour, not only because they have no patron-client relationship with 'landlord-capitalist' ('substantial PCPs'), but also due to their *will* to dispose of their labour all year round to meet beyond subsistence aspirations. Some of them even manage to transform themselves into capitalist farmers, while others have become members of the classes of labour. Contrary to the neo-populist view which explains the willingness of the PCPs to work harder mainly because the shift in the household demography, particularly when there are more 'mouths that need to be fed' (van der Ploeg, 2013: 33), we have shown that the eagerness of the PCPs to sell their labour all year round despite having met their 'simple reproduction' needs indicates the PCPs' response to the accumulation dynamics in their place. It is doubtless that they try to follow the line of capitalist farmers.

With such contradictory class locations, the class tendency of PCPs depends on specific historical conjunctures that have been mentioned in the literature (Harris-White, 2012).

The classes of labour also illustrate the importance of having 'varied positions within similar class situations'. In *Njomplang*, where 'semi-proletariat farmers' require land control, either to complement their small land-holding or to substitute their class reproduction, they are generally in a patron-client relationship with 'landlord-capitalist'. In this case, for the 'semi-proletariat farmers' in *Njomplang*, it is structurally more difficult for them to share interests with other members of the classes of labour: 'proletariat-farmers' and the FFP. In contrast, since most 'semi-proletariat farmer' in *Timpang* own their land and have no clientelistic relationship with 'landlord-capitalist', they are more inclined to share interests with the classes of labour.

This nuanced account of class locations is indispensable for our understanding of class relations in the two villages. The struggle of the classes of labour in *Njomplang* and *Timpang* is similar, with the crucial exception of the absence of open debate over agricultural wages and working conditions using a specific institutionalised mechanism (the 'village meeting'). Our study fills the gap in the studies of agrarian change in Java which significantly has overlooked the way in which agricultural wages are adjusted and how class relations between capitalist farmers and classes of labour shape the wage rates. This also applies to the literature of agrarian change in oil palm which hardly pays attention to the wage negotiations. In *Timpang*, the chances of an overt class struggle are hampered by the variations in class locations and the labour market within the village, which prevent the effective consolidation of the classes of labour. Moreover, *Timpang* has no institutionalised space for collective bargaining in the form of a 'village meeting', as *Njomplang* does. Thus, while in *Timpang*, there is no patron-client relationship between the agrarian ruling class (particularly 'landlord-capitalists') and the classes of labour (plus PCPs), the collective action of the classes of labour has hardly been organised. On the other hand, *Njomplang*'s case may represent a wasted opportunity for overt class struggle. The skewed class composition and the 'village meeting' in *Njomplang* should have paved the way for a collective struggle between the capitalist farmers and the classes of labour. However, the patron-client relationship has effectively tamed the class struggle, since many 'semi-proletariat farmers' and PCPs are tied up in the hands of the 'landlord-capitalists'. As for the 'proletariat-farmers' and FFP, they have neither the organisational capability nor the experience to collectively organise themselves.

Class situation has also been experienced and handled differently over time and has shaped the different nature of class relations. In the 1960s, strong organisations of the classes of labour in both villages (the BTI in *Njomplang* and SARBUPRI in the neighbouring village of *Timpang*) managed to unite the responses of the classes of labour in promoting their class interests. This was the time of 'class in the making'. However, after the massacres and the detention without trial of the union members, the power of the classes of labour in both villages was effectively destroyed. The national un-making of the working class throughout the country has had a detrimental impact on the current generation of classes of labour in the villages. They neither have the experience nor knowledge to advance their class interests. As a result, the characteristic of class relations in the contemporary two villages has been 'everyday resistance' (Scott, 1989) or 'subtle resistance and negotiations' (Pincus, 1996). This shows that the recent persistence of such class relations is not simply due to the presence of the life-threatening risk of joining an open class struggle and a lack of the organisational capacity to organise collective struggle (Scott, 1989). The recent absence of overt class struggle owes much to the destruction of the labouring class in the previous struggle. Any attempt at re-making the classes of labour will only be possible if such progressive organisations of the past present themselves again in the contemporary villages.

Notes

1 This also depends on the duration of the fixed rent. A longer term of fixed rent provides a greater incentive for tenants to improve land productivity than a shorter one.

2 This is, for example, popular in India, where larger landowners sharecrop the land from smaller farmers.

3 In the village, a hectare of paddy field is generally measured as six *irings* (parcels) of land. Each *iring is* 1600–1700 m^2. Six *irings* of land may or may not equal precisely 10.000 m^2. We include all households owning six *irings* as capitalist farmers. Hence, for the sake of simplicity, Table 1 uses one hectare of land as the minimum threshold for capitalist farmers, and it includes landholders of around 0.95 hectares into the category of $\geq$ 1 hectare.

4 By 'agrarian ruling class' we mean the propertied-class within agricultural sector which manage to extract surpluses (either via wage labour or rent). In our Javanese village, the 'agrarian ruling class' constitutes the 'overall ruling class' in the village given the agrarian nature of the village. Whilst in our Sumatra village, the 'agrarian ruling class' is only part of the wider 'ruling class' in the village, since agriculture is not the only important sector in the village. See also the next section on 'The agrarian ruling class and family ties'.

5 The reliable 'farming contractors' require 'personal trust' in the sense that the landowners must know personally the contractors (the track record of their conduct and their performance in land cultivation). Thus, the contractors are generally the landowners' neighbours in the village. However, since the contractors also have to take care of their own land and depend mostly on local workers in the village, their ability to receive orders from the 'landlord-capitalists' is limited.

6 The minimum requirement to receive an SP from a factory (a local processing plant) is control of over 20 hectares of palm oil. The local agents (palm oil traders) who own land less than 20 hectares might still receive an SP if they manage to secure loyal farmers (equivalent to 20 hectares of palm oil) who regularly supply them with bunches of palm oil.

7 As for tractor hiring for land preparation, farmers do not hire in wage labour (tractor operator) but paying agricultural service to tractor's owners.

8 The tractors are hired out to the villagers and the income from the service (minus the wage for the tractor operators and fuel costs) goes to the POKTAN account.

9 To get the tractor as a grant from the state, the chairman, using the name of POKTAN, generally needs to pay 'bureaucratic fees'. For instance, Budi, the chairman of one of the POKTANs and one of the key political figures in the village (see Chapter 7) paid Rp. 8

million to the Local Office of Agriculture to secure the tractor grant. Those who did not pay the 'fees' did not receive the grant.

10 There were 13 tractors and 17 tractor drivers in 2017.

11 On 17 November 2014, the government raised the gasoline price from Rp. 4,500/litre to Rp. 6.500/litre and diesel from Rp. 5,500/litre to Rp. 7,500/litre.

12 In some cases, the share was 30-70 or 50-50, but the fuel cost was borne by the driver. The share depended on the bargaining power between the driver and tractor owner.

13 In the 2014 village meeting, Mantili one-sidedly initiated a move to remove the free lunch from the wage packet of the planters. She told the planting workers: 'from now on, a free lunch is not provided for planting, okay?' At the time, the planting workers were shocked but did not really give a proper response to Mantili's proposal. While the planters' wage was increased to Rp. 100 thousands/*iring* from the previous Rp. 80 thousands/*iring*, the free lunch was omitted from the wage stipulation.

References

Ambarwati, A et al 2016, 'Land tenure and agrarian structure in regions of small-scale food production', in J.F McCarthy & K Robinson (eds), *Land and development in Indonesia: Searching for the people's sovereignty*, Singapore, ISEAS-Yusof Ishak Institute, 265–296.

Bernstein, H 2010, *Class dynamics of agrarian change*, Sterling, VA, Kumarian Press.

Chayanov, A.V 1966, *The theory of peasant economy*, Homewood, Richard D. Irwin.

Hadiz, V 1997, *Workers and the state in Indonesia*, London, Routledge.

Hadiz, V.R 2002, 'The Indonesian labour movement: Resurgent or constrained?' *Southeast Asian Affairs*, pp. 130–142.

Harris-White, B 2012, 'Capitalism and the common man: Peasants and petty production in Africa and South Asia', *Agrarian South: Journal of Political Economy*, vol. 1, no. 2, pp. 109–160.

Harris-White, B & Goptu, N 2000, 'Mapping India's world of unorganised labour', *Socialist Register*, no. 37, pp. 89–118.

Lucas, A 2009, 'Berjuang diatas Perahu: Livelihood, contestation and declining marine resources on Java's north coast', in C Waren & J.F McCarthy (eds), *Community, environment and local governance in Indonesia: Locating the commonweal*, London and New York, Routledge, 59–88.

Pincus, J 1996, *Class power and agrarian change: Land and labour in rural West Java*, London, MacMillan Press.

Ploeg, J.D 2013, *Peasants and the art of farming: A chayanovian manifesto*, Winnipeg, Fernwood Publishing.

Robinson, G.B 2018, *The killing season: A history of the Indonesian massacres, 1965–66*, Princeton University Press.

Scott, J.C 1989, 'Everyday forms of resistance', *The Copenhagen Journal of Asian Studies*, vol. 4, no. 1, pp. 33–62.

Wiradi, G 2009 [1961], *Seluk Beluk Masalah Agraria, Reforma Agraria dan Penelitian Agraria*, Yogyakarta, STPN Press.

Wood, E.M 1982, 'The politics of theory and the concept of class: E.P. Thompson and his critics', *Studies in Political Economy*, vol. 9, no. 1, pp. 45–75.

Wood, E.M 2002, *The origin of capitalism: A longer view*, London and New York, Verso.

6 Agricultural Production in Java and Sumatra

Introduction

One of the major blind spots of the current understanding of Indonesia's agrarian change is the neglect of the nature of agricultural production. The agrarian populist sentiment in the dominant literature has undermined the dynamics of production relations and dedicated their main attention to the relation between the assumed egalitarian farmers/smallholders versus corporations or the state. Meanwhile, neo-classical economists tend to view production relations simply from the technical aspect while ignoring the social aspect of production. This chapter shows how a social organisation in the form of class dynamics plays a prominent role in shaping the nature of production relations. After showing how class dynamics shape the nature of land tenure, the dynamics of sharecropping in Java receive special attention, given their pertinence in current capitalist agriculture. The chapter continues by explaining the dynamics of the labour arrangements in Java and Sumatra. The discussion of credit provisions and technological development that are inextricably linked to class dynamics in the two villages follows. The last section of the chapter describes the dynamics of land productivity and the income from 'own-account' farming of both rice and oil palm production across different agrarian classes. This chapter enables an overall discussion of class relations and production relations, issues that have largely been overlooked by the existing literature.

Land Tenure

Based on empirical information from our fieldwork, there are several types of land tenure in the two villages. As mentioned in the methodology (Chapter 4), the survey covers the land tenure information of the respondents. However, the survey was designed to provide detailed information about each of the different class categories in the two villages, not to provide a quantitative overview of each village as a whole. We, therefore, complement the survey information with qualitative information and wider observations to gauge the incidence of each type of land tenure yielding a rough estimation. This approach to information gathering was taken because our main concern is to explain the processes and mechanisms that shape the nature of land tenure over time.

DOI: 10.4324/9781003267348-6

Today, one common land tenure system in *Njomplang* is sharecropping. As shown in Table 6.1, it involves the class sections of 'landlord-capitalists' and 'politico-bureaucrat capitalist farmers' to represent the landowners (patrons) who grant land cultivation rights to both 'formal PCPs' and the classes of labour as their clients. This 'normal sharecropping' (larger landowners sharecrop out lands to smaller landowners or landless) is the common sharecropping arrangement while there is no 'reverse sharecropping' in the village. Of course, there is also a more 'symmetrical contract' of sharecropping among classes of labour and PCPs. However, these are exceptional cases and confined largely to some households who have no family labour to cultivate their tiny land (e.g. widow or too old farmers with no children available) and manage to find willing sharecroppers.[1] Another common form of land tenure is ownership of land, where capitalist farmers cultivate their land using wage labour, while PCPs and the classes of labour harness their own family labour. A rather limited practice of land tenure is fixed land rent. Another limited practice of land tenure is 'land contracting', where capitalist farmers pay fixed production costs per hectare to a 'farming contractor', someone from PCP or the classes of labour, who is responsible for the whole cultivation process, while the full outcome goes to the landowner. The incidence of this land tenure is limited given both the technical limitations (labour availability) and social trust issues between the capitalist farmers and the 'land contractors', as briefly discussed in Chapter 5. The least common form of land tenure in the village is land pawning.

The high incidence of sharecropping in *Njomplang* has been the case since the colonial period. While we have no precise figures, there is a strong indication from the villagers that sharecropping was more widespread up to the 1990s, both in terms of land covered and the number of farmer households involved. In the 1990s, the incidence of sharecropping declined partly due to the rise of the fixed land rent practice. Capitalist farmers and PCPs who were in great need of cash money to send their children to school and college rented their parcels of land out to both the classes of labour and PCPs. Only in the last ten years has the incidence of fixed rent become a rarity, now that many capitalist farmers plus landlord-capitalists' and PCPs' children have completed their education. The decrease in sharecropping intensified in the 2000s when 'land contracting', a new way of land cultivation, was introduced into the village. This arrangement was initiated by widows who hired 'farming contractor' to take care of their *sawah* when the male labour in the family was not available. 'Farming contractor' is generally someone from PCP or the classes of labour, who is responsible for the whole cultivation process, while the full outcome goes to the landowner. When the arrangement proved to be more profitable than sharecropping, capitalist farmers followed suit in adopting such an arrangement. When sharecropping was considered less profitable in the 2000s (see next section), self-cultivation by wage labour went on the rise. Land pawning was known in the 1980s, where it mostly involved capitalist farmers who craved cash money for consumption activities (custom ceremonies). Today, such a practice is virtually non-existent in *Njomplang*[2] due to religious considerations.[3]

Table 6.1 Land tenure in *Njomplang*, Central Java

Types of land tenure	*Classes involved*	*The interest*	*The incidence*
Sharecropping	'Landlord-capitalists' and 'politico-bureaucrat capitalist farmers' with sharecroppers from the formal PCP, semi-proletariat farmers and proletariat-farmers	For the 'landlord-capitalists', they have no option but to sharecrop out in order to secure labour, although it is less profitable than using wage workers. For the 'politico-bureaucrat capitalists', it is a way of securing political supporters. For sharecroppers, it is a way of receiving a steady income.	It used to be more common in the past. Recently it has become less common.
Ownership of land	• Capitalist farmers with wage workers from the formal PCP and the classes of labour • PCPs with family labour and sometimes with other's labour from the classes of labour • Semi-proletariat farmers and proletariat farmers with their own family labour	For capitalist farmers, it is now more profitable than sharecropping. For those working as wage labourers, it is a way to earn a wage for survival.	Recently common. It is now more common than in the past.
Fix land rent	• Capitalist farmers with PCPs and the classes of labour • PCPs with other PCPs and the classes of labour	Capitalist farmers need to earn cash money to pay for their children's education at college, while for PCPs and the classes of labour who lease-in land, it is an opportunity to add to their land cultivation and, thus, their income from farming PCPs lease out land to finance their children's school education, and for those who lease-in the land, it is to add to their land cultivation and income from farming	Recently limited. It used to be more common in the 1990s and 2000s

(*Continued*)

Table 6.1 Continued

Types of land tenure	*Classes involved*	*The interest*	*The incidence*
Land pawning	Among capitalist farmers and 'landlord-capitalists'	For those pawning the land, it is to earn cash money for consumption ends, while for those taking on the land, it is a way of raising easy money through high interest charges	Recently negligible practice There used to be limited practice in the past (1980s)

Source: fieldwork

The situation in *Timpang* is quite the opposite of *Njomplang*. In *Timpang*, sharecropping is negligible. As we can see in Table 6.2, this generally only involves absentee landowners (owning less than four hectares) or capitalist farmers and local proletariat-farmers or semi-proletariat farmers. The share between landowners and sharecropper varies from 65-35 to 50-50.

The most common form of land tenure in *Timpang* is ownership of land (Table 6.2). This arrangement has been in place since the inception of small-holder oil palm production in the early 1990s. Ownership of land for capitalist farmers means they generally rely on wage workers to cultivate their land while for PCP and 'semi-proletariat farmers' use their own family labour. In other occasions, capitalist farmers with ownership of land may hire in a 'farming manager' to take care of their land. Since its inception in the early 1990s, the arrangement has mostly involved 'absentee-capitalist farmers' who live outside of the village (usually in the city, like Medan) and the local villagers, who play the role of foreman, organising the production processes: organising the labour (recruitment, control), supplying production inputs (fertilisers and pesticides), and selling the output. The 'farming manager' receives a monthly salary, regardless of the output of the harvest.

A limited practice of land tenure is land pawning. It generally involves transaction among semi-proletariat farmers, PCPs and capitalist farmers (see Table 6.2). Land pawning is the last resort when landowners are no longer able to access other credit sources. Unlike in *Njomplang*, especially after the 1990s, when land pawning was condemned as morally inappropriate, the practice in *Timpang* has generally been regarded as a normal market transaction due to the diverse religious composition in the village. Hence, the incidence of land pawning in *Timpang* is higher than in *Njomplang*.

Fixed land rent for oil palm fields, which has been known since the early 1990s, is also a limited practice in *Timpang*. It usually only involves neglected

Table 6.2 Land tenure in *Timpang*, North Sumatera

Types of land tenure	*Classes involved*	*The interest*	*The incidence*
Ownership of land	• Capitalist farmers with wage workers from the PCP and classes of labour • PCPs with family labour and, sometimes, with other's labour from the classes of labour • Semi-proletariat farmers and 'proletariat farmers with their own family labour	For capitalist farmers, it is the most efficient way of securing labour	It has been common since the 1990s
Land pawning	Semi-proletariat farmers, PCPs with capitalist farmers and vice versa	• For semi-proletariat farmers and PCPs who are in great need of cash money to conduct customary ceremonies (weddings) or to buy consumption goods • For capitalist farmers who need cash money and who have some neglected oil palm fields to be pawned	Limited practice since the 1990s
Fix land rent	Capitalist farmers with PCPs and the classes of labour	Capitalist farmers who need cash money and they have some neglected oil palm fields to be leased out For both PCPs and the classes of labour who lease-in the fields, it provides an opportunity to earn extra income	Limited practice since the 1990s
Sharecropping	• Absentee landowners (owning less than four hectares) with sharecroppers from the PCP and classes of labour • Capitalist farmers with sharecroppers from the PCP and classes of labour	• The land is too small to hire a 'farming manager' • Capitalist farmers pass the improvement costs of their neglected oil palm fields on to sharecroppers	It has been a negligible practice since the 1990s due to the less intensive nature of oil palm production

Source: fieldwork

oil palm fields. Capitalist farmers (either present or absentee) rent out their neglected oil palm fields to both PCPs and the classes of labour to recover the abandoned oil palm at minimum cost. Capitalist farmers may lease out some of their fields and they may harness the money received from the leasing to be invested either in farm (other fields of oil palm) or non-agricultural (trading) businesses. Land leasing generally takes place over a period of three to five years. In this period, fixed tenants may optimise the land by applying as much fertiliser as possible to increase the yield in a short period of time to reap maximum profit.

The Trajectory of Sharecropping in Njomplang

Regarding land tenure in the two villages, the significance of sharecropping in *Njomplang* is of special interest. The fact that sharecropping remains common in a village with already advanced capitalist social relations needs to be explained. Without adequately comprehending the nature and trajectory of sharecropping, we may not be able to understand the class dynamics of agrarian change in contemporary Java at all.

While sharecropping has been the dominant form of land tenure in *Njomplang* for centuries, we need to look at its internal dynamics at play. The sharing between landowners and sharecroppers in *Njomplang* is complex. It differs across different categories of *sawah* and seasons. In the village, there are three land categories. Based on the local practice, land category A is the first-class quality *sawah* because of its strategic location in many respects: closest access to the main irrigation system; ideal land elevation, where it is easy to pump out the excess water, if necessary; and nearest to the village settlement, which makes land supervision much easier. These pieces of land are the most fertile ground for paddy cultivation in the village. However, land category A is only limited, maybe less than a third of the total *sawah*. Land category A is only located in the southern part of the village.

Land category B and C do not share the privileges of land category A. Both land categories often face temporary flooding during the rainy season, since their land elevation is lower. Land category B is considered only slightly better than category C in terms of the distance from the settlement. This means land category B and C are generally rolled into one category when the sharing out of sharecropping is concerned. Most parcels of land category B and C are located in the southern part of the village, given the small portion of *sawah* which is located in the northern part of the village (less than a quarter of total *sawah*). The season also plays a crucial role in the sharing out between landowners and sharecroppers. The rainy season generally produces a higher yield than the dry season. Landowners prefer to grant lower shares for their sharecroppers during the rainy season than the dry season.

It is difficult to give a precise account of the trajectory of the share allocation within sharecropping over time in *Njomplang*, since the share of sharecropping depends mainly on the individual agreements between the landowners and

Table 6.3 The trajectory of sharecropping in *Njomplang*, Central Java

Period	*Land category*	*Season*	*Sharing α*
1980s	Land category A	Dry	60-40('Morolimo')
	Land category B and C	Rainy	70-30 ('Mretelu')
		Dry	50-50 ('Maro')
		Rainy	60-40 ('Morolimo')
2000s	Land category A	Dry	50-50 ('Maro')
	Land category B and C	Rainy	60-40 ('Morolimo')
		Dry	50-50 ('Maro')
		Rainy	60-40 ('Morolimo')
Mid-2010s	Land category A	Dry	All 50-50('Maro')
	Land category B and C	Rainy	
		Dry	
		Rainy	

Source: fieldwork
α: landowner's share is mentioned first.

sharecroppers. These are not decided through 'village meetings'. As a result, there is no uniform share for certain land categories and seasons. With this caution, what we have tried to do is to sketch a general pattern of its development, although with several pivotal qualifications.

As shown in Table 6.3, the general trend is that the share for sharecroppers has been increasing over time at the expense of the 'landlord-capitalists'. The recent share of 50-50 between the 'landlord-capitalists' and their sharecroppers is the result of the long-established class relations operating over decades. We need to bear in mind that the share of 50-50 does not necessarily mean that the sharecroppers receive exactly 50 percent of the yield simply because they must bear the input cost (about 15 percent, see Appendix 3). Nonetheless, the share for sharecroppers in *Njomplang* has increased over the last three decades.

In the 1980s, the share for land category A was only 30 percent for sharecroppers during the rainy season and 50 percent during the dry season. The important 'landlord-capitalists', such as Prapto (Prawiro's father), however, only offered 40 percent shares for sharecroppers in the dry season. Since this family is the biggest landowner in the village, many sharecroppers had no other option but to accept such a low share. This is particularly true when the other landowners who offered the standard share during the dry season (50 percent) had already found their sharecroppers. When agricultural labourers were abundant at the time, the bargaining position of sharecroppers was weak *vis-à-vis* landowners. The 50-50 share was also the case for land category B and C for the dry season. In the rainy season, landowners only granted sharecroppers of land category B and C a 40 percent share, which was lower than the 50 percent share of land category A. This was mostly because the yield during the rainy season in land category B and C was lower than in land category A. However, Prapto-Prawiro's family again offered a lower share than the norm (40 percent share for the dry season). In other cases, some sharecroppers of land category B and C were granted a higher share than in common practice (a 50 percent share during the rainy season), because the landowners were their close relatives or their employers.

A major transformation in the village took place in the 1990s. The surplus of labour that was the norm in the previous decade turned into a state of relative shortage of labour in the mid-1990s. In 1995, one of the most important typical capitalist farmers, Hadikusomo, first mobilised about 50 labourers from mountainous villages in the northern part of the district (about 35–45 km from *Njomplang*) for planting, sowing and harvesting, given the lack of workers in the village. The shortage of labour was felt more seriously when, two years later, some areas of *sawah* were not harvested in time. Hadikusomo's move to import migrant workers was followed shortly after by other capitalist farmers who had the capability to bring workers in. Along with capital availability, social networks were crucial in mobilising the labour from the mountainous areas.

The decline of available agricultural workers in the village was predominantly due to the out-migration of the unmarried villagers in the 1980s, while the married workers were getting older and entering their retirement from the laborious agricultural tasks. The unmarried villagers, who were mostly from the classes of labour's families, like Tarmi's (see Chapter 5), moved out from the village, because nothing could be expected for them there. Tarmi worked in a factory in Bekasi, while other unmarried villagers sold their labour for plantations in Sumatra, worked as daily labourers in big cities and took other casual jobs available in the country. Working as a factory worker in Jakarta and Bekasi remains common for unmarried villagers in *Njomplang* today.

In the 2000s, the willingness of the capitalist farmers to import migrant workers was also connected to the rising dissatisfaction of many sharecroppers who gave up their land cultivation rights as a protest against the landowners. The general economic deterioration after the Asian economic crisis in 1998, especially for the classes of labour, provided the impetus for the demand for a greater share. They told the landowners that 'there was nothing left for us if that was our only share'. The economic crisis apparently offered different circumstances for the sharecroppers. While Breman and Wiradi (2002), in their study in West Java, reported that the elites in the villages faced no real economic harm, in *Njomplang*, some of them were experiencing an economic improvement.[4] They improved their houses, thus raising the demand for construction labour. The rise of the construction sector was not only peculiar to *Njomplang*, but it was part of a national trend after the economic crisis (Agung et al., 2009: 53) in the context of de-industrialisation and the boom in commodity export products, such as oil palm and coal (Habibi & Juliawan, 2018). Some sharecroppers in *Njomplang* left their agricultural jobs to join the construction sector which was offering higher wages, while others kept their land cultivation rights and became stonemasons or coolies in their spare time. This doubling of jobs served as a warning to the landowners that if the sharecroppers' demands were not properly accommodated, they would easily take their foot out of agriculture and follow the other foot which had already moved out.

The sharecroppers' demand was accommodated to some degree. The share for land category A increased from 30 to 40 percent during the rainy season. However, some landowners, like Prapto's family, continued to offer only a third of share until the 2010s. In the same category, the share remained at 50 during the dry season. For land category B and C, the general trend was for the share to remain at 50-50 and 60-40 for the dry and rainy season, respectively (Table 6.3). However, some sharecroppers reported that they received an increased share of 50 percent for the rainy season. The structural change caused by the rise of construction employment was weighing in favour of the bargaining power of sharecroppers. But, again, Prapto-Prawiro's only offered a 40 percent share during dry season for land category B and C, lower than the 50 percent now being offered as common practice. To deal with the grievance of the sharecroppers, this family granted more land to their loyal sharecroppers from the land which had been given back to them from their former sharecroppers who were not satisfied with the share. This enabled them to secure labour from sharecroppers who received bigger parcels of land cultivation rights, although the number of their sharecroppers declined. Some of the loyal sharecroppers now hold more than a hectare of land after previously cultivating less than half a hectare of *sawah*. This may explain the increase in the number of landholders controlling between a half and one hectare in the last two and half decades, as village land registration has indicated (Chapter 5).

The pressure on patron landowners was intensified in the early 2010s when agricultural labourers became scarce again. There were two developments at the time: the supply of labour from the mountainous areas was cut by half from the previous decade and the unison timing for planting and harvesting in the neighbouring villages created what White and Wiradi (1989) call a 'temporary shortage of labour' in *Njomplang*. This will be discussed in detail in the next section. With the lack of workers for planting and harvesting, the need of 'landlord-capitalists' to secure labour was increasing. With the widespread demand from the sharecroppers and the great need to secure labour, the patron landowners had no other option but to agree to an increase in the share for sharecroppers. For the first time in the village, the share was 50-50 (*Maro*) between the landowners and sharecroppers for all land types and all seasons. However, Prawiro's family only increased the share for sharecroppers to 50 percent for the dry season, while for the rainy season the share was kept at 40 percent. Only after the death of Prawiro in 2016 did all of his sharecroppers meet Sari (Prawiro's wife) and urge her to raise the share for the rainy season. Being a widow with little knowledge or experience of farming and her children being busy with their studies in Yogyakarta, Sari agreed to accommodate this demand.

The trajectory of sharecropping shares is important in understanding the pertinence of sharecropping in current *Njomplang*. The need to secure a sufficient number of workers through sharecropping remains important, because rice cultivation is still predominantly dependent on manual labour. It is only in land preparation, which has been mechanised by tractor, that there is a reduced labour need. Meanwhile, planting and harvesting still require manual labour.

Njomplang might represent the situation where class dominance is low and, at the same time, the labour process is under-mechanised, making sharecropping a desirable form of land tenure, as Pearce (1983) suggests (Chapter 2). However, Pearce fails to explain the reasons for the under-mechanisation of the labour process. *Njomplang* shows that this is partly due to the relative balance of the bargaining power between capital and labour itself (low class dominance), along with the technical problems of the current planting and harvester machines, as will be shown in the section entitled 'Technological Development'.

What is also missing from Pearce's account is the political consideration of the patrons (the 'politico-bureaucrat capitalist farmers') who favour sharecropping as a means of securing political support, as we have seen in Karto's case (Chapter 5). This can also be seen with Agung, Prawiro's son, who, in 2017, became the village secretary and received 1.5 hectares of salary land. He grants six sharecroppers all his salary land to sharecrop, with each of them receiving a quarter of a hectare. Agung's decision to sharecrop out his lands to secure political supporters is the pivotal way of keeping open the possibility of running for village head.

In intensive crop cultivation like rice, and where becoming a village official remain a lucrative avenue for non-agricultural activities (see Chapter 7), sharecropping is used as a means of securing political support, rather than simply of securing labour. Instead of disappearing, this patron-client relationship between capitalist farmers and the classes of labour continues to be crucial, despite the advanced penetration of capitalist social relations. As Scott (1972) notes, this is mainly due to landowners ('landlord-capitalists') retaining the material resources, while the tenants/sharecroppers (classes of labour) are not in a well-integrated position regarding political power. In *Njomplang*, events in 1965 turned well-organised labour into its current state of disorientation (Chapter 5).

Labour Arrangements

Securing Labour

Before explaining labour system in two villages, it is important to note how labour supply is secured to perform agricultural tasks. For 'proletariat-farmers' and 'semi-proletariat farmers' in *Njomplang*, they normally depend on their family labour to perform rice cultivation. They only hire in labour occasionally when their family labour is insufficient to perform agricultural task, due to a variety reasons (ill, travel outside the district). There is indeed certain agricultural task namely planting which requires regular hiring in labour. This is because planting is exclusively performed by female workers. If a household only has a single female worker, they need to hire in female workers to perform planting.[5] In this arrangement, a female worker helps to plant on her colleague's land and, in return, her colleague will plant on hers in the next round of planting. Cash payment is only involved when one of them exceeds the day's work of her colleague. This 'horizontal labour hiring'[6] is different from a more 'traditional labour exchange' in which all social classes in the community are involved (including the propertied class) while cash payment is barely involved. It is also different from 'normal wage labour hiring' under capitalism when capitalist farmers hire in wage labour from other classes while they never sell back their labour to others. While such 'vertical labour hiring' indicates the economic power possessed by capitalist farmers to command other's labour, 'horizontal labour hiring' among the member of classes of labour signals their lack of alternative but to 'hire' in their neighbours. PCPs may involve in either 'horizontal labour hiring' or 'vertical labour hiring'. They are doing the latter occasionally when they cultivate additional land (either due to lease in land or additional land cultivation rights under sharecropping) and their family labour is technically no longer sufficient to perform the required agricultural tasks.

The situation is similar to *Timpang*. Here, 'proletariat-farmers' and 'semi-proletariat farmers' even more depend solely on their family labour to perform all oil palm's cultivation tasks, given the much lower intensity of oil palm cultivation. 'Horizontal labour hiring' only takes place occasionally when the member of family labour is not available for some reasons. Like in *Njomplang*, PCPs in *Timpang* may perform either 'horizontal labour hiring' or 'vertical labour hiring'. However, since the incidence of land leasing and sharecropping is rare in oil palm context, the chance for PCPs here to perform 'vertical labour hiring' is less. Similar to their fellow in Java, capitalist farmers in *Timpang* also depend entirely on other's labour to perform agricultural tasks. In both villages, a few agricultural tasks such as applying fertilisers and herbicides are sometimes performed by capitalist farmers themselves as part of their hobby, and in *Timpang* it especially relates to trust issues towards agricultural workers. There is little doubt that in both villages, the greatest demand for agricultural labour is from capitalist farmers.

In *Njomplang*, the supply of labour, up to the mid-1990s, was predominantly met by local labourers. As mentioned earlier, only since the mid-1990s, have capitalist farmers imported labour from outside the village, mainly from mountainous village areas. Local villagers call the workers from these areas 'mountain people/*wong gunung*', which has the pejorative meaning of 'less-modern people'. Migrant workers have been mostly deployed to perform planting and harvesting. In the 2000s, importing such labour was a common practice for capitalist farmers who were not involved in sharecropping arrangements. At a much smaller level, labour has also been imported from neighbouring villages, but not the other way around, since the 2010s (see below). Planting (with sowing) and harvesting should be seen as a package for hiring labour. Landowners only grant the right of harvesting to those who agree to plant (and sow) in the first place. When there are not a sufficient number of these workers to perform the harvesting, additional harvesters may be recruited. Some PCPs have also invited migrant workers, but these were mostly their relatives. For a different reason, importing labour is also important for the traders (*penebas*) (see Chapter 5). During this period, migrant workers account for about half of the total labour for both planting and harvesting.[7] Without migrant workers, rice cultivation in the village would be impossible. These favourable conditions, however, were halted in the early 2010s when the number of migrant workers from the mountainous areas plummeted to less than half of the previous decade. Since then, the total number of labourers in *Njomplang* for planting and harvesting has met less than three-quarters of the demand for labour in the village.

One immediate impact of this labour shortage is the extension of both planting and harvesting time. Planting has been extended from about four weeks to five or six weeks and harvesting from about two to three weeks (more time is needed in the rainy season) to four to five weeks. This means the capitalist farmers cannot freely determine the timing of their planting, since it is dependent on the availability of labour. The female planting workers in *Njomplang* punish the 'stingy capitalist farmers' by putting them at the end of the waiting list while prioritising 'generous capitalists'. They especially take revenge on the capitalist farmers who had previously invited migrant labour to do their planting. The ideal timing of planting is in the middle of the planting season (the second/third week). Planting too early or too late means there is a much higher risk that the young paddy stalks will be damaged by snails, which tend to attack the first available paddy. During the harvesting, the dry stalk paddy that grows much earlier than the rest of the paddy in the area is also the first to invite rats. With the sabotage by the local planting labourers, some capitalist farmers have already complained about the deficiency of their yield due to the poor timing of the planting.

The fall in the migrant labour supply follows several developments. First, in the early 2010s, the villagers in the mountainous areas started to tap coconut trees.[8] The daily return from this activity is about the same as from planting and only half of the daily return from harvesting in *Njomplang*.[9] However, planting (and sowing) only took up about 10 to 20 days of work per year, while harvesting only about six to eight weeks. It is clear that tapping coconut trees provides a much higher annual income. One would expect that the labourers could do both activities by working in *Njomplang* during the planting and harvesting season while tapping coconut trees for the rest of the year. But there is something peculiar about tapping coconut trees. The coconut stalk should be tapped every day, otherwise, it will stop generating sap and it needs to be chopped off. Most former migrant workers preferred to leave their paddy jobs for tapping coconut trees. Migrant workers who are still going to *Njomplang* are those who do not grow coconut trees or who rent their coconut trees out to their neighbours, because they already have yet another job (stonemason). Masons keep going to *Njomplang* given it offers a lucrative return during the short period of harvesting. Since the tappers are only male, planting workers who are female should be able to continue working in *Njomplang*, especially when their daily work of producing handmade bamboo food boxes (*besek*) promises a much lower return (only about one-third). However, as *Njomplang* is located about 35–45 km from their homes, the female workers have needed the company of their male co-workers, who were usually employed to sow the rice. Now that their co-workers are occupied with tapping coconut, it is very difficult for the female workers to come to *Njomplang*.

The incentive for male workers not to return to *Njomplang* to accompany their female co-workers is also provided by the introduction of the government Village Fund ('Dana Desa') program since 2015. For the workers from poor villages in the mountainous areas, the grant from the national government to build local infrastructure offers valuable extra income. Some villages schedule their project work during the off-season (August to October), which allows its villagers to attend the planting and harvesting seasons in *Njomplang*. However, other villages are working on their projects throughout the year (or in a scattered manner), preventing their workers from going to work outside the village. Even when male co-workers are available, however, the availability of female agricultural workers in the mountainous villages is on the decline due to generational issues. Many female workers who have stopped coming to *Njomplang* are in their sixties, while the younger generation have either migrated out of their home village or are not interested in agricultural work.

The recent lack of labour for planting and harvesting in *Njomplang* is also, crucially, due to the unison timing of planting and harvesting in the neighbouring villages. Up to the 2000s, the rice cultivation used to start in the eastern sub-districts and wove across to the western sub-districts. The difference in timing of planting and harvesting between *Njomplang* and the surrounding villages used to be two to three weeks. This provided adequate time for the workers from the surrounding villages to arrive for work in *Njomplang* after completing their tasks in the eastern villages. With the improvement of the irrigation systems in the eastern sub-districts since the 2010s, the interval time of harvesting is only a week, which means the planting and harvesting for most villages in the area is now done almost simultaneously. This effectively prevents harvesters from neighbouring village to come to *Njomplang* and, at the same time, hinders the possibility of *Njomplang*'s workers going to work in the neighbouring villages.

It turns out that some workers from the mountainous areas who used to work in *Njomplang* and several other surrounding villages (because the timing was in sequel order) have chosen not to working any more in *Njomplang* since the timing has changed. They now work only for the capitalist farmers in the neighbouring villages who offer the highest bids, since they still provide a free lunch and, sometimes, even cover transportation costs. This punishes capitalist farmers in the 'stingiest village' of *Njomplang* (see Chapter 5). The move from migrant workers that cannot easily be followed by local workers, as most of them are tied to 'landlord-capitalists' through sharecropping arrangements.

This simultaneous timing mostly affects the capitalist farmers and '*penebas*' in *Njomplang*, who now have great difficulty in securing labour, especially for harvesting. At the same time, it also brings losses to the classes of labour and PCPs in *Njomplang* who are no longer able to join the planting and harvesting, which offers higher returns, in the surrounding villages.

The dynamic in *Timpang* is quite the opposite. Since the early inception of oil palm in the 1990s, labour has been supplied by local workers. This owes much to the less intensive nature of oil palm production. With the current technology (manual sickles and threshing machines), rice harvesting requires about 48 times more workers than oil palm harvesting.[10] Calculated on a yearly basis, the number of harvesters required per hectare for rice remains four times higher than oil palm.[11] Overall, when considering all agricultural tasks, rice cultivation needs many more workers, since harvesting is the only labour-intensive agricultural task in oil palm production. With such less intensive cultivation, the labour supply for oil palm production in *Timpang* has effectively been provided by local workers. Even when the population density in the village is very low, even by Sumatra's standards (Chapter 4), labour is in relative surplus, reflecting the national trend (Habibi & Juliawan, 2018). Only a few workers have been absorbed by companies operating in *Timpang* and the neighbouring villages. This means own-account employment outside of agriculture is the most common type of work that overrides farming.

Therefore, there is no need for capitalist farmers in *Timpang* to secure labour, either from outside the village or through sharecropping arrangements. For the workers, finding a steady income all year round is the priority rather than demanding higher wages and better working conditions. This is especially so when selling their labour in the neighbouring villages to obtain a higher reward is not an easy option given the trust issues that exist with the employers there.[12] This highlights their similarity to those workers in *Njomplang* who cannot easily punish their capitalist farmers. However, while in *Njomplang*, this is mainly due to the patron-client tie of sharecropping, in *Timpang*, it is about the nature of the relative surplus of workers in the village.

The Dynamics of the Labour Arrangement

This background is important when we are now discussing the dynamics of the labour arrangement in the two villages. In *Njomplang*, the most common labour system is contract by task (*borongan*). This covers all the agricultural tasks except weeding and harvesting. Daily wage labour is applied only to weeding and other unspecified agricultural tasks. Payment-in-kind is used for harvesting. The labour arrangement in *Njomplang* becomes more complex, since we have to take into account the provision of a meal (free lunch) that is attached to each labour arrangement. With this additional caution, the most common labour arrangement in the current *Njomplang* is contracted by task with no free lunch.

The prominent incidence of this arrangement in *Njomplang* is a result of a rather complex transformation of each agricultural task. As shown in Table 6.4,

Table 6.4 The dynamics of the labour arrangement in *Njomplang*, Central Java

Period	*Land Preparation*	*Sowing*	*Planting*	*Applying fertilisers*	*Applying herbicides*	*Weeding*	*Harvesting*
1970s	Contract by task plus free lunch	Labour exchange	Contract by task plus free lunch	-	-	Daily wage plus free lunch	Open harvest (payment-in-kind)
1980s	↓	Contract by task plus free lunch	↓	Daily wage, no free lunch	-	↓	↓
1990s 2000s	Contract by task, no free lunch	↓	↓	Contract by task, no free lunch	Daily wage, no free lunch	Daily wage, no free lunch	Closed harvest (payment-in-kind)
2010s	↓	Contract by task, no free lunch	Contract by task, no free lunch	↓	Contract by task, no free lunch	↓	↓

Source: fieldwork

some agricultural tasks (sowing, planting and weeding) have only been transformed into contract by task with no free lunch since the 2010s, while others (applying fertilisers and land preparation) had already adopted the arrangement earlier (in the 1990s and 2000s, respectively). Land preparation used to be performed for contract by task plus free lunch in the 1970s, when manual ploughing was the norm, up to the 1990s, when tractors replaced manual labour. The change in the 2000s to get rid of the provision of free lunch was initiated by both the capitalist farmers and the classes of labour. While, for the former, it was to lower the production cost, for the latter, it related to the food waste provided to tractor drivers.[13] More importantly, the number of tractor drivers was limited compared to workers, as a whole, even if they were part of the classes of labour. With pressure from both sides, a free lunch was easily ruled out as early as the 2000s.

The earliest arrangement of contract by task with no free lunch was introduced for those applying fertilisers, in the 1990s. Applying fertilisers was not widely practiced in *Njomplang* in the 1970s. There were a few farmers who applied organic fertilisers (cow manure or tree leaf), but most of them did not put any fertilisers at all. When chemical fertilisers began to be widely used in the 1980s, the labour arrangement was daily wage with no free lunch. Following a decade of experience, the workers realised that such an arrangement was detrimental to them, since their labour was being extracted throughout the day to apply fertilisers to as many pieces of land as possible but for only one wage. 'Slowing down the work', as was practiced in *Timpang*, was not an available option as the supervision on the *sawah* was much more effective (the land was closer to the village settlements and could be seen easier) than in oil palm fields. The labourers demanded a change to contract by task with no free lunch to obtain a higher share. When *Njomplang* first experienced the shortage of labour in the 1990s, the bargaining power of the classes of labour was in such a position that this demand could not easily be ignored by the capitalist farmers. However, the abolition of the free lunch put more burdens on the female workers, since they had to prepare meals for her and her partner in the very early morning.

Among the last tasks to adopt contract by task with no free lunch is planting. For about four decades since the 1970s, planting was performed through contract by task with free lunch. Actually, up to the 1990s, the system included the element of daily wage. At the time, the number of workers needed to plant of one *iring* (0.16 hectares) of land was supposed to be eight. Each of them could easily move and join a new group of workers to plant on another piece of *sawah* when her quota of planting had been completed. From the workers' perspective, this was a kind of daily wage, since they were paid based on how many 'quotas' or 'rounds' of planting each of them were involved in a day. However, from the employers' point of view, it was simply a contract by task job, since the cost was fixed per *iring* for eight workers, whoever they were. In the 2000s, the element of the daily wage was banished. The quota of eight workers per *iring* could not be sustained with the falling labour supply. Today, the practice is that the cost of planting per *iring* is fixed but the number of workers to perform such a task is in the hands of the workers. The workers involved in planting are more satisfied with this system, since they no longer need to hurry from one field to another in order to provide higher income security for themselves. The capitalist farmers have also agreed to this system because, with the decline of the labour supply, the new labour system is effective in securing workers.

However, in 2014, the provision of free lunch for planting and sowing workers was abolished. As shown in Chapter 5, this initiative came from the agrarian ruling class (capitalist farmers and 'landlord-capitalists'), in the name of simplicity. Considering the labour shortage had been in effect since early 2010, it seems quite strange that the agrarian ruling class managed to get rid of the provision of free lunch from the labourers' wages. Apart from the fact that some compensation was given by the agrarian ruling class in the form of a slight increase in the planting wage, this also relates to the nature of the labour shortage. The labour shortage was only relative (a reduction of about a quarter of the ideal labour supply) and it did not affect all the agrarian ruling class in the village. This is why it is useful to look into the internal dynamics of the agrarian ruling class. Mantili, who initiated the removal of the free lunch for planting, is a 'landlord-capitalist' who has many sharecroppers. She can effectively secure labour for planting on her own land from her sharecroppers. This also applies to Sari (Prawiro's wife), who has even more sharecroppers at hand. At the same time, many 'semi-proletariat farmers' and PCPs have been effectively tied to their patron. This prevents the classes of labour from effectively challenging the capitalists' arrangements (Chapter 5).

Another agricultural task that has only adopted contract by task with no free lunch since the last decade is sowing. It used to be performed by labour exchange (*sambatan*) in the 1970s. In this arrangement, villagers (mostly capitalist farmers) invited labourers to sow their rice seeds and, in return, the host provided a decent free meal (including chicken as a side dishes) to be taken home by the workers. The hosts, in return, were required to attend the invitation from other landowners who wished to sow their seeds. It is unclear why the practice was replaced by contract by task with free lunch in the 1980s. It might be related to the inception of the new modern seeds (IR 64) in 1979. With the lower paddy stalk, the task of sowing was presumably easier and required fewer workers per hectare. However, the provision of a free meal was kept to attract the labourers. The practice lasted for three decades which to some extent, owes much to the significant rise in the bargaining position of the classes of labour after the mid-1990s. The abolition of the free lunch only came about in the 2010s alongside the inception of the new arrangement of planting mentioned earlier.

Applying herbicides has also been performed for contract by task with no free lunch since the 2010s. Applying herbicides was unknown in the village during the 1970s and 1980s. This related to the limited supply at the time. It was only widely applied in the 1990s when private companies' networks offered mass supplies of their herbicides to villagers. The daily wage was the labour arrangement at its inception. As in the case of applying fertilisers, the workers realised that daily wage was unfair to them. However, it took two decades before daily wage was replaced by contract by task with no free lunch which arrived in the 2010s. A relative labour shortage at the same time may have been responsible for advancing the bargaining power of the classes of labour to initiate the change. The same labour shortage in the mid-1990s did not have the same effect since the daily wage arrangement for applying herbicides was applied some years before.

Weeding and other unspecified agricultural tasks (such as burning paddy straw and tidying up the field after it is tractorised) are the only agricultural tasks performed by daily wage labour. It has been the case since the 1990s. In the two previous decades, these tasks were performed by daily wage labour but with free lunch. The change was initiated by the capitalist farmers to minimise labour costs. In the context of a relative surplus of labour in the early 1990s, the classes of labour in the village had little power to resist such an initiative. One might ask why daily wage for weeding was not replaced with contract by task in the recent *Njomplang*. This mainly relates to the nature of the weeds. Since there is no way to predict how rampant the weeds may be in advance, one cannot pre-determine the labour cost per piece of land through the fixed cost arrangement of contract by task.

The peculiar labour arrangement in the Javanese rice cultivation is payment-in-kind for harvesting (the *bawon* system). This labour arrangement is favourable for both the landowners and harvesters. For the former, payment-in-kind lowers risk in the case of a harvest failure, while for the latter, the value of the proportional share is over and above what a standard daily wage would be. A harvester (*wong nderep*) generally will receive one tonne of dry grain paddy as their share (*bawon*) from a harvesting season. If there are three members of a household joint harvesting, their *bawon* is about equal to the yield of owning *sawah* of half a hectare. The lucrative earning for harvesters is the result of a one-seventh share from the total harvested yield which has been in effect since the 1980s. In the previous decades, the share was only one-tenth to one-twelfth.

Such improvements for harvesters owe much to the changing balance of power. We have mentioned that the major changes in the 1980s were the inception of a new paddy variety in the late 1970s (IR 64) and the widespread application of chemical fertilisers (see above). The higher yield produced from the new variety provided the impetus for harvesters to demand a rise in their *bawon*. Given the out-migration in the 1980s and, thus, the increase in the bargaining power of the workers, the capitalist farmers were effectively forced to increase the *bawon* to one-seventh. While one-seventh has become the norm in recent *Njomplang*, there are some exceptions. Some farmers grant a higher share (one-sixth) when the harvesters are their close relatives, especially if they come from mountainous areas. However, *penebas* like Cokro generally offer a lower share (one-eighth) to their *tebasan*. This discrepancy is a way of securing a profit from *tebasan* activity, which is heavily speculative in nature (see Chapter 5). The variation of *bawon* is made possible because it is not uniformly stipulated by village rules through the 'village meeting'.

The lucrative nature of rice harvesting attracts harvesters from elsewhere to come to *Njomplang*. Up until the mid-1990s, *Njomplang* employed an open harvesting system whereby everyone was welcome to harvest in the village. With the harvesters overcrowding the fields, however, a common result was rice damage. Too many anonymous harvesters also created the problem of supervision for landowners. Rice pilfering was widespread under the open harvest system (see similar cases in Northern Central Java, Hart, 1986; and West Java, Pincus, 1996). For both reasons, the loss of the yield to the landowners (ultimately, capitalist farmers) was only the obvious result. To deal with such unfavourable circumstances, the capitalist farmers and *penebas* in *Njomplang* banned open harvesting in the mid-1990s and has since employed a closed harvest system. Harvesting is not closed in the sense of spatial closure (for migrant workers), but it means closed to those who are not invited. Only harvesters who have been asked in advance by the landowners can join harvesting. The initiative, by the capitalist farmers, to get rid of the open harvest system was not challenged by the classes of labour in the village, since the closed harvest system increased the security of their *bawon*, because in the context of the relative labour shortage, they did not have to compete with too many harvesters. It provided a higher return for many of them.

While *Njomplang* represents the uniformity of the labour arrangement for each agricultural task in a single village, in *Timpang*, the labour arrangement is varied across agricultural tasks, hamlets and individual farmers. This owes much to the absence of village rules to regulate a uniform labour arrangement. Without a uniform rule, many agricultural tasks are organised according to more than a single labour arrangement. Against such a backdrop, when there is more than one labour arrangement for certain agricultural tasks, we may only be able to speak about the 'general practice' when we want to indicate that one labour arrangement is more widespread than another. Another implication of the absence of village rules in *Timpang* is the detachment of the meal provision from the wages component. Meal provision is mainly dependent on the employers. While the labour arrangement in *Timpang* is much less regulated by the village apparatus, it does not necessarily mean that everything is simply determined via market mechanisms operating on the supply and demand function. As will be shown, the dynamics of labour arrangement in *Timpang* owes much to the class relations following the uneven development of the village.

Today, the most common labour arrangement in *Timpang* is contract by task. Most agricultural tasks from planting, applying herbicides and cutting off the midribs to harvesting are generally performed under contract by task. Daily wage may be applied for applying herbicides and harvesting, but mostly in the peripheral hamlets. In central hamlets, it is generally applied for applying fertilisers and weeding. The percentage system is another labour system, but this is applied only rarely, and it only applies to harvesting.

The common practice of contract by task in *Timpang* can be traced through the trajectory of each agricultural task over time. As shown in Table 6.5, contract by task has been the only labour arrangement performed for planting and cutting of midribs since the 1990s. The practice has lasted for three decades, since it is favoured by both employers (mostly capitalist farmers) and workers. It promises a higher return for labourers, while for the capitalist farmers, it lowers the risk of being played by workers through them 'slowing down the work' (Chapter 5). For applying herbicides, contract by task is generally practiced, along with a lower incidence of daily wage, which is applied mostly in the peripheral hamlets. This has only been the case since the 2000s. In the 1990s, daily wage for applying herbicides was also applied in the central hamlets. However, the labourers in the hamlets found that such an arrangement provided them with lower returns. They collectively urged the capitalist farmers to change the arrangement into contract by task. The capitalist farmers accepted the demand, since it was less likely to invite labourers from the peripheral hamlets who received a higher wage rate than the workers in the central hamlets. Workers in the peripheral hamlets, in contrast, were in favour of daily wage, because they could slow down the work for the reason that has been explained earlier.

A similar process also applies to harvesting. Before the 2010s, contract by task was generally applied for harvesting, along with daily wage, which was mostly confined to the peripheral hamlets. It continued through the 2010s, although the incidence of daily wage in the peripheral hamlets declined and was replaced by contract by task. It should be noted that harvesting is not only about dropping oil palm fruits, but also bringing the fruit to a certain point where a truck can pick it up. One important development is the road improvements in the hamlets, thanks to the villager's endowment fund and the Foster Father scheme.[14]At the same time, the oil palm boom following the 2000s has provided a lucrative return that has enabled more villagers to buy motorcycles to be modified as 'along-along' to carry oil palm. This has cut the harvesting time by half (from two to three days to a day). This means there is no reason for workers to keep daily wage as it is no longer profitable. However, other workers remain eager to harvest under daily wage when they are sure that they can slow down the work. Other labourers still favour the daily wage arrangement when they harvest only a small field of oil palm (a hectare), which is less lucrative if it is performed under contract by task.

Harvesting in the 2010s also introduced a new labour arrangement. The percentage system is when employers pay the harvesters a fixed portion (20 percent) of the total yield harvested that has been cashed. It is a way for employers to lower risks when their fields are small (less than two hectares) and not well maintained. This system, however, is currently negligible in *Timpang*.

Agricultural tasks that are still predominantly performed by daily wage in *Timpang* are applying fertilisers and weeding. Applying fertilisers has been generally conducted through daily wage except for a few hamlets in the central village, where contract by task is widespread. The variation within the central

Table 6.5 The dynamics of the labour arrangement in *Timpang*, North Sumatera

Period	*Planting*	*Applying Fertilisers*	*Applying Herbicides*	*Weeding*	*Cutting off the midribs*	*Harvesting*
1990s	Contract by task as the only practice	• Daily wage (general practice) • Contract by task (limited practice, mostly limited in the few central hamlets)	• Contract by task (general practice) • Daily wage (limited practice both in the central and peripheral hamlets)	Daily wage as the only practice	Contract by task as the only practice	• Contract by task (general practice) • Daily wage (limited practice, mostly in the peripheral hamlets)
2000s	↓	↓	• Contract by task (general practice) • Daily wage (limited practice, mostly in the peripheral hamlets)	↓	↓	↓
2010s	↓	↓	↓	• Daily wage (general practice) • Contract by task (limited practice, mostly in the central hamlets)	↓	• Contract by task (general practice) • Daily wage (limited practice, mostly in the peripheral hamlets and less widespread than in the past • Percentage system (exceptional case)

Source: fieldwork

hamlets relates to the nature of capitalist farmers. In the few hamlets which apply contract by task, influential 'absentee-capitalist farmers' are dominant. With the larger scale of production and the absentee nature of the landowners, the problem of supervision is naturally greater. Performing fertiliser application through contract by task is the reasonable option to lower the risk of being played by the labourers. This is not the case for other hamlets among the central hamlets, where the capitalist farmers own smaller plots and are present in the village. This has also led to the demand of the workers in these hamlets to adopt contract by task for applying fertilisers to be rejected by the capitalist farmers. Again, the opposite applies for the peripheral hamlets, where daily wage is favoured by the labourers for the reason mentioned earlier. This combination of labour arrangements for applying fertilisers in *Timpang* has been employed since the 1990s.

Daily wage labour is also a common arrangement for weeding. Up to the 2000s, daily wage was the only labour system applied for weeding. Similar to *Njomplang*, since it is difficult to estimate in advance the level of mowing which might be required, it is difficult to set a fixed rate for weeding for a piece of land. However, the inception of lawnmowers (produced by home industry) in the 2010s to mow the grass surrounding the oil palm trees, enables both the workers and employers to estimate the fixed cost of mowing the lawn. The adoption of contract by task for weeding in the 2010s was the initiative of big capitalist farmers like Bungaran, who sought lower risk in weeding. This is why it mostly applies in the central hamlets rather than the peripheral hamlets.

In some cases, daily wage has a meal provision attached to attract labour. This is common in the peripheral hamlets, since labour is more expensive here, while it can be found in only a few cases in the central hamlets. For the capitalist farmers who provide a free lunch, it is a way of lowering the risk of being cheated by the labourers (pilfering in applying fertilisers, herbicides and harvesting). The different degree of feeling secure among capitalist farmers shapes their decision to provide a free lunch or not which, from the workers' point of view, positions capitalist farmers as a stingy boss or a generous one. The provision of a meal is, to some extent, shaped by religious considerations. Muslim workers generally refuse to eat the meal provided by Christian employers to avoid any food that is forbidden for Muslims. This, fortuitously, justifies Christian capitalist farmers in not serving a free lunch.

Credit Provision

Another aspect that is crucial for agricultural production is credit provision. In the two villages, credit plays different roles for the different agrarian classes. As shown in Table 6.6, for the capitalist farmers in *Njomplang*, acting as a creditor is a prominent means of non-agricultural accumulation. This is the case for Hadikusumo, a typical capitalist farmer, who opened the only agricultural shop in the village and who provides the credit for agricultural inputs. When capitalist farmers are debtors, they manage to secure large amounts of credit, both for

Table 6.6 Credit provision in *Njomplang*, Central Java

Types of credit	*Scheme*	*Class involved*	*Utilisation*
Agricultural shop credit • Established by a capitalist farmer in the 2000s and has been the common credit provision since then	• Agricultural inputs credit (seeds, fertilisers, pesticides, etc.) • No collateral • Flat interest rate of 3.3% per month for four months due	• Creditor: capitalist farmer • Debtor: PCPs and the classes of labour	• For capitalist farmers as creditors, extracting the interest rate is a crucial form of off-farm accumulation • For PCPs and the classes of labour: to make up a shortage of cash money and more convenient than buying agricultural inputs elsewhere
KUR-BRI Micro • Introduced in 2008, but the current terms and conditions have only been in operation since 2016 and have been the common credit provision in the village	• Cash money credit to a maximum of Rp. 25 million • Neither collateral nor meticulous verification required • Flat interest rate 0.41% per month for three to five years	• Creditor: the state • Debtor: modest capitalist farmers, PCPs and the classes of labour	• Capitalist farmers harness it to finance their children's education at college • PCPs and the classes of labour make use of the credit for both productive activities (leasing-in *sawah*, opening up petty businesses, paying children's education fees) and consumption (buying motorcycles, paying for the family ceremonies of weddings and childbirth, and for daily food consumption)
Cooperative • 'Neighbourhood Association' (RT) Cooperative and POKTAN's cooperative • Introduced in the 2000s and 2010s respectively and yet they can only cover a limited number of debtors in the village (about a quarter of total households)	• Cash money credit for maximum Rp. 2 million • No collateral but membership is required • Flat interest rate 1% per month for ten instalments	• Creditor: cooperative • Debtor: capitalist farmers, PCPs and the classes of labour	• Capitalist farmers join only to avoid social exclusion • PCPs harness the credit to complement their earning to lease-in *sawah* or to make small home improvements • Classes of labour use the money for daily consumption, especially in the middle of rice cultivation season

• The *Projo Seliro* cooperative, established in 1998 by capitalist farmers and only involved in a very limited number of households (around a tenth of total households)	• General cash money credit for maximum Rp. 25 million divided between three debtors • No collateral but membership is required • Flat interest rate 1% per month for ten instalments	• Creditor: cooperative • Debtor: capitalist farmers and PCPs, no classes of labour	• In the beginning, capitalist farmers used it simply as a political vehicle to overthrow the incumbent village head • Now, for both capitalist farmers and PCPs, it serves as additional cheap credit, other than KUR-BRI, to finance children's education or other non-farm needs
'Bank Plecit' (loan shark organisation disguised as a credit cooperative)			
• the staff were sent to the village in the 2000s from its central office to offer credit and since then has served a limited number of classes of labour (about a tenth of total households)	• Cash money credit for maximum Rp. 1 million • No collateral • Flat interest rate 8% per month in two and a half month instalments	Creditor: private companies Debtor: classes of labour	• This is last resort for the classes of labour to sustain their daily consumption in the middle of rice cultivation season, though some of them make use of the money to run their petty businesses
Credit from Patrons			
• only in rare cases	• Cash money credit, generally to a maximum of Rp. 2 million • No collateral, interest rate nor fixed due date of repayment	• Creditor: 'landlord-capitalists' • Debtor: classes of labour	• A way of 'landlord-capitalists' to maintain the loyalty of their sharecroppers • Classes of labour need to sustain their daily consumption and to pay medical costs, children's education and visits to distant relative elsewhere
Other Credits			
From relatives and neighbours • only in rare cases	See above	• Creditor: sometimes PCPs but mostly the classes of labour • Debtor: classes of labour	• Mostly for daily consumption and children's education

Source: fieldwork

'own-account' farming and non-agricultural activities. PCPs and the classes of labour cannot be creditors, except for small levels of credit (less than Rp. 2 million) offered to their relatives or neighbours. Mostly, they are debtors subjected to different creditors: capitalist farmers, the state, private companies and cooperatives. Private companies, under their guise as credit cooperatives, charge the highest interest rates, followed by capitalist farmers. The state provides the cheapest credit (KUR-BRI Micro), which makes it very popular with PCPs and the classes of labour in the village. The local cooperatives also offer cheap credit. The credit enables PCPs to consolidate their simple reproduction (by leasing more land or financing their children's education). For the classes of labour, it helps them to meet their daily consumption needs.

There are several reasons for the common practice of agricultural input credit. Many 'proletariat-farmers' and 'semi-proletariat farmers' have little choice but to borrow when they are short of cash money during the planting season, and the nominal debt is considered small given their limited need for fertilisers and herbicides. Others complain that they cannot easily obtain the inputs if they buy them for cash. For PCPs, it is more convenient to obtain the agricultural inputs in the village than from elsewhere, and it is also a way to save cash money. On the other hand, the capitalist farmers manage to avoid this credit by buying their input elsewhere. For state-subsidised credit (KUR-BRI Micro), apart from it being cheap, its popularity owes much to the procedural simplicity to access it. Since 2016, the prospective debtors have only been required to present their identity card and a letter of confirmation from the village office concerning their business to BRI. 'Proletariat-farmers', 'semi-proletariat farmers' and PCPs can apply for this credit, since they can claim their land cultivation rights as their business. For the FFP, however, it is more difficult to access this credit, since they have no land cultivation rights. This is why, in some cases, the 'proletariat-farmers' hold on to their tiny land cultivation rights if only to enable them to apply for this credit. Meanwhile, the cooperatives only maintain a limited number of members, although they offer cheap credit. This is because the obligation to apply for credit and pay regular instalments is seen as too demanding for PCPs and, especially, the classes of labour, who may be in great need of cash money. If the PCPs and classes of labour cannot access any of the credits mentioned, their last resort is to borrow money, either from their patrons, relatives, neighbours or the *Bank Plecit*.

Similar to *Njomplang*, credit plays a different role for different agrarian classes in *Timpang*. We see in Table 6.7 that when capitalists act as creditors, they can earn lucrative revenue from their non-agricultural accumulation through oil palm trading, although they generally do not charge interest rate for credit less than Rp. 5 million. Since the debtors must sell their oil palm to them, this provides good earnings for the capitalist farmers-cum-oil palm traders. But certain capitalist farmers, like Sofian, even charge an interest rate (Rp. 20/kg lower than market price) for credit below Rp. 5 million, which means they receive double the profit (from trading and the interest rate). When capitalist farmers are the debtors, they are able to borrow huge amounts of

Table 6.7 Credit provision in *Timpang*, North Sumatera

Types of credit	*Scheme*	*Class involved*	*Utilisation*
Credit from palm oil traders • Introduced in the 1990s by capitalist farmers and has been a common credit provision since then	• Cash money credit from Rp. 5 million to Rp. 50 million • No collateral, only a commitment to sell the palm oil to the creditor • No interest rate for credit below Rp. 5 million • Credit between Rp. 5 to Rp. 20 million, interest rate is a sale price of Rp. 20–30 per kg lower than market price • Credit above Rp. 20 million, interest rate is the lower sale price of Rp. 50/kg	• Creditor: capitalist farmer-cum-traders and capitalists outside agriculture • Debtor: capitalist farmers, PCPs and classes of labour	• For capitalist farmers as creditors, credit is a form of off-farm accumulation via trading and extracting interest rates • For capitalist farmers as debtors, they may borrow up to Rp. 50 million to finance their children' education at college • PCPs mostly use their Rp. 5 million credit to buy agricultural inputs and pay medical costs. When they borrow Rp. 20 million, it is mostly for conducting customary ceremonies (weddings, funerals) and house improvement • Classes of labour generally only borrow maximum Rp. 5 million, to purchase agricultural inputs, pay medical costs and children's education
KUR-BRI Micro • see *Njomplang* above	• Cash money credit to maximum of Rp. 25 million • Neither collateral nor meticulous verification required • Flat interest rate 0.32% per month (since 2018) for three to five years	• Creditor: the state • Debtor: modest capitalist farmers, PCPs and classes of labour	• Capitalist farmers harness it to buy more land and add capital for trade business • PCPs use the money for both productive activities (rent-in palm oil fields, buy agricultural inputs, open shrimp farms, pay for children's education) and consumption (house improvement and daily consumption) • Classes of labour make use of the credit to plant or replant palm oil, finance children's education and run their petty businesses

(*Continued*)

Table 6.7 Continued

Types of credit	*Scheme*	*Class involved*	*Utilisation*
BTPN Syariah (Commercial Bank) • It claims to be a Syariah bank (based on Islamic values) but charges six times higher interest rate than KUR-BRI • It offered its service to villagers in the 2010s and since then has covered a limited number of debtors (about a tenth of total households)	• Cash money credit with an initial credit of Rp. 2 million, which could be doubled based on the performance of the debtor • No collateral • Flat interest rate of 2.08% per month for 24 instalments	• Creditor: private company • Debtor: PCPs and classes of labour	• For PCPs, the credit is harnessed to complement the capital for their petty trade • The classes of labour use the credit to meet daily consumption, rent-in palm oil fields and a little house maintenance
BAKRI/'Batak Kredit' (loanshark disguised as a credit cooperative) • The staff were sent to the village in the 2000s from its central office in Medan to offer credit and since then it has gained a limited number of debtors	• Cash money credit to a maximum of Rp. 5 million • No collateral • Flat interest rate 15% per month in daily instalments (40 days) • Flat interest rate of 10% per month for weekly instalments (8 weeks)	• Creditor: private companies • Debtor: classes of labour	• This is last a resort for the classes of labour to run their petty trades, pay medical costs and pay for children's education
Personal loan shark • It is only used in rare cases	• Cash money credit with no specific limit • No collateral • Flat interest rate of 10% per month until the debt is fully repaid	• Creditor: capitalist farmers and capitalists outside of agriculture • Debtor: classes of labour	• A lucrative off-farm avenue for capitalist farmers • Classes of labour in dire need of cash to sustain their daily consumption and to pay medical costs, children's education

(*Continued*)

Table 6.7 Continued

Types of credit	*Scheme*	*Class involved*	*Utilisation*
Other Credits Credit from relatives and neighbours • It is also only used in rare cases	• Cash money credit with no certain limit (generally only less than Rp. 2 million) • No collateral, interest rate nor fixed due date of repayment	• Creditor: sometimes PCPs but mostly classes of labour • Debtor: classes of labour	• They mostly use it to meet daily consumption

Source: fieldwork

money to expand their oil palm business or finance their children's education at college. For instance, Budi, a significant big capitalist farmer (see Chapter 5), earns credit of Rp. 400 million to pay the fees for three of his children to attend college. Similar to *Njomplang*, the PCPs and classes of labour in *Timpang* have no capacity to be creditors, except offering small sums of money to their relatives or neighbours. They are subject to being debtors to several creditors: capitalist farmers, capitalist non-agriculture, private companies and the state. Unlike *Njomplang*, the cheapest credit in *Timpang* is generally provided by oil palm traders. The most expensive credit in our oil palm village is offered by both the loan shark and BAKRI (a pseudo credit cooperative). The credit may 'consolidate' the PCP's simple reproduction by providing cheap agricultural inputs, while it may also endanger it when the credit for consumption spending puts them in a relentless debt cycle. As for the classes of labour, cheap credit from the state helps them to meet daily survival needs and yet when, due to several reasons, they only have access to expensive credit from loan sharks, they end up losing their basic means of subsistence. Some villagers have reported that several villagers from the classes of labour have lost their houses to local loan sharks.

The popularity of credit from oil palm traders owes much to the cheap interest rates involved in the credit schemes. Nonetheless, 'proletariat-farmers' and 'semi-proletariat farmers' may not be able to obtain sufficient credit from local traders when their oil palm is not properly managed and only produces a meagre yield. In these circumstances, KUR-BRI also becomes a popular credit option. In a different situation, the classes of labour may need bigger credit than Rp. 5 million to meet the required initial capital for agricultural production (planting or re-planting oil palm), financing their children's education or to complement the capital they have for their petty trade businesses. Some PCPs who need higher credit (Rp. 20 million) prefer the KUR-BRI over the credit from the local oil palm traders, since the former promises more predictable interest rates than the latter, whose rates depend mostly on market price dynamics. In other cases, some stingy local traders may only grant maximum credit of between Rp. 10–15 million to their client farmers, much lower than the KUR-BRI of Rp. 25 million. Of course, applying for credit to both local traders and the KUR-BRI is also technically possible for some PCPs. However, the instalment for both credits would be too difficult to raise.

It is often said that informal credit charges higher interest rates than formal credit (Pincus, 1996). For both *Njomplang* and *Timpang*, however, this might not be as straightforward as it may seem. It is true that in *Njomplang*, the informal personal credit for agricultural inputs charges much higher interest rates than the formal government subsidised credit of the KUR-BRI. However, it is also true that the formal micro financing of corporation-based cooperative credit (Bank Plecit) charges much higher interest than the informal community-based credit cooperative (Table 6.6). In *Timpang*, the informal credit from the local oil palm traders carries a lower interest rate than the formal KUR-BRI and, of course, the corporation-based credit cooperative (BAKRI). On the other hand, the informal credit of loan shark invokes much higher interest rates than the formal KUR-BRI (Table 6.7). It seems that when the state provides a significant subsidy, credit through formal institutions can be cheap, while informal credit can also be generous, as far as it is collectively established from below.

Pincus (1996), in his study in West Java, highlights how capitalist farmers manage to access formal credit that is cheaper than informal credit and lower their overall production cost. The practice in *Njomplang*, Central Java, supports this view, but for different reason. Despite the cheap credit in the form of KUR-BRI being available for the classes of labour and PCPs, they rather harness the cheap credit for a higher return in agricultural activity, like leasing-in *sawah*, than for buying agricultural inputs.

Technological Development

The development of production techniques, both in *Njomplang* and *Timpang*, may represent a mixed development. In *Njomplang*, traditional seeds were replaced with modern seeds in 1969 and 1979. IR 64, which was introduced in the late 1970s, remains common today in *Njomplang*, along with the new variety of seed called *Ciherang*, introduced in the 2000s. Chemical fertilisers have been widely used since the 1980s, while chemical herbicides arrived a decade later. While the chemicalisation of agriculture has been the case, mechanisation has largely stalled. Land preparation is the only agricultural task that has been mechanised through the inception of the tractor in the 1980s. Planting, weeding and harvesting are still heavily dependent on manual labour. *Ani-ani* (simple hand-held knives) for harvesting was only replaced by the sickle in the late 1970s. Water pumps were introduced in the 1990s, and these have been crucial for *sawah* in the northern part of the village to enable harvesting twice a year. Threshing machines were only introduced in the mid-2010s to replace manual threshing. They ease the work and reduce the working time by half.[15] From an international perspective, the mechanisation of Javanese rice cultivation is far behind the advanced countries like the US, Japan and South Korea.

The most pivotal development of production technique in *Njomplang* has been trialling combine harvester machine. It was first introduced by *penebas* for some plots of *sawah* in the dry season of 2016, a time when harvesters were fewer (see previous section). The trial by the *penebas* proved to be economically more profitable for them. It offered 30 percent lower cost than harvesting through the *bawon* system.[16] The use of the harvester machine also reduced the harvesting and threshing losses almost to zero, compared to about 15 percent loss by the *bawon* and conventional threshing (Simatupang & Timmer, 2008: 70). Harvesting time is also reduced to about a quarter of the time needed for manual harvesters.[17] This has attracted the interest of the capitalist farmers in *Njomplang*. Nevertheless, using the machine is not an easy option as there are both technical problems and social challenges.

The first technical issue with the harvester machine is that it does not work properly during the rainy season. The wheels get jammed in the wet paddy field and the machine cannot harvest the lying paddy stalk due to heavy rain. One cannot use the services of the harvester machine during the dry season while hire harvesters for the rainy season. This is socially unfeasible, since the harvesters could boycott the harvesting during the rainy season as their revenge for being abandoned in the dry harvesting season. Another problem in both dry and rainy seasons is that the harvester machine cannot be used for *sawah* that is surrounded by other paddy fields which have not been harvested. Javanese *sawah* is generally scattered across different parts of the village rather than consolidated in a single location, making it difficult for the mobility of the harvester machine. Harvesters who are also sharecroppers can easily block the harvesting by not allowing the machine to pass through their controlled paddy fields. The trial in 2016 was successful only because the *penebas* had bought the rights to harvest a group of plots of *sawah* in one location that enabled the harvester machine to pass through.

Even if such problems have been successfully addressed, the combine harvester machine still cannot be used when planting, which needs a lot of workers, is not yet mechanised. As discussed in the previous sections, planting is often tied to harvesting. Workers can only be guaranteed harvesting rights if they have participated in the planting. Should such harvesting rights be abolished by the introduction of the harvester machines, there is no longer sufficient incentive to attract workers to participate in the planting. Using the harvester machine without mechanising planting will only create acute production problems, similar to what Byres (1995) has described for cotton production in the US during the early twentieth century. Rice planting machines have been used in the neighbouring villages of *Njomplang* in the last few years. However, a bulk of trays is needed to plant the seeds. It is considered not only impractical but also more expensive than using manual labour. The machine in the neighbouring villages has not been used during the rainy season.

With such acute technical obstacles, the classes of labour have effectively prevented the partial application of harvester machines (during the dry season) in *Njomplang*. There is a widespread threat from the classes of labour and PCPs that they would not perform any agricultural tasks if the capitalist farmers used harvester machines in the dry season. 'Let us see if they dare to use the harvester machine, who would plant their paddy?' they rhetorically ask. Many capitalist farmers have mentioned their fear that labour would take revenge on them if they used the harvester machine for the dry season. 'It is difficult for now to use the harvester machine because of labour grievances. We are still waiting for harvesting and planting machines to be perfected', a capitalist farmer said. With this stalemate, the production techniques in *Njomplang* have neither significantly accelerated the production process nor raised the yield over the last few decades. The stalled mechanisation in *Njomplang* is not merely due to the resistances from the labouring class, as Scott (1976) may suggest, but also the acute technical problems of the machines.

The desperation of the current government to increase rice productivity may shorten the waiting period for capitalist farmers to apply new technology. When planting machines and harvester machines have settled their technical issues, capitalist farmers would be in a strong position to abolish the social obstacles to the harvester machine (access to *sawah*) by withdrawing land cultivation rights of sharecroppers. Should this happen, sharecropping, which has been the norm in Javanese rice cultivation for centuries, might face a significant blow. Sharecropping may only be maintained by a few 'politico-bureaucrat capitalist farmers' for political reasons, not for production purposes.

Oil palm production in *Timpang* is even less mechanised, although it shares a similar degree of chemicalisation of agriculture. Chemical fertilisers and herbicides were simultaneously applied in the 1990s when oil palm was introduced to the village. At the accumulative level, chemicalisation in *Timpang* may be less intrusive than in *Njomplang* only because some, mostly non-capitalist, farmers do not apply any fertilisers or herbicides to their fields. Some point to the reduction in production cost, while others simply believe that fertilisers have no significant role to play in increasing the yield and that weeding can be done without the help of chemical herbicides. However, at the individual level, especially with significant capitalist farmers, they have heavily relied upon chemical fertilisers and herbicides.

Mechanisation is largely absent in *Timpang*. There was the introduction in the 2010s of lawnmower machines for weeding by the 'big capitalist farmers'. Another technological change in *Timpang* is the inception of the 'along-along' (a modified motorcycle) in the 2000s, used to pick up the oil palm fruit from the field and put it on the roadside to be carried away by mini-truck to the local agents (oil palm traders) or processing plants. As discussed earlier, this 'along-along' has effectively shortened the harvesting time by about a half. The last development is the adoption of aluminium-fibre fruit picker poles for harvesting the oil palm to replace the bamboo-made poles, the former being a more comfortable and efficient tool for harvesting. Technological developments in *Timpang* have more shortened the production process than increased the yield.

Output and Land Productivity

As discussed earlier, each of the production factors, from land arrangement, the labour system, credit provision to the technological development, play an indispensable role in producing the agricultural output. Based on the recent available production factors, our survey in *Njomplang* shows the yield is, on average, about six tonnes (6.2) of dry stalk paddy per hectare or one tonne (1.03) per *iring* (Table 6.1). There is no inverse relationship between larger and smaller land cultivation. This is similar to Pincus's study in West Java (1996). The yield in *Njomplang* is higher than the national average by about 20 percent (see Chapter 3). However, since the inception of a new variety of seeds in the late 1970s and the widespread use of chemical fertilisers in 1980s, the yield has been stagnant at about six tonnes. There is also the question of the decline of soil fertility. Recently, with 60 percent higher input of fertilisers than in the 1980s, the soil still produces about the same level of yield.[18] The yield stagnation and soil degradation only mirror a national trend (Simatupang & Timmer, 2008). Farmers apply more fertilisers to obtain higher yields but, in return, the soil fertility is degraded and only produces a lower yield. To keep the previous yield, farmers then apply more fertilisers, which only makes the soil degradation worse. At this point, *Njomplang* may have arrived at its metabolic rift (Foster, 2000). On the other hand, the application of organic fertilisers is only a rare case. For the PCPs and classes of labour, organic fertilisers only mean more laborious work to do, which prevents them from taking paid jobs elsewhere.

A similar trend applies to *Timpang*. The output per hectare of oil palm (per harvest) has been stagnant at about 1.6 tonnes since the 1990s (Table 6.9). This is about a third to a half of the national average (see Chapter 3). The fertility of the soil has also declined, if we consider that the application of fertiliser is twice as high now as in the 1990s but only produces a similar level of yield.[19] However, apart from soil degradation, the stalling of the land productivity in *Timpang* is also due to the widespread use of second class seeds (un-certified seeds). This is not only because the certified seeds are expensive[20] but also because they are difficult to obtain. Related to this is replanting. Many oil palm trees in the village are too old (more than 25 years) and they need to be replaced with newly qualified seeds if the productivity of the oil palm field is to increase. However, this is not easy considering the high cost it will incur, but also the loss of a source of income for at least four years.[21] At the same time, the government's support for replanting programs is negligible (see Chapter 3).

In *Timpang*, instead of an 'inverse relationship' of farm size and productivity between bigger and smaller cultivation, we see the trend of 'economies of scale', where the bigger cultivators generate higher land productivity. As shown in Table 6.9, the capitalist farmers produce the highest land productivity at 1.9 tonnes/month. They generate 10 percent higher productivity than PCPs (1.7 tonnes) and almost 30 percent higher than semi-proletariat farmers (1.2 tonnes). Since the incidence of 'proletariat-farmers' in *Timpang* is negligible, as mentioned in Chapter 5, they are not included in the survey. On average, capitalist farmers separate themselves from non-capitalist farmers by producing 25 percent higher output. As shown in Appendix 4, the secret of the capitalist farmers for generating higher yields is that they spend almost three times more on fertilisers than the average non-capitalist farmer. They are not only applying a greater volume of fertilisers, but also using premium brands. On the other hand, the 'semi-proletariat farmers' and, to a lesser degree, PCPs, who sell their labour all year round, are thus otherwise occupied with this work, and they often treat their own fields poorly or even completely abandon them.

Land productivity in both *Njomplang* and *Timpang* could have been higher, even with the current production factors available, if different production process had been used. Land productivity in *Njomplang* could have been higher if the loss during harvesting and threshing had been reduced to almost zero by the adoption of the harvester machine (see above). Furthermore, in *Njomplang*, where more than three-quarters of *sawah* is served by irrigation, it is possible to plant and harvest three times a year, instead of twice. However, the main problem is that planting only at some plots of *sawah*, and not all, would attract the pests that would easily destroy the paddy. Some capitalist farmers tried this in the past but ended up with acute failure. The 'proletariat-farmers' and 'semi-proletariat farmers' are simply not interested in planting for a third time during the peak dry season (August to October), because the need to use water pumps increases the production cost (between 20 and 40 percent).[22] With their insubstantial land control (most of them are sharecroppers), planting in this situation is only a 'waste of our labour'.

At the same time, it is neither desirable nor practical for capitalist farmers to rent-in the land from other agrarian classes in the village. First, it requires a huge amount of initial capital to lease-in the vast amount of land in the village, while the rise of production cost, although modest, makes the risk too high. Moreover, cooperation among capitalist farmers is required to fully cultivate large portions of paddy fields in the village. However, cooperation among capitalist farmers is not a straightforward option given the internal differences that have been discussed in Chapter 5. For example, there would be no incentive for 'politico-bureaucrat capitalist farmers' and 'professional-capitalist farmers' to cultivate rice with a higher risk when they are occupied with their non-agricultural activities.

The production process is also inseparable from the non-agricultural activities of the farmers' households. In *Timpang*, land productivity could have been higher if some capitalist farmers, like Budi (Chapter 5), a member of the agrarian class who generate the highest productivity, had not allocated their funds to financing their children at college at the expense of reducing agricultural inputs. For example, by cutting the fertilisers costs by half, they decrease the oil palm yield by about a third. Their priority for non-agricultural activities, such as their children's education, highlights the high-risk nature of oil palm production, despite the fact that current oil palm capitalist farmers acquire a higher rate of profitability than rice capitalist farmers, to which we now turn our concern.

The Income from 'Own-Account' Farming

The central aspect of our survey was to map the income from 'own-account' farming of different farmers. As mentioned in the methodology, the Survey was designed to provide a rather crude estimation than a precise figure of 'own-account' farming's income from different agrarian classes. The income is deducted from the total value produced minus total production cost. The details of total production cost and total value produced for each agrarian class in *Njomplang* can be found in Appendix 3. Our survey shows that capitalist farmers reap the highest income in rice cultivation. They earn Rp. 39.1 million per season from their average land cultivation of 2.25 hectares (Table 6.8). In monthly terms, this income amounts to almost seven times the district's minimum wage.[23] It is difficult to situate the farming income for capitalist farmers in *Njomplang* in a broader context. At the national level and Central Java, BPS only reveals the average 'rate of profit' (income from 'own-account' farming)

Table 6.8 Land productivity and the income from 'own-account' farming of agrarian classes in *Njomplang*, Central Java

Class	*Average land cultivation*	*Average land productivity (per season)*	*Average income from 'own-account' farming/season*	*Comparison of monthly income from 'own-account' farming to monthly district's minimum wage*
Capitalist farmers	2.25 ha	6.2 tonne/ha (1.03 tonne/*iring*)	39.1 million	6.5:1
PCPs	0.84 ha	1.02 tonne/*iring* (6.1 tonne/ha)	10.8 million	1.8:1
'Substantial PCPs'	0.67 ha	1.05 tonne/*iring* (6.3 tonne/ha)	13.1 million	2.2: 1
Formal PCPs	0.93 ha	1.01 tonne/iring (6.1 tonne/ha)	8.7 million	1.5: 1
Classes of labour				
'Semi-proletariat farmers'	0.47 ha	1.05 tonne/*iring* (6.3 tonne/ha)	5.4 million	0.9: 1
'Proletariat-farmers'	0.30 ha	1.02 tonne/*iring* (6.1 tonne/ha)	4.1 million	0.7: 1

Source: fieldwork

for *all* rice farmers as a general category, regardless of their class location (see Chapter 3).

If we compare the 'own-account' farming income of capitalist farmers (of any types), who cultivate their land with wage labour for one hectare of *sawah* with 'landlord-capitalists' who sharecrop out their land, the former earns at least 30 percent higher than the latter.[24] This is in contrast to Hüsken's calculation (1979: 150) in Northern Central Java four decades ago when sharecropping (on a *mretelu* basis) was between 20 and 30 percent more profitable than cultivation with wage labour. As shown in Chapter 5, given the more profitable nature of hiring wage labour, there is little surprise that many capitalist farmers prefer to cultivate their land with wage labour than sharecropping out the land.

The income from 'own-account' farming for PCPs in *Njomplang* is much lower than for capitalist farmers. With an average of land cultivation of 0.84 hectares, PCPs only generate less than a third of the capitalist farmers' income (Table 6.8). Their monthly income from 'own-account' farming is about Rp. 2.7 million. This income for PCPs is about 80 percent higher than the district minimum wage (excluding the income from *bawon*). The group of 'substantial PCPs' earns a higher income than the group of 'formal PCPs' and the PCP's average. This owes much to the fact that the former has no land rent cost to be paid while the latter must bear a significant land rent cost (see Appendix 3). The group of 'formal PCPs' also tends to bear a higher labour cost, since the practice of performing all the tasks by using family labour is less common for 'formal PCPs' than 'substantial PCPs', because the former cultivates a larger amount of land than the latter, even though they receive a lower yield due to sharecropping arrangements.

For the group of classes of labour, like the 'semi-proletariat farmers' in *Njomplang*, the income from 'own-account' farming per season is only about a seventh of the capitalist farmers (Rp. 5.4 million). With the average land cultivation of 0.47 hectare, the monthly income of 'semi-proletariat farmers' is slightly below of the district minimum wage (Table 6.8). This is insufficient to meet their subsistence. The income from farming is even lower for the group of 'proletariat-farmers'. Having the smallest amount of land cultivation (0.30 hectare on average), their average income is only Rp. 4.1 million, which amounts to only a ninth of the capitalist farmers' incomes. In monthly term, their income is only three-quarters of the district minimum wage. For both the 'semi-proletariat farmers' and 'proletariat-farmers', their minimal income from rice cultivation effectively forces them to sell their labour elsewhere, if they wish to sustain their subsistence.

Why the classes of labour continue with paddy cultivation despite its meagre income is at least for two reasons. First, as mentioned earlier, land cultivation rights under sharecropping, in many cases, is attached to the right of harvesting (*bawon*), which is the most lucrative agricultural task. If we include the average earning from *bawon* for a household with two labourers,[25] the monthly income for those classes of labour would rise significantly. For the group of 'semi-proletariat farmers', their monthly income would increase to Rp. 2.75

million. This is about 80 percent higher than the district minimum wage. The income of the 'proletariat-farmers' would rise to Rp. 2.4 million, which is around 60 percent higher than the minimum wage. Another reason for the classes of labour continuing with their meagre rice cultivation is strategic, in that it helps them to obtain cheap credit. As shown in the previous section, those running small businesses (such as rice cultivation) have easier access to cheap credit through the BRI-KUR scheme than members of the FFP, who have no such businesses.

Similar to *Njomplang*, different agrarian classes in *Timpang* receive different level of incomes from 'own-account' farming. However, while for *Njomplang* this difference is owed exclusively to the different size of farming among the agrarian classes, *Timpang*'s case reveals another crucial factor: that of the differentiation of land productivity. As mentioned earlier, capitalist farmers in *Timpang* generate higher land productivity than PCPs and the group of semi-proletariat farmers. There is also a difference between the group of capitalist farmers and other agrarian classes as far as sale prices are concerned. On average, the sale price for capitalist farmers is similar to the sale price of non-capitalist farmers (Rp. 1460/kg for capitalist farmers, Rp. 1375/kg for PCPs and Rp. 1345 for semi-proletariat farmers). However, if we only look at 'big' capitalist farmers (owning more than eight hectares, see Chapter 7), they manage to sell their oil palm at a rate 15 percent higher (Rp. 1585/kg) than the other agrarian classes. The main reason for this is the ability of 'big' capitalist farmers to sell their oil palm directly to local processing plants.

Like their compatriot in Java, capitalist farmers in *Timpang* reap the highest 'own-account' farming income.[26] The detailed figures of total value produced and total production cost for each agrarian class in our oil palm village is shown in Appendix 4. Since the number of 'formal PCPs' and 'proletariat-farmers' is negligible in the village, for the reason that was discussed in Chapter 5, we exclude them from our survey of the income from 'own-account' farming. As shown in Table 6.9, capitalist farmers reap a higher rate of income than PCPs (in this case, we mean the group of 'substantial PCPs') and 'semi-proletariat farmers'. Oil palm capitalist farmers, with their average land cultivation of 8.30 hectares, receive income from farming of Rp. 185.6 million/year. Similar to capitalist farmers in *Njomplang*, the monthly income of capitalist farmers in *Timpang* from their farming amounts to almost seven times the district minimum wage.[27] As in Java, however, we cannot compare this income with the national or provincial figures provided by BPS, since they only cover the average for all farmers.

The income from 'own-account' farming for PCPs in our oil palm village is only about a third of the capitalist farmers'. With the average land cultivation of 2.30 hectares, PCPs earn Rp. 51.5 million per year (Table 6.9). The income for the PCPs mentioned is the result of a common practice in the village, where they perform all the agricultural tasks with their own labour. For some PCPs who have two jobs and cannot perform certain tasks and have to hire in other's labour (harvesting), their income is slightly

Table 6.9 Land productivity and the income from 'own-account' farming of agrarian classes in *Timpang*, North Sumatra

Class	*Average land cultivation*	*Average land productivity (per month)*	*Average 'own-account' farming income/year*	*Comparison of monthly 'own-account' farming income to monthly district's minimum wage*
Capitalist farmers	8.30 ha	1.9 tonne/ha	185.6 million	6.7: 1
PCPs				
Substantial PCPs'	2.30 ha	1.7 tonne/ha	51.5 million	1.9: 1
Classes of labour				
'Semi-proletariat farmers'	0.70 ha	1.2 tonne/ha	17.9 million	0.6: 1

Source: fieldwork

lower. The monthly 'own-account' farming income for PCPs is around 90 percent higher than the district minimum wage stipulated in 2018. This is similar to PCPs in *Njomplang*.

The least income from 'own-account' farming on oil palm production in *Timpang* is received by the group of 'semi-proletariat farmers'. They only generate about a tenth of the income of capitalist farmers. Their average land cultivation of 0.70 hectares only delivers them yearly earnings of Rp. 17.9 million (Table 6.9). In monthly terms, this is only about two-third of the minimum wage in the district. In this regard, the group of 'semi-proletariat farmers' in *Timpang* is in a worse situation than their comrades, the 'semi-proletariat farmers' in *Njomplang* (excluding *bawon*). With this minuscule income from oil palm cultivation, these members of the classes of labour in *Timpang* must sell their labour elsewhere throughout the year to meet their survival.

In both *Njomplang* and *Timpang*, if we look at the yearly income *per hectare*, the income from paddy cultivation (Rp. 34.8 million) is higher than oil palm production (Rp. 22.4 million) by about 35 percent. Nonetheless, the figure is quite the opposite in class terms. Owing much to the larger average land cultivation, oil palm capitalist farmers in North Sumatra earn higher total income from 'own-account' farming (in millions) than rice capitalist farmers in Central Java (Table 6.8 and 6.9). This suggests that in farming terms, current capitalist farmers in oil palm production are wealthier than their associates in rice cultivation. However, if we look at the household total incomes, that depends on what they do outside farming. This will be the focus of the next chapter.

The superiority of oil palm capitalist farmers over rice capitalist farmers in farming should not be seen as a static and permanent situation. By being exposed to the global market, the sale price for oil palm has been highly volatile, resulting in changes in the level of income from 'own-account' farming. It can be estimated that a 25 percent drop of the sale price would decrease the income from oil palm per hectare by about 35 percent, while a fall to half the price would bring down the income to only a third of the normal level. Both scenarios occurred at the end of 2018, forcing the government to remove the export levies for oil palm products (Chapter 3). This undoubtedly harmed the oil palm capitalist farmers in *Timpang*.

The falling sale price had an even more detrimental impact on the PCPs and 'semi-proletariat farmers' in the village. With the decline of the sale price by half, the PCP's 'own-account' farming income was reduced to only about 40 percent, making their monthly earnings equal to 20 percent below the district minimum wage. This is the point when they were transformed into being members of the classes of labour. This highly volatile market seems to provide the impetus for the situation where PCPs in *Timpang* are eager to dispose of their labour all year round. For 'semi-proletariat farmers', the 50 percent price plummet brought down their earnings by 60 percent, making their monthly income from 'own-account' farming only a quarter of the minimum wage in the district.

The decisive contrast between the capitalist farmers and non-capitalist farmers, especially the classes of labour, can be found in the share of the total farming income allotted to capital and to labour. In current *Timpang*, labour only receives about a tenth, while the rest of the total share is obtained by capital. This share for labour in *Timpang* is much lower than that in *Njomplang*. There, they gain almost a third of the share, whereas capital earns about two-thirds of the total. This reflects the much higher intensive nature of rice cultivation than oil palm production (about three times). However, the share between capital and labour is not only determined by the cultivation nature of the crops. To understand this, we need to see the change in share overtime.

In *Njomplang*, it is possible to calculate the change of the 'share' of total income between capital and labour overtime, since a reliable dataset on wage levels in the previous period (2001) is available from the notes of the 'village meeting'. The detailed procedure to estimate real wages can be found in Appendix 5. The same cannot be done for *Timpang* as the data is unavailable. In *Njomplang*, the real wage has increased twice in the last one and a half decades and so has labour's 'share' of the total farming income. This rise to the detriment of capital owes much to the class dynamics in *Njomplang* (Chapter 5). From the capital point of view, their share of total farming income in the mid-2010s was 15 percent lower than in the early 2000s. The decline resonates with the finding of a previous study in one of the Subang villages in West Java (Pincus, 1996). With this deterioration, the capitalist farmers have tried to restore their share through the mechanisation of agriculture. As this effort is still facing technical difficulties, they have become more reliant on non-agricultural revenues, as we shall see in the next chapter.

Non-Main Crops Agricultural Production

Apart from the main crop production in *Njomplang* (rice) and *Timpang* (oil palm), farmers in both villages grow other crops. In *Njomplang*, they grow other crops during the off-season (August to October). The most common crop in this season is mung bean. For capitalist farmers, growing mung bean is predominantly a hobby in farming and is used for owner consumption, since the income is meagre. This explains why this farming activity is confined exclusively to 'typical capitalist farmers'. Some of them grow fruit or vegetables. Watermelon is seen to be too risky because of the unpredictable weather, although the profit is desirable.[28] For vegetables, they are considered less profitable given the cost of using the water pump when the price of the vegetables is unfavourable.

Mung bean is also common for PCPs. Other than using it for owner consumption, growing mung bean is an opportunity to earn extra income.[29] This, however, assumes that they have their own water pump. If they have no water pump, the cost is 50 percent higher and, thus, the profit falls by about 12 percent. While growing this crop provides considerable extra income, PCPs who do not have a water pump do not grow mung beans. They prefer to dispose of their labour elsewhere which offers a higher income. For both 'semi-proletariat farmers' and 'proletariat-farmers', they would rather sell their labour than grow mung bean just to earn quick cash money, which they desperately need for their daily consumption. This makes growing mung bean or other crops involves a few farmers in *Njomplang*, while most large areas of *sawah* are left untouched during the off-season.

Timpang is quite the reverse of *Njomplang*. Here, rice is the most common crop after oil palm. This is not surprising, given that *Timpang* used to be one of the rice baskets of the district (Chapter 4). For capitalist farmers in *Timpang* who grow rice, it could mean extra income if there is a surplus after allocation for owner consumption. But rice can also constitute the class position of the capitalist farmers themselves. When their ownership of oil palm is less than the minimum amount for capitalist farmers in *Timpang* (four hectares) and yet they own considerable paddy field, the earning from rice cultivation can be harnessed to hire in labour for oil palm production. This, by definition, makes them capitalist farmers. However, today, fewer capitalist farmers in *Timpang* are growing rice than PCPs, because the capitalist farmers have sufficient initial capital in their hands to transform their former paddy fields into oil palm, which is currently more profitable, while for the PCPs, this is not so easy given their limited capital. Apart from owner consumption, PCPs are generally able to sell some of their rice. For 'semi-proletariat farmers' and 'proletariat-farmers' in *Timpang*, they are keen to lease-in paddy field to grow rice for securing their daily household consumption rather than buying it from the market.

Akin to main agricultural production, in both *Njomplang* and *Timpang*, the members of the classes of labour ('semi-proletariat farmers' and 'proletariat-farmers') have no much significant income from non-main agricultural production. They prefer to dispose of their labour elsewhere to earn higher income or just quick cash money. For PCPs, non-main agricultural production can help not only their consolidation but also their class transformation into capitalist farmers, given their income from main agricultural production is higher than both the 'semi-proletariat farmers' and 'proletariat-farmers'. For some capitalist farmers, especially in *Timpang*, second crop cultivation provides additional capital, while for others it even constitutes their very class position.

Conclusion

It has been argued in this chapter that the nature and the change in land arrangement, labour system, credit provision and technological development that, all together, are pivotal to land productivity and the income from 'own-account' farming have been crucially shaped by the dynamics of class power. The relentless incidence of sharecropping in *Njomplang*, despite the advancement of capitalist relations, owes much to the class structure and class relations in the village. In Pearce's terms (1983), *Njomplang* represents the low incidence of 'class dominance' while, at the same time, the 'labour process' is under-mechanised. However, Pearce tends to take the labour process for granted. As shown in *Njomplang*, the under-mechanisation of agriculture is mainly due to the relative balance of the bargaining power between capital and labour and the technical problems of mechanisation. Moreover, where filling the posts of village officials remain lucrative avenues for non-agricultural activities, sharecropping is a crucial instrument to secure political support, particularly for 'politico-bureaucrat capitalist farmers', instead of simply securing labour.

Class power also plays a crucial role for the inception of the currently dominant labour arrangement (contract by task) in the two villages. *Njomplang* confirms Pincus's argument in West Java (1996), where class power is more crucial in shaping labour arrangements than the technical aspects of production suggested by neo-classical economists. Nevertheless, while Pincus's account only provides anecdotal evidence on the processes and mechanisms that shape the labour arrangement (White et al., 1998), our study has explained more comprehensively the processes and mechanisms by tracing them back over the last few decades. For *Timpang*, we have contributed to the understanding of the dynamics of the labour system in oil palm production that has been largely overlooked in the literature.

We have also seen that class dynamics are intertwined with gender. The recent decline of the labour supply in *Njomplang* is related to the complex gender-based division of labour of the migrant workers in their village of origin. At the production site, the change in certain labour arrangements, such as the abolition of the free lunch as a component of the wage in *Njomplang*, has added more burdens to female workers, since they must prepare the meal for themselves and their male partner in the early morning. Wage-wise, female workers in the two villages receive lower wages than their fellow male workers for the same agricultural tasks they perform. The literature has depicted this gender pay gap elsewhere (Huyer, 2016). The gender pay gap in *Timpang* is higher than in *Njomplang*. This largely owes much to the intensive labour process of rice cultivation in *Njomplang* that needs certain crucial agricultural tasks (planting and weeding) to be performed by female workers. Under such circumstances, female workers in *Njomplang* have a higher bargaining position than their comrades in the less intensive oil palm production in *Timpang*, though they still experience the double burden of taking care of domestic tasks and a wage job at the same time (Bhattacharya, 2017).

The technological development of agricultural production cannot be separated either from the social relations, especially from the class relations at play in the specific context. In *Njomplang*, the resistance of the labouring class to the adoption of combine harvester machines and planting machines resonates with what has already been mentioned in the literature (Scott, 1985). Nonetheless, the acute and complex technical problems concerning both machines have also played a crucial role in the stalled mechanisation in the village. Should the technical problems be resolved, the stronger bargaining power would then be in the hands of the capitalist farmers to pursue full mechanisation and the abolition of sharecropping. Meanwhile, in *Timpang*, the inception of the lawnmower to perform through contract by task has been the initiative of 'big' capitalist farmers in the central hamlets to lower the risk of being played by labour in the daily wage arrangement.

For credit provision, local class dynamics intertwine with state intervention through the credit programs. It is often perceived that informal credit charges higher interest rates than formal credit (Pincus, 1996). However, this may not be an obvious conclusion. In both *Njomplang* and *Timpang*, the nature of credit (interest rate) in rural areas is more shaped by the state's intervention and the initiation of the credit (from the collective-below versus individual-above) than simply the division between formal and informal. We have shown that credit provided by formal institutions could be cheap if the state supplies sufficient subsidy and informal credit could also be generous when it is collectively organised from below.

The class dynamics that drive the land arrangement, labour system, credit provision and technological development eventually form the level of land productivity. In *Njomplang*, there are neither economies of scale nor an inverse relationship between the size of the farming and productivity. Land productivity across different agrarian classes is similar. Land productivity in the village has been stagnant in the last few decades. Instead of solely focusing on technology and policy, as mainstream economists suggest, land productivity in *Njomplang* owes much to social organisation, especially class dynamics (Bernstein, 2010). The resistance against mechanisation in *Njomplang* owes much to the class structure that allows the continuation of sharecropping that can be used by the classes of labour to block the further application of combine harvester machines and, thus, the advancement of land productivity. At the same time, soil degradation that contributes to the halt in land productivity may signal that *Njomplang* has reached its 'metabolic rift' (Foster, 2000) given that the higher level of fertiliser application still only generates the same output. The stalling of land productivity is also the case in *Timpang*, though it has not reached its 'metabolic rift'. Nonetheless, big cultivators (capitalist farmers) generate higher productivity than the smaller cultivators (non-capitalist farmers). This is not simply the result of 'economies of scale' as mainstream economists have often championed. PCPs and 'semi-proletariat farmers' generate lower productivity because their oil palm fields are poorly tended, or can be completely abandoned when the owners have been occupied by working for others all year round.

The income from 'own-account' farming is also significantly different across agrarian classes. Capitalist farmers, both in *Njomplang* and *Timpang*, earn a higher income than non-capitalist farmers. Capitalist farmers generate income from farming three times greater than PCPs and more than six times more than the classes of labour. For PCPs in *Njomplang*, their farming income is about 30 percent higher than the minimum wage, while for PCPs in *Timpang*, it is 50 percent greater. They also receive income from non-main agricultural production, although at a much lower level than capitalist farmers. Despite these incomes from 'own-account' farming, they are still ready to sell their labour throughout the year, with the exception of some substantial PCPs in *Njomplang*. This negates the view of the neo-populist supporters who often regard the will of PCPs to work harder is simply because of the demographic dynamics in their household (Ploeg, 2013: 33). We suggest that the PCPs' willingness to sell their labour to buy more land is rather a response to the wider accumulation dynamics in the countryside and beyond. They are keen to follow their materially-successful neighbour of capitalist farmers.

'Semi-proletariat farmers' and 'proletariat-farmers' receive the lowest income from their 'own-account' farming. In *Njomplang*, if the revenue from *bawon* is excluded, they obtain lower than the district minimum wage. When it is included, their income is slightly higher than the minimum wage; this puts them in a much better position than their comrades in *Timpang*, who can only generate an income lower than the district minimum wage. The 'own-account' farming income for 'semi-proletariat farmers' in our oil palm village is squeezed further when the price of oil palm falls. At the same time, the income from non-main agricultural production in *Timpang* (rice) is only enough for own consumption, while in *Njomplang*, only rarely are they involved in this non-main agricultural production (vegetables or fruit) even though the income is considerable. Their significant need to earn a cash income during the off-season forces them to sell off their labour elsewhere rather than growing a second crop. With the dismal income from overall farming activity (both the main and second crop), the classes of labour in the two villages have to dispose of their labour all year round for the sake of survival.

The opposite fate of the capitalist farmers and classes of labour is also reflected in the share of total farming income. In *Njomplang*, where the data is available, the share to labour has increased two-fold as the real wage has doubled in the last one and half decades. This means the share for capital is lower by 15 percent from the previous decade. This decline is similar to Pincus's case of 'South Subang' village (1996), where the change was due to the larger incidence of 'middle farmers' and lower inequality, than his 'North Subang', where there was more widespread landlessness. However, while Pincus does less to depict the class relations that shape such a decline, our study has shown the struggle of the classes of labour have effectively urged wage improvement through the 'village meetings' that since democratisation have revealed their progressive nature. This is the value of looking into the class relations at play rather than simply providing a static picture of class structure.

With this lower share and considering the soil degradation and stalling land productivity, the capitalist farmers in *Njomplang* need to mechanise rice cultivation if they wish to restore their share levels. So long as a standstill remains, given the acute technical problems and the resistance from the labouring classes, farming in *Njomplang* does not appear to be a promising avenue for accumulation. In *Timpang*'s oil palm production, the capitalist farmers are generating higher average income than their compatriots in *Njomplang*. However, the high volatility of the oil palm price and the stagnant land productivity of the last few decades prevent them from depending solely on oil palm production for their accumulation strategy. Because of the limitations experienced in both villages, the capitalist farmers in *Njomplang* and *Timpang* are looking elsewhere outside of farming to consolidate their class position. This will be the concern of the next chapter.

Notes

1 The willing sharecroppers are usually their relatives who sharecrop in the land out of pity. If they (widows or too old farmers) do not have relatives available to sharecrop, they need to hire 'farming contractor' to take care of their land.
2 The only land pawning transaction found involved Karto, the politico-bureaucrat capitalist farmer, who pawned his parcels of land to another capitalist farmer, in order to buy a car.
3 Until the 1980s, *Njomplang* was a much more 'secular' village, even though most of the villagers were Muslims. The change came in 1990s, when a villager established a *Pondok Pesantren* (Islamic Boarding School) and invited a qualified Islamic teacher (Kyai) to live in the village. *Njomplang* has been gradually transformed into a more religious village. The practice of land pawning is now strongly condemned by most villagers.
4 This may relate to the rise in remittances from their children elsewhere and the significant increase (two-fold more than in the previous period) of salary for civil servants since the era of President Abdurahman Wahid's administration in 2001.
5 A few households perform planting entirely by their family labour when the husband joins his wife to plant.
6 Others might see it as 'symmetric labour relation' (Stoler, 1977a).
7 It is estimated that the workers (all female) involved in the planting season in the 2000s numbered between 85 and 90. Local workers accounted for about 43, while migrant labourers were 44. For harvesting, migrant workers alone numbered between 190 and 210. The number of local harvesters was about the same as migrant labourers.
8 It was initiated by a petty entrepreneur from Probolinggo, East Java. The male villagers previously only grew fruit and sold the coconut fruit (which is much cheaper than the latex from coconut tress), while the female dwellers made bamboo boxes.
9 The daily earning from tapping coconut (at least 30 trees) is about Rp. 126 – 132 thousand. For planting, a female worker can receive Rp. 120 thousand per day. The same earning applies to male workers for sowing. Harvesting is the most lucrative. If, on average, each harvester received one tonne of dry stalk paddy as their share (*bawon*) from

three weeks work, their daily earnings, with the price of the dry stalk paddy, in 2017 was about Rp. 214 thousand.

10 Harvesting one hectare of palm oil in a day only needs one worker, while a hectare of paddy field requires at least 48 harvesters. The number is even higher if we calculate rice harvesting in a normal day's work (eight hours), given the practice in *Njomplang* is that the harvesters works for 9–11 hours per day.

11 If harvesting of palm oil is twice a month, in a year, the harvesting of a hectare of palm oil needs 24 workers. For rice, it requires 96 workers when the paddy is harvested twice a year.

12 Once, they were paid a lower harvesting fee (premi) than the agreed deal.

13 One tractor (usually only has one driver, while some have two) in one day may prepare several pieces of land owned/controlled by different landowners/landholders. When each of the landowners provided a meal on the same day for the drivers, it was conceivable that food would be wasted.

14 In this Foster Father relationship, businessmen (palm oil traders from the city) agreed to improve road conditions by putting more rocks down to make the road more resilient (before, the road was simply fragile ground which could be washed away during the rainy season), and in return, the local farmers had to sell their palm oil fruit to this businessmen at Rp. 25/kg lower than the market price.

15 It was introduced by a local mechanic who modified a diesel generator to move the thresher. It is sold for Rp. 2.2 million per threshing machine.

16 The cost for a combine harvester machine's services is Rp. 500 thousand per *iring* or Rp. 3 million per hectare. The service includes the delivery of the yield to the landowner's house. If the share of the *bawon* per *iring* is about 142 kg (with the average yield per *iring* being one tonne) then, using the average price of dry stalk paddy for capitalist farmers in 2017 (Rp. 4610/kg), the cost for the *bawon* is about Rp. 655 thousands/*iring* (31 percent higher than the cost of the harvester machines).

17 A combine harvester machine only needs twelve hours to harvest one hectare of paddy field, using three operator workers. Manual harvesting requires six working days (nine to ten hours per day) with eight harvesters to perform such a task.

18 From the interview in the village, in the 1980s, the average application of fertilisers was about 240–300 kg per hectare per season. In recent *Njomplang*, it is 420–480 kg per hectare. The average increase per decade is about 60 kg/hectare. The figures are about 20 percent higher for *sawah* in the northern part of the village.

19 In the 1990s, the fertiliser per hectare of palm oil per year was about 272 kg–304 kg and in the contemporary *Timpung*, it is about 544 kg–608 kg.

20 The price of certified seeds is two to four times higher than non-certified seeds.

21 To replant one hectare of palm oil, one needs at least Rp. 60 million.

22 The cost includes the rent for the water pump and fuel. For the rent, it costs Rp. 200 thousands (a fifth of the normal production cost). For fuel, each session of water pumping costs about Rp. 167 thousand or almost a fifth of the normal production cost. If they have a water pump, they still have to pay the fuel costs.

23 The minimum wage in Purworejo was Rp. 1.5 million per month in 2017.

24 With the average output of capitalist farmers for one hectare is 6171 kg, 'landlord-capitalists' only receive a half from the total output under sharecropping, although they do not bear any production cost. As a result, their net profit is 3085 kg multiplied by the price per kg of dry stalk paddy (Rp. 4,610). Meanwhile, for capitalist farmers, although they bear the production cost (Rp. 8.7 million), they earn all the output that makes their net profit at least 30 percent higher profit than 'landlord-capitalist'. See more details in Appendix 3.

25 In money term, the *bawon* may provide the income about Rp. 1.4 million/month all the year round.

26 The calculation of total production value has been adjusted to include the period of harvest decline (*Masa Trek*) for three months in the year. During this period, the output is generally 30 percent lower than in the rest of the year. With proper maintenance however, some capitalist farmers have managed to avoid this problem.

27 Langkat's minimum wage in 2018 was Rp. 2.3 million/month.
28 The income from this activity is about Rp. 25 million per hectare of watermelon with favourable weather (only a little rain during the growing season).
29 Using their own labour, one *iring* of mung bean cultivation generally generates between Rp. 2.6 and 3.3 million. This additional yearly income means an extra income of Rp. 241 thousand per month or about one seventh of the minimum wage.

References

Agung, B et al. 2009, 'Competitiveness of the Indonesian construction industry', *Journal of Construction in Developing Countries,* vol. 14, no. 1, pp. 51–68.

Bernstein, H 2010, *Class dynamics of agrarian change*, Sterling, VA, Kumarian Press.

Bhattacharya, T 2017, *Social reproduction theory: Remapping class, recentering oppression*, London, Pluto Press.

Breman, J & Wiradi, G 2002, *Good times and bad times in rural java: Case study of socio-economic dynamics in two villages towards the end of the twentieth century*, Leiden, KITLV Press.

Byres, T.J 1995, 'Political economy, agrarian question and comparative method', *Economic and Political Weekly*, vol. 30, no. 10, pp. 507–513.

Foster, J.B 2000, *Marx's ecology: Materialism and nature*, New York, Monthly Review Press.

Habibi, M & Juliawan, B.H 2018, 'Creating surplus labour: Neo-liberal transformations and the development of relative surplus population in Indonesia', *Journal of Contemporary Asia*, vol. 48, no. 4, pp. 649–670.

Hart, G 1986, *Power, labor and livelihood: Processes of change in rural Java*, Berkeley, CA, University of California Press.

Hüsken, F 1979, 'Landlors, sharecroppers and agricultural labourers: Changing labour relations in rural java', *Journal of Contemporary Asia,* vol. 9, pp. 140–151.

Huyer, S 2016, 'Closing the gender gap in agriculture', *Gender, Technology and Development*, vol. 20, no. 2, pp. 105–116.

Pearce, R 1983, 'Sharecropping: Towards a Marxist view', *The Journal of Peasant Studies*, vol. 10, no. 2–3, pp. 42–70.

Pincus, J 1996, *Class power and agrarian change: Land and labour in rural West Java*, London, MacMillan Press.

Ploeg, J.D 2013, *Peasants and the art of farming: A chayanovian manifesto*, Winnipeg, Fernwood Publishing.

Scott, J.C 1972, 'The erosion of patron-client bonds and social change in rural Southeast Asia', *The Journal of Asian Studies*, vol. 32, no. 1, pp. 5–37.

Scott, J.C 1976, *The moral economy of the peasant: Rebellion and subsistence in Southeast Asia*, New Haven, Yale University Press.

Scott, J.C 1985, *Weapons of the weak: Everyday forms of peasant resistance*, New Haven, CT, Yale University Press.

Simatupang, P & Timmer. C.P 2008, 'Indonesian rice production: Policies and realities', *Bulletin of Indonesian Economic Studies*, vol. 44, no. 1, pp. 65–80.

Stoler, A.L 1977, 'Rice harvesting in Kali Loro: A study of class and labor relations in rural Java', *American Ethnologist*, vol. 4, no. 4, pp. 678–698.

White, B & Wiradi, G 1989, 'Agrarian and nonagrarian bases of inequality in nine Javanese villages', in G Hart, A Turton & B White (eds), *Agrarian transformations: Local process and the state in Southeast Asia*, Berkeley, CA, University of California Press, 266–302.

White, B, Djurfeldt, G & Lerche, J 1998, 'Book reviews', *The Journal of Peasant Studies*, vol. 25, no. 2, pp. 159–167.

7 Class Reproduction in Java and Sumatra

Introduction

It should be emphasised from the outset that this chapter deals with class reproduction and not social reproduction. While social reproduction is focused on the reproduction of social capitalist relations (Bhattacharya, 2017), our concern with class reproduction focuses on what agrarian classes do with their economic gains from agricultural production (Bernstein, 2010). In previous chapter, we are informed that capitalist farmers reap a higher income from 'own-account' farming than PCPs and the classes of labour. The first section of the chapter will describe the 'own-account' farming and non-agricultural strategies of capitalist farmers in investing their surplus from production. This will be followed by explanations of the 'own-account' farming, selling labour out to other's farms and non-agricultural activities of PCPs to reproduce themselves. The similar activities of the members of the classes of labour employed to meet their basic needs will be discussed in the following section. It also shows how class reproduction is inextricably linked with gender, clanship and generational issues. The discussion of class reproduction in this chapter completes our previous understanding of class dynamics and agricultural production, and provides a completely different picture of Indonesia's agrarian change from the dominant view of agrarian populism.

Capitalist Farmers (with 'Landlord-capitalists') and Accumulation

The Investments in 'Own-Account' Farming

Land-buying has been noted in the literature as one of the major investment activities in 'own-account' farming for capitalist farmers. From the village registration, we may observe the activity in the land market in the two villages. In *Njomplang*, the land market has not been very active in the last five years (2012–2017) where only 32 transactions have been registered. Furthermore, the data on land transaction is not straightforward as far as the class backgrounds of the buyers and sellers are concerned. In *Njomplang*, almost half of the total land transactions (1.04 out of 2.4 hectares) in 2012 and 2017 involved

DOI: 10.4324/9781003267348-7

non-*Njomplang* residents, making it difficult to locate their class position. Some of them can be identified as the children of capitalist farmers in *Njomplang* who, while living in the big cities (Jakarta, Semarang and Surabaya) were buying their family paddy fields. However, when the buyers were from the neighbouring villages, such land transactions were unlikely to be intra-family.

Considering the difficulty of locating the class position of those outsiders, we have confined our analysis to land transactions which merely involved *Njomplang* dwellers. While this prevents us from having a complete understanding of the agrarian classes' activities in the land market, given the limitation of data available, we are still able to get a picture of the majority of land market activity in the village. As Table 7.1 shows, the capitalist farmers have neither accumulated more land nor have been dispossessed of their land (-0.04 hectares). However, focus on one village alone has often ignored the activity of capitalist farmers purchasing lands beyond it (Breman, 1982; Pincus, 1996). Apparently, capitalist farmers, like Cokro, bought 0.48 hectares of paddy fields in the neighbouring villages during the five-year period concerned. To our knowledge, during this period, Cokro was the only capitalist farmer in the village to buy land outside of *Njomplang*. His activity was an exception rather than the rule. If we adjust Table 7.1 with Cokro's activity, capitalist farmers in *Njomplang* are indeed the main land accumulators (+ 0.44 hectares). This accumulation is lower than in Pincus' case (1996) of South Subang (+ 2.08 hectares) and East Subang (+ 4.04 hectares), while higher than North Subang (- 1.25 hectares).

The modest land-buying of rice capitalist farmers is often explained in relation to the lower profitability of 'own-account' farming compared to non-agricultural investments, and the capability of smaller landholders to retain their land (White & Wiradi, 1989; Pincus, 1996; Jun-Kim, 2002). As will be shown in the next section, this view also applies to *Njomplang*. Moreover, the share of total income of capitalist farmers *vis-a-vis* labour has even declined in the last two decades (Chapter 6).

Even when *Njomplang* supports the argument in the literature of Javanese rice production about the modest nature of capitalist farmers' accumulation in their farming, the literature hardly explains why some capitalist farmers are still keen to invest in farming, while others are not. This is a flaw in ignoring

Table 7.1 The net result of land transactions of each class in *Njomplang* Central Java, 2012–2017

Resident capitalist farmers	- 0.04 hectares (+ 0.44 hectares, adjusted)
Resident PCPs	+ 0.31 hectares
Resident 'Semi-proletariat farmers'	- 0.35 hectares
Resident 'Proletariat-farmers'	0
Resident FFP	+ 0.13 hectares

Source: calculated by author from the Village Register

the internal differences between capitalist farmers. In *Njomplang*, for 'typical capitalist farmers', such as Cokro, non-agricultural accumulation is not always an easy option. Political accumulation is put aside, since Cokro is not popular enough to run for village office (because of his actions in the 'village meetings'). Meanwhile, opening a highly propitious rice hulling business is not a straight forward option given another capitalist farmer (Supri) has monopolised the business in the village. Neither is opening an agricultural inputs shop considering it requires an official license, which is currently in the hands of Hadikusumo, another capitalist farmer. The only lucrative non-agricultural avenue left for Cokro is rice trading. With this limited option of non-agricultural accumulation, 'own-account' farming accumulation in the form of land-buying provides a good option for Cokro, although he must find the land in the neighbouring villages.

Another 'own-account' farming activity of capitalist farmers is purchasing production technology (machinery). Similar to land-buying, purchasing more machinery, like tractors, is also a limited activity, since the potential use of tractors has reached its limit. Nowadays, planting machines and combine harvesters that promise to cut production cost significantly have attracted the interest of capitalist farmers, especially 'typical capitalist farmers'. They were ready to buy the machines had there been no technical problems.[1] When the problems are resolved, the interest in capitalist farmers investing in machinery will likely be lifted and this will resurrect the interest in acquiring more land and expanding 'own-account' farming accumulation as a whole. This might provide the impetus for the acceleration of land concentration and class polarisation.

In *Timpang*, land transactions are much more prevalent. In only three years (2015–2017),[2] there were 82 land transactions, involving 34.4 hectares. The active land market in *Timpang* shows the dynamics of the new frontier, where land commoditisation started only about a half-century ago. It has accelerated while the oil palm boom has flourished over the last three decades. Land prices have risen in this period. However, with the availability of uncultivated land in the village, the land price is still relatively low. The price of a hectare of land in *Timpang* is only a sixth to a tenth of that in *Njomplang*. With this cheap land available, the strategy to accumulate in 'own-account' farming, for both the companies and capitalist farmers, is to extend by acquiring more land rather than intensify by focusing on improving the land productivity (see also Chapter 3).

Unlike *Njomplang*, the village register in *Timpang* shows that most of the total land transactions from the total land transacted in three years (34.4 hectares), around 60 percent (20.1 hectares), has involved *Timpang* dwellers. This means that intra-villager land transaction in *Timpang* is slightly higher than in *Njomplang*. Hence, although we confine our analysis only to village dwellers, it still covers the majority activity of the land market in *Timpang*. Since the number of 'proletariat-farmers' is negligible in our oil palm village, as discussed in Chapter 5, they are excluded from our calculation. As shown in Table 7.2, capitalist farmers have purchased more land than they sold (+ 1.70 hectares).

Table 7.2 The net result of land transactions of each class in *Timpang* North Sumatra, 2015–2017

Resident capitalist farmers	+ 1.70 hectares
Resident PCPs	- 2.23 hectares
Resident 'Semi-proletariat farmers'	- 6.94 hectares
Resident FFP	+ 7.49 hectares

Source: calculated by author from the Village Register

However, since we know little about the buying activities of the capitalist farmers outside their village borders,[3] we may treat our calculations as merely a rough indication of the capitalist farmers' activity in the land market. Unlike other cases, where the second generation of oil palm farmers may lose their land to corporations (Li, 2017), in *Timpang*, such expansion had already taken place decades earlier (Chapter 4). This implies the current generation of farmers may not be in great danger from 'land dispossession by displacement'.[4]

Unlike rice cultivation agrarian change, oil palm capitalist farmers' activity in the land market has not received adequate attention. Our fieldwork suggests that the modest activity of *Timpang*'s capitalist farmers in buying land relate to both the limited income from 'own-account' farming and the high-risk nature of oil palm production, as far as the global CPO price is concerned. As discussed in Chapter 6, profitability per hectare of oil palm is lower than per hectare paddy cultivation. Capitalist farmers depend mainly on the size of their farm to increase their income from 'own-account' farming. However, considering the unstable nature of the global price of oil palm (Chapter 3), putting their money only into one basket of oil palm production by purchasing more land is too risky, when non-agricultural business offers lower risk and can be more profitable.

Akin to *Njomplang*, the decision of capitalist farmers in *Timpang* to become involved in certain non-agricultural activities is shaped by competition between them. For instance, occupying politico-bureaucratic positions in the village is not an open option for every capitalist farmer. Bungaran, a 'typical capitalist farmer', economically is able to run for the position of village head. However, he only moved permanently to *Timpang* in the 2010s. His new village dweller's status is simply not ideal to stand for election. Furthermore, unlike either Sofian or Luhut, who have vast family-clanship networks in the village, Bungaran has no such connections. It is inconceivable for him to depend solely on money politics without having a social circle that he can trust.

The activity in 'own-account' farming in the form of adopting more new production techniques (machinery) in *Timpang* is more limited than in *Njomplang*. The introduction of lawnmowers has had no significant impact on productivity. This means only a few capitalist farmers in *Timpang* have shown an interest in adopting the machine. The only substantial production technology for them is the mini-truck, used to carry their fresh fruit bunches to the local processing plants or factories. With this modest mechanisation, the need for investment by capitalist farmers in *Timpang* in new technology is limited.

Non-Agricultural Accumulation Strategies

Considering the limitations of accumulation from 'own-account' farming, non-agricultural accumulation is crucial for capitalist farmers in both *Njomplang* and *Timpang*. In *Njomplang*, the most common non-agricultural investment is in children's education. Our survey and wider observations in the village indicate that all types of capitalist farmers ('typical', 'professional', 'politico-bureaucrat') and 'landlord-capitalists' send their children to college. It has been suggested by Javanese agrarian change literature that this move is to both avoid land fragmentation and to provide a decent livelihood for the children (Pincus, 1996). *Njomplang* shows a similar pattern, although here, we also must take into account the decline of the share of total income of capital versus labour in recent years (Chapter 6). Furthermore, sending children to college is also crucial for capitalist farmers as far as the remittances from their children are concerned.

Here, there is a difference between the 'modest' capitalist and 'big' capitalist farmers/'landlord-capitalists'. We use the former term for the group of capitalist farmers/'landlord-capitalists' owning between one hectare of paddy field, this being the minimum threshold of landownership needed to be capitalist/'landlord-capitalist' (Chapter 5), and two hectares of *sawah*, as double the size of the minimum threshold. Those owning more than two hectares of *sawah* are considered to be 'big' capitalist farmers/'landlord-capitalists'. Given their larger land cultivation, they earn a higher return on farming than 'modest' capitalist farmers/'landlord-capitalists' and, thus, have a larger financial capacity to finance their non-agricultural activities. This difference delivers a prominent impact on both the pattern of their children's education and the comparison between their total income from 'own-account' farming and non-agricultural activities.

As far as children's education is concerned, our survey and wider observations inform us that 'big' capitalist farmers/'landlord-capitalists' (Cokro, Sari, Mantili, Hadikusumo, etc.) have managed to send all of their children to higher education. 'Modest' capitalist farmers/'landlord-capitalists', however, are usually only able to send some of their children, given the limited resources they have. They must sell some parcels of their land if they wish to finance a college education for all of their children. But this is generally avoided, since the children who do not go to college accept their position, knowing they will inherit the paddy fields once their parents retire from farming.[5] Male and female children both have the same rights of inheritance, as has been reported in other Javanese villages (Ambarwati et al., 2016). During this waiting period, married children can help their parents with the farming or, if they are unmarried, migrate out to work elsewhere.

This educational accumulation has a profound impact on the regeneration of rice capitalist farmers and their transformation (the general pattern can be

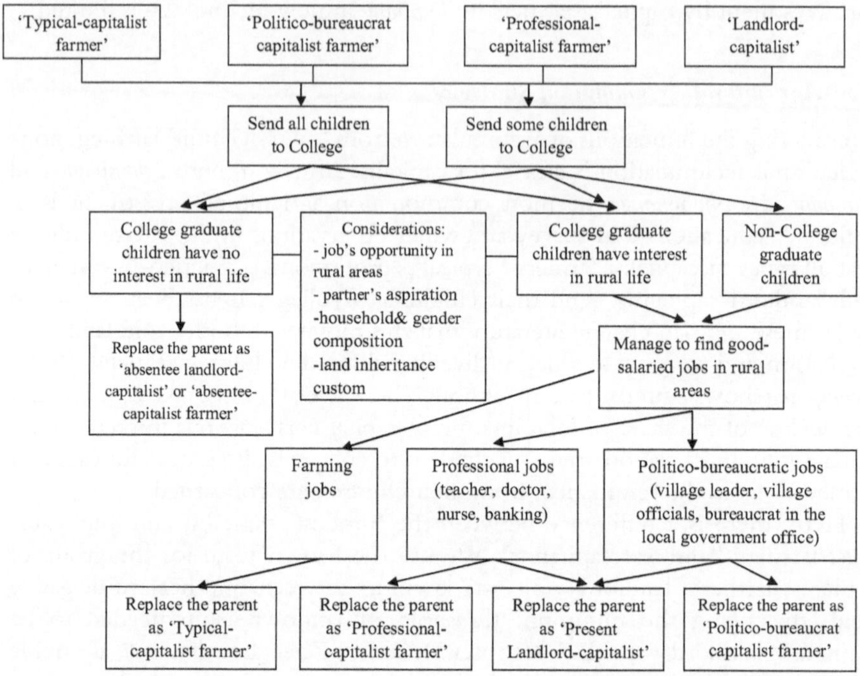

Figure 7.1 Class and generational reproduction of the agrarian ruling class in the two villages. (Source: author)

seen in Figure 7.1). Let us consider the case of Cokro, a 'big typical capitalist farmer', who has two female children. His older daughter is married to a rich entrepreneur who is not interested in agriculture, while the younger daughter still attends university and is not interested in agriculture either. As Cokro gets older, the only option he has is to ask the older daughter, who is staying in the village, to replace him. However, given the vast amount of land and being fully occupied by her domestic duties, she may well not have sufficient spare time to replace Cokro as a full-time 'typical capitalist farmer'. She will probably share-crop out the land, and that would transform her into a 'landlord-capitalist', receiving a lower income from 'own-account' farming than a 'typical capitalist farmer' (Chapter 6).

This might be different for 'modest typical capitalist farmers', such as Darsam, a 62-year-old man who owns 1.2 hectares of *sawah*. Of his three female children, one holds a bachelor's degree and lives in the city. The other two are only high school graduates and become housewives. One lives in the village, while the other lives elsewhere. The former is now helping Darsam with the farming. She will probably replace Darsam when he retires in the near future. With only modest land ownership, his daughter should be able to control the daily rice cultivation and, thus, maintain the status of 'typical capitalist farmer' of Darsam.

For the already 'landlord-capitalist' like Sari, there will be no way for her heirs to be a 'typical capitalist farmer'. Instead, her children will probably be either 'present landlord-capitalists' or 'absentee landlord-capitalists'. After being appointed as the village secretary, Agung will continue what Sari and Prawiro have performed as 'present landlord-capitalists', while, at the same, time serve the role of 'politico-bureaucrat capitalist'. Meanwhile, Sari's daughter, who has finished her college education, will be expected to work elsewhere in the city and replace her mother as an 'absentee landlord-capitalist' when she receives her share of the land inheritance.

Any type of capitalist farmers and 'landlord-capitalists' can be an 'absentee landlord-capitalists' in the future if they do not have children who want to stay in the village. With their high level of education, their children would stay in the village only if they could find well-paying jobs in rural areas, either as professionals (teachers, nurses, doctors, banking) or political-bureaucrats (local civil servants, village officials, village head). The decision to stay in the village or elsewhere is also shaped by their partner's aspiration to live a rural or urban life. It shows that the class reproduction of capitalist farmers is inextricably linked with generational and gender issues in the certain type of capitalist farmers involved. This suggests that generational problems may be more complex than suggested in the literature (White, 2012a, 2020).

Apart from avoiding land fragmentation, the children's higher education provides capitalist farmers with potential sources of income. They make use of the remittances for political accumulation, significant house improvements and help in financing the college education of their younger siblings. The oldest child of Karto, for instance, works as a member of a ship's crew and sends money back home to pay for significant house improvements and to finance political campaigns that have brought Karto to be village head. For others, remittance is also harnessed to financing younger siblings at college.

Another common non-agricultural activity is providing tractor services. Almost all the tractor service providers are capitalist farmers (of all types) except one PCP, who owns a tractor. However, this activity offers much less income than a child's education. In each paddy season, the income from tractor services for capitalist farmers is between Rp. 1.25 and Rp. 7 million.[6] This limited income is unsurprising, since they have to share the service revenue with their tractor drivers instead of paying them a daily wage. Annually, the incomes from tractor services are much lower than 'own-account' farming. Capitalist farmers view this tractor business as merely a source of an additional income. Their main concern with the use of the tractor is to prepare their own paddy fields. This explains why most tractors are owned by 'big' capitalist farmers, since 'modest' capitalist farmers, who are financially able to buy one, have no proper incentive to do so.

From our wider observations in the village, the less common non-agricultural strategy for capitalist farmers in *Njomplang*, despite offering a lucrative income, is rice trading. This is generally confined to 'typical capitalist farmers', since neither 'professional-capitalists' nor 'politico-bureaucrat capitalists' have the time to manage the business. Meanwhile, 'landlord-capitalist' look to see whether they have other more rewarding activities to engage in to prevent them from joining the rice trade business. Local rice traders in *Njomplang* sell their un-hulked paddy to big rice traders (both at a regional and national level). With the net profit per tonne being between Rp. 100 and Rp. 300 thousand, depending on the market price fluctuations, 'big' capitalist farmers, like Cokro, could earn from Rp. 25.2 to Rp. 75.6 million in a single harvesting season. In annual terms, the maximum revenue is lucrative, although it is slightly lower than his income from 'own-account' farming, considering his five hectare land ownership. For 'modest' capitalist farmers, their income is only about half of that of the 'big' capitalist farmers, since their rice sale is only half the volume. The yearly income from this non-agricultural venture could be lower or higher than the annual income from 'own-account' farming. It is lower when 'modest' capitalist farmers, like Darsam who own 1.2 hectares, only reaps minimum net profit per tonne (Rp. 100 thousand) and it is higher if he receives a higher net profit per tonne (Rp. 200 or 300 thousand). It may suggest that the income comparison between 'own-account' farming and non-agricultural activities depends on the farming size of the capitalist farmers and the nature of their non-agricultural incomes.

This lucrative rice trade however, is only possible because a trade oligopoly is operated by the capitalist farmers-cum-rice traders in *Njomplang*. Fewer than ten local rice traders (most of them capitalist farmers, while the rest are PCPs) effectively ban outsider rice traders, who offer higher prices, from the neighbouring villages to come and purchase the rice in *Njomplang*. The PCPs, 'semi-proletariat farmers' and 'proletariat-farmers' complain that they are missing the chance to obtain the better price offered by the outsider rice traders (Rp. 100 thousand per tonne higher). They could sell their rice outside the village to find a better price but it is not worth if they have to bear the transportation costs to carry their paddy. This shows that the capitalist farmers not only control and dominate the other classes, specifically the classes of labour, at the production site but also in non-agricultural activities that are crucial for their accumulation.

As common non-agricultural activity such as rice trading is political accumulation. 'Politico-bureaucrat capitalist farmers' and their families are the main actors involved in this activity. The 'landlord-capitalists' might also join the political competition if they have a good reputation or if their children are living in the village. The 'professional-capitalist farmers' are only able to pursue political positions when they have retired from their professional jobs. 'Typical capitalist farmers' are generally not interested in politics, but their children, with a higher education, might join the competition, since they have no intensive experience or interest in farming as their parents do.

Political and bureaucratic positions in the village office remain attractive for capitalist farmers and 'landlord-capitalists'. In *Njomplang*, the land salary (*Tanah Bengkok*) is the largest incentive to be a village official. The village head is granted four hectares, while the village secretary is given 1.5 hectares. Each ordinary village official is given a half hectare of land salary. The literature often characterises political activity as a part of the non-agricultural accumulation of capitalist farmers (Pincus, 1996). Nonetheless, with the significant land right cultivation granted to the village officials, the politico-bureaucratic positions may only represent partial non-agricultural accumulation, since some of their total incomes from these political-bureaucratic positions are produced by 'own-account' farming from their land salary. The incomes from non-agricultural activities are mainly obtained by extracting 'administration fees' for the public services they perform. The most lucrative one is the fee from land transactions (*Pologoro*), although the land market in *Njomplang* is not very active. Each land transaction is charged with a 4 percent fee based on the total value of the transaction. Although this practice was banned in 2018 by the district government, the village officials in *Njomplang* have refused to obey the law.[7] Another income is extracted from land certification.[8] The village officials also expect a donation for each administrative service they perform (birth certificate, family card, identity card, etc.). While, officially, the administration fees are free, the general practice is that the villagers are expected to give a proper donation if they wish their administrative affairs to be taken care of promptly. The Village Fund, since 2015, has provided considerable additional income for village officials when they occupy a supervisory position on a development project. Since 2019, the Jokowi Administration has granted the village officials across the country a monthly salary equal to a public civil servant's. This is a rise from previous salary, which was equal to the minimum wage stipulated in the district.[9] Although it is difficult to provide exact comparisons between the income from 'own-account' farming and non-agricultural activities for 'politico-bureaucrat capitalist farmers', with the significant portion of salary land involved, it may be suggested that the income from 'own-account' farming is higher than the non-agricultural income.

With such promising earnings, capitalist farmers and 'landlord-capitalists', as the backbone of the ruling class in the village, compete among themselves to occupy these public officials' positions. Their combining against the classes of labour at the 'village meetings' is underplayed when it comes to lucrative opportunities. One of the most important competitions among the ruling class can be seen in the village head election of 2012. At the time, the leading candidate was Fadli, the son of Cipto, the incumbent village head. As discussed in Chapter 5, they represented the establishment family block of Prapto. The contender was Karto, with support from his son's remittances and his family networks in the village. Cipto's political campaign did not involve money politics, since he was confident that what he had given to the villagers in the past would make them support his son. He granted land cultivation rights for most of his salary land (20 *iring* out of 24 *iring*) to villagers, regardless of their class. Each household received one *iring* per paddy season. Using a rotation mechanism, during his 14 years of leadership, almost all the households in the village were granted his land salary for free. On the other hand, Karto bought the vote for Rp. 300 thousand per person and Rp. 500 thousand for some influential figures. He also promised to grant a few of his salary lands (only six *iring*) to his supporters under a sharecropping arrangement, not for free as Cipto had done. The election result was a surprise, with Cipto's son losing by 12 votes. Cipto's family networks had managed to secure support from the PCPs and classes of labour, who were sharecroppers in their paddy fields. However, the key to Karto's triumph was the mobilisation of more than 20 of his distant relatives who lived in the city but still held *Njomplang* identity cards and thus were eligible to vote. He covered their transportation costs and provided a significant allowance to them. Without this 'spatial relatives-mobilisation', the village head position would be still have been in the hands of the Prapto family block.

Another political competition within the ruling class was the selection of the village secretary,[10] in 2017. There were nine candidates, all of them from 'landlord-capitalists'/capitalist farmers' backgrounds except one, who was the son of a 'proletariat-farmer'. The eight candidates were from Prapto's family block, since neither Karto's block nor Hadikusumo's family network had eligible nominees (there were no children of Karto or Hadikusumo who lived in the village). Under these circumstances, the battle for village secretary was a fight within Prapto's block. This might explain the absence of money politics in the selection process. Agung, the son of Sari, eventually won the competition after obtaining the highest test score.

The least common non-agricultural accumulation for capitalist farmers/'landlord-capitalists' in *Njomplang*, but one which provides a lucrative return, is money-lending. Here, propitious money-lending takes the form of the interest from loaning to purchase agricultural inputs. Hadikusumo, the only owner of an agricultural shop in the village, earns between Rp. 22.7 and Rp. 28.9 million per paddy season.[11] He sold 70 tonnes of fertilisers alone in one season (not including pesticides) with 90 percent of them paid for after harvesting and with 20 percent interest. While this non-agricultural yearly earning is promising, it is still slightly lower than his income from 2.3 hectares of rice cultivation. This gainful venture is made possible, since Hadikusumo is the official distributor of agricultural inputs, mandated by the local GAPOKTAN when its chairman was Hardjo, the older brother of Hadikusumo (Chapter 5). Meanwhile, as discussed in Chapter 6, extracting interest from personal credit relations is not a straightforward option for capitalist farmers given the availability of cheap credit provided by the state (KUR-BRI) and the rising bargaining power of sharecroppers, and the classes of labour in general *vis-a-vis* capitalist farmers. Personal credit provided by capitalist farmers generally does not involve interest as it is mostly designated to attract labour.

Another lucrative non-agricultural investment is rice hulling. In *Njomplang*, the only rice hulling machine in the village is owned by Supri, the son of Cipto (former village head) and the son-in-law of Guntur (Chapter 5). Supri's main business is rice trading. He uses his rice huller mostly to mill his own dry stalk paddy to be sold as rice. He purchases the dry stalk paddy from the village and neighbouring districts. The revenue from this rice hulling business is among the most lucrative non-agricultural business for capitalist farmers in the village.[12] This revenue was lower before he installed the new oven machine.[13] If we only estimate the minimum revenue from this rice hulling-trading, its income is still much higher than his income from 'own-account' farming (2.5 hectares). With such lucrative revenue from rice hulling-trading and being occupied by his business, it is not surprising that a 'typical capitalist farmer' like Supri is not interested in local politics.

In *Timpang*, children's education is also the most common non-agricultural accumulation strategy for capitalist farmers. Our survey and wider observations indicate that all types of capitalist farmers ('typical', 'politico-bureaucrat' and 'professional-capitalist') send their children to college. However, the literature on oil palm agrarian change has said little to explain this widespread non-agricultural activity. In *Timpang*, it is predominantly a cautionary response to the risks of the volatile market for oil palm and to set up a decent livelihood for their children, especially the daughters. Since the female children in Batak tradition have no priority right of inheritance, they must achieve a higher education if they wish to live a decent life without relying on their husbands. Here, the children's remittances for capitalist farmers are less pronounced than in *Njomplang*. It seems that the income from oil palm farming is higher than the salary or income obtained by the children outside the village that makes the parents prohibit their children from sending money back to them.[14]

In *Timpang*, there is also a different nature between a 'big' capitalist farmer and a 'modest' capitalist farmer. Since the minimum threshold of land ownership to be capitalist farmer in *Timpang* is four hectares (Chapter 5), we categorise 'modest' capitalist farmers as those owning between four and eight hectares of oil palm. The owners of more than eight hectares of oil palm are considered as 'big' capitalist farmers. With their greater financial capacity, 'big' capitalist farmers, like Bungaran and Budi manage to send all of their children to college, while 'modest' capitalist farmers, like Subandi, are only able to support some of their children. For the 'modest' capitalist farmers from a Batak background, the daughters are generally prioritised to go to college rather than the sons as the males would receive the largest share of land inheritance from their parents. For other clanships, the oldest child, either male or female, is generally given the first chance to obtain higher education, as in *Njomplang*.

The impact of children's education on the regeneration and transformation of the capitalist farmers in *Timpang* is notable (see the general pattern in Figure 7.1). It should be noted that not all capitalist farmers' children in *Timpang* who go to college manage to complete their studies. Some of them fail due to the widespread trafficking of drugs and juvenile delinquency in the village. This failure leads them to be either 'typical capitalist farmer' or 'politico-bureaucrat capitalist farmer'. They are definitely not eligible to be 'professional-capitalist farmers' like their parent, as in the case of Ucok's children, who failed to complete their studies. For 'typical capitalist farmers' whose children complete college education, they might be replaced by their children as 'professional-capitalist farmers' if they both manage to find professional job and want to live in the village. This is the possibility for Budi's daughter, who might open a medical practice in the village after receiving her doctor's permit. They might also compete for politico-bureaucrat capitalist farmers' positions if there are any suitable ones compatible with their higher education background (village head or secretary).

For college graduates, the most unlikely outcome is to be a 'typical capitalist farmer' because they do not want to waste their higher education. Some of them may become 'absentee capitalists' if they work in the city yet hold land inheritance from their parents. Many of them, especially the male heirs from a Batak background, may become 'present capitalists' (either professional-capitalists or politico-bureaucrat capitalists), since their strong patrilineal tradition would expect one of the sons to stay in the village to continue the clanship name. Regarding this, his wife must come to live in the village even though she may originate from and prefer to live in the city. This suggests that not only is the class reproduction of capitalist farmers inextricably linked with generational and gender issues, as *Njomplang* indicates, but, in *Timpang*, those webs closely intersect with clanship.

The less common non-agricultural accumulation strategy in *Timpang* with a promising propitious return, is oil palm trading. There are dozens of local oil palm traders, or *toke*, in the village who are capitalist farmers. For oil palm traders who hold a cover letter (SP),[15] the monthly income from their trade is between Rp. 8.4 and Rp. 19.6 million.[16] In annual terms, the minimum income is about equal to the income from 'own-account' farming of 'modest' capitalist farmers. As far as the maximum income is concerned, it is more or less parallel to the income from 'own-account' farming of 'big' capitalist farmers. If 'modest' capitalist farmers-cum-oil palm traders only earn a minimum yearly income from oil palm trading, their income from 'own-account' farming is about equal to their non-agricultural income whereas if they obtain the maximum income on trading, their 'own-account' farming's income is less profitable than their non-agricultural revenue. For 'big' capitalist farmers-cum-oil palm traders, their income from 'own-account' farming is significantly higher than for non-agricultural activities if they only earn minimum profit from oil palm trading. Meanwhile, their comparison of income between 'own-account' farming and non-agricultural would be equal if they received maximum profit from their oil palm trading.

This is precisely the reason why 'big' capitalist farmers are not involving themselves in local oil palm trading. They more focus on their own oil palm and sell it directly to local processing plants. 'Modest' capitalist farmers are the dominant players among oil palm traders. However, it also depends on the type of capitalist farmers. Neither 'professional-capitalist farmers', such as Ucok, nor 'politico-bureaucrat capitalists', like Luhut, are interested in oil palm trading, since they have no adequate spare time to manage the trade. It is only 'typical capitalist farmers' who have such a chance. In contrast to *Njomplang*, where an oligopoly is the prerequisite to earn lucrative income from trading, the competition among local oil palm traders is the norm in *Timpang*. The sale price competition is a competition among the traders to attract local farmers to sell their oil palm to them, including the provision of credit without interest to farmers. Competition also takes place in the form of credibility. Cheating on weighing the fresh fruit bunches of oil palm is the norm among the *toke*.[17] Local farmers normally choose the least cheated one. In many cases, however, the cheating is acceptable to the local farmers so long as they are offered a good sale price and provided with credit when they need it.

Political accumulation is also about as common as oil palm trading as a non-agricultural activity of capitalist farmers in *Timpang*. Political accumulation in *Timpang* is a lucrative avenue, although the village official positions do not offer a land salary, as they do in *Njomplang*. Without the return from land, political accumulation in *Timpang* is more of a fully-fledged non-agricultural accumulation than in *Njomplang*. First, every month and during Eid, dozens of companies operating in *Timpang* grant what is called 'syrup money' (*Uang Sirup*) to village officials.[18] Another propitious venture is from the village levy placed on the company vehicles which pass along the village road. Considerable revenues from this levy are distributed as an incentive to the village officials.[19] Village officials are also the biggest beneficiaries of the development project in the village. From the railway construction project, they can earn significant regular earnings.[20] The authority of having a village office position enables the officials to extract lucrative administration fees from the villagers. The most propitious administration fee is from land transactions. With the active land market in *Timpang*, the revenue from land transactions is substantial, since they charge a 10 percent fee for each transaction.[21] Other administration fees, for birth certificates, identity cards, family cards and land certificates, add more revenues for village officials.[22] By occupying a supervisor's position in a development project of the Village Fund, village officials also reap another source of income. They have also been granted a monthly salary equal to a civil servant's salary, as is the case in *Njomplang*. It is difficult to estimate and compare the income from political accumulation with 'own-account' farming, since it is dependent on the rank of the village official, as well as the number of projects available, and the number of villagers who need to take care of their administrative affairs in a given year. However, it should be at least the same as the income from the 'own-account' farming of 'modest' capitalist farmers, which makes many capitalist farmers interested in occupying positions at the village office.

The competition among capitalist farmers in *Timpang* over politico-bureaucrat positions can be seen in the village head election in 2013. Of the four contenders, all of them were capitalist farmers except one candidate from a 'semi-proletariat farmer' background. Sofian, Luhut and Budi were capitalist farmers and the only real contenders. They represented three different influential family-clanship networks in the village (Chapter 6). Gultom, the anomaly candidate, was only a puppet nominee of Sofian, set to defeat Budi in his own hamlet.[23] With the absence of salary land and sharecropping in *Timpang*, unlike in *Njomplang*, making political promises and dispensing patronage relationships through land is not a feasible option for the candidates. In this case, money politics expressed itself in its most vulgar form. The night before the election,

Sofian bought the vote in a stylish style.[24] This money politics, combined with the strategy of using Gultom, was successful and Sofian was elected for the second time.

Money lending is another lucrative non-agricultural venture for capitalist farmers in *Timpang*, although it is a limited practice. Extracting interest is not an easy option for capitalist farmers given the availability of cheap credit provided by the state (KUR-BRI) and local oil palm traders. A few loan sharks, however, have managed to earn good returns. By charging a monthly 10 percent fixed interest rate, they have been able to take over some houses from the local debtors who normally are members of the classes of labour. Loan shark lenders are generally confined to the 'typical capitalist farmers' or non-agrarian capitalists, while neither 'politico-bureaucrat capitalist farmers' nor 'professional-capitalist farmers' are prepared to put their reputations on the line to get involved in this.

There are also other less lucrative avenues for non-agricultural accumulation in *Timpang*. Livestock-rearing (cattle) is quite common for 'typical capitalist farmers'. They use the livestock as a backup when their other businesses, both 'own-account' farming and non-agricultural (oil palm trading), face losses. Only a few capitalist farmers, like Sofian, are involved in agricultural inputs trading, and they only act as brokers, without owning their own shop. This is due to the low demand for agricultural inputs in the village. 'Big' capitalist farmers, both present and absentee, take care of their own agricultural inputs from outside the village, while PCPs and the classes of labour ('semi-proletariat farmers' and 'proletariat-farmers') only require a limited amount of such inputs. A small number of capitalist farmers have opened food stalls or sold traditional liquor (*tuak*) but that only offers a small income.

In both *Njomplang* and *Timpang*, it is quite clear that non-agricultural activities are an indispensable accumulation avenue for capitalist farmers/'landlord-capitalists'. However, its weight, in relation to 'own-account' farming, depends mostly on the nature of their involvement in such activities. Some of them engage in more than one lucrative non-agricultural activity, which makes their income from non-agricultural businesses higher than their income from 'own-account' farming. Others only engage in one non-agricultural activity, but a lucrative one, so their incomes from 'own-account' farming are about the same as non-agricultural incomes. Some of them join some different non-agricultural activities but not the propitious ventures, making their non-agricultural incomes lower than 'own-account' farming. The variation can also be shaped by the size of their landownership. The greater it is, the higher the income from 'own-account' farming tends to be higher than from non-agricultural activities, even the lucrative ones.

If we must make a rough comparison with the caveats above, 'modest' capitalist farmers/'landlord-capitalists' tend to have a relatively balanced income between 'own-account' farming and non-agricultural contributing to total income. For the 'big' one, however, their non-agricultural incomes tend to be less than half of their total income. With the bigger land cultivation, their 'own-account' farming incomes is higher than for 'modest' capitalist farmers/'landlord-capitalists' and, thus, its contribution to total income is higher. Apart from productive non-agricultural accumulation, the capitalist farmers/'landlord-capitalists' in the two villages spend their surpluses for consumption purposes. Buying cars and motorcycles, making substantial house improvements and purchasing electronic devices are among the most common activities.

The importance of non-agricultural accumulation has been explained in the literature. In Javanese rice cultivation, Hüsken (1989) labels 'large farmers' who engage in non-agricultural accumulation as 'hesitant capitalists', since they are not willing to put all their surpluses into 'own-account' farming. Nevertheless, this perspective might put too much emphasis on their agency in exercising choice. *Njomplang* shows that their decision is made within the context of class relations that squeeze their profits, while the stalled mechanisation and the continuing degradation of the soil restricts the options for the capitalist farmers to accumulate on farming. Competition among the ruling class in the village and the concern over children's future also play a role in their investment strategies. In the literature concerning oil palm (McCarthy, 2010; Fortin, 2011), however, this theme is virtually absent. *Timpang* suggests that the nature of non-agricultural accumulation is shaped by the highly volatile price of oil palm, competition among capitalist farmers/'landlord-capitalists' and their concern on the future of their children.

PCPs and the Dynamics of Simple Reproduction

The Activities in 'Own-Account' Farming

In *Njomplang*, the common reproductive activity in 'own-account' farming of PCPs is buying and selling land. As shown in Table 7.1, PCPs manage to acquire more land, although in small parcels, than they sell. However, this is only possible with the help of lucrative non-agricultural income from skilled jobs (masonry), rice trading or remittances. The remittance-senders are the family members who work in formal employment (manufacturing factories in Greater Jakarta or the army). The ability to buy more land has generated higher income from 'own-account' farming. Nonetheless, they have not reached the point where their additional land ownership/control transforms them into capitalist farmers. On the other hand, PCPs may sell the land due to economic pressure, which could transform them into members of the classes of labour.

A less common activity in 'own-account' farming yet one offering lucrative incomes for PCPs is leasing-in land. In a season, the income from this land lease is about half of the income from the average PCP's land control/ownership (Chapter 6).[25] It greatly supports the reproduction of the PCPs. This practice, however, only involves a few PCPs. Nowadays, leas-in land is less common than it used to be (Chapter 6). At the same time, land available for rent from Village Lands (*Tanah Kas Desa*) is also limited. Each year, there are only 20 pieces of land (each 800 m^2) rented out to the villagers, regardless of their class. The renters are drawn through a random lottery.[26] This offers an opportunity for the capitalist farmers at the expense of other agrarian classes, including the PCPs. With a decline in the supply of land to be rented in, PCPs in *Njomplang* have been prevented from earning higher income from 'own-account' farming and, thus, the possibility of transforming themselves into capitalist farmers.

When it comes to production technology, the PCPs in *Njomplang* have no ownership over substantial production machinery like tractors, but do have ownership over the basics, such as water pumps, threshing machines and other manual tools. There is one exception, whereby Kirun, a member of the substantial PCP owns a tractor. However, he must pay a high price for this unusual situation. None of his three children have been able to complete high school and he has no motorcycles, while the floor of his house is only coated with cement. Other PCPs in *Njomplang* have not followed this extreme self-exploitation and for them, buying a tractor is not an option.

Similar dynamics of PCPs' activity in 'own-account' farming is seen in *Timpang*. The main difference in *Timpang* is the rare incidence of land rent (Chapter 6). For PCPs, this has restricted their chances to leasing in land either to consolidate or transform their class position. The more dynamic 'own-account' farming activity for PCPs in *Timpang* is selling and buying land. In Table 7.2, PCPs sell more land than they buy. They generally sell some of their small parcels of land (0.05 to 1 hectare) to finance ritual ceremonies (marriages, funerals) or to finance their children's education. For others, they give up their land to start non-agricultural businesses. Those who manage to buy more land owe it to their salaries from working as wage labour elsewhere (agriculture or non-agriculture, companies-plantations or individual oil palm fields). Only by selling their labour all year round, the savings for the year can be harnessed to purchase more land, although only a little (one or half of a hectare).

The impact of land transactions on PCP's reproduction is prominent. Some PCPs buy land to consolidate their simple reproduction. However, there are PCPs for whom their accumulative buying of land over the years has transformed them into capitalist farmers, as shown earlier (Subandi in Chapter 5). On the other hand, there are also PCPs who are transformed into the classes of labour through land fragmentation (Rustam in Chapter 5). This usually happens when a PCP has some children and none of them goes to college. This makes it difficult to get good salaried jobs elsewhere. However, the tendency of land fragmentation is lower in the Batak clanships given their patrilineal customs. This scrutiny of PCP reproduction is crucial to understanding class differentiation among oil palm smallholders, something that has largely been overlooked in the literature (McCarthy, 2010; Fortin, 2011).

As far as production technology is concerned, PCPs in *Timpang* have no ownership of substantial oil palm production machinery. They generally only buy a modified motorcycle (an *along-along*) and manual tools, such as aluminium poles, sickles (*egreks*), axes and loose fruit collection baskets.

Selling Labour out to Other's Farms

The most common activity for PCPs in *Njomplang* outside their 'own-account' farming is selling their labour as agricultural workers. They generally sell their labour all year round while some 'substantial PCPs' only sell their labour for some agricultural jobs.[27] Harvesting is the most lucrative agricultural employment for PCPs.[28] For male workers, the lucrative agricultural jobs are being a tractor driver or a seeding worker.[29] One worker cannot do both jobs, since they are performed at the same time of the year. The less well-paid tasks are applying fertilisers and herbicides. As for female workers, weeding is the most lucrative agricultural job, more so than planting.[30] The workers required for weeding are usually the same required for planting. In *Njomplang*, the common practice is that a PCP household consists of a male (performing either seeding or tractor driving and applying fertilisers/herbicides) and a female worker (performing both planting and weeding), while one or both of them work as harvesters.[31] Their income from agricultural jobs is between equal and twice to their income from 'own-account' farming. This means that agricultural wages contribute between half and more than two-thirds of PCPs' total income. It only signals the importance of agricultural wage labour in the total income for PCP households. Income from harvesting (*bawon*) plays the most important role, accounting for more than half of the total income from agricultural wages. This also suggests that agriculture as an economic sector, via providing agricultural wages, still matters for the overall reproduction of PCPs. At the same time, however, the significant contribution of agricultural wages to the total income of PCPs should not be seen as their being dependent on wage income to meet their subsistence. As has been discussed in Chapter 6, the income of PCPs from 'own-account' farming is sufficient to meet their simple reproduction. We have shown that some substantial PCPs and all formal PCPs in *Njomplang* sell their labour both through agricultural and non-agriculture avenues throughout the year to meet their aspirations beyond subsistence.

Similar to *Njomplang*, the common activity for PCP in *Timpang* outside their 'own-account' farming is disposing of their labour in agricultural jobs. They work for company plantations and individual capitalist farmers. With the company, harvesting offers the highest income.[32] As for individual capitalist farmers, the income from harvesting is about equal to the income from working at the company.[33] The company even pays higher wages for weeding.[34] However, for applying herbicides, capitalist farmers offer slightly higher wages than companies, since they perform the task with a contract by task arrangement rather than a daily wage. To a lesser extent, PCPs also work as foremen and security guards for absentee-capitalist farmers.[35] All of these jobs are largely confined to male workers. Female workers only work for capitalist farmers and the companies to perform weeding and apply herbicides.[36] In some cases, they also work for capitalist farmers in paddy cultivation.[37] With the limited demand for female workers, only some of them are active workers, while others are housewives and family workers growing their own oil palm.

The incomes for the household with two active workers depend largely on the workplace and type of agricultural tasks the husband and wife perform. In a household where the husband performs harvesting and the wife is doing non-harvesting tasks, both for the company, their income from agricultural employment is almost equal to the average income of PCP from 'own-account' farming. This is the highest income for a household performing agricultural tasks. However, it is less common practice, since the household needs some time to take care of both their domestic duties (especially if they have little children) and their own oil palm fields. Wider observation in the village indicates that the more common pattern is when only one worker in the household (either the husband or wife) is working for the company (whatever tasks) while the other sells her/his labour to capitalist farmers in the village. Their income is between half and three-quarters of the PCP's income from 'own-account' farming. This also applies to households where both of their workers sell their labour to individual capitalist farmers, whatever tasks they perform. These total earnings from agricultural jobs are considerably lower than for PCPs in *Njomplang*, given the more intensive nature of rice cultivation than oil palm.

The income from agricultural jobs is lower for the households where, due to some reason, they only have one active worker. The female worker is generally the one who cannot perform the wage job. The most common reason for this is when she has to take care of her little children (before they enter primary school). Another reason is when she has been occupied with domestic duties and taking care of their oil palm. For this type of household, the income is only about half of those households with two workers. In this case, their income from agricultural jobs is only between a quarter and a third of PCP's income from 'own-account' farming.

Similar to *Njomplang*, the significant contribution of an agricultural wage income to the total income only indicates the importance of agriculture as an economic sector (from agricultural wage labour) in providing indispensable income for PCPs. However, as in our Java village, this does not necessarily mean that PCPs in our Sumatra village mainly depend on agricultural wages to support their simple reproduction. Instead, most substantial PCPs in *Timpang* sell their labour all year round to achieve their consumption and productive dreams beyond subsistence.

Non-Agricultural Activities

Along with selling their labour in agricultural jobs, another common activity for PCPs outside their 'own-account' farming is selling their labour in non-agricultural employment. In *Njomplang*, they generally work as masonry and construction work during the off-season. Masonry provides higher returns, although it is more difficult to find this skilled job than a construction job. The earnings from being a mason are about 25 to 30 percent higher than for construction workers.[38] They perform these non-agricultural jobs mostly during the off-season (August-October) and earn between Rp. 3.2 and 3.9 million. In some cases, masons also work during the off-peak part of the season, usually a month after the planting period. When doing so, they must hire in other's labour to take care of their land cultivation. For PCPs-cum-masons, their yearly income from being a mason is around a quarter of the income from 'own-account' farming, whereas for PCPs-cum-construction workers, their income is about 25 percent lower than that. If the average gain from non-agricultural employment above is combined with the income from the agricultural jobs discussed before, the share of income from wage labour for PCPs is greater than the 'own-account' farming. Income from wage labour contributes to between half and more than two-thirds of the total income of PCPs.

For non-agricultural employments, unlike *Njomplang*, PCPs in *Timpang* have no off-season and are unable to sell their labour for non-agricultural jobs all year round. They (male workers) have to choose between working in agricultural or non-agricultural jobs. When they decide to do agricultural tasks, it is only the wives who can work in non-agricultural employment. They usually open petty trade businesses. The common non-agricultural jobs are daily wage jobs working for factories, local processing plants, the railway project and infrastructure projects sponsored by the Village Fund. Construction workers and masons are less common, although masonry offers the highest wage of all other non-agricultural employment.[39] Female workers are largely excluded from these jobs. All the jobs offer similar daily wages.[40] The monthly income from these non-agricultural jobs is about half of the PCP's income from 'own-account' farming.

Because of the absence of an off-season in agricultural production, the comparison between a household's income from agriculture and non-agriculture for PCPs in *Timpang* is not easy to make. There are two types of PCP households as far as the origin of their income is concerned. The first is the 'agricultural-oriented PCP', where they choose agricultural jobs to support their 'own-account' farming. This household is similar to the PCPs in *Njomplang*, in which 'agriculture as an economic sector' keeps playing an important role in the overall reproduction of PCPs by providing agricultural wages. However, when they prefer to work in non-agricultural employments to complement their 'own-account' farming as 'non-agricultural-oriented PCPs', 'agriculture as an economic sector'(via wage labour income) is much less important for their reproduction. This suggests that as an economic sector, agriculture is less important in *Timpang* than in *Njomplang*.

However, when it comes to the comparison between the contribution of 'own-account' farming and wage labour (both in agriculture and non-agriculture) to total income, the contribution of 'own-account' farming to the total income of PCPs in *Timpang* is higher than in *Njomplang*. 'Own-account' farming continues to contribute between half (for 'non-agricultural-oriented PCPs') and two-thirds (for 'agricultural-oriented PCPs') of total income of PCPs in *Timpang* whereas in *Njomplang*, 'own-account' farming only contributes between a third and half of the total income. This shows that the income from 'own-account' farming for PCPs in *Timpang* is more crucial for class reproduction than for their compatriots in *Njomplang*, although agriculture as an economic sector is less important in *Timpang*.

Another activity outside 'own-account' farming for PCPs is 'self-employment'. In *Njomplang*, 'self-employment' is quite rare. Some practices include tractor services and non-rice trading. Tractor services are an exception given only one PCP in the village owns a tractor. Similar to capitalist farmers, the income from tractor services is less lucrative than rice trading. However, Kirun's earnings from tractor services are higher than those for capitalist farmers because he does not need to share the income with the driver (his own son is the driver).[41] The income from tractor services is around half of the income from his 'own-account' farming, which brings Kirun's total income to be higher than the average for a PCP in *Njomplang*. On the other hand, the rare petty grocery stores and petty trades[42] promise much less income than tractor services (only about a quarter) and, thus, only provide a small amount of additional income to contribute to the PCP's total income. This makes the total income of PCP-cum-petty traders slightly lower than the average of a PCP in the village.

A rare 'self-employment' venture for PCPs in *Njomplang*, and yet one which offers a lucrative income is rice trading. There are only a few PCPs who are rice traders. As explained in the previous section, with their limited capital, PCPs-cum-rice traders usually team up with 'modest' capitalist farmers to supply the minimum quota to big rice traders (national and regional players). To do so, they are, at the same time, acting as *penebas* (Chapter 5). In annual terms, their income is similar to those 'modest' capitalist farmers-cum-rice traders mentioned in the previous section. However, since the PCP land cultivation is smaller than capitalist farmers', the income from rice trading for PCPs is about the same as the income from 'own-account' farming when rice trading only generates a minimum profit (Rp. 100 thousand per tonne), while it is higher than an 'own-account' farming if rice trading yields the maximum gain (Rp. 300 thousand per tonne). With this lucrative income, their total income is higher than the average PCP in *Njomplang*.

In *Timpang*, the role of self-employment outside of agriculture depends on the nature of the PCPs' households. Agricultural-oriented PCPs generally have no activity in self-employment outside agriculture, since they are occupied with agricultural wage jobs to complement their own-account farming. As for non-agricultural-oriented PCPs, one of the most lucrative practices is oil palm trading, yet it only involves a small number of PCPs. The monthly income from this trading is similar to those 'modest' capitalist farmers-cum-oil palm traders discussed earlier. If they earn minimum profit from trading (Rp. 8.4 million), PCPs' income from trading is about twice the income from their 'own-account' farming and it is much higher if they manage to secure maximum revenue from the trading. A much less lucrative 'self-employment' is petty trades. The income from this activity is only around a third of the average income of PCPs from 'own-account' farming.

Since PCPs' daily needs have been met by the earnings from 'own-account' farming, they make use of the income from outside 'own-account' farming for several activities. In *Njomplang*, they harness their income for renting-in land, buying basic production technology, paying for the children's education and, to a lesser extent, purchasing land. When the opportunity to renting-in land is rare, while there is no need to pay for the children's education anymore, and the chance to buy land is small, they harness the money for consumption goods.

The most common non-agricultural utilisation of the income for PCPs in *Njomplang* is sending children to high school. Our survey and wider observations in the village indicate that most PCPs send their children to high school. They finance their children with minimal state assistance, since they are not below the poverty line and, thus, are not eligible for assistance (see the comparison with the classes of labour in the next section). After completing school,[43] the graduates work in the big cities in Java (Greater Jakarta and Lampung). Working as factory workers in Greater Jakarta is the most common goal for both young males and females despite the fact that some of them have to pay intermediary fees to a middle man to get the jobs.[44] This does not apply to those who have a connection with the factory, usually when their distant relatives already work there. While working in the factory is laborious, the higher steady income they receive is better than that from agricultural jobs, and this attracts many high school graduates in *Njomplang* to take up factory work. Other destinations for migration are urban jobs such as security guards, clerks in shipping, drivers, mechanics and various casual jobs. A few others join the army if they can meet the physical eligibility demands and their parents have a connection to help with the enrolment. The remittances from these migrant workers are harnessed to renting-in land, purchase basic production technologies and, in rare cases, to buy small parcels of land. For those who still have younger siblings at home, the remittances are harnessed to pay their education fees up to high school.

The activity of PCPs in sending their children to high school has had some profound impacts on the regeneration and the reproduction of their class (the general pattern can be seen in Figure 7.2). In *Njomplang*, apart from limited employment options at home, out-migration to urban areas by high school graduates is because they are generally less familiar with farming and this makes them less interested in agriculture. When most young workers leave agriculture, their parent PCPs must work further into their old age. This has been described as a generational problem in the literature (White, 2012a, 2020). However, it does not necessarily always mean that these parents will have no successor, especially in the case of 'substantial PCPs'.

In many cases, the migrant children of 'substantial PCPs' abandon their less lucrative jobs in the city and come back to the village. If all the children are migrant workers, the successor depends on the economic situation of each sibling, the genders of the children, the husband-wife relationship and their interest in agricultural or village life. When one child stays at home and helps the

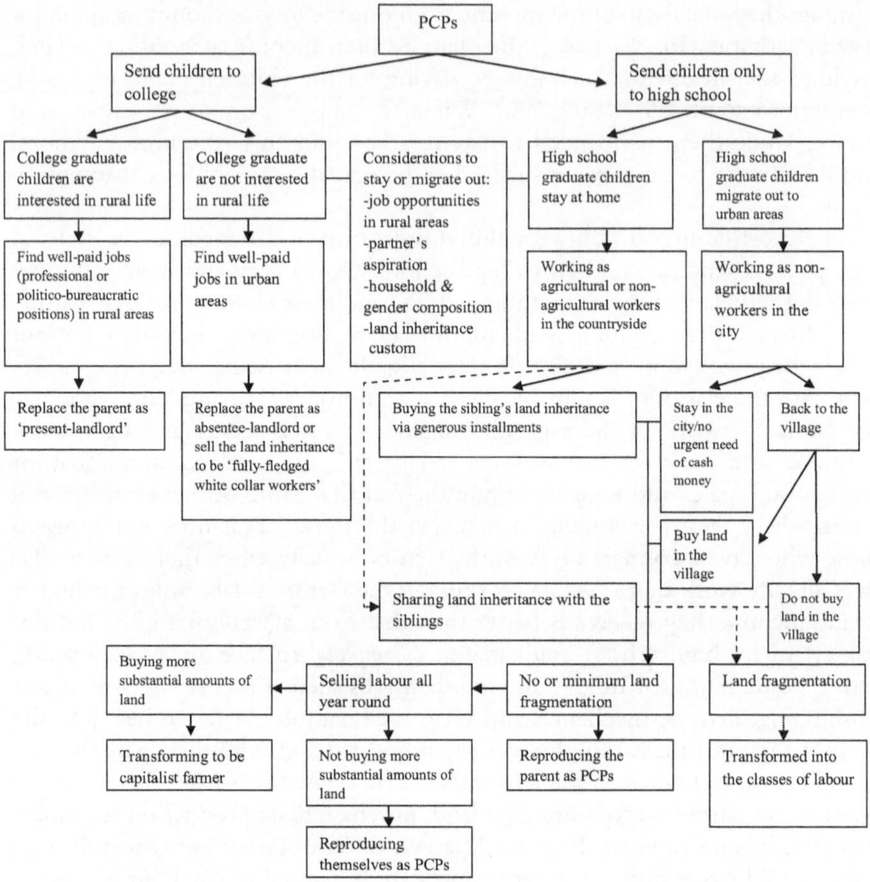

Figure 7.2 Class and generational reproduction of PCPs in the two villages. (Source: author)

parents with their farming, she/he inherits the land, with generous instalments to be paid to the siblings. However, if the siblings are in great need of cash money, they may demand the sale of the land, which can lead to land fragmentation and transform all of the children into 'semi-proletariat farmers' or FFP.

For 'formal PCPs', the chance to find their successor is smaller. Their children have no strong obligation to come back to the village, since their parents have no land ownership but only land cultivation rights. However, there is a pattern where one of the children comes back to the village when the parents are too old or have passed away, to take over the parental home. Whether she/he takes over land cultivation rights from her/his parents would depend on the availability of other employment in the village and their interest in farming. When the children are neither interested nor able to continue their parents' land cultivation rights, their 'formal PCP' status is transformed into FFP.

This is slightly different for the few PCPs in *Njomplang* who have managed to send their children to college. Their ability to do this has been due to their ability to rent-in significantly more land (more than one hectare). This is the case of the PCPs like Sutikno (see Chapter 5). For him, the higher education of his children effectively prevented land fragmentation, since they could find well-paid employment elsewhere. However, the reproduction of their class position as PCPs is in question. If neither of his children wanted to stay in the village, then the PCP status is not reproduced. The children outside the village might behave as 'absentee landlords' if they decide to sharecrop out the land to the villagers. Even if one of the children lives in the village, she/he might not continue to be a PCP if they keep their paid employment. The paddy field is likely to be sharecropped out to others, making the owners 'present landlords'.

Similar to *Njomplang*, PCPs in *Timpang* harness the income from outside 'own-account' farming for several activities. Buying land, renting-in land (oil palm or paddy), paying children education fees and spending for consumer goods are among the common activities. For some PCPs, sending children to college is the top priority aspiration to prevent their children work laborious job in the oil palm field as they do. However, if for some reason their money is not enough to finance the education or to buy lands while land rent is rare, the next option is to purchase consumption goods. Buying more land is an option when the money is available and there is no need to finance the children's education anymore.

Sending children to high school is one of the common non-agricultural activities for PCPs in *Timpang*. Similar to *Njomplang*, PCPs in *Timpang* manage to pay for their children's education without state social assistance. When they complete high school, however, working for an oil palm plantation in their own village is not a straightforward option for the graduates. Having been occupied by their studies, they are not familiar with working in oil palm production, which needs special skills, especially in harvesting (*Ngegrek*). Moreover, juvenile delinquencies (oil palm pilfering, gambling, drinking liquor) have also diverted their attention from farming. However, even for those who manage to acquire the skills, they are left behind by those junior school graduates who started their careers in oil palm much earlier, and have been able to obtain more *ancak* at individual oil palm fields. For high school graduates, they generally have to accept jobs with companies that offer less autonomy. With these limited options, high school graduates from *Timpang* normally migrate out to Riau, South Sumatra, and other provinces in Sumatra. Some of them go to Malaysia. Selling their labour as a worker in the oil palm plantations (mostly with the companies), shipping, driving for the companies and being construction workers are the common forms of employment that they find.

Nonetheless, this out-migration is less than it used to be in the 1990s, when oil palm production had not been developed in the village. Today, women are more likely to migrate out than men, since oil palm provides fewer jobs for female workers (limited to applying fertilisers and herbicides or weeding). In addition, their wages are lower than males for the same jobs. Furthermore, as mentioned before, the daughters from Batak families have little chance of receiving land inheritance. Unlike the daughters of capitalist farmers who could attend college, the daughter from PCPs must find manual jobs elsewhere. Working as shopkeepers or factory workers in Medan are common options. Some migrant workers (both female and male) do not send remittances given the limited earnings they obtain and their aspirations to save money to start their own families. When remittances are sent, they are used for financing younger siblings' education, renting-in land (oil palm or paddy) and buying land.

PCs' desire to send their children to high school has a notable impact on their class reproduction (see Figure 7.2). For substantial PCPs, who are in the majority in *Timpang*, the son is the natural successor, particularly for Batak families. When a PCP retires from farming, the oldest son normally takes over the position. When there are several sons, land fragmentation can be prevented if the oldest son, as the largest inheritor, offers to buy his brothers' share through generous instalments. However, this is only the case when the brothers are not in great need of cash money. When the opposite situation occurs, land fragmentation might happen, although to a lesser extent in *Njomplang*, where daughters have similar rights to land inheritance. For non-Batak households, the reproduction of the 'substantial PCP' in *Timpang* is similar to that in *Njomplang*. For 'formal PCPs', who are negligible in *Timpang*, a successor may be difficult to find. They only have a limited fixed land rent arrangement, which lasts for a couple of years that provides little chance for their children to be 'formal PCPs'.

A different mechanism applies for the few PCPs in *Timpang* who manage to send their children to university. Apart from their oil palm fields, this capacity is owed to their significant paddy field ownership (almost a hectare) which provides crucial additional income to their oil palm production and the money saved from their previous jobs abroad (Malaysia). For these substantial PCPs, their reproduction depends on the inextricable link through generational, gender and clanship ties (Figure 7.2). Unlike *Njomplang*, where the college graduate children might become a landlord, in *Timpang*, this is rare, since sharecropping is negligible. The bigger chance is that they will be transformed into capitalist farmers (either absentee or present) who hire in labour all year round to take care of their inherited oil palm while they focus on their salaried occupations.

Occupying political-bureaucratic positions in the village is also a common non-agricultural activity for PCPs in *Timpang*. Some of them are the head of their hamlet in the village. Some PCPs who become head of hamlet give up their own farming and hire in workers to take care of their oil palm fields, apart from applying fertilisers or herbicides. This usually happens when the hamlets are lucrative hamlets which occupy strategic positions such as being the centre of developmental projects (both local and national) and where the hamlets are the key entrance to a company's plantations. For PCPs-cum-politico-bureaucrat officials, their total income is higher than the average PCP's income.

Concerning both *Njomplang* and *Timpang*, there is little doubt that income sources from beyond 'own-account' farming play an indispensable role in PCP reproduction. Literature has stated that the so-called 'off-farm' activity of 'middle farmers' crucially helps their consolidation (White & Wiradi, 1989). We see this in *Njomplang*. By the same token, non-agricultural activities, like sending children to college, could endanger their 'simple reproduction'. The effort to send their children to higher education signals the PCP's aspirations to move beyond subsistence. Moreover, at least with the oil palm village of *Timpang*, outside 'own-account' farming activities of PCPs do not only assist their 'simple reproduction', but also facilitate PCPs transforming themselves into capitalist farmers. They are eager to exchange their 'relative autonomy from the labour market' for economic gain by selling their labour in order to buy more land. With this level of differentiation, instead of assuming the reproduction of PCPs is due to their inherent superiority, it merely epitomises their 'contingent resilience' (Zhang, 2015).

Classes of Labour and their Survival

The Struggles in 'Own-Account' Farming

As mentioned in Chapter 5, regarding the members of the classes of labour, only 'semi-proletariat farmers' and 'proletariat-farmer' are involved in 'own-account' farming and, thus, only they can obtain income from such farming. FFPs, on the other hand, are neither involved in 'own-account' farming nor do they receive income from it. When they are involved in 'own-account' farming activities such as renting-in land or buying land, they are, by definition, no longer FFP but have become either 'proletariat-farmers' or 'semi-proletariat farmers'. For 'semi-proletariat farmers' in *Njomplang*, the common 'own-account' farming activity is buying and selling land. As shown in Table 7.1, 'semi-proletariat farmers' are on the negative side of the equation concerning land transactions. This vulnerability to dispossession is closely related to their smaller income from 'own-account' farming compared to PCPs (Chapter 6), which means their total income is lower than that of PCPs, even though they engage in similar outside 'own-account' farming activities (see the next section). As for 'proletariat-farmers', their equation in land transaction is zero, since they neither own land to be sold nor have any ability to buy or own land. The only exception was in the 2000s when one of the 'proletariat-farmers' bought a tiny parcel of land (0.08 hectares) with the help of a remittance.

What is interesting is the ability of members of the FFP to buy land indicated in Table 7.1. There are two groups of workers who have managed to do this. The first group is the 'white collar workers' (generally working in banking or as government officials) living in the village. They buy the land as an investment for their retirement. Another group of workers is the 'migrant blue-collar workers' working in the factories around Jakarta. From this formal employment, their monthly salary is about three times the minimum wage stipulated in the district, which enables them[45] to buy a meagre portion of land in their home village (several *iring*). They also buy the land for their retirement in the village. In both cases, before their retirement, their land is currently cultivated by their family members in the village. The landowner generally receives not more than a half return from their land. Especially for those migrant 'blue-collar workers', they can grant a higher share for their family members, since by doing that, they also reduce the duty of sending regular remittances back home.

Another common activity in 'own-account' farming for the classes of labour in *Njomplang* is leasing-in land. As discussed in the PCP section, the incidence of land rent is lower than it used to be in the 2000s. Nowadays, most land rent depends on the offer from the Village Lands (*Tanah Kas Desa*), which are limited in number. The classes of labour condemn the random lottery mechanism which still provides a chance for capitalist farmers to have access to the Village Lands. One member protested that 'it is not fair if those who are in more need like us cannot access Village Lands that are given to the *Juragan* (capitalist farmers)'. The limited supply of land being rented out in the village cannot meet the high demand for leasing in land, although the rent fee is not cheap.[46] The small chance of acquiring leasing in land for 'semi-proletariat farmers' and 'proletariat-farmers' means they must earn additional income from the outside of 'own-account' farming.

A more difficult situation must be faced by the FFP. They are usually only able to renting-in land when they receive additional earnings from rearing livestock (sheep). They are only interested in leasing-in land to grow their own rice for their own consumption. When the FFP leases-in land for a couple of years, they become members of the 'proletariat-farmers' or 'semi-proletariat farmers'. But when their contract is over and they fail to find another land contract, they fall back again into the ranks of the FFP in the village.

For all the members of the classes of labour in *Njomplang*, remittances have generally been harnessed for daily consumption instead of being used to leasing in land. In only a few cases, those who have no children at school, can the money from remittances be saved to leasing in land. With the chances of renting in land decreasing, the classes of labour's attempts to meet their subsistence are getting harder.

The 'own-account' farming activities of the classes of labour also involve buying basic production technology. They generally own a threshing machine for harvesting. Owning this tool is a top priority given harvesting is the most lucrative agricultural task (*bawon*). This also applies to the FFP, who own neither land nor land cultivation rights. They join the harvesting by withdrawing themselves temporarily from their regular employment (petty trades, petty home industries, non-agricultural casual jobs). With a limited labour supply of harvesters, the FFP are invited by the landowners. Another important production technology for the classes of labour is a water pump. However, this is usually only owned by sharecroppers in the northern part of the village or those who are eager to grow mung beans during the off-season.

As with PCPs, the main difference between the classes of labour in *Timpang* and *Njomplang* is the incidence of land rent. In *Timpang*, the chance of leasing-in oil palm is smaller given there is a more limited supply of land to rent. For the few 'proletariat-farmers' who lease-in oil palm, the returns are highly lucrative and they greatly help them to meet their subsistence.[47] However, many classes of labour have no access to leasing in land. This situation has decreased their chances of generating a higher income.

The more common 'own-account' farming activity for the classes of labour in *Timpang* is buying and selling land. For 'semi-proletariat farmers' in *Timpang*, they experience negative net results in their land market activity (Table 7.2). As with PCPs, 'semi-proletariat farmers' in this village sell their land to raise money to conduct their ritual customs and to send their children to school. In some cases, they sell their land to open up non-agricultural businesses. It should be noted that most of their land is not bought by either capitalist farmers or PCPs. As shown in Table 7.2, it is the FFP that has the highest positive net result in the land market (+ 7.49 hectares). This indicates that land transactions mostly occur within the classes of labour, especially between 'semi-proletariat farmers' and the FFP. Only a tiny parcel of land is involved in each land transaction.

The ability of the FFP in *Timpang* to buy land is hardly surprising. Similar to *Njomplang*, local 'white collar workers' and 'migrant blue collar workers' are among those who manage to buy these small pieces of land (in *Timpang*, it is around 0.10 to 2.0 hectares). The former are usually workers who work at the oil palm companies, while the latter are migrant workers working in Malaysia's oil palm plantations.[48] Both want to make some investments for their retirement. Unlike *Njomplang*, however, in *Timpang*, there are 'local blue-collar workers' who manage to buy land. This is made possible by three mechanisms. First, they use their savings from their agricultural and non-agricultural wages. With land being relatively cheap in *Timpang* (compared to *Njomplang*), they may purchase a small piece of land (half of a hectare). Nonetheless, the classes of labour in *Timpang* take years of saving at the expense of consumer spending to do this.[49] Most importantly, they are able to save some money when they have no children of high school age as this costs a lot of money (see next section). The second way is rearing livestock (cows) along with disposing of their labour throughout the year. They must work more than ten hours a day, since, after completing their agricultural wage jobs, they have to take care of their own livestock. This 'self-exploitation' to purchase a small piece of land could take a decade.[50] Another mechanism is through generous intra-family loans. The FFPs may be offered by their siblings a lower price than the land market price and second, they can pay through many small instalments and without interest. This ability to buy land effectively transforms members of the FFP into 'semi-proletariat farmers'.

When buying land in their village is too difficult, the classes of labour in *Timpang* purchase oil palm fields outside of their district, mostly in Aceh province. For *Timpang*'s workers, Aceh is a favourite place to buy land, since the price is only about a fifth to a third of the price in *Timpang*.[51] The location is also not that far from the village, since *Timpang* is located close to the border between North Sumatra and Aceh (Chapter 4). They purchase the lands to prepare the future of their children in a new place. While this buying of land does not directly increase the income from 'own-account' farming for the classes of labour's households, it effectively prevents land fragmentation of the 'semi-proletariat farmers' in *Timpang* and transforms the FFP into 'semi-proletariat farmers' in the new location. In this case, the 'semi-proletariat farmers' are generationally reproduced through 'spatial-relocation'.

On the other hand, the 'semi-proletariat farmers' in *Timpang* may also lose their land. Their land dispossession is mostly due to non-agricultural rather than agricultural activities. There are 'semi-proletariat farmers' who sell their only land to pay the debt for financing their many children at high school. Others sell the land to finance traditional rituals; this is confined largely to the Batak clanship. More commonly, they may lose their land due to land fragmentation. If their children become high school graduates and cannot find the means to buy their own land or live independently outside the village, land fragmentation is unavoidable. Without these causes, land dispossession is generally avoided. Cash money shortages are coped with by consumption reduction.

Similar to the PCP, the classes of labour in *Timpang* generally only manage to purchase basic production technology, such as aluminium poles, sickles, axes, loose fruit collection baskets and a modified motorcycle. The modification, which may cost a few hundred thousand rupiah, is prioritised to support their job. By accelerating the harvesting process, they can move to another *ancak* more quickly.

Selling Labour Out to Other's Farms

With such meagre incomes from 'own-account' farming, both 'semi-proletariat farmers' and 'proletariat-farmers' are struggling to meet their subsistence and need to sell their labour all year round. In *Njomplang*, the most common activity outside 'own-account' farming for the classes of labour is working in agricultural production. Their activities and incomes are similar to the PCP discussed earlier. The main difference lies in the income comparison from 'own-account' farming and agricultural wages given the PCP's incomes from 'own-account' farming are higher than those of the classes of labour (Chapter 6). For 'semi-proletariat farmers', their incomes from agricultural jobs is from twice to four times greater than their incomes from 'own-account' farming. For a 'proletariat-farmer' household with the same labour composition (two workers in a household), their income from agricultural employment is between two and half times and five times that of 'own-account' farming given that they receive smaller income from 'own-account' farming than 'semi-proletariat farmers'. Even if, for some reason, there is only one source of labour from a household, either male or female, the minimum income for both 'semi-proletariat farmers' and 'proletariat-farmers' from agricultural jobs remains at least the same to twice the income from 'own-account' farming.

In *Timpang*, similar activities of the classes of labour can be found. The pressure to complement 'own-account' farming with the income from wage labour is even higher for the classes of labour in Sumatra's oil palm industry than *Njomplang* considering their lower 'own-account' farming income compared to their comrades in Java (Chapter 6). However, different from *Njomplang*, both agricultural and non-agricultural employment is crucially important for the classes of labour in *Timpang*. As discussed earlier, the activities and the income from these jobs are similar to PCPs in *Timpang*. The crucial difference is the share between the incomes from 'own-account' farming and outside 'own-account' farming given that the incomes from 'own-account' farming for PCPs are higher than those of the classes of labour. For 'semi-proletariat farmers' in *Timpang*, their incomes from agricultural jobs are from twice to four times greater than their income from 'own-account' farming. Similar to *Njomplang*, the minimum income for 'semi-proletariat farmers' in *Timpang* from agricultural jobs remains at least the same as to twice the income from 'own-account' farming when there is only one labourer in the household, either male or female. It highlights the low income from 'own-account' farming in oil palm and the high dependency of 'semi-proletariat farmers' on wage income.

In both *Njomplang* and *Timpang*, similar to PCPs, we are informed the importance of income from agricultural wages to the total income of 'semi-proletariat farmers' and 'proletariat-farmers'. However, different from PCPs in which their income from 'own-account' farming is sufficient to sustain their 'simple reproduction' and thus their selling labour activity rather indicating their aspiration to achieve their dreams beyond subsistence, the selling labour of 'semi-proletariat farmers' and 'proletariat-farmers' represents their survival activity simply because their 'own-account' farming is hardly adequate to meet their subsistence.

Non-Agricultural Means of Survival

Similar to PCPs, another important activity outside of 'own-account' farming for the classes of labour is selling their labour outside agriculture. In *Njomplang*, before the inception of the Village Fund in 2015, most workers in *Njomplang* were unemployed with only a little farming feasible in the break season (Chapter 6). Some male workers do manage to find construction jobs in the neighbouring villages or in the downtown of the district. With the Village Fund infrastructure projects, the classes of labour in the village are offered a steady job for about three months every year (August to October). The jobs, however, are only available for male workers. As with the PCPs, the income from the job is between Rp. 3.2 and Rp. 3.9 million, depending on whether they are ordinary construction workers (coolies) or masons/supervisors. This earning alone is about half of the 'own-account' farming of 'semi-proletariat farmers' and around 80 percent of 'proletariat-farmers' income from 'own-account' farming. However, not all male workers can be absorbed into the infrastructure projects.[52] Furthermore, since the projects depend on a state budget, the jobs will simply disappear when the program is over.

In *Njomplang*, 'semi-proletariat farmers' and 'proletariat-farmers' generally take non-agricultural jobs, mentioned above, during the off-season while working in agricultural employment during the on-season. If we combine their early incomes both from the agricultural and non-agricultural employment noted above, the share of income generated from wage labour is getting bigger than that from own-account farming. For 'semi-proletariat farmers', their wage labour earnings contribute to about two-thirds to three-quarters of their total income. As for 'proletariat-farmers', the contribution of 'own-account' farming is only between a quarter and a fifth of the total income. This suggests that agricultural wages play an indispensable role in the reproduction of both 'semi-proletariat farmers' and 'proletariat-farmers'. Thus, the main issue for the classes of labour is to capture higher income from agricultural wages (outside of 'own-account' farming) to boost their total income when the option to demand bigger land cultivation ('own-account' farming) through land redistribution is not feasible.

In *Timpang*, the classes of labour have no such off-season as *Njomplang*. Throughout the year, they must decide whether to work in agricultural or non-agricultural jobs. For 'semi-proletariat farmers', their income from wages (both agricultural and non-agricultural) contribute to about two-thirds (for 'non-agricultural-oriented PCPs') and three-quarters (for 'agricultural-oriented PCPs') of their total income. This indicates that more of the classes of labour's income is obtained from wages than 'own-account' farming. The political implication for this situation is worth mentioning. In *Njomplang*, where agricultural wages are the most important component of the classes of labour's total income, it is easier to find a common platform among them. This is more difficult in *Timpang*, where the classes of labour are divided along the lines of 'agricultural-oriented' and 'non-agricultural-oriented households'.

Another activity outside 'own-account' farming for the classes of labour is 'self-employment' outside agriculture. In *Njomplang*, this includes non-rice trading and petty trades and home industries. A few of them open petty grocery stores, selling snacks for the children attending school in the village, and making *tempe*, which are mostly managed by female workers. Similar to PCPs, the income from these activities for the classes of labour is meagre. With the combination of non-rice trading or petty home industries managed by the wife and the income from agricultural jobs and construction work performed by the husband, the total income for 'semi-proletariat farmers' is slightly lower (15 percent) than those who have two sources of labour (husband and wife) doing agricultural jobs all year round,[53] while for the 'proletariat-farmers', it is about the same having two labourers in agriculture and a combination of one agricultural labourer and one non-agricultural labourer, since they obtain lower income in 'own-account' farming than 'semi-proletariat farmers'. The female workers usually give up an agricultural job to join non-agricultural employment when they get older (50 or 60 years old) because of the laborious nature of agricultural jobs (especially planting and harvesting).

In contrast to PCPs, the classes of labour mostly use their income for daily survival. Some members of the classes of labour in *Njomplang* have to take on debt to meet these needs. Others avoid such debt by reducing their consumption level, signalling the mode of 'self-exploitation'. The state does provide cash assistance for poor households.[54] However, the goal of this support is only to keep the poor alive. It has limited coverage and there is regular misallocation of funds.[55] This concern over survival hampers the classes of labour wishing to invest in their 'own-account' farming. Apart from the 'semi-proletariat farmers', other members of the classes of labour need the help of cheap credit (KUR-BRI) to leasing in land.

Similar to PCPs, the classes of labour in *Njomplang* also harness their incomes to send their children to high school. Unlike PCPs, who generally manage to finance the education from their own resource, the classes of labour rely on state assistance. The state provides BOS,[56] which makes schooling up to junior school free. The parents of the students only need to cover the cost of the stationery and supply a daily allowance. However, the state assistance is not adequate enough to make high school free.[57] With the combination of the school fees, stationery costs and the allowance, the monthly cost for a high school student is between a third and a half of the minimum wage in the district. The cost is even higher for those who are studying at a vocational high school, since they must pay extra fees in the form of fees for the obligatory period(s) of practical work. In this situation, the state assistance, such as PKH and BSM,[58] is not sufficient.[59] Compared to the past up to the 1980s, the parents' burden today is also higher, since school-going teenagers no longer get involved in work that earns money to support the household (White, 2012b). Similar to most PCPs, many classes of labour in *Njomplang* send their children to vocational high school to equip them with a skill so they are ready to work after graduating.

With such aspirations, the classes of labour are usually willing to apply for cheap loans (KUR-BRI) to finance their children's education. When the loan is not available for some reason (for instance, because the previous instalment had not been paid off) they borrow money from their wealthier neighbours. For the sharecroppers, sometimes they borrow money from their 'landlord-capitalist' patrons. With such a difficult life, some of the classes of labour and PCPs rear livestock (sheep) solely to finance their children's education. After their children finish their school, rearing livestock usually stops because of the laborious nature of the job, especially when it is combined with their agricultural wage employment.

The aspirations of the classes of labour to provide a better future for their children are not easily met. As with the PCPs, the high school graduates, both male and female, from the classes of labour households in *Njomplang* mostly migrate out to Greater Jakarta to work as rank and file workers. Regarding the classes of labour migrants, their remittances are mostly harnessed to meet the daily needs and to pay the education fees of their younger siblings at home. Only when these priorities have been met, can the remaining money be used to renting-in land or purchase basic production technology. There are 'proletariat-farmers' who buy a tiny parcel of land with the help of the remittances sent from their children working in big company factories. This remittance effectively transforms them into 'semi-proletariat farmers', although they are still members of the classes of labour.

The activities of the classes of labour in sending their children to high school have an impact on the reproduction of their class (Figure 7.3 illustrates the general pattern). The generational reproduction of 'semi-proletariat farmers' who own lands is similar to the PCPs who *only* manage to send their children to high school, as mentioned earlier. While for 'semi-proletariat farmers' who only control lands without owning, their reproduction is similar to 'proletariat-farmers'.

As for 'proletariat-farmer' households, they only inherit a house and land control (no *sawah* ownership). Usually the sibling (either male or female) who stays at home when their parents pass away would continue the land control and inherit the house following the payment of generous instalments to any other siblings. However, should any of the siblings be in great need of cash money and demand the sale of the house, it would be questionable if the successor were to become a 'proletariat-farmer'.

A quite different form of reproduction applies to the FFP. Since the members neither own land nor land cultivation rights, their children are likely not familiar with farming. When one of the children (either a migrant worker or local worker) takes over the parent's house after they pass away, they are unlikely to be interested in farming. However, if farming provides a higher income, they would be pleased to receive land cultivation rights as sharecropping, and become 'proletariat-farmers' or 'semi-proletariat farmers'. Such a chance in *Njomplang* is considerable. Nonetheless, when farming offers lower income, they will focus on wage employment, either in agriculture (*bawon* from harvesting) or non-agriculture in the village. Either way, they will continue their parent's role as a member of the FFP.

As in *Njomplang*, the classes of labour in *Timpang* also make use of their income to meet basic daily needs. As mentioned earlier, they manage to lease-in or buy tiny plots of land only when they effectively minimise their spending, both on consumption and educational costs (high school), while maximising their additional income by rearing livestock.

They also harness their income to send their children to high school. They mostly rely on state assistance, like their compatriots in *Njomplang*. Like *Njomplang*, high school in *Timpang* district collects fees from students[60] due to the limited state assistance they receive. If we combine the school fees (including the cost of books), stationery and the allowance, the monthly cost for a single high school student is around a third to a half of the district minimum

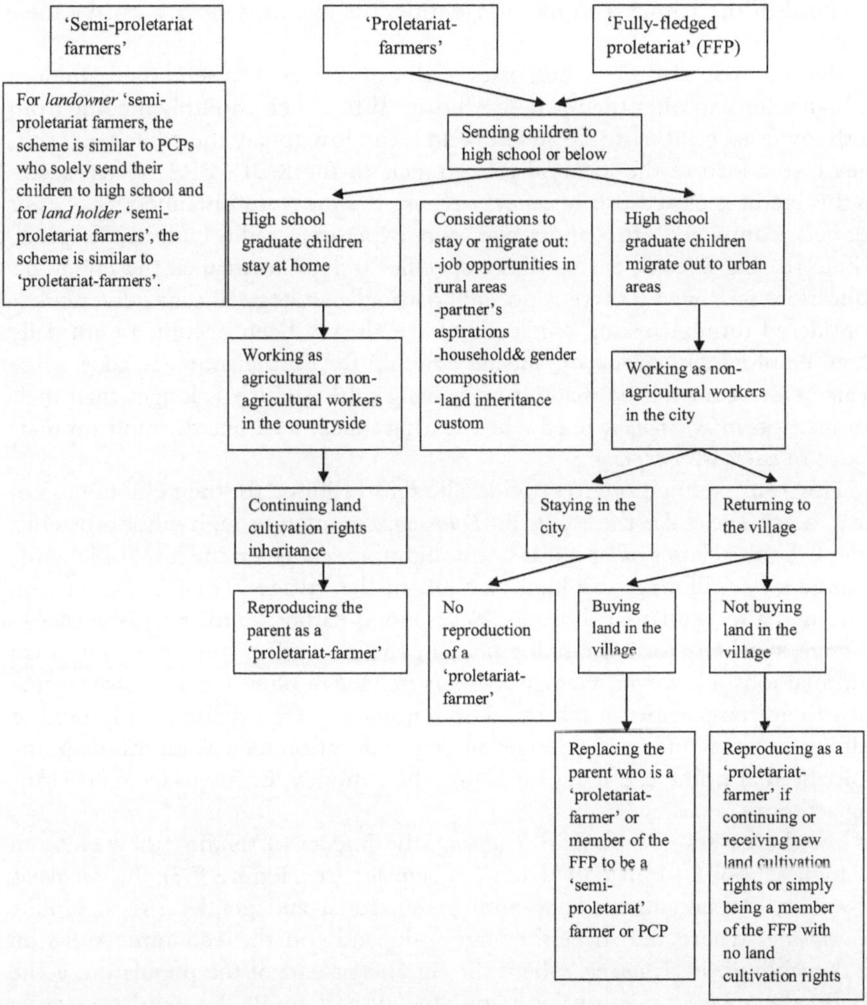

Figure 7.3 Class and generational reproduction of the classes of labour in the two villages. (Source: author)

wage. In household terms, it amounts to about a quarter to a third of total household expenditure. The cost is even higher when they send their children to vocational high school. Similar to *Njomplang*, many parents in *Timpang* from the classes of labour prefer a vocational high school in the hope of improving their children's chances of getting a job as soon as possible after graduating. It may well be that the interest in technical schools is a national trend rather than merely a local response. The state rhetoric and programs that prioritise 'link and match' between education and industry are largely responsible for this trend. In *Timpang*, the problem with state assistance is more pronounced because of the rampant nepotism dispensed by the village officials (including the head of the hamlets) to the non-entitled recipients, who are usually their relatives.[61]

Despite these obstacles, the classes of labour are eager to send their children to high school to offer them a better future. When their monthly income from both 'own-account' farming and beyond is too low to pay the education costs, they take a loan to the local oil palm traders or the KUR-BRI. When access to this credit is closed (for instance, because the previous instalments have not yet been completed), they must take more expensive credit. Unlike *Njomplang*, where rearing livestock is used as a specific strategy to finance the children's education, in *Timpang* there is no such particular strategy. Rearing livestock is considered too exhausting when they have already been occupied with daily wage employment inside or outside agriculture. Furthermore, it takes some years before cash can be made from rearing cattle, which is longer than their compatriots in *Njomplang* need when rearing sheep, let alone the rampant incidence of theft in *Timpang*.[62]

This 'self-exploitation' to provide a better livelihood for their children is not easy to achieve. Like the PCPs in *Timpang*, completing high school for children from the classes of labour is not straightforward given the level of juvenile delinquency (pilfering, drinking alcohol) in the village. Their out-migration pattern is also similar to those PCPs discussed earlier. Similar to *Njomplang*'s migrant workers, formal employment in the city offers higher income than informal jobs. However, factory workers in Medan often receive lower wages than their compatriots in Jakarta. The remittances are predominantly used to fulfil daily needs and assist younger siblings' education fees. With this help, the household at home can focus on saving their money for 'own-account' farming activities.

For the classes of labour in *Timpang*, the impact of sending their children to high school is similar to that in *Njomplang* (see Figure 7.3). In *Timpang*, however, clanship intertwines with generational and gender issues. Unlike *Njomplang*, where the successor largely depends on the economic situation of the siblings, in *Timpang*, where the significant part of the population is the Batak, the successor is usually a son. In contrast to PCPs, 'semi-proletariat farmers' who own a tiny parcel of land have no possibility of sharing the land between all the sons. Land fragmentation is avoided when the oldest son, who is the largest recipient of land inheritance, is allowed to buy his brothers' share with generous instalments, and vice versa. For non-Batak households, their pattern of reproduction is similar to that of the 'semi-proletariat farmers' in *Njomplang*.

For 'proletariat-farmers' and the FFP in *Timpang* who own no land, one of their children will inherit the house and its yard. In *Timpang*, 'proletariat-farmers' have no right to inherit land cultivation rights as their comrades in *Njomplang* have because of the different nature of the fixed land rent arrangement and sharecropping. Again, for Batak households, the inheritor is predominantly the son. The daughter only has a chance to inherit the house if she is the only child. The heirs of 'proletariat-farmers' and the FFP have only a small chance of becoming 'proletariat-farmers', since land rent is rare in *Timpang*. This renders them able to buy a tiny piece of land only by committing to 'self-exploitation'. Some are successful in transforming themselves into 'semi-proletariat farmers', while others fail to do so and just follow through the line of their parents to become either 'proletariat-farmers' or members of the FFP.

Similar to what we have seen with the PCPs, the classes of labour, both in *Njomplang* and *Timpang*, are reproduced generationally through re-migration by migrant workers returning from the city. The successors come back to the village at a relatively young age (30s or 40s). The son, with his nuclear family, is usually more likely to re-migrate to the village than the daughter. In *Timpang*, this is due to the patrilineal land inheritance customs. In both villages, as housewives, women usually follow their husbands' decisions on where to live. Unlike the offspring of PCPs (especially 'substantial PCPs') who may come back to the village and cultivate an adequate piece of land for their household, the descendants of the classes of labour's family must struggle to collect money in the city to buy their own land, if they wish to live off their own farming when they get back home. If they fail to do so, farming is merely a last resort of survival.

This re-migration trend has been precipitated by the limited amount of formal employment in the city. There is also the expansion of labour flexibility regime since the 2000s that has increased the precariousness of formal employment, especially the rank and file positions (Tjandraningsih, 2013). Nowadays, it is difficult to find a permanent long-term job in formal employment, such as working in a factory or holding a rank and file job in a private company. The companies also prefer to hire in younger workers (in their twenties) for the sake of productivity. Furthermore, most workers in Indonesian cities now work in precarious informal employment because of the stall in industrialisation in the last two decades (Habibi & Juliawan, 2018).

With such gloomy prospects in urban life, many migrant workers from the rural areas consider their activities in the city as being temporary. While the rural economy may not offer higher returns, it does offer lower living costs. This has been the main reason for re-migration to rural areas after the economic crisis of 1998 (Hugo, 2000). The workers wish to come back to their villages after collecting some initial capital they need to re-settle in the village. They use the capital to buy some pieces of land in the village while they are still working elsewhere. This late entry to farming to replace the ageing older farmers is discussed in the generational problem literature (White, 2012a, 2020). However, this ageing issue might not necessarily lead to chronic generational problems, since there are now successors to replace the old farmers.

The way the classes of labour in *Njomplang* and *Timpang* reproduce themselves suggests that we cannot take their reproduction strategy for granted. It is often said in the literature that the classes of labour have increasingly engaged in rural income diversification (Veltmeyer & Wise, 2016). However, the origin of increased income diversification as 'non-political strategies of reproduction' has been overlooked in the discussion, despite the fact that agricultural wages still contribute a significant portion to the total income for 'semi-proletariat farmers' and 'proletariat-farmers' (except for 'non-agricultural-oriented' households in *Timpang*). In *Njomplang* and *Timpang*, 'political strategies of reproduction' in the form of protests and strikes used to be more important in the early 1960s. They demanded land reform (to increase the income from 'own-account' farming) and the increase of general wages (to improve the income from wages). After the massacre of millions of members of the classes of labour across the country in the mid-1960s and the brutal authoritarian control that followed, the political strategies of reproduction have been wiped from the memory of the current generation of classes of labour.

Conclusion

The chapter has argued that agricultural production shapes the reproduction of the agrarian classes. *Njomplang* and *Timpang* highlight the pattern of class reproduction that has been discussed in the literature (Bernstein, 2010). Capitalist farmers harness their abundant agricultural surpluses to accumulate, through both 'own-account' farming and non-agricultural activities. Having only modest 'own-account' farming surpluses, PCPs mostly make use of them for their 'simple reproduction', although when there are chances available, they transform themselves into capitalist farmers. Similar to the FFP who produce no agricultural commodities and rely entirely on wage labour to survive, both 'semi-proletariat farmers' and 'proletariat-farmers', obtaining only a tiny income from farming, are forced to dispose of their labour throughout the year to cope with their subsistence squeeze. However, the nature of reproduction for each agrarian class is contingently shaped by specific settings. In *Njomplang* and *Timpang*, class reproduction intertwines closely with generations, gender and clanship. This complex web of reproduction adds to our understanding of agrarian change that has been largely overlooked in Indonesia.

In generational terms, there is a general tendency for all agrarian classes to come back to the village after working for some time in the city. However, different agrarian classes have different structural reasons for coming back to their village of origin. Their return to replace the older generations may add to the understanding of the generational problem farming today, echoed in the generational literature (White, 2012a, 2020). The class and generational issues are closely related to gender. As shown earlier, the women's position in land inheritance and job position matters. Javanese women (mainly from the PCP and the classes of labour) in our Javanese village tend to have more economic equality than their fellow Batak women in North Sumatra, although women in both villages still experience 'double burdens' in selling their labour in the labour market and preparing the needs of their husbands and children for free, to the 'capital doorsteps' (Bhattacharya, 2017).

As for capitalist farmers in *Njomplang* and *Timpang*, they accumulate through 'own-account' farming as much as from non-agricultural activities, as mentioned in the Indonesian literature (Jun-Kim, 2002; McCarthy, 2010; Li, 2014). However, the literature tends to over-generalise the homogeneity of capitalist farmers. In fact, there is an important difference between those 'modest' capitalist farmers and 'big' capitalist farmers. In absolute figures, the share of non-agricultural accumulation for 'big' capitalist farmers is larger than for 'modest' capitalist farmers. In proportional terms, however, 'modest' capitalist farmers tend to have a larger share of non-agricultural *vis-a-vis* 'own-account' farming accumulation, than 'big' capitalist farmers. Generationally speaking, the smaller proportional share of non-agricultural accumulation for 'big' capitalist farmers apparently leads to the transformation of their children to different types of capitalist farmers (present, absentee, professional-capitalist, politico-bureaucrat capitalist, etc.), while this is not the case for 'modest' capitalist farmers, who proportionally have a larger share of non-agricultural accumulation.

The literature also largely fails to explain why some capitalist farmers are still keen to accumulate via 'own-account' farming activities, while others are not, when the income from 'own-account' farming is considered lower than non-agriculture. As discussed before, it relates to the competition among different types of agrarian ruling class (capitalist farmers and 'landlord-capitalists') in the village. The importance of non-agricultural accumulation, especially in terms of children's education, provides an impetus for the generational reproduction of the capitalist farmers. Both villages show that different types of capitalist farmers ('typical capitalist', 'politico-bureaucrat capitalist' and 'professional-capitalist') and 'landlord-capitalists' have different patterns of generational reproduction. This is further complicated by the clanship (Batak) aspect that holds patrilineal land inheritance as a custom. The different nature of the successors from their parents undoubtedly delivers a profound impact on the dominant nature of capitalist farmers in the future. Only by looking at the internal dynamics of agrarian ruling class more closely, might we be able to sketch the future of capitalist farmers, 'landlord-capitalist' and farming itself. Another crucial factor for class reproduction of agrarian ruling class is state assistance. In Indonesia, this includes delivering subsidies for agricultural inputs, promoting land certification instead of agrarian reform, providing lucrative incentives to village officials, and sponsoring technological development to lower agricultural production costs.

For PCPs, such state policies deliver a mixed impact. While input subsidy is undoubtedly helpful to PCPs, the contra-agrarian reform agenda and the promotion of technological advancement that reduces manual labour might threaten the aspirations of PCPs beyond simple reproduction. With their considerable land ownership ('substantial PCPs') or land control ('formal PCPs'), their income from 'own-account' farming, both in *Njomplang* and *Timpang*, have been sufficient to meet their subsistence (if this means basic food, settlement, clothes and enough basic education for the children that enables them to replace their parents' role as PCPs). However, except for some 'substantial

PCPs' in *Njomplang*, most of them are keen to sell their labour all year round at the expense of their relative autonomy from the labour market to realise their beyond simple reproduction aspirations, such as sending their children to college. The ability or the failure of having college graduate children shapes different patterns of class reproduction among PCPs, which are also closely linked to gender and clanship. With their eagerness to sell their labour throughout the year to meet their beyond simple reproduction aspirations, it is highly doubtful that PCP reproduction represents their inherent superiority, as neo-populist supporters often argue. It rather mirrors their 'contingent resilience' (Zhang, 2015) although the defensive nuance of the term 'resilience' might not do justice to PCPs who successfully transforms themselves into capitalist farmers.

The possibility of being capitalist farmers is inconceivable for the members of the classes of labour. 'Semi-proletariat farmers' and 'proletariat-farmers' can only earn meagre income from 'own-account' farming. With their negligible land ownership and control, the state subsidy for agricultural inputs only provides a little help. Under such circumstances, wage incomes contribute to the largest portion of their total earnings, which greatly shapes their generational reproduction. The most crucial aspect is the children's education. The classes of labour are not able to send their children to college, which is no surprise given they must rely on state assistance just to send their children to high school. With this failure, the pressure for land fragmentation is augmented, especially for 'semi-proletariat farmers' ('proletariat-farmers' do not own land). The ability of 'semi-proletariat farmers' to cope with land fragmentation depends on the demographic composition of the household, the economic situation of the siblings, gender and clanship. However, Batak households tend to face lower pressure of land fragmentation given their patrilineal land inheritance customs. This highlights the inextricable link between generations, classes, genders, and clanship. This also applies to 'proletariat-farmers' the successor of whom depends on the factors mentioned above, plus the nature of land rent. The successors of 'proletariat-farmers' under the sharecropping arrangement in *Njomplang* are easier to find than under the fixed land rent in *Timpang*. When they consider sharecropping or fixed land rent is not worth their efforts, they are simply being members of the FFP, relying entirely on wage incomes for their survival.

With the state's policy being to ignore agrarian reform, their aspirations to obtain more land for cultivation and increase their income from 'own-account' farming are hard to achieve. At the same time, their overwhelming dependence on agricultural wages to survive is under threat by the state's promotion of technological advancement that replaces manual labour, at least in rice cultivation. Under such circumstances, it is often said in the literature that the classes of labour have diversified their rural income generation (Veltmeyer & Wise, 2016). Nonetheless, the literature tends to underplay the origin of such 'non-political strategies of reproduction'. Both *Njomplang* and *Timpang* show that the domination of the current reproduction strategies for the classes of labour goes back to the annihilation of the 'political strategies of reproduction' (land reform and pro-labour wage policy) in the past. The future reproduction of the classes of labour will undoubtedly depend on whether this political struggle can be re-enacted to accompany their 'non-political strategies of reproduction'.

Notes

1 Big 'typical capitalist farmers', like Cokro, are interested in buying medium-sized combine harvester machines that would cost him about Rp. 120 to Rp. 200 million, while modest 'typical capitalist farmers', such as Darsam, have an interest in purchasing small harvesters (Rp. 80 to Rp. 120 million).

2 As this is the only data available, we cannot make a five-year comparison to *Njomplang*. However, the point is that, even within a shorter period, the land market in *Timpang* has been more active than *Njomplang*.

3 Wider observations in the village point to the activity of capitalist farmers, PCPs and semi-proletariat farmers in buying land outside the village, usually in the neighbour provinces (Aceh or Riau) which offer cheaper property. However, it is difficult to gauge the scope of their transactions in the village without a baseline-household census.

4 In the 2000s, the expansion of corporations mainly involved the claiming of uncultivated wetlands in the village. The companies, along with local intermediaries (mainly capitalist farmers, such as Luhut), successfully navigated such expansion at the expense of the local fishermen.

5 When this happens, the parents are only given a meagre share, just enough to support their basic retirement, although the land ownership is still under their name on paper.

6 The lowest calculation points to the case where the share between a tractor owner and a driver is 50-50, and the tractor services only cover about 20 *iring* (3.3 hectares) of paddy field. The maximum calculation is when the share is 70-30 for the tractor owner, while the tractor cultivates about 80 *iring* (13.3 hectares) of rice field for a season.

7 They keep asking the land buyer for the 4 percent fee. However, those who already know about the new rule refuse to pay and the officials, in turn refuse to complete the administrative process of the land transaction. Eventually, some compromises are found when the fee is reduced to 1 or 2 percent.

8 Land certification is carried out by the authority of the National Land Agency (BPN) and is supposedly free. The role of the village officials is to recommend the priority for land certification in their village. Capitalist farmers are willing to pay millions of rupiah to village officials as long as their lands are given priority and the certificate.

9 This decision has been highly political since it was introduced in March 2019, only a month before the general election in April. The village head receives a minimum salary per month of Rp. 2.4 million, while the village secretary receives Rp. 2.2 million and the remaining village apparatus, Rp. 2 million.

10 Village secretary and other village officials are not elected but appointed by village heads in consultation with the sub-district head.

11 The calculation involves the lowest price of most common used fertiliser that is Urea (Rp. 1800/kg) and the highest price of the fertilisers that of NPK Phonska (Rp. 2300/kg).

12 Supri refused to state the profit from this business. However, the literature indicates that the profit from the milling of dry stalk paddy to be sold as rice in Java is around Rp. 2.5 million per tonne (Putri et al., 2013: 149). In a month, Supri can mill between 60 and 120 tonnes of dry stalk paddy, although the huller does not work all year round as dry stalk paddy is only available to be milled for six to ten months.

13 He installed the oven in 2014 and it cost him more than Rp. 120 million.

14 When they send substantial amounts of money back home, it is usually to buy land in their names and not for their parents.

15 For those who hold no cover letter, their volume of sale is only about a half of those who do have one and, thus, their return from palm oil trading is only about half of the calculation above.

16 It depends on the volume of sale to local processing plants. The range is from 5 to 10 tonne per day.

17 The *toke* generally steals from 10 to 30 percent of the total weight. They do this by 'playing their hands' on the scales and understating the weight of the produce brought by the customers. This is only possible because they use manual scales instead of digital ones.

18 Literally, 'syrup money' means the money to buy bottles of syrup. Of course, it is only a euphemism, since, in fact, the companies regularly provide hundreds of thousands of millions of rupiah to village officials.

19 For instance, in only four months, the revenue from the levy is Rp. 75 million.

20 The village head receives Rp. 200 thousand, while other village officials, including the head of hamlets obtains Rp. 150 thousand per day.

21 This is technically legal, since the laws provide for the discretion of the village to earn its own revenues. This has been banned in *Njomplang*'s district.

22 These are supposedly free of charge. Some classes of labour have reported that they had to pay from Rp. 150 to Rp. 200 thousand to get their administrative letters processed.

23 Since Gultom is living in the same hamlet as Budi, Sofian needed Gultom to divide the voters for Budi, whom he regarded as the main contender, given the already bad reputation of Luhut in the village.

24 At his house, Sofian held a party by cooking *lemang* (sticky rice cooked inside a segment of bamboo). He inserted Rp. 50 thousand in each of the *lemang*. More than thousand *lemang* were distributed at that night.

25 By renting-in land between two and four *iring*, the return is about half of the return from sharecropping in 0.93 hectares (the average land cultivation of formal PCPs' in *Njomplang*) and less than half the return from landownership of 0.67 hectares (the average land cultivation of substantial PCPs in the village): see Chapter 6.

26 The initiation of such a mechanism is unclear. However, since it advantages capitalist farmers who also occupy village offices, it seems that they have played a prominent role in advancing it.

27 The variation within substantial PCP relates to the aspiration of the household. The households who have aspirations to send their children to college tend to sell their labour throughout the year, and vice versa.

28 If there are three members of a household joint-harvesting, their *bawon* is about equal to the yield of owning a *sawah* of half a hectare. A worker could receive a one tonne share of dry stalk paddy (*bawon*) during a harvesting season. In money term, this is around Rp. 4.2 million per season.

29 The return per season for tractor drivers is between Rp. 1.25 and Rp. 3 million (see also from the tractor owner's point of view in the previous section), while for a seeding worker, it is from Rp. 1.5 to 2.1 million. A single seeding worker can cover up to 25 *iring*, 50–100 *iring* for two workers, and more than 100 *iring* for three seeding workers. The share among the workers is distributed equally. Meanwhile, applying fertilisers is around Rp. 800 thousand–Rp. 1.6 million per worker, whereas applying herbicides is only half of that.

30 For weeding, the per worker income for a season is from Rp. 2.1 to 4.2 million, and for planting it is Rp. 1.5–3 million. In a season, a group of two female workers can cover 25 to 50 *iring*, while a group of eight female workers might cover from 100 to 125 *iring*.

31 Since harvesting is a laborious job, some households only provide one labour (husband) when the wife is seen to be 'too old' to perform harvesting.

32 The monthly income for a worker harvesting at the company is between Rp. 2.3 and 2.5 million. Other tasks only offer an income of around Rp. 1.6 million. Male and female workers are paid equally by the company for the same job.

33 It depends on how many *ancak* they have. For PCPs with eight *ancak*, they earn Rp. 2.2–2.6 million per month, while those who own four *ancak* receive half of that. For those who own less than eight *ancak*, they usually also work for a company, making their total income about equal to those who own eight *ancak*.
34 The daily wage for weeding at the company is Rp. 62 thousand compared to individual capitalist farmers earning Rp. 40 thousand.
35 As for the foreman and security guard, their daily wage is about Rp. 66 thousand but their work is much less laborious than that of other workers. They also receive a bonus every harvest.
36 For the same job, female workers receive 25 percent lower wages than male workers.
37 The income is about equal to non-harvesting palm oil tasks.
38 The daily wage for a mason in the village is Rp. 80 to Rp. 90 thousand, while construction workers get Rp. 60 thousand. However, the same positions for development projects funded by the village fund offer lower wages, that of Rp. 55 thousand for masons and supervisors and Rp. 45 thousand for construction workers. The village apparatus argues that this policy is taken to provide more jobs for more workers. The lower wages, nonetheless, remain attractive given they are offered regularly during every off-season.
39 The daily wage for a mason in *Timpang* is Rp. 120 thousand. Their earnings equal harvesters who hold at least 10 *ancak*. Construction workers' wages are about the same as other daily wages.
40 The daily wage is generally Rp. 80 thousand.
41 With the coverage of tractor services being 40 *iring* (2.4 hectares), Kirun's net income is around Rp. 5 million per season.
42 In *Njomplang*, overall there are only less than ten households involve in petty trades (vegetables and fruits, snacks, grocery) and petty home-crafts activity (*Tempe* production). The absence of local marketplace in the village might explain this rarity of non-rice trading. The local marketplace is located in the neighbouring village where agriculture is much less important than in *Njomplang*.
43 While a high school degree is not an absolute requirement to get a job, PCPs and the classes of labour households generally aspire to sending their children to high school to meet the social norm. The parents view education as the best thing that they can give to their children, whereas for the children, remaining at school is to some extent 'a way to postpone 'real' work' (White, 2012b: 94).
44 The fee ranged from Rp. 1.5 to Rp. 3 million. This was equal to about half to a monthly minimum wage stipulated in Jakarta in 2017.
45 Especially if they earn severance payment after they are laid off from a factory.
46 The cost of land rent is between Rp. 1.5 and Rp. 2 million per *iring* per season or Rp. 3 to 4 million per year for one *iring* (0.16 hectares) of paddy field.
47 The income from 'own-account' farming via leasing in land contributes to around a half of their total income.
48 In the 2000s, their wages were about three times higher than the wages in *Timpang*. However, in 2010s, the wages in Malaysia were only half times higher than in *Timpang*. Nowadays, fewer workers from *Timpang* migrate to Malaysia.
49 They prefer to live in houses made only from woven bamboo or simple wood, with a dirt floor in order to buy a small piece of palm oil field. They also eat simple meals, avoiding chicken or even eggs for their side-dishes, let alone meat.
50 A member of the FFP is able to purchase one hectare of land after selling a cow every year for ten years.
51 The average price for a hectare of land in *Timpang* is about Rp. 70–120 million, while the price in Aceh is from Rp. 15 to Rp. 40 million.
52 It absorbs around 60 workers, which is only about a third of the total households involved in agriculture.
53 Rp. 31.7–Rp. 41.9 million compared to Rp. 36.6–Rp. 54.3 million per year.

54 In 2007, the state introduced PKH (conditional cash transfers) to poor households. Cash transfers consist of two types: fixed and component fund. The fixed fund grants Rp. 550 thousand per household per year. The component fund gives cash transfers to each specific member of the household: pregnant mothers (Rp. 2.4 million/year), infants (Rp. 2.4 million/year), elementary school students (Rp. 0.9 million/year), junior school students (Rp. 1.5 million/year), high school student (Rp. 2 million/year), severely disabled (Rp. 2.4 million) and elderly (Rp. 2.4 million/year). Each household may receive component fund grants for a maximum of four members. However, with the state budget limited, it is rare that a household receives the maximum grant.

55 Some households from the classes of labour complain that they receive no assistances. There are also complaints from 'proletariat-farmers' when their neighbours from the PCP with much better housing conditions receive state assistance.

56 BOS (school operational assistance) was introduced in 2005 by the national government to cover the direct annual operational costs of the school. It generally covers the costs for primary and junior school all around the country. For high school, however, the state assistance is very small. In some provinces and districts, high school is free, since their provincial and district government provides an additional subsidy to cover the school fees. Unfortunately, this is not the case for *Njomplang* district.

57 In Purworejo, the fee was about Rp. 200 thousand per month in 2017.

58 To complement the BOS, in 2008, the state introduced BSM (cash transfer to students from poor households). It annually grants a primary school student Rp. 450 thousand, a junior school student Rp. 750 thousand and a high school student Rp. 1 million. Recently, it covered around a third of total students who receive BOS.

59 The fee for one session of practical work can be a few million rupiah. In one calendar academic year, the student might have several mandatory practical works. PKH assistance of Rp. 2 million and BSM grants of Rp. 1 million per year for high school students is barely adequate to cover the practical work's fees alone. In fact, it is rare that a household receives both PKH and BSM at the same time. With a limited budget and to avoid social jealousy, it is often that PKH and BSM are split between different households for the sake of 'equity'.

60 The fee is similar to *Njomplang*, which was around Rp. 200 thousand per month in 2018.

61 One of the heads of the hamlets openly declared that, as the distributor of the grant, he had the right to get the assistance as well.

62 It is very common considering the rampant criminality in the village. See Chapter 4.

References

Ambarwati, A et al 2016, 'Land tenure and agrarian structure in regions of small-scale food production', in J.F McCarthy & K Robinson (eds), *Land and development in Indonesia: Searching for the people's sovereignty*, Singapore, ISEAS-Yusof Ishak Institute.

Bhattacharya, T 2017, *Social reproduction theory: Remapping class, recentering oppression*. London, Pluto Press.

Bernstein, H 2010, *Class dynamics of agrarian change*, Sterling, VA, Kumarian Press.

Breman, J 1982, 'The village on Java and the early-colonial state', *The Journal of Peasant Studies*, vol. 9, no. 4, pp. 189–240.

Fortin, C.J 2011, 'The biofuel boom and Indonesia's oil palm industry: The twin processes of peasant dispossession and adverse incorporation in West Kalimantan', paper presented at the *International Conference on Global Land Grabbing*, University of Sussex, UK 6–8 April.

Habibi, M & Juliawan, B.H 2018, 'Creating surplus labour: Neo-liberal transformations and the development of relative surplus population in Indonesia', *Journal of Contemporary Asia*, vol. 48, no. 4, pp. 649–670.

Hugo, G.J 2000, 'The impact of the crisis on internal population movement in Indonesia', *Bulletin of Indonesian Economic Studies*, vol. 36, no. 2, pp. 115–138.

Hüsken, F 1989, 'Cycles of commercialization and accumulation in a central Javanese village', in G Hart, A Turton & B White (eds), *Agrarian transformations: Local process and the state in Southeast Asia*, Berkeley, CA, University of California Press, 303–331.

Kim, H.J 2002, 'Agrarian and social change in a Javanese village', *Journal of Contemporary Asia*, vol. 32, no. 4, pp. 435–455.

Li, T.M 2014, *Land's end: Capitalist relations on an Indigenous frontier*, Durham, NC, Duke University Press.

Li, T.M 2017, 'Intergenerational displacement in Indonesia's oil palm plantation zone', *The Journal of Peasant Studies*, vol. 44, no. 6, pp. 1158–1176.

McCarthy, J.F 2010, 'Processes of inclusion and adverse incorporation: Oil palm and agrarian change in Sumatra, Indonesia', *The Journal of Peasant Studies*, vol. 37, no. 4, pp. 821–850.

Putri, T.A, Kusnadi, N, Rachmina, D 2013, 'Kinerja Usaha Penggilingan Padi: Studi Kasus Pada Tiga Usaha Penggilingan Padi Di Cianjur, Jawa Barat', *Jurnal Agribisnis Indonesia*, vol. 1, no. 2, pp. 143–154.

Pincus, J 1996, *Class power and agrarian change: Land and labour in rural West Java*, London, MacMillan Press.

Tjandraningsih, I 2013, 'State-sponsored precarious work in Indonesia', *American Behavioral Scientist*, vol. 57, no. 4, pp. 403–419.

Veltmeyer, H & Wise, R.D 2016, *Agrarian change, migration and development*, Halifax, Fernwood Publishing.

White, B 2012a, 'Agriculture and the generation problem: Rural youth, employment and the future of farming', *IDS Bulletin*, vol. 43, pp. 9–19.

White, B 2012b, 'Changing childhoods: Javanese village children in three generations', *Journal of Agrarian Change*, vol. 12, pp. 81–97.

White, B 2020, *Agriculture and the generation problem*, Halifax, Fernwood Publishing.

White, B & Wiradi, G 1989, 'Agrarian and nonagrarian bases of inequality in nine Javanese villages', in G Hart, A Turton & B White (eds), *Agrarian transformations: Local process and the state in Southeast Asia*, Berkeley, CA, University of California Press, 266–302.

Zhang, Q.F 2015, 'Class differentiation in rural China: Dynamics of accumulation, commodification and state intervention', *Journal of Agrarian Change*, vol. 15, no. 3, pp. 338–365.

8 Conclusion

To properly grasp the nature of contemporary capitalist agrarian change in Indonesia, this book challenges the dominant agrarian populist view which mainly focuses on the relation between the assumed homogeneous farmers/smallholders and corporations or the state through an investigation into the internal dynamics of agricultural producers. We have shown the power of class dynamics in the twenty-first century by looking at Sumatra's oil palm production and rice production in Java. Contrary to the agrarian populism image of smallholders as a homogeneous community, it has been shown the nature of class structures and class relations among those smallholders. A few political economy studies in this field predominantly perceive class location from a Weberian gradational class approach and have thus failed to understand class structure as a socially distinct location in the production relationship that emphasises the exploitation of relations between classes. With their emphasis on class structure, the previous studies have also largely downplayed their attention to class relations. Our study avoids this caveat by, in the first place, explaining the class location of the agrarian classes before delineating their class relations. Moreover, it goes beyond descriptive terms commonly used in the literature, such as 'prosperous farmers', 'rich farmers' or 'big farmers', as we also argue that the ruling class in the agricultural production of Sumatra's oil palm is best viewed as capitalist farmers, taking into consideration their ownership and control over land that enables them to hire in other's labour all year-round.

A similar argument has been made for Javanese rice cultivation. With a few exceptions, the understanding of class location in the Javanese rice field tends to share the caveat of the Weberian class analysis above. Our approach to Java is similar to that of Sumatra—i.e. to properly understand class relations, we need to explain the class structure first. As shown in Chapter 5, Javanese rice farmers in *Njomplang* have been structurally differentiated into different agrarian classes that expose the exploitation relations between them. Different from the descriptive term of 'large farmers' or 'commercial farmers' commonly held by both scholars and activists, we depict the nature of those exploiting classes of labour as capitalist farmers and 'landlord-capitalists'. From our theoretical standpoint, they are not simply the 'elite classes' as Pincus suggests. Neither do they represent the 'hesitant capitalists' championed by Hüsken, who,

DOI: 10.4324/9781003267348-8

previously, favoured calling them 'landlords'. Our account of class dynamics in contemporary rural Java adds to the burgeoning, and yet outdated, agrarian change literature in the twentieth century that significantly contradicts the agrarian populism image of Javanese farmers highlighted by the contemporary literature of agrarian conflict.

Class structure, both in Javanese rice cultivation and Sumatra's oil palm production, reveals how a handful of capitalist farmers (and 'landlord-capitalists' in Java) are in charge of commanding, all year round, labour from the classes of labour, which includes 'semi-proletariat farmers', 'proletariat-farmers' and the 'fully-fledged proletariat' (FFP). Apart from the two classic classes, we also see some farmers or smallholders who possess considerable means of production that enables them not to hire in other's labour all year-round, while they are also not forced by *market compulsion* to hire out their own labour throughout the year. The number of these PCPs is much smaller than that of the classes labour in the village, although it is slightly greater than the number of capitalist farmers.

What makes the two villages quite different from each other is the nature of their agrarian class structure. Our comparative study illuminates how land ownership/control needs to be combined with the position in the labour relation to locate class structure, as others have suggested. To be more precise, land size is not sufficient to locate class location, it is crucial also to look at crop value. With a much higher crop value per hectare in rice cultivation in Java than in Sumatra's oil palm, to be capitalist farmers in Java requires much less land ownership/control as a cut-off point for when a landowner hires in other's labour all year round, compared to their compatriots in Sumatra.

The class composition in Javanese rice production has experienced some changes in the last three decades. The class composition of the residents shows the growing number of PCPs which, to some extent, stalls further class polarisation. This change owes much to the changing labour market and class relations in the village discussed in Chapter 5. In *Timpang*, we have no firm conclusion on the changing class composition in the last few decades. However, class differentiation has clearly taken place, along with the expansion of oil palm described in Chapters 4 and 5. Class differentiation went hand-in-hand with the dispossession by displacement of smallholders/non-corporate producers by both the state and private companies. Under these circumstances, *Timpang* has experienced the twin processes of class differentiation and dispossession by displacement known from the literature. Because of the new frontier nature of *Timpang*, the process of dispossession in the 1980s signals primitive accumulation by which the creation of capitalist relations begins (Chapter 4). However, it does not necessarily imply that the recent neoliberal capitalist expansion signals primitive accumulation throughout Indonesia's countryside. *Njomplang*, on the other hand, has no experience of dispossession by displacement, since rice cultivation barely involves corporate-agricultural producers, and its primitive accumulation took place much earlier, in the early nineteenth century.

What has been largely missing from the literature on agrarian class structure is attention to the internal dynamics within the agrarian ruling class. There has been a tendency to treat them as a non-varied group, and this prevents us from identifying different groups within this privileged class, often glued together by family ties, and how this has an impact on class relations. Our comparative study has identified several types of capitalist farmers in Sumatra's oil palm and Javanese rice cultivation: 'typical capitalist farmers', 'politico-bureaucrat capitalist farmers' and 'professional-capitalist farmers'. In Java, apart from capitalist farmers, another member of the agrarian ruling class is 'landlord-capitalists'. The differences between them concern their involvement in the production process and pattern of accumulation. Their impact on class relations cannot be overlooked. From *Njomplang*, we see that the 'politico-bureaucrat capitalist farmers' who have a political position in the village and wish to stay in office, tend to be more compromising and less antagonistic in defending their class interests *vis-à-vis* the classes of labour, whereas 'typical capitalist farmers' and 'landlord-capitalists', who have much fewer social burdens, are more straightforward against labour.

Class relations in the Javanese rice village show that in this specific setting, a 'village meeting' (*rembug desa*), mediates the relations between the agrarian ruling class (*Juragan*) and the classes of labour in negotiating wages and working conditions. The meeting provides the space for collective bargaining between capitalist farmers plus 'landlord-capitalists' and the classes of labour that, potentially, could lead to overt class struggle. However, the patron-client arrangement prevents this from coming to fruition. The 'landlord-capitalists' have effectively established a paternalistic relationship with the PCPs and a segment of the classes of labour ('semi-proletariat farmers') through a sharecropping arrangement. As Scott points out, without a changing balance of power between the landowners and labourers, the paternalistic relationship only evolves along with the advance of commodification. On the other hand, other segments of the classes of labour (the 'proletariat-farmers' and FFP) have neither got the experiences nor organisational capacities to collectively organise themselves against the capitalist farmers and 'landlord-capitalists'. This means their fight against their *Juragan* takes the form of 'everyday resistances' or 'subtle resistances'. The everyday resistance, like 'slowing down the work', pilfering and complaining are also the dominant forms of class relations in *Timpang*. Here, they have no 'village meeting' as *Njomplang* has, and, thus, there is no institutional space for collective bargaining power to take place between capital and labour. Furthermore, the variation of class structures and the labour market within the village, between the central hamlets and the peripheral hamlets, weakens the overall bargaining power of the classes of labour against the capitalist farmers.

A problematic aspect of the everyday resistance literature is that it hardly provides a historical account of such resistance. Scott mainly explains the widespread use of everyday resistances as a result of the life-threatening risk of open class struggle and the lack of an organisational capacity to organise a collective struggle. There is no more exploration of why this is the case. Referring to *Njomplang*, we show that historically, there were well-organised classes of labour under the banners of the BTI and PKI, which performed overt class struggle in the countryside. Following the bloody massacre of the leftist powers in the country and their mass prosecution without trial in the mid-1960s, the current generation of classes of labour in the village has virtually no imagination concerning how to organise themselves collectively. This makes them waste their chance of launching an overt class struggle, which exists given the institutionalised collective bargaining power available to them (the 'village meeting'). This is, to a lesser degree, also the case in *Timpang*, where a strong organisation of classes of labour in the plantations, the SARBUPRI under the PKI's influence, was annihilated in the same period. The defective current model of farmers groups (POKTAN) in both villages only exacerbates the apathy among the classes of labour for joining a collective organisation. This New Order regime's legacy of state-sponsored farmers groups, dominated by capitalist farmers, is the complete opposite of those of the BTI and SARBUPRI. A different trajectory of recent class relations in *Njomplang* and *Timpang* could have occurred if progressive working organisations such as in the past were present in the contemporary villages.

Class dynamics, both in Sumatra's oil palm areas and the Javanese rice villages, have subsequently shaped the dynamics of production relations. We have seen that the popularity of sharecropping in current *Njomplang* owes much to the class structure and class relations in the village. The persistence of sharecropping, despite the expansion of capitalist social relations, owes much to what Pearce points to as the low incidence of class dominance and the under-mechanisation of the labour process. However, Pearce hardly explains why the labour process was under-mechanised. In *Njomplang*, this owes much to the resistance and the technical problems associated with mechanisation. Pearce also plays down the political consideration of capitalist farmers who are in favour of sharecropping more than cultivating with wage labour. Our study suggests that as long as village officials' positions keep providing lucrative incomes for capitalist farmers, instead of merely securing labour, sharecropping may be used as a means of providing political support, especially for the 'politico-bureaucrat capitalist farmers'. *Njomplang* is also instructive in illuminating how class dynamics shape the changing share received by landowners and sharecroppers overtime, where the share of the sharecroppers has been on the rise over recent decades. The popularity of sharecropping as a dominant form of land arrangement in rural Java, however, is not found in Sumatra. In *Timpang*, the most popular land tenure is ownership of land, either using hired labour or own family labour. The much less intensive nature of oil palm production provides no need for landowners to secure labour all year round through sharecropping.

Class dynamics have also shaped the changing pattern of labour arrangements. The transition to contract by task as the most dominant form of labour arrangement in both contemporary Javanese rice cultivation and Sumatra's oil palm is the result of the class power dynamics in the two villages. In *Njomplang*, our findings substantiate Pincus's argument in his rural West Java context. While Pincus's account mainly provides anecdotal evidence of the process and mechanism involved in this transformation of the labour system, our treatment presents a systematic account of the process and mechanisms of the changing labour relations in all agricultural tasks over the last few decades. As far as *Timpang* is concerned, our treatment of the dynamics of labour relations contributes to the burgeoning literature on agrarian change in Sumatra's oil palm industry, which, so far, has paid little attention to the production relations. Without an understanding of this aspect of production, particularly the labour arrangements, we may fail to fully grasp the nature of class dynamics and the reproduction of agrarian classes in rural Sumatra.

The power of class dynamics has also been crucial in relation to the development of production techniques. The stalling of the mechanisation of Javanese rice cultivation since the end of the Green Revolution is well known. Only since the mid-2010s has the attempt to advance mechanisation through the introduction of combine harvester machines and planting machines been initiated by the state. However, its application is varied across regions given both the limited resources of the state and the class relations. In *Njomplang*, the effort is largely a non-state initiative by capitalist farmers. Their initiative meets the threat from the labouring classes, who receive their highest agricultural wage from harvesting. Their resistance might resonate with similar types of resistance against mechanisation discussed in the literature (Scott, 1985). However, the arrested mechanisation also owes much to the technical problems (Byres, 1996) facing both combine harvesters and planting machines. When these obstacles have been resolved, it is likely that the situation will favour capitalist farmers to advance mechanisation at the expense of the classes of labour. Meanwhile, significant attempts to mechanise oil palm production have been virtually absent. However, class dynamics can also be seen in the inception of a new method of weeding. In *Timpang*, to avoid being played by the workers under the daily wage arrangement of manual weeding, capitalist farmers have introduced lawnmowers contracted by task to lower risk.

Credit provision is another key aspect of production that has been shaped by class dynamics. The literature shows that capitalist farmers tend to have easier access to formal credit, which is cheaper than informal credit and bears lower costs of production (Pincus, 1996). Our findings from *Njomplang* confirm Pincus's case in West Java but for a different reason. The agrarian classes other than the capitalist farmers (PCPs, 'semi-proletariat farmers' and 'proletariat-farmers') actually manage to access subsidised-formal credit from the state (KUR-BRI). However, they keep buying their agricultural inputs through informal credit from local shop owners, because they would rather harness their formal credit for higher 'own-account' farming income activity (rent-in *sawah*) and for urgent non-agricultural needs. Pincus's account, however, is not supported by the practices in Sumatra's oil palm. In *Timpang*, it is true that, with the exception of capitalist farmers, other agrarian classes mainly access informal credit to obtain their agricultural inputs. Yet, this informal credit provided by local oil palm's traders is free of interest, making it even cheaper than formal credit. Similar to *Njomplang*, the PCPs and classes of labour in *Timpang* mostly make use of their formal credit received from the state (KUR-BRI) for non-agricultural purposes. In both *Njomplang* and *Timpang*, we also find that the formal credit is not always cheaper than the informal, as the literature suggests. Formal credit may charge a higher interest rate (corporation-based cooperative credit, both 'Bank Plecit' in Java and 'Batak Kredit' in Sumatra) than the informal community-based credit cooperative. It prompts the view that the nature of micro-finance depends largely on the state intervention and the initiative from below. Formal credit can be cheap as long as the state delivers adequate subsidy, and informal credit can also be generous if it is organised collectively from popular initiatives.

The dynamics of land arrangements, the labour system, technological development and credit provision that have been shaped by class dynamics decide the level of land productivity. In *Njomplang*'s rice village, we find neither the 'economies of scale' often mentioned by mainstream economists nor the 'inverse relationship' favoured by neo-populist supporters. Our case from Central Java resembles Pincus's village in West Java, where there is no significant difference in land productivity across different agrarian classes. *Njomplang*'s land productivity is higher than the national and international standards. However, it is lower than the major rice producers of Vietnam, China, Japan and South Korea. Moreover, land productivity in the village has been arrested in the last few decades, which mirrors the national trend. Contrary to the mainstream economists who explain the halt of land productivity as mainly a result of the lack of proper technology and policy, based on *Njomplang*, we argue that social relations in the form of sharecropping—formed by a specific class structure and class relations—play a major role in stalling the further increase in land productivity. On the other side of the coin, we also need to look at the environmental limits of the land under the expansion of capitalist agriculture. *Njomplang* may have reached the point of 'metabolic rift', since the application of higher amounts of fertilisers in the last few decades has only delivered the same level of rice output. This provides a barrier to further agricultural accumulation. The stalled improvement of land productivity has also been the case in *Timpang*'s oil palm village. Unlike *Njomplang*, however, *Timpang* witnesses a strong, direct relationship between farming size and land productivity, where the capitalist farmers (the largest cultivators) achieve much higher land productivity than the non-capitalist farmers. However, these 'economies of scale' may not simply relate to the given function of efficiency but largely correspond to the dynamics of wider social relations. PCPs and 'semi-proletariat farmers' in *Timpang* obtain lower levels of land productivity, because they only take care of their oil palm fields half-heartedly, with some farmers even abandoning their land. Having disposed of their labour all year-round, they have only a little spare time to take care of their own fields. This half-hearted care or abandonment can only take place because oil palm is not the daily food they consume. This would be inconceivable in *Njomplang*, where rice is the food crop for daily consumption, and half-hearted care or complete neglect of the fields would endanger their own consumption needs.

A decisive class division can be seen clearer from the 'own-account' farming income. The capitalist farmers earn the highest incomes from their farming since they cultivate more land than the other agrarian classes. However, the capitalist farmers in *Timpang* generate even higher farming incomes simply because they obtain a higher level of land productivity than the other classes. The capitalist farmers in this village earn a farming income three times that of the PCPs and about ten times that of the 'semi-proletariat farmers'. A lower gap is the norm in *Njomplang*. The 'own-account' farming income for capitalist farmers is three times more than that of PCPs while seven times greater than that of the 'semi-proletariat farmers' and almost ten times that of the 'proletariat-farmers'. In absolute terms, the capitalist farmers in oil palm receive higher average farming income than their compatriots, the rice capitalist farmers, although, per hectare, rice is more profitable than oil palm. Nonetheless, when the average oil palm price goes down to a half—due to global volatility, as was the case at the end of 2018—the farming income of oil palm capitalist farmers and rice capitalist farmers is similar. With minimum state intervention, the capitalist farmers in oil palm production are much more vulnerable than the rice capitalist farmers. Meanwhile, the 'own-account' farming income obtained by the PCPs, both in *Njomplang* (excluding *bawon*) and *Timpang*, is sufficient to enable them to meet their subsistence. The income from 'own-account' farming for PCPs in both villages is almost twice the stipulated district minimum wage (it is 80 percent and 90 percent higher than the minimum wage in the districts of *Njomplang* and *Timpang* respectively). Among the bottom echelon, the 'semi-proletariat farmers' in *Timpang* are facing a worse situation than their colleagues in *Njomplang*. The 'own-account' farming income of the 'semi-proletariat farmers' in rice cultivation (excluding *bawon*) amounts to almost equal to the district minimum wage, while for their comrades in oil palm in *Timpang*, the earnings only contribute about two-thirds of Langkat's minimum wage.

The incomes from 'own-account' farming above are closely related to the wages levels, especially for those who depend on others' labour in their cultivation. The neo-classical perspective often sees wages and profit as simply a function of the supply and demand for labour. This has been rejected by Pincus, particularly with regard to Hayami and Kikuchi's findings in rural West Java. Our study substantiates Pincus's argument that class power plays a major role in determining wages and profits (income from 'own-account' farming). We have highlighted the process and mechanism of negotiation between the capitalist farmers and classes of labour in both Sumatra's oil palm village and Javanese rice cultivation. While in *Timpang*, class relations signal a rather scattered individual negotiation between the capitalist farmer and the members of the classes of labour, in *Njomplang*, we witness a systematic exercise of collective bargaining power between the capitalist farmers plus 'landlord-capitalists' and the classes of labour mediated by the 'village meeting'. It has also been shown that the dynamic of the level of wages is the result of this class relationship, which is inextricably linked to gender. In both villages, female workers receive lower wages than the males for the same agricultural tasks they perform. This only mirrors what has been reported elsewhere in the literature. The higher gender pay gap is found in *Timpang*. Given the nature of the intensive labour process of rice cultivation, which requires female workers for certain prominent agricultural tasks such as planting and weeding, the female agricultural workers in *Njomplang* tend to have greater bargaining power than their fellow female workers in *Timpang*, although both of them continue to experience the 'double burden' of taking care of unpaid domestic tasks and being active workers.

The changing level of wages shapes the share received by capitalists from total 'own-account' farming income. *Njomplang* illustrates how, in the last two decades, the share of total farming income to labour has increased markedly when the real wage has doubled over the previous decade. This implies that the share of total income from 'own-account' farming for capital fell by 15 percent over the two periods concerned (see Chapter 6). The same procedure to estimate the changing share of capital and labour cannot be applied to *Timpang*, because of the unavailability of the wage data in the previous decade. *Njomplang*'s case is similar to Pincus's findings in rural West Java, particularly in his South Subang village. Pincus points to the class structure in the village as being responsible for this, where 'middle farmers' are more present (than in North Subang) to challenge the capitalist farmers. Class composition in our Central Java village of *Njomplang* might be similar to South Subang. However, while Pincus's explanation relies heavily on a static picture of class structure and anecdotal class relations, our account offers a more comprehensive treatment of class relations by explaining the struggle between capital and labour through the 'village meeting'. Given a lower share in the last two decades, the arrested improvement of land productivity and the soil degradation, the capitalist farmers in *Njomplang* are now compelled to advance the mechanisation if they wish to restore their share levels. Nonetheless, because of both the acute technical problems and the resistance from the classes of labour, the future of mechanisation is bleak, especially given the limitation of the state resources to overcome the technical shortcomings. This has created unfavourable conditions for the capitalist farmers to invest solely in rice production. A similar situation is faced by the capitalist farmers in *Timpang*. While we have no information on whether their share against labour has increased or declined over the last two decades, it is clear that they are constantly vulnerable to the global market volatility when state intervention has offered little to protect them. Moreover, they face rather stalled land productivity. These two threats effectively prevent them from relying on palm production as their only accumulation strategy.

These dynamics of agricultural production have undoubtedly had a prominent impact on the way in which the agrarian classes reproduce themselves.

For the capitalist farmers in both Sumatra's oil palm and Javanese rice cultivation, they make use of their agricultural surplus to accumulate further. However, given the threats and problems of agricultural production that they face, the capitalist farmers in both *Timpang* and *Njomplang* have invested their agricultural surplus in non-agricultural activities as much as 'own-account' farming. This illuminates the trend mentioned in both the Javanese literature and that of the outer islands. However, the literature tends to over-generalise the accumulation nature of capitalist farmers. Our study reveals that there is a crucial difference between 'modest' capitalist farmers and 'big' capitalist farmers. The former earns lower farming income than the latter. This means that the dependency on 'own-account' farming tends to be higher for the 'big' capitalist farmers than the 'modest' capitalist farmers. The literature has also largely failed to explain why some capitalist farmers keep investing their surpluses into 'own-account' farming activities considering the unfavourable conditions that prevail. Based on *Njomplang* and *Timpang*, we are informed that this closely relates to the competition among the agrarian ruling class in the village. When favourable non-agricultural ventures (trade, village offices, services) have been dominated by certain capitalist farmers or 'landlord-capitalists' in the village, other latecomer capitalist farmers and 'landlord-capitalists' have little option but to accumulate inside agricultural production. Competition among the agrarian ruling class is also closely linked to family ties in the village. Without identifying the pattern of the family ties and the competition within the agrarian ruling class, we might not be able to adequately understand their non-agricultural activities.

The significant nature of non-agricultural accumulation in the two villages prevents the expansion of a fully-fledged 'accumulation from below', as discussed in the literature. This owes much to the nature of state intervention. While in Javanese rice cultivation, the 'necessary but limited support' (Chapter 3) only provides inadequate means for the capitalist farmers to advance their 'own-account' farming accumulation; in Sumatra's oil palm, it is the minimal protection from the state that exposes the vulnerability of the farmers to global market volatility and, to some lesser degree, to the threat from the expansion of corporate-scale producers. The prominent level of non-agricultural accumulation in both rural Java and Sumatra means there has been less pressure on land acquisition and, thus, proletarianisation. Especially in Java, the subsequent impact is that agrarian class polarisation is unlikely to sharpen, as the literature has often suggested. *Timpang* might also share a similar tendency, although, as a new frontier, 'own-account' farming activity in land-buying and selling is more prevalent than the old frontier of *Njomplang*.

As for PCPs in both Sumatra's oil palm production and Javanese rice cultivation, they harness their considerable income from 'own-account' farming to meet subsistence and pursue beyond subsistence aspirations. To some extent, this is possible given the continuing state subsidy for agricultural inputs and credits, which are also enjoyed by other agrarian classes. The reproduction of some PCPs delineates the pattern of 'simple reproduction', as discussed in the literature. What is interesting about *Njomplang* and *Timpang* is that, despite their basic needs having been met through the income from 'own-account' farming, the PCPs keep selling their labour all year round. They are doing it to achieve beyond their 'simple reproduction' aspirations, such as becoming capitalist farmers, sending their children to college or purchasing consumption consumer goods at the expense of their 'autonomy from the labour market'. This negates the view of the neo-populist supporters who often regard the desire of PCPs to work harder is simply because of the demographic shift in their households. We suggest that the PCPs' willingness to sell their labour to buy more land is rather a response to the wider accumulation dynamics in the countryside and beyond. They are keen to follow their materially-successful neighbours: the capitalist farmers. From their different activities in the labour relation, we see that some PCPs have managed to transform themselves into capitalist farmers while others have been transformed into members of the classes of labour. This shows that the PCPs' capacity to retain their class position simply represents 'contingent resilience', instead of the inherent one (Zhang, 2015), although the defensive nuance of the term 'resilience' might not do justice to the PCPs who have successfully transformed themselves into capitalist farmers.

The aspiration to be capitalist farmers is simply inconceivable for the classes of labour. With their meagre income from 'own-account' farming, both 'semi-proletariat farmers' and 'proletariat-farmers' have to struggle to meet their daily needs. This is even more so for the FFP, who produce no agricultural output. Their reproduction pattern does indeed reflect their 'subsistence squeeze'. They must sell their labour throughout the year, both in agriculture and non-agriculture jobs, out of market compulsion. For the classes of labour, the market reveals more of its compulsion than its opportunity. The state's bias towards capitalist farmers by promoting anti-land reform effectively prevents the classes of labour from acquiring more land for cultivation and higher income from 'own-account' farming. Moreover, the state's push on technological advancement that threatens manual labour, particularly in rice cultivation, endangers the agricultural jobs available, i.e. those which have been a prominent contributor to the classes of labour's total income. While social policy, such as rice for the poor, is helpful to some of the classes of labour, some of them have received nothing, either because of the limited state resources or the corruption in the village office. More importantly, this social assistance only mirrors what has been called the 'management of poverty' instead of getting rid of poverty. Given these unfavourable conditions, the literature has indicated that the classes of labour will eventually diversify their rural income generation through 'non-political strategies', such as 'self-employment' or migration. What has been missing from the discussion, however, is the origin of such 'non-political strategies of reproduction'. From both *Njomplang* and *Timpang*, this strategy of reproduction in the village has only been possible since the annihilation of the leftist power in the mid-1960s and the rural de-politicisation that followed it. With such destruction, the recent generations of the classes of labour in both villages have no imagination of what their 'political strategies of reproduction' might be.

Class reproduction is inextricably linked to generational reproduction. This has received less attention in the literature on class reproduction. On the other hand, the literature on generational issues tends to detach its discussion from class reproduction. Our study illuminates how different types of capitalist farmers and 'landlord-capitalists', both in Sumatra's oil palm and Javanese rice production, espouse different forms of generational reproduction, which have a prominent impact on the future of farming. For instance, 'typical capitalist farmers', especially those who manage to send all their children to college, may have great difficulty in finding a successor. Although one of their children may reside in the village, others, with their higher educational background would not be the 'typical capitalist farmer' their parents were but would rely instead on a sharecropping arrangement to cultivate the inherited land. This would make them 'landlord-capitalists' who have little interest in farming.

Class and generational reproduction are also intertwined with gender and clanship. In Batak oil palm production, where land is exclusively inherited by the sons, the chance of the daughter becoming the successor of her parents' capitalist farmer status is extremely small. However, they are fortunate enough since they generally manage to enjoy higher education at university. The chances for women here are higher than in the Javanese village of *Njomplang*, where the customs pertaining to land inheritance are quite different. The close relationship between generational ties, gender and clanship can also be seen in the class reproduction of PCPs. The PCPs who are able to finance college education for their children have a bigger problem trying to find their successor as a PCP. In gender terms, the daughters of PCPs in the Batak village are less likely to inherit the land than those women from the Javanese village; yet the women's aspirations in both villages to access a university education are less than those of the women from the capitalist farmer's families. A similar pattern is seen in the reproduction of the classes of labour. The classes of labour are not able to send their children to college, since they depend on state assistance just to pay for their children to attend high school. Given the failure to send their children to university, the challenge of facing land fragmentation is greater. For 'semi-proletariat farmers', success in avoiding land fragmentation depends on complex interrelated situations: the demographic composition of the household, the economic situation of the siblings, gender and clanship. This complex generational and class issue also applies to 'proletariat-farmers'. A successor for a 'proletariat-farmer' is easier to find in *Njomplang* where sharecropping is widespread. However, if sharecropping or fixed-rent is perceived to be less profitable than wage jobs, the successor may prefer to abandon their land cultivation rights and rely exclusively on wage jobs as a member of the FFP.

We have seen throughout our comparative study that class dynamics have prominently shaped production relations and class reproduction. Our study substantiates Bernstein's insistence on the need for an understanding of class dynamics from the two dimensions of class: class structure (economic sociology) and class relations (political sociology). Such a class approach taken in our comparative study has proven to be useful in illuminating the class dynamics which have eventually shaped the pattern of production relations and class reproduction. Nonetheless, our study does not simply apply the existing framework of class to understand Indonesia's agrarian changes, particularly in our specific setting of Javanese rice cultivation and Sumatra's oil palm production. Drawing on those existing approaches, we have rather developed our own analytical framework based on our particular settings. From our comparative study, we have shown that a nuanced account of the class analysis is required to illuminate the complexity of class location of the capitalist farmers plus 'landlord-capitalist', PCPs and classes of labour, and their impacts on class relations. The complexity of class dynamics matters both to agricultural production and the pattern of class reproduction.

Agrarian change literature has barely embarked on a systematic investigation of the complexity of class location of capitalist farmers plus 'landlord-capitalists' and its impact on class relations. There is little doubt that the literature has thrown some light on this issue. However, some studies have merely identified the different strategies of the capitalist farmers' accumulation and said little about the impact on class relations, while others have explained the class relations involving capitalist farmers without carefully identifying the factions which exist within them. Our comparative study has systematically identified different groups within the capitalist farmers and the impact of this on class relations. We have delineated that there are at least three different types of capitalist farmers ('typical-capitalist farmers', 'politico-bureaucrat capitalist farmers' and 'professional-capitalist farmers') based on their involvement in the production process and the nature of their accumulation. This internal difference within the capitalist farmers matters to class relations. It has been shown that certain groups of capitalist farmers ('typical-capitalist farmers') along with 'landlord-capitalists' tend to be more antagonistic towards the classes of labour, while other capitalist farmers ('politico-bureaucrat capitalist farmers' and 'professional-capitalist farmers') are less so. The differences between the capitalist farmers also crucially shape the agricultural production. We have also illustrated that a certain group of capitalist farmers ('typical-capitalist farmers') tends to generate higher land productivity and agricultural surpluses than other types of capitalist farmers, given their main focus on farming. As far as class reproduction is concerned, our study has also depicted different patterns of class reproduction, which is closely linked to generational reproduction, across different types of capitalist farmers and 'landlord-capitalists'.

The literature has paid even less attention to the complexity of the PCPs and its impact on class relations. It is often assumed in the literature that farmers who sell their labour all year round are automatically part of the labouring class. Our study of PCPs, however, shows that it is not always the case. It has been shown that while the income from 'own-account' farming of the PCPs alone enables them to pursue simple reproduction, they maintain disposal of their labour throughout the year to pursue their aspirations beyond subsistence. We have called them 'aspiring PCPs' given their choice to harness market opportunities (Chapter 5). This indicates that they are different from 'disguised wage labour' and thus they are not necessarily part of the classes of labour. We have also identified a smaller group of 'classical PCPs' who meet their 'simple reproduction' needs through the income from 'own-account' farming but choose not to sell their labour all year round. One needs to take into account whether farmers' activity of selling labour is a form of harnessing market opportunities or the result of market compulsion by investigating their 'own-account' farming incomes and whether these can meet their subsistence.

This matters if we wish to adequately explain the process of class differentiation of the PCPs. The literature often perceives that how PCPs can be transformed into capitalist farmers or members of the classes of labour relates largely to their market competitiveness in their farming (Bernstein, 2010). Yet, our comparative study reveals that wage labour activities play a prominent role in PCP reproduction. Selling labour as the main activity of PCPs outside 'own-account' farming is crucial for their aspirations to be capitalist farmers. For the 'aspiring PCPs', their slogan seems to be 'only by selling more of our labour power, can we become closer to be capitalist farmers'.

The position of the PCPs in class relations has received much less attention than it deserves. Our comparative study adds to this rather thin literature by carefully identifying the different groups within the PCPs. The 'classical PCPs' tend to be indifferent to the class relations between capital and labour given their independence from the labour market. However, their number is much smaller than the 'aspiring PCPs' who share the interest with labour since they sell their labour all year round. Nonetheless, their class position towards capitalist is also shaped by labour relations. We have mentioned that the 'formal PCPs' (predominantly in Javanese rice cultivation) are in a sharecropping relationship with the landowners ('landlord-capitalists'), which exposes them to a dependency relationship with their landowners. This situation makes the PCPs tend to align themselves with the agrarian ruling class. In contrast, the 'substantial PCPs' (largely in Sumatra oil palm production) have no such paternalistic relationship, and it is easier for them to align themselves with the classes of labour in the village in demanding higher wages and better working conditions. Our study highlights how class relations in a particular setting involve the struggle between capital and labour, which only re-emphasises what has been discussed by Marx in the classical critical political economy tradition. The PCPs' class position, whether they align themselves with capital or labour, depends on the specific context. What is clear is that they only seek the alliance that suits their material interests in a given situation.

In the literature, a more nuanced account of class location has been devoted to the rural working class. Bernstein coined the concept of the 'classes of labour' to highlight the fragmented nature of the contemporary labouring class in the peripheral world. This has been applied and developed in several ways by others. Despite their different emphases, they seem to refuse to accept the stereotypical view of the working class as merely those who have nothing but the power of their labour. Instead, those who retain a meagre means of production, such as land (marginal farmers), yet must sell off their labour all the year round to meet their subsistence needs, should be included as members of the classes of labour, mainly because their reproduction is dependent on their received wages. However, this literature has neither offered a systematic account of the complexity of classes of labour nor the impact of such complexity on class relations. Others have paid attention to the competition among the classes of labour and its impact on class relations and yet it has given little systematic treatment to their class location.

Our comparative study has carefully identified different members of the classes of labour. We highlight how a marginal farmer (in our account, this is the 'semi-proletariat farmers' and 'proletariat farmers') is different from a PCP in the sense that, while the income from 'own-account' farming of the PCPs alone enables them to pursue 'simple reproduction' without selling off their labour, the 'own-account' farming income of the 'semi-proletariat farmers' and 'proletariat farmers' has no such capacity. Although both the 'semi-proletariat farmers' and 'proletariat farmers' are compelled to sell their labour out of market compulsion, they share different natures of class location. Given their land ownership and/or a larger land control, 'semi-proletariat farmers' have 'something to lose', whereas 'proletariat farmers' tend to have 'nothing to lose'. 'Proletariat-farmers' share similar features with the FFPs who neither own nor control any land. However, when it comes to class relations, the response of the different members of the classes of labour is not only shaped by their class location but also by the nature of their labour relations. With their position of having 'something to lose', the option for the 'semi-proletariat farmers' to work against capitalist farmers and 'landlord-capitalists' is ambiguous at best. Hence, when the paternalistic relationship exists under sharecropping arrangement (such as in the Javanese rice cultivation), 'semi-proletariat farmers' are more inclined to support their 'landlord-capitalists'. When such a paternalistic relationship is absent (as in Sumatra's oil palm production), it is easier for them to align themselves with other members of the classes of labour (the 'proletariat farmers' and the FFPs) to bargain against capitalist farmers. Our comparative study suggests that the 'proletariat farmers' and FFPs are the only members of the classes of labour who can take a clear-cut oppositional position towards the agrarian ruling class (capitalist farmers and 'landlord-capitalists'). For 'semi-proletariat farmers', their relationship with the capitalist farmers depends on the dominant labour relation. This urges us to devote our attention again to production relations, particularly land tenure and labour arrangements in a particular setting, if we wish to properly explain the nature of agrarian class relations.

Our account of class implies the need to look more seriously at the 'own-account' farming and non-agricultural activities and the earnings generated from both to fully grasp the nature not only of agrarian class reproduction but also the very nature of class structure itself. The literature on part-time farming and pluriactivity has devoted great attention to this issue. However, since their main concern is largely to understand the livelihood aspect of farming and non-farming activities in rural areas, they barely bring their insight to bear on the theoretical discussion on class, production and class reproduction. Our comparative study has thrown some light on this subject when we conceptualise the complexity of the class location of agrarian classes from their 'own-account' farming and non-agricultural activities, and their impact on agricultural production and class reproduction.

The power of class dynamics in Indonesia's agrarian change complicates the agrarian populist movements that have been on the main stage of the current agrarian struggle. We have demonstrated that farmers/smallholders are not a homogeneous community and reveal the class exploitation relations among farmers/smallholders both in Java and Sumatra. The agrarian populist campaign to unite the farmers/smallholders under one banner against the corporation or the state is thus rather problematic than illuminating. Different agrarian classes (capitalist farmers, PCPs, classes of labour) possess different capacities and respond to the corporation or state. Rice capitalist farmers (with 'landlord-capitalists') receive the largest subsidies from the state, and the state protects them from any agrarian reform initiative at the expense of PCPs and 'semi-proletariat farmers' and proletariat farmers'. Oil palm capitalist farmers may be endangered by corporations. However, they have a more powerful negotiation capacity to get proper compensation from corporation expansion than the PCPs and 'semi-proletariat farmers'. Sometimes, using their political power in the village office, oil palm capitalist farmers even actively facilitate the expansion of corporations at the expense of PCPs and 'semi-proletariat farmers'. This complex class relation needs to be taken into account if any campaign against corporations hopes to succeed. Instead of uniting the farmers/smallholders under a single class against corporations, as agrarian populists propose, it is clear that capitalist farmers cannot be included, since they share different class interests from PCPs and classes of labour. Moreover, hiding class exploitation of capitalist farmers and the PCPs plus classes of labour under the banner of 'people of the land' contradicts the ideal of the emancipation of agrarian populists themselves. Any real emancipation effort in the Indonesian countryside (and beyond) would only be a realistic endeavour if one starts from a proper understanding of agrarian class dynamics and how these different classes each relate to the corporation or state.

Class-based political struggle also challenges the sectoral resistance of the agrarian populists. We have shown that the Indonesian state is not simply anti-farmers/smallholders. This populist understanding has its roots in their sectoral attention to state intervention in export crops, particularly palm oil. However, if one looks at the broader picture, state intervention in agriculture (palm oil and rice) rather signals the anti-workers of the state to facilitate capital accumulation in agriculture and beyond. The state's anti-worker policy in agriculture is manifested in the contra-agrarian reform policy for the sake of accumulation by both capitalist farmers (with 'landlord-capitalists') and corporations. To attack only the state means the omission of the capitalist farmers (with 'landlord-capitalists') from the picture of exploitation relations. Apart from agriculture, the anti-workers of the Indonesian state also take place outside agriculture in the form of cheap (manufacturing) labour to attract foreign capital. To focus solely on demanding a pro-agricultural workers' program of agrarian reform, without taking into account the interest of the non-agricultural workers, would only end up in a lack of support from non-agricultural workers. Any sectoral resistance to dealing with the wider anti-workers' environment, both in agriculture and beyond, will only result in acute failure. Inter-sectoral and class-based political struggle is not without precedent in Indonesia. The country experienced this broad (inter-sectoral) class struggle between workers and capital before the mid-1960s. Only with mass killings was this struggle crushed and expunged from the memory of Indonesian workers. It is only by re-exposing the class dynamics in the countryside and beyond that the disorganised classes of labour across economic sectors may be re-organised to powerfully oppose both capitalist farmers (with 'landlord-capitalists') and corporate capitalists.

Appendixes

Appendix 1

The Village Head and Family Ties in Njomplang, *Central Java*

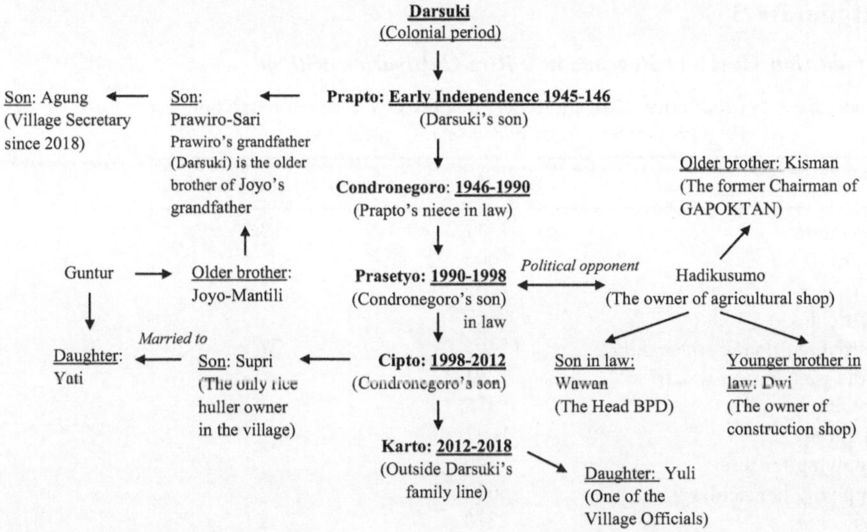

Appendix 2

The Village Head and Family Ties in Timpang, *North Sumatera*

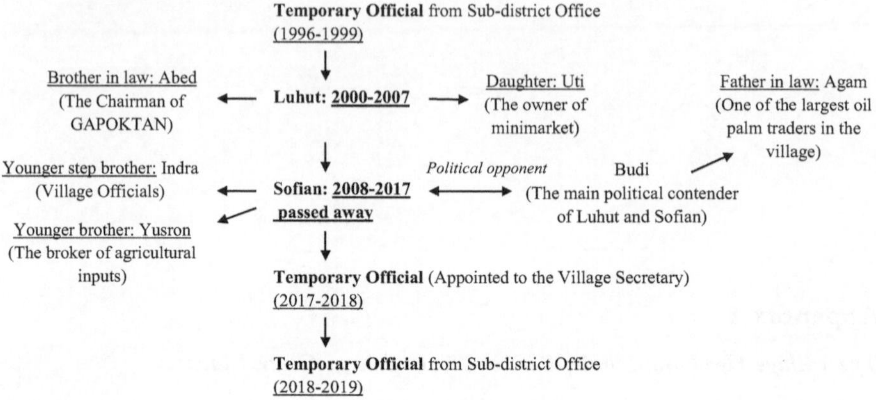

Appendix 3

Production Cost and Revenue in a Rice Cultivation Village

Appendix 3.1 Production Cost and Revenue of Rice Cultivation of Capitalist Farmers per Season in *Njomplang*, Central Java

	(In thousands Rupiah)	*(In percentage)*
Input cost	*3571*	*18.2*
Seeds	1006	
Fertilisers	2235	
Pesticides	329	
Labour cost (tractor service included)	*15401*	*78.7*
Land preparation (tractor)	1291	
Sowing	816	
Planting	1621	
Applying fertilisers	540	
Applying herbicides	632	
Weeding	2270	
Harvesting and threshing	8237	
Other cost	*606*	*3.1*
Land tax	325	
Others	281	
Total production cost	**19578**	**100**
Total revenue	58646	
Net income per season	39068	

Notes

In the survey, we calculate production cost by including what local farmers actually pay for production. In *Njomplang*, land rent cost for PCPs, semi-proletariat farmers and proletariat-farmers is deduced from the yield share under sharecropping that goes to landowner minus input cost born by sharecropper. In both villages, the components under the category of 'others' include transportation costs and consumption costs to provide lunch, snacks or drinks to workers.

Appendix 3.2 Production Cost and Revenue of Rice Cultivation of PCP per Season in *Njomplang*, Central Java

	(In thousands Rupiah)	*(In percentage)*
Input cost	*1374*	*14.8*
Seeds	436	
Fertilisers	822	
Pesticides	117	
Labour cost (tractor service included)	*2131*	*23.0*
Land preparation (tractor)	409	
Sowing	114	
Planting	219	
Applying fertilisers	33	
Applying herbicides	33	
Weeding	92	
Harvesting and threshing	1370	
Land rent cost	*5520*	*59.6*
Other cost	*250*	*2.6*
Land tax	121	
Others	129	
Total production cost	***9275***	***100***
Total revenue	20102	
Net income per season	10827	

Appendix 3.3 Production Cost and Revenue of Rice Cultivation of 'Semi-Proletariat Farmers' per Season in *Njomplang*, Central Java

	(In thousands Rupiah)	*(In percentage)*
Input cost	*733*	*11.6*
Seeds	215	
Fertilisers	432	
Pesticides	86	
Labour cost (tractor service included)	*1355*	*21.5*
Land preparation (tractor)	317	
Sowing	76	
Planting	141	
Applying fertilisers	9	
Applying herbicides	14	
Weeding	90	
Harvesting and threshing	696	
Land rent cost	*4073*	*64.6*
Other cost	*148*	*2.3*
Land tax	72	
Others	76	
Total production cost	***6309***	***100***
Total revenue	11660	
Net income per season	5351	

Appendix 3.4 Production Cost and Revenue of Rice Cultivation of 'Proletariat-Farmers' per Season in *Njomplang*, Central Java

	(In thousands Rupiah)	*(In percentage)*
Input cost	*447*	*8.8*
Seeds	129	
Fertilisers	275	
Pesticides	43	
Labour cost (tractor service included)	*479*	*9.4*
Land preparation	248	
Sowing	20	
Planting	73	
Applying fertilisers	4	
Applying herbicides	7	
Weeding	19	
Harvesting and threshing	108	
Land rent cost	*4065*	*80.1*
Other cost	*84*	*1.7*
Land tax	42	
Others	42	
Total production cost	***5075***	***100***
Total revenue	9181	
Net Profit per season	4106	

Appendix 4

Production Cost and Revenue in an Oil Palm Village

Appendix 4.1 Production Cost and Revenue of Capitalist Farmers per Year in *Timpang*, North Sumatera

	(In thousands Rupiah)	*(In percentage)*
Input cost	*20631*	*37.6*
Seeds	325	
Fertilisers	17303	
Pesticides	3003	
Labour cost	*27542*	*50.2*
Applying fertilisers	1391	
Applying herbicides	843	
Weeding	2881	
Harvesting	19557	
Cutting the midribs	2870	
Other cost	*6683*	*12.2*
Land tax	860	
Others	5823	
Total production cost	*54856*	*100*
Total revenue	240469	
Net income per year	185613	

Appendix 4.2 Production Cost and Revenue of PCP per Year in *Timpang*, North Sumatera

	(In thousands Rupiah)	*(In percentage)*
Input cost	*2853*	*45.6*
Seeds	71	
Fertilisers	2066	
Pesticides	716	
Labour cost	*2692*	*43.0*
Applying fertilisers	37	
Applying herbicides	0	
Weeding	0	
Harvesting	2479	
Cutting the midribs	213	
Other cost	*711*	*11.4*
Land tax	271	
Others	440	
Total production cost	***6256***	***100***
Total revenue	57745	
Net income per year	51489	

Appendix 4.3 Production Cost and Revenue of 'Semi-Proletariat Farmers' per Year in *Timpang*, North Sumatera

	(In thousands Rupiah)	*(In percentage)*
Input cost	*1193*	*74.8*
Seeds	25	
Fertilisers	961	
Pesticides	207	
Labour cost	*245*	*15.4*
Applying fertilisers	1	
Applying herbicides	21	
Weeding	0	
Harvesting	221	
Cutting the midribs	2	
Other cost	*156*	*9.8*
Land tax	88	
Others	68	
Total production cost	***1594***	***100***
Total revenue	19592	
Net income per year	17998	

Appendix 5

Real Wage in Njomplang *2001 and 2017 (in Thousands Rupiah)*

Agricultural tasks	*Real wage 2001*	*Real wage 2017 (basis year)*
Contract by task		
Planting	59.2	110
Seeding	23.7	60
Applying fertilisers	20.8	40
Daily wage (weeding)		
Male	8.9	15
Female	7.4	14

Note: the calculation of the real wage is based on Laspeyres Index. It normally requires the Consumer Price Index (CPI) to weight the change of wage in different periods. However, the data of CPI in the district (Purworejo) is not available. In Indonesia, BPS only surveys 82 districts and cities to calculate CPI every year. Purworejo, nonetheless, is not one among those districts. When a reliable CPI is unavailable, we use the rice price to serve as denominator. Rice as the staple food in the country is still one of the largest contributors to inflation. It is also reported by BPS that during the harvesting season in March, deflation usually follows. This only proves the significant account of rice as a denominator. The data on rice price for both periods is gathered from BULOG's local office.

Land preparation by tractor is excluded from the wage. It is considered as the service provided by tractor's owners.

Index

Note: **Bold** page references indicate tables, *Italic* page references indicate figures.

absentee landlord-capitalists 93, 98–99, 130, 193
accelerated production process 172
accessing formal credit 170
accumulation: in agriculture (*see* agriculture, accumulation in); capitalist farmers and 27–30; description 28; by dispossession, concept of 15; primary actors of 28–29
The Act of Killing 124
affordable staple food 6, 41, 47, 50, 63, 70
agrarian change: in 2000 84; Capitalist Thesis (CT) 21; generalised commodity production, description 22–23; in Indonesia and State (*see* class dynamics); 'labour bondage' 22; literature on 2, 241; non-economic coercion of labour process 23; and reproduction of classes (*see* reproduction of agrarian classes); 'semi-Feudalist Thesis' (SFT), aspects 21–22; un-free labour and capitalism 22
agrarian change under capitalism, class dynamics of 3–9; anti-farmer state 4; based on Marxist political economy 4–5; capitalist farmers and 'landlord-capitalists' 8; in contexts of oil palm and rice 6; dynamics of agricultural producers 6–7; dynamics of classes in Javanese rice cultivation 8; exploitative relations, propertied class within agriculture 4; income from 'own-account' farming 4; labour's platform of agrarian reform 7; land redistribution programs 6; levels of income from production 5; low-wage working population 6; nature of production in rural Indonesia 8; notion of a homogeneous 'peasantry' 8; own-account' farming 5; positions of farmers in the division of labour 4; relation between farmer-employer 5; state and capitalist rice farmers, relationship 4; state intervention in agriculture 7; use of income from production 8
agrarian classes in Indonesia 64–66; agricultural landholders **64**; class composition of rice farmers 65; data of landholding categories 65; declining trend in agricultural profit rate 64; increase in 'near-to-(absolute) landless 64; rice landholders in Indonesia **66**; trajectory of class composition in oil palm 66
agrarian class location 8, 18–21, 34, 117, 137, 138; *see also* class location in villages and composition
agrarian class structure 88, 231, 232
agrarian populism in Indonesia 1–3; class differentiation, impact on agricultural production 3; concept of 'sharing poverty' by Geertz 1–2; impact of oil palm expansion 3; legacy of Suharto's authoritarian regime 1–2; literature on agrarian change 2; partial bias, change in the outer islands 3; social movements against land grabbing 3
agrarian ruling class and family ties 103–106, 140n4; Budi's family-clanship networks 106; close-knit extended families 103; Cokro 104; economic resources and political power 104; Hadikusumo 104; linked with ethnicity 105; Luhut, family-clanship block 105;

marriage among capitalist families 105; Prawiro and Sari in *Njomplang* 103–104; Sofian, family 105–106; *see also* nature of agrarian ruling class
agrarian transition approach 13
agrarian village 77, 85
Agricultural Involution (Geertz) 2
agricultural landholders in Indonesia **64**
agricultural production in Java and Sumatra: credit provision 163–170; income from 'own-account' farming 175–179; labour arrangements 151–163; land tenure 142–151; non-main crops agricultural production 179–181; output and land productivity 173–175; technological development 170–173; *see also specific entries*
agricultural real wages: in estate crops **61**; in food crops **57**; wage income 204
agriculture, accumulation in: 'American path' 28; characteristics of 29; in peripheral countries 29; 'Prussian path 28
agriculture liberalisation 48–49
'*aksi sepihak*' (one-sided action) 122
alcohol and drugs selling 84
aluminium-fibre fruit picker poles 172
anti-colonial nationalism 42
articulation of mode of production 42
Asiatic mode of production 42
aspiring PCPs 107–111, 242

Bachriadi, D. 64
Bardhan, P. 19
Basic Agrarian Law (BAL) 45, 47
basic production technology 207, 212, 214, 218
basic share tenancy law (BSTL) 45
Bernstein, H. 5, 15, 16, 31, 32, 240, 242
Bhaduri, A. 22
'big' capitalist farmers 86, 87, 177, 182, 191, 193, 194, 197, 198, 200, 223, 238
BOS (school operational assistance) 217, 228n56
bos or *toke* (employer) 91
BPDP (Endowment Fund Body for Oil Palm) 62
Brass, T. 22
Breman, J. 149
BRI-KUR scheme 177
BTI (Indonesian Farmer's Front) 44, 233
Buttel, F.H. 20
buying and selling land 201, 213–214
Byres, T.J. 5, 22, 25, 171

cacah system 52
Camfield, D. 18
capital class, notion of 13
capitalism: agrarian change and class dynamics 12–21; description 14; *vs.* feudalism 21
capitalist agrarian change under neoliberalism 15–17; commodification of subsistence 16; conception of accumulation by dispossession 15; corporate-and non-corporate-agricultural producers 17; dispossession by displacement 16; generalized commodity production 16; market dependence 16; phenomena of 'land grabbing' 16; primitive accumulation (PA) process 15; 'stereotypical approach' 15–16
capitalist farmers 232; investments in 'own-account' farming 187–191; with 'landlord-capitalists' and accumulation 187–201, 225nn1, 4; non-agricultural accumulation strategies 191–201
capitalist rice farmers and 'landlord-capitalists' 90
capitalist social relations ('primitive accumulation') 4, 6, 12, 15, 16, 27, 33, 34, 103, 147, 151, 233
'Capitalist Thesis' (CT) 21
capitalist transition and class differentiation 12–15; agrarian transition' approach. 13; capital-wage labour relations 13; differentiation of PCP 15; expanded reproduction 14; 'extra-economic means' to 'economic means' transformation 13; 'landless labour' 13; Marxist understanding of primitive accumulation 13; notion of capital class 13; semi-proletarian farmers or 'marginal farmers' 14–15; small peasants 13; tenant-farmers 13; tradition of commercial capitalism 12
capital-wage labour relations 13
cash circulation in rural Java 42–43
Chamber of Commerce and Industry Indonesia (KADIN) 134
cheap credit by state (KUR-BRI) 166, 169, 170, 196, 217, 234, 235
cheating on weighing 199
children's education, in *Timpang* 197–198, 220
Ciherang, new variety of seed 170
clanship 220
class and generational reproduction 240; of agrarian ruling class in the two villages

192; of classes of labour in two villages *219*; of PCPs *208*
class antagonism between capital and labour 122
class as social expression of exploitation 20–21
class-based political organisations 50
class-based political struggle 244–245
class composition, in Javanese rice production 231
class composition of rice farmers 65
class differentiation 17–21; agrarian class location 18–19; class as the social expression of exploitation 20–21; 'classes of labour' 20; 'class exploitation,' Marxist perspective 17–18; combination of synchronic and diachronic approaches 18; economic sociology and political sociology aspects 18; empty dogmatism 18; hiring/selling labour in farming 20; impact on agricultural production 3; market relations, types 19; middle class and lower-middle class 17; objective exploitation 18; 'off-farm' activities 20; 'on-farm' activities or 'own-account' farming 20; property ownership and market relations 19; qualitative approach of Zang 19; 'relational approach' of class 18; 'semi-proletariat farmer' 20; social expression of exploitation 19; Weberian approach of class 17
class dominance 24, 151, 181, 233
class dynamics 233, 240–241; of agricultural producers 31; impact on crucial labour relations 34; power of 234; and production relations 21–27; and state (*see* class dynamics and state)
class dynamics and state: acceleration of 'dispossession by displacement' 51; affordable staple food 47; agriculture liberalisation 48–49; annihilation of communist power 46–47; Basic Agrarian Law (BAL) 45; basic share tenancy law (BSTL) 45; BTI (Indonesian Farmer's Front) 44; class-based political organisations 50; class relations and the state 50; Consensus Forest Land Use Plan 48; developmentalism 47; 'dispossession by displacement' 48; dominance of the HKTI 48; expansion of corporate-scale producers 51; food sovereignty 50; forestry and plantations 49; households of oil palm farmers 51; integration with the global market via liberalisation 49; KPPA (Prime Cooperative for Credit Members) 50; liberalisation 48; low-rank landed gentry 46; material benefits to the rural elites 47; *Nahdatul Ulama* party 46; nationalisation of foreign-owned plantations 45; nationalism and Islamism 50; NES program/scheme 48–49; offensive by PKI and BTI 46; patron-client relationship 51; PKI (the Indonesian Communist Party) 44; revolutionary ideas 44; revolution of landless labourers and the BTI 46; role of the state under the New Order 48; SARBUPRI (Estate Workers' Union of the Republic of Indonesia) 44; skill of the GAPOKTAN 50; state fertiliser subsidy 50; Suharto's New Order 47
classes of labour, traits of members 111–117; farming manager' positions 116; FFP 116; fully fledged proletariat 113; horizontal labour hiring 112; labour in non-agricultural work 115; landlord-capitalist 112, 117; less vocal against individual capitalist farmers 114; patron-client relationship 114; politico-bureaucrat capitalist farmer 117; professional-capitalist farmer 117; proletariat-farmers 112, 115–117; semi-proletariat farmers 111, 112, 114, 117; state and the privately-owned companies 117; 'struggles over class' 111; typical capitalist farmer 117
classes of labour and survival 20, 32–33, 211–222; agricultural and non-agricultural employment 215; basic production technology 212; buying and selling land 213–214; cheap credit (KUR-BRI) 217; clanship 220; high school education 217, 227n43; intra-family loans. 213; labour migrants 218; land rent 213; leasing-in land in *Njomplang* 212; local 'white collar workers 213; members of FFP to buying land 212; migrant blue collar workers 213; nepotism 220; non-agricultural jobs 216; non-agricultural means of survival 215–222; non-agricultural-oriented households 216; off-season 216; parent's role as member of the FFP. 218; rearing livestock 212–213; re-migration by migrant workers 221; rural income diversification 221–222; self-employment outside agriculture 216;

self-exploitation 217, 220; selling labour out to other's farms 214–215, 222; struggles in 'own-account' farming 211–214; Village Lands 212; water pump 212
class exploitation: Marxist perspective 17–18; and women's oppression 27
classical PCPs 107, 109, 242
class location: in *Njomplang*, Central Java **118–119**; in *Timpang*, North Sumatera **119–120**
class location in villages and composition 90–95, 138; *bos* or *toke* (employer) 91; buying of land and trucks 91; capitalist rice farmers and 'landlord-capitalists' 90; dominance of capitalist farmers and 'landlord-capitalists 94; groups of farmers as '*juragan*' 90; landholding in *Njomplang* **93**; landholding in *Timpang* **94**; land ownership/control 90; non-resident landholding 94–95; official land registration 92; oil palm farmers as PCPs 91–92; ownership of plot of *sawah* 91; PCPs in non-agricultural work 91; petty self-employment 92; selling of labour 91; skilled artisan jobs 90; *wong mburuh* (workers) 91
class power, role of 181–182
class relations and variation 132–137; disputes over agricultural wages and working conditions 137; female workers in weeding 135; generous capitalist farmers 135–136; New Order's state-sponsored labour union, SPSI 136; PCPs 133–134, 138; pension rights 137; peripheral hamlets 133; pilfering 136; 'premi' system 133; risk of accident 136–137; risk of work-related accidents 133, 136–137; yellow labour union, the SPSI 137
class reproduction 66–69, 240; capitalist farmers 66–67; classes of labour 69; PCP 68–69; reproduction strategies 69; second neoliberal cycle 69
class structure 231
class struggle in villages before 1965 117–126; '*aksi sepihak*' (one-sided action) 122; class antagonism between capital and labour 122; corruption in the POKTAN and GAPOKTAN 125; GAPOKTAN 123; KBKI 124; mass killing 124–125; mass murder of PKI members 122–123; non-corporate producers 125; patronage of capitalist farmers by POKTAN and GAPOKTAN 126; PKI's program 122; PNI 122; POKTANs 123; regular allowances 125; SARBUPRI 124; traditional theatrical performances by PKI 122; Village Unit Cooperative (KUD) 123
Cohen, G.A. 17, 18
colonial mode of production 42
combine harvester machine services 185n16–17
commercial capitalism, tradition of 12
commodification: commodity production-based farmers. 14; generalised commodity production 14; under the neoliberal wave 33; reproduction of PCP 14; of subsistence 16
communist power, annihilation of 46–47
competitions among the ruling class 195–196
Consensus Forest Land Use Plan 48
Consortium for Agrarian Reform 1
contemporary class relations in Njomplang and Timpang
contingent resilience 30, 211, 224, 239
contract by task *(borongan)* 155, 160–161; with no free lunch is planting 157–158
corporate-agricultural producers 17, 34
corporate-and non-corporate-agricultural producers 16, 17, 34
corporate food regime 29
corporate-scale producers 62; expansion of 51; power of 63
corruption in POKTAN and GAPOKTAN 125
cost of planting 158
Cousins, B. 28
CPO price, rise of 63–64
credit provision 163–170, 182, 234–235; accessing formal credit 170; credit provision in *Timpang*, North Sumatera **167–169**; formal micro financing of corporation-based cooperative credit 170; informal credit charges 170; KUR-BRI 169–170; in *Njomplang*, Central Java **164–165**; oil palm traders 169; private companies 166; reasons for practice of agricultural input credit 166; state, cheapest credit 166; state-subsidised credit (KUR-BRI Micro) 166
criteria and indicator of capitalism 42

data collection 54; 'big' capitalist farmers 86; household survey 85–86; income from 'own-account' farming 86; information on social groups 87–88; interviews and observation

85; 'landlord-capitalists' in *Njomplang* 86; 'modest' capitalist farmers 86; for *Njomplang* 85; secondary data 88; 'semi-proletariat farmers' 87; 'substantial PCPs' and the latter 'formal PCPs' 86; thematic issues 88
data of landholding categories 65
decline of profit 57, 70
'defensive' nature of current rice capitalist cultivation 59
de-industrialisation 149
demand for labour from capitalist farmers 152
developmentalism 32, 47
dispossession by displacement 16, 48, 51, 231; or class differentiation 34
disputes over agricultural wages and working conditions 137
dominance of capitalist farmers and 'landlord-capitalists 94
Dutch colonial state in Java 42
dynamics of agricultural production 237–238
dynamics of land arrangements 235

earning from tapping coconut 184n9
economic crisis 48, 149, 221
economic sociology and political sociology aspects 18
educational accumulation 191–192
employment: agricultural and non-agricultural 215
empty dogmatism 18
enclosure 1, 16, 31, 33, 48, 51
expanded reproduction *see* accumulation
expansion and deepening of capitalist social relations 12
expansionist strategy 62
expansion of export crops 1, 29, 30
exploitation: Marxist perspective 17–18; objective 18; oppression and class exploitation 27; relations 230; social expression of 19; and women's oppression 27

falling sale price 179
family labour for rice cultivation 151
farming contractors 99, 140n5, 143
farming managers 100–101; positions 116; salary 145
feminisation of agriculture 27
fertilisers **163**, 173
feudal slavery system 45
fixed land rent for oil palm fields 145–147
fixed-rent leasing 90, 140n1
food sovereignty 1, 50
forestry and plantations 49
formal micro financing of corporation-based cooperative credit 170
formal PCPs 86, 108–111, 130, 138, 143, 176, 177, 203, 208, 210, 223, 242
Foster Father relationship 185n14
Frank, A.G. 21
free labour 43
free lunch: abolition of 157–158, 181
fully fledged proletariat (FFP) 113, 116, 231

GAPOKTAN 50, 53, 71n3, 123
Geertz, C. 2, 41
gender oppression and class 34
generalized commodity production 16, 44; agrarian change and 21–23; class dominance 24; class exploitation and women's oppression 27; description 22–23; feminisation of agriculture 27; 'indicator' of process of capitalist development 23; labour process 24; labour relations in agricultural production 23–24; metabolic rift 26; ownership structure 26; patron-client relationship 25; and production relations in peripheral world 23–27; resistance to mechanisation 24–25; sharecropping 24; social organisation of production 26; surpluses generated 23; wage and agricultural profitability 26; wage levels and level of profit 26–27
generous capitalist farmers 135–136
global informal working class 33
'golden era of rice' 84
Gooptu, N. 111
Gordon, A. 42
Green Revolution 7, 29, 47–49, 53, 59, 67–70, 76, 123, 234

Hall, D. 15
Harris-White, B. 68, 111
harvester machine's services cost 185n16
Harvey, D. 15
Hayami, Y. 26, 236
hectare of paddy field, measurement 140n3
herbicides 158–159, 170
hesitant capitalists 201, 230
higher education for children 207
highest income for capitalist farmers, in *Timpang* 176–177
high school education 217, 227n43
hire wage labour 95
hiring/selling labour in farming 20
HKTI, dominance of 48

horizontal labour hiring 112, 152
household joint-harvesting 226n28
household survey 85–86
Hüsken, F. 176, 201, 230

IMF-led liberalisation policies 57
incentives and Village Fund 154
income, 'big' capitalist farmers-cum-oil palm traders 198
income from 'own-account' farming 86, **175**, 175–179, **183**; of agrarian classes in *Timpang*, North Sumatra **178**; BRI-KUR scheme 177; falling sale price 179; highest income for capitalist farmers 176, 177; lease income for semi-proletariat farmers **178**; oil palm village 177; for PCPs in *Njomplang* 176; of the 'proletariat-farmers' 177; for 'semi-proletariat farmers 176; superiority of oil palm capitalist farmers 178–179
Indonesia Logistics Bureau (BULOG) 88
informal credit charges 170
information on social groups 87–88
integration with the global market via liberalisation 49
interviews and observation 88
intra-family loans 213
investments in 'own-account' farming 187–191
irrigation system 58, 59, 77, 81, 84, 147, 154
islands 'outside' Java 9n1

Java: accumulation under the Green Revolution 42; *cacah* system 52; cash circulation in rural Java 42–43; Dutch colonial state in 42; emergence of generalised commodity production 44; free labour 43; liberalisation 42–43; private capitalists in 1870 43; private companies 43; proletarianisation 43–44; revolt against the Dutch rule 43; sharecropping in paddy cultivation 52; VOC as the ruling class 42
Jokowi 7, 53, 67, 195
'jumping squirrels'/*Bajing Loncat* 83–84
'*juragan*', groups of farmers as 90

Kautsky, K. 30, 31
KBKI 124
Kikuchi, M. 26, 236
KPPA (Prime Cooperative for Credit Members) 50
KUR-BRI 169–170, 234–235

labour: bondage 22; migrants 218; in non-agricultural work 115; *see also* securing labour
labour arrangements 151–163, 233–234; applying fertilisers **163**; applying herbicides 158–159; contract by task 155, 160–161; contract by task with no free lunch is planting 157–158; cost of planting 158; daily wage labour for weeding 163; detachment of the meal provision from the wages 160; level of mowing 163; meal provision attached to daily wage 163; in *Njomplang*, Central Java **156**; out-migration in the 1980s 159–160; payment-in-kind (*bawon* system). 155, 159; removal of free lunch for planting 158; rice pilfering 160; road improvements in the hamlets 161; slowing down the work 157; task of sowing 158; in *Timpang*, North Sumatera **162**; transformation of agricultural task 156–157; weeding 159; *see also* securing labour; state and labour arrangements
labour process 23, 24, 151, 181, 233, 237
labour relations: in agricultural production 23–24; of production in oil palm 53
labour shortage 153, 158–160
labour system 80, 88, 133, 151, 155, 158, 160, 163, 173, 181, 182, 234, 235
Laclau, E. 21
land arrangements 235; *see also* dynamics of land arrangements
land-buying of rice capitalist farmers 188–189
land categories 147, 148
land certification 195, 223, 225n8
land concentration and proletarianisation 52
land contracting 98–99, 143
Land for the People (Lucas and Warren) 1, 2
land fragmentation 110–111, 191, 193, 202, 208–210, 214, 220, 224, 240
land grabbing 16, 33; social movements against 3
landholding, in *Njomplang* **93**
landholding, in *Timpang* **94**
landless labour 13, 24, 25, 46
landlord-capitalists 98–100, 103, 112, 117, 232; in *Njomplang* 86; and sharecroppers, share of 50-50 148
land ownership/control 90; fixed-rent leasing 90; gap between land ownership and land control 89–90; in Njomplang and Timpang 89–90; sharecropping 90

land pawning 143, 145, 184n3
land productivity 77
land rent 213
land tenure 142–151; farming contractor 143; farming manager, salary 145; fixed land rent for oil palm fields 145–147; incidence of fixed rent 143; land contracting 143; land pawning 143, 145; in *Njomplang*, Central Java **144–145**; normal sharecropping 142; ownership of land 143, 145; reverse sharecropping 142; self-cultivation by wage labour 143; sharecropping 142; symmetrical contract' of sharecropping 142; in *Timpang*, North Sumatera **146**
land transactions 188; in *Timpang* 189–190, **190**
Langkat's GDP 78
'large farmers'as 'hesitant capitalists' 201
lease income, for semi-proletariat farmers **178**
leasing-in land in *Njomplang* 212
leas-in land 201–202
Lenin, V.I. 28, 30, 67
Lerche, J. 20
liberalisation 43, 48; agriculture 48–49; IMF-led policies 57; indication of primitive accumulation 43; integration with the global market via 49; and privatisation 31; rice cultivation in 42
livestock rearing 200, 212, 213
local white collar workers 213
low-rank landed gentry 46
Lucas, A. 2

Mamdani, M. 28
'management of poverty' policies 33, 239
Mantili's proposal 129, 141n13
marginal farmers 14, 23, 32–33, 243
market: compulsion 231; dependence 16; relations, types 19
Marxist political economy 2, 5
Marxist understanding of class 12, 89
Marxist understanding of primitive accumulation 13
mass killing 122–125, 245
meal provision: attached to daily wage 163; detachment from the wages 160
mechanisation 54, 234; absence in *Timpang* 172, 182; modest 191; problems of 181; resistance to 24–25
metabolic rift 26, 34, 59, 173, 182, 235
migrant blue collar workers 211, 213
migrant children of substantial PCPs 207–208
migrant labour supply: fall in 153–154
migrant workers, import of 149
migration 239; decline in permanent 84
'mode of production' under Dutch rule 41
modest and big capitalist farmers/landlord-capitalists 191–193
modest capitalist farmers 86, 238
modest mechanisation 191
money lending 49, 196, 200
movement of 'land for the people' 1

Nahdatul Ulama party 46
nationalisation of foreign-owned plantations 45
nationalism and Islamism 50
nature of agrarian ruling class 95–103, 140n4; absentee landlord-capitalists 98–99; agrarian ruling class and family ties 103–106; case study 97; farming managers 100–101; hire wage labour 95; landlord-capitalists 98, 103; and lord-capitalists 99–100; petty commodity producers and characteristics 106–111; politico-bureaucrat capitalist farmers 96, 101–102; present landlord-capitalists 99; professional-capitalist farmers 97–98, 100, 102; rice capitalist farmers as political leaders 96; rice trading 96; traits of the members of the classes of labour 111–117; typical capitalist farmers 96
near-to-(absolute) landless, increase in 64
Neocosmos, M. 28
neoliberal approaches 29
nepotism 220
NES scheme 48–49, 81
New Order regime 50, 104; state-sponsored labour union, SPSI 136
New Road' strategy 71n2
non-agricultural accumulation strategies 30, 191–201, 238; 'absentee landlord-capitalists' 193; buying cars and motorcycles 201; cheap credit by state (KUR-BRI) 196; cheating on weighing 199; children's education in *Timpang* 197–198; competition over politico-bureaucrat positions in *Timpang* 199–200; competitions among the ruling class 195–196; difference between modest and big capitalist farmers/ landlord-capitalists 191, 223; educational accumulation 191–192; income for 'big' capitalist farmers-cum-oil palm traders 198; 'large farmers' as 'hesitant capitalists' 201; livestock-rearing 200;

modest and big capitalist farmers/ landlord-capitalists 191–193; money lending 200; partial non-agricultural accumulation 195; political accumulation 194–195, 199; rice hulling 197–198; rice trading 193–194; sale price competition 198–199; spatial relatives-mobilisation 196; supervisor's position 199; tractor services 193; Village Fund 195; village secretary, selection 196, 225n10
non-agricultural activities 174, 204–211, 216, 243–244
non-agricultural means of survival 215–222
non-agricultural-oriented households 216, 222
non-corporate-agricultural producers 16, 17
non-corporate producers 78, 125
non-economic coercion of labour process 23
non-main crops agricultural production 179–181; crops during the off-season 180; leasing-in paddy field 180; Mung bean, growing 180
non-political strategies 69, 221, 225, 239
non-resident landholding 94–95
normal sharecropping 90, 143

objective exploitation 18
off-farm activities 20, 211
official land registration 92
off-season 69, 107, 108, 114, 154, 180, 183, 204, 205, 212, 216; absence of 205
oil palm, change in total real revenue and production cost **60**
oil palm capitalist farmers activity 190
oil palm farmers as PCPs 91–92
on-farm activities or 'own-account' farming 20
open class struggle 140, 232–233
out-migration 149, 159, 207, 209–210, 220; in the 1980s 159–160
output and land productivity 173–175; bigger cultivators and higher land productivity. 173; need to use water pumps 173; new variety of seeds 173; non-agricultural activities 174; output per hectare of oil palm 173; rent-in the land, problems 173; use of chemical fertilisers 173
output per hectare of oil palm 173
own-account farming 8, 187, 223; activities in 201–202; employment 155; income 236–237; land-buying of rice capitalist farmers 188–189; land transactions 188–190, **190**; modest mechanisation 191; and nonagricultural activities 20; oil palm capitalist farmers' activity 190; part-time farming 20; property relations and market relations 21; result of land transactions in *Njomplang* Central Java **188**
ownership of land 91, 143, 145
ownership structure 26

parent's role, as member of FFP 218
partial bias, outer islands change 3
partial non-agricultural accumulation 195
Patnaik, U. 18, 22
patronage of capitalist farmers by POKTAN and GAPOKTAN 126
patron-client relationship 25, 46, 51, 111, 112, 114, 135, 138, 139, 151
payment-in-kind (*bawon* system). 155, 159
PCPs and simple reproduction 30–32, 201–211; absence of off-season 205; activities in 'own-account' farming 201–202; cheap food commodities with less labour cost (wages) 31; class and generational reproduction of PCPs *208*; contingent nature of 30–32; contingent resilience 30; contribution of agricultural wage income 204; de-peasantization 31; disposing of labour in agricultural jobs 203; global agrarian movement 31; higher education for children 207; impact of education on class reproduction 210; impact of land transactions o 202; income generation of PCP households 32; incomes for the household 204; land fragmentation 209; liberalisation, privatisation and deregulation 31; limited leas-in land 201–202; migrant children of 'substantial PCPs 207–208; non-agricultural activities 204–211; no off-season in *Timpang* 205; 'off-farm' activity of 'middle farmers' 211; out-migration 209–210; PCPs-cum-construction workers 205; political-bureaucratic positions 210–211; production technology 202; remittance-senders 201; role of self-employment in *Timpang* 206; self-employment 206; self-exploitation 30; sending children to high school and college 209; survival of PCPs 30; university education 210; vertical concentration 31; wage labour

and 'own-account' farming 205–206; women in PCP households 32
PCPs-cum-construction workers 205
Pearce, R. 24, 25, 151, 181, 233
Peasant and the Ruler (Rachman) 2
peasant households, dynamics of 35n2
peasant-plantation in Java 42
'peasant rights' 1
Pemuda Marhaen (the Youth organisation of PNI) 122
pension rights 116, 124, 137
peripheral hamlets 133
peripheral world 6, 7, 12–16, 23, 24, 33, 35n1, 242
'Petani dan Penguasa' *(Peasant and the Ruler)* (Rachman) 2
Petty Commodity Producers (PCPs) 5, 14, 106–111, 133–134, 138, 238–239; aspiring PCPs 107; class differentiation of 242; classical PCPs 107; formal PCPs 108; impact on class relations 241–242; land fragmentation and classes of labour 110–111; in non-agricultural work 91; patron-client relationship 111; PCPs' transformation into capitalist farmers 106; position in class relations 242–243; relationship with patrons 108–109; and 'semi-proletariat farmers 235; substantial PCPs 107; transformation to capitalist farmers 106, 109–110
petty self-employment 91, 92
pilfering 136, 137, 160, 163, 209, 232
Pincus, J. 26, 170, 173, 181, 183, 184, 188, 230, 234–237
PKH (conditional cash transfers) 228n54
PKI, Indonesian Communist Party 44, 71n2, 122, 233
PNI, Indonesian National Party 122, 124
POKTAN 71n3, 123, 140n9, 233
political accumulation 49, 67, 189, 193–195, 199; in *Timpang* 199
political-bureaucratic positions 96, 195, 210–211
politico-bureaucrat capitalist farmers 96, 101–102, 117, 232
pre-capitalist labour arrangement 41–42
'premi' system 133
pressure on patron landowners 150
primitive accumulation (PA) and capitalist agriculture 41–44; articulation of mode of production 42; Asiatic mode of production 42; colonial mode of production 42; criteria and indicator of capitalism 42; Dutch colonial state in Java 42; 'mode of production' under Dutch rule 41; peasant-plantation in Java 42; pre-capitalist labour arrangement 41–42
primitive accumulation (PA) process 15; agrarian change in *Njomplang* 80; capitalist relations during the colonial period 80; first rice huller 81; individual-permanent land ownership 80–81; Islamic rebellion in Aceh in 1958 (DI-TII) 80–81; land value 81; migration of labours 82–83; NES scheme from oil palm company 81; and the origin of main crop cultivation 80–83; social differentiation in Java 80; social formations in *Timpang* 80; violence in land acquisition 81–82; violence to take over the lands 81–82
private capitalists in 1870 43
private companies 43, 48, 49, 77, 78, 82, 158, 166, 169, 231
pro-agricultural workers' program of agrarian reform 245
production cost and revenue: in an oil palm village 250–251; in rice cultivation village 248–250
production technology 189, 190, 202, 207, 212, 214, 218
professional-capitalist farmers 97–98, 100, 102, 117, 232
pro-labour legislation 33
proletarianisation 3, 15, 16, 19, 31, 43–44, 52, 82, 238
proletariat-farmers 112, 115–117, 231
property ownership and market relations 19
Purworejo 76; share of agriculture in Purworejo's GDP 77

qualitative approach, household's involvement in market relation 19

Rachman, N.F. 2
rate of profit: per hectare of oil palm of farmer/smallholders **59**; wet paddy cultivation **54**
real wage, in *Njomplang* 2001 and 2017 252
regular allowances 124–125
relational approach of class 18
re-migration by migrant workers 221
remittance-senders 201
rent-in the land, problems 173
reproduction of agrarian classes: accumulation, description 28; capitalist farmers and accumulation 27–30;

classes of labour searching for survival 32–33; contingent nature of PCPs' simple reproduction 30–32; expanded reproduction or accumulation 27–28; expansion of 'corporate food regime' 29; expansion of export crops 29, 30; 'global informal working class' 33; 'management of poverty' policies 33; marginal farmers 32–33; neoliberal approaches 29; non-agricultural accumulation 30; primary actors of accumulation 28–29; pro-labour legislation 33; rural emigration 33; rural income diversification 33
resistance to mechanisation 24–25
result of land transactions in *Njomplang* Central Java **188**
reverse sharecropping 90, 143
revolt against the Dutch rule 43
revolution of landless labourers and the BTI 46
rice: capitalist farmers as political leaders 96; commercialisation 52; hulling 197–198; landholders in Indonesia **66**; pilfering 160; for the poor 239; trading 96, 193–194
road improvements in the hamlets 161
rubber farming 83
Rudra, A. 22
rural elites, material benefits to 47
rural emigration 33
rural income diversification 33, 221–222

sale price competition 198–199
SARBUPRI (Estate Workers' Union of the Republic of Indonesia) 44, 124, 233
Scott, J.C. 25, 151, 172, 232
season, role of 147
secondary data 88
secular' village 184n3
securing labour 151–155; cash payment 152; demand for labour from capitalist farmers 152; fall in migrant labour supply 153–154; family labour for rice cultivation 151; horizontal labour hiring 152; incentives and Village Fund 154; inception of oil palm 1990s 155; labour shortage 153; own-account employment 155; package of planting and harvesting 152–153; planting by women 152; vertical labour hiring 152; workers from mountainous areas 155–156
seeds: modern 170; new variety of 170, 173
self-cultivation by wage labour 143
self-employment 206, 239; outside agriculture 216
self-exploitation 30, 213, 217, 220, 221
selling labour out to other's farms 187, 203–204, 214–215, 222
semi-Feudalist Thesis (SFT), aspects 12, 21–22
'semi-feudal' social formations 34
semi-proletarian farmers 14–15, 20, 87, 111, 112, 114, 117, 176, 231
sharecropping 24, 142, 172, 235; benefits of 53; under capitalism 24; class dominance 24; in paddy cultivation 52; sharecroppers' demand 149–150; symmetrical contract of 142
sharecropping in Njomplang 147–151, **148**; boom in commodity export 149; de-industrialisation 149; economic crisis 149; import of migrant workers 149; internal dynamics 147; land categories 147; landlord-capitalists' and sharecroppers, share of 50-50 148; pressure on patron landowners 150; season, role of 147; sharecroppers' demand 150; shortage of labour in the mid-1990s 149; state of disorientation 151; surplus of labour 149; trajectory of the share allocation 147–148; trend of 50-50 and 60-40 share 150; under-mechanised labour process 151
sharing poverty, concept of 1–2
Sidel, J.T. 44
simple reproduction 243; *see also* PCPs and simple reproduction
skilled artisan jobs 90
social differentiation and demographic differentiation 35n3
social diversity 79
social organisation 2, 7, 26, 34, 142, 182
socio-economic features of *Njomplang* and *Timpang* 76–80; agrarian village 77; characteristics 77; land productivity 77; Langkat's GDP 78; map of the village in Central Java and North Sumatera *79*; proper irrigation system 77; 'small-holders oil palm village 78; social diversity 79; stereotyping of different ethnicities and religions 79–80
soil degradation 26, 58, 173, 182, 184, 237
sowing 149, 152, 158
spatial relatives-mobilisation 196
state and agricultural production 52–64
state and agricultural profit 54–64; agricultural real wages in estate crops **61**; agricultural real wages in food crops **57**; BPDP (Endowment Fund Body

for Oil Palm) 62; change in total real revenue and total production cost **55**; composition of the oil palm production cost of oil palm **60**; composition of wet paddy cultivation cost per hectare **56**; corporate-scale producers 62; data collection method 54; decline in the oil palm profit rate 59–60, **59–60**; decline of profit 57; defensive nature of rice capitalist cultivation 59; expansionist strategy 62; fall in the share of labour cost 55; farm-gate price **58**; IMF-led liberalisation policies 57; inability to introduce new production techniques 58; increase in farm-gate rice price 58; land productivity of oil palm **61**; land productivity per hectare of wet paddy field **58**; oil form, change in total real revenue and production cost **60**; power of the 'corporate-scale producers 63; profit decline in Oil palm 59–60; rate of profit of wet paddy cultivation **54**; rate of profit per hectare of oil palm of farmer/smallholders **59**; rise of the CPO price 63–64; state-sponsored farmers association 59; surge of the labour cost 61; upsurge in the labour cost 60; World CPO Price *62*, 62–63
state and labour arrangements 52–54; benefits of sharecropping 53; *cacah* system 52; GAPOKTAN. 53; Green Revolution 53; Jokowi's administration 53; labour relation of production in oil palm 53; land concentration and proletarianisation 52; mechanisation 54; nature of the crop 52; rice commercialisation 52; sharecropping in paddy cultivation 52
state fertiliser subsidy 50
state of disorientation 151
state policies for PCPs 223–224
state-sponsored farmers association 59
state's role under the New Order 48
state-subsidised credit (KUR-BRI Micro) 166
'stereotypical approach' 15–16
stereotyping of ethnicities and religions 79–80
struggles over class 111
subsistence-oriented and egalitarian community 33
substantial PCPs 86, 87, 107–108, 111, 117, 130, 135, 138, 175–178, 183, 202–204, 207, 210, 221, 223
Suharto 1, 2, 7, 46–51, 62, 67, 82, 123, 125, 127; authoritarian regime 1–2; New Order 47
Sultan Langkat 77–79, 81, 100, 116, 124, 236
superiority of oil palm capitalist farmers 178–179
supervisor's position 199
surplus of labour 149, 159
synchronic and diachronic approaches, combination of 18
syrup money 199, 226n18

technological development 3, 5, 8, 88, 101, 142, 151, 170–173, 181, 182, 223, 235; absence of mechanisation in *Timpang* 172, 182; accelerated production process 172; aluminium-fibre fruit picker poles 172; chemical herbicides 170; *Ciherang*, new variety of seed 170; modern seeds 170; sharecropping 172; threshing machines 170–171; trialling combine harvester machine 171; trialling combine harvester machine, use and problems 171; water pumps 170
tenant-farmers 13, 25
Thompson, E.P. 18
threshing machines 91, 170–171, 202
Tichelman, F. 42
total production value calculation 185n26
tractor services 127, 140nn7–8, 193, 206
traditional theatrical performances by PKI 122
trajectory of the share allocation 147–148
transformation, extra-economic means to economic means 13
transformation of agricultural task 156–157
transition to the oil palm economy 83–85; administrative change in *Timpang in* 1996 83; agrarian change in 2000 84; alcohol and drugs selling 84; decline in permanent migration 84; 'golden era of rice' 84; 'jumping squirrels'/*Bajing Loncat* 83–84; rubber farming replaced 83
trialling combine harvester machine, use and problems 171
typical capitalist farmers 96, 117, 232

under-mechanised labour process 151
un-free labour and capitalism 22
university education 210, 240

vertical labour hiring 152
Village Fund 51, 69, 154, 195, 205, 215

village head and family ties: in Njomplang, Central Java 247; in Timpang, *North Sumatera* 248
Village Lands 77, 201, 212
village map, in Central Java and North Sumatera *79*
village meeting in Njomplang and class relations 126–132, 139, 232, 237; Cokro's proposal 127–128; decision-making mechanism of the *musyawarah* 127; de-politicisation policy 130–131; everyday resistance 132; formal PCPs 127; increase in the planting tariff 128–129; labour exchange in land preparation 126; New Order's ideology 127; raise in the tractor tariff 128; rejection of classes of labour's proposals 129–130, 139; strategy, to pit labourers against each other 127; village meeting 126, 131; wages for agricultural tasks in *Njomplang*, Central Java **130**
village secretary, selection 196, 225n10
Village Unit Cooperative (KUD) 123, 125
VOC as the ruling class 42

wages 237; and agricultural profitability 26; incomes 224; labour and 'own-account' farming 205–206; labour domination over sharecropping 52; levels and level of profit 26–27
Warren, C. 2
water pumps 170, 173, 212
Weberian approach of class 12, 17, 230
weeding 159, 226nn30, 34; daily wage labour for 163; women workers in weeding 135
willing sharecroppers 143, 184n1
Wiradi, G. 64, 149, 150
women: household reproduction 34–35; lower wages 181; oppression and class exploitation 27; in PCP households 32; planting by 152; workers in weeding 135
wong mburuh (workers) 91
Wood, E.M. 16, 18
work-related accidents, risk of 133, 136–137
World CPO Price *62*, 62–63

yellow labour union, the SPSI 137

zero landholder 71n5
Zhang, Q.F. 19, 20, 29